The Pandemic and the Working Class

The Pandemic and the Working Class

How US Labor Navigated COVID-19

Edited by
NICK JURAVICH and
STEVE STRIFFLER

UNIVERSITY OF
ILLINOIS PRESS
Urbana, Chicago, and Springfield

This book will be made open access within three years of
publication thanks to Path to Open, a program developed
in partnership between JSTOR, the American Council of
Learned Societies (ACLS), University of Michigan Press,
and The University of North Carolina Press to bring
about equitable access and impact for the entire scholarly
community, including authors, researchers, libraries,
and university presses around the world. Learn more at
https://about.jstor.org/path-to-open/

Library of Congress Cataloging-in-Publication Data

Names: Juravich, Nick, 1984– editor. | Striffler, Steve,
    1967– editor.
Title: The pandemic and the working class : how US labor
    navigated COVID-19 / edited by Nick Juravich and
    Steve Striffler.
Description: Urbana : University of Illinois Press, [2025]
    | Series: The working class in American history |
    Includes bibliographical references and index.
Identifiers: LCCN 2024047465 (print) | LCCN
    2024047466 (ebook) | ISBN 9780252046520
    (cloth) | ISBN 9780252088643 (paperback) | ISBN
    9780252047848 (ebook)
Subjects: LCSH: Working class—United States—Economic
    conditions—21st century. | Labor policy—United
    States—History—21st century. | COVID-19 Pandemic,
    2020–2023—Influence | COVID-19 Pandemic, 2020–
    2023—Economic aspects—United States. | Collective
    bargaining—United States—History—21st century.
Classification: LCC HD8072.5 .P36 2025 (print) | LCC
    HD8072.5 (ebook) | DDC 331.0973—dc23/eng/20250115
LC record available at https://lccn.loc.gov/2024047465
LC ebook record available at https://lccn.loc.gov/2024047466

Contents

Introduction

NICK JURAVICH and
STEVE STRIFFLER

The health and economic crises brought on by the COVID-19 pandemic affected working people across the United States and the world deeply and dramatically. The pandemic triggered the worst jobs crisis since the Great Depression and led to a massive contraction of the global economy, made worse by the fact that the nation was not prepared to respond. Decades of rising inequality and plummeting union density, combined with the dismantling of the social safety net, meant that most working people found themselves without the support or resources to navigate a complex crisis of this scale.

In the early months of the pandemic, millions of people lost their jobs, fell behind on rent or house payments, struggled to put food on the table, and saw their limited savings evaporate. Low-wage workers were hit particularly hard, despite being elevated from disposable to "essential" in the blink of an eye.[1] Many of their jobs evaporated, especially in the service sector, stranding workers who were poorly positioned to weather the crisis in the first place. It was a horrible time to be living paycheck to paycheck; to lack healthcare, sick leave, or childcare; or to work in close, unsafe conditions. And yet, as we know, this was the situation many workers found themselves in for much of the early pandemic.

Two subsequent factors mitigated the hardships of the crisis for thousands of working people while also putting the brakes on the exponential growth of inequality. An emergency government response that kept millions from falling into poverty and effectively redistributed (some) wealth downward was followed by a rapid increase in demand for labor as businesses and the economy opened back up. Government support and the demand for labor gave some workers a bit of newfound leverage, allowing them to improve their situation by demanding better wages and working conditions or by simply switching jobs.

By 2021 it was clear that the pandemic was producing something of a significant moment for labor. Work, and workers, had become visible in new and unprecedented ways in the harsh light of COVID-19. Virtually all workplace arrangements, as well as the production and consumption of most goods and services, were dramatically disrupted by the pandemic. Work was on our minds, in the media, and at the center of political and policy debates. It was in this context that the contributors to this book first came together in March 2022, roughly two years after the start of the pandemic, to begin writing the essays that follow in order to make sense of these chaotic, confusing years for labor and working-class struggles.

• • •

The contradictions and high-relief contrasts of early pandemic work experiences remain familiar, even with years of distance from March 2020. Hotel, restaurant, entertainment, and tourism workers were laid off en masse as their industries ground to a halt. Food and healthcare workers became "heroes" even as they worked brutal hours in unsafe conditions. Middle-class professionals kept their jobs but brought them home, upending their work and family relations simultaneously. And the closing of schools and daycare centers scrambled essential systems of care work and social reproduction for working people, both in their homes and on the job.

The collapse of interconnected relations of production, care, and service provision pushed working people to look beyond the boundaries of their own homes and jobs. Workers struggled to find basic consumer goods, confronted an overwhelmed healthcare system, and desperately sought childcare. Over time, this led to a collective political revelation, perhaps the most glaring of the pandemic: our government was grossly ill-equipped to deal with a health and economic crisis of this magnitude, and the billionaires whose wealth shapes election outcomes cared only to "return to normal" as quickly as possible. Workers have suffered the consequences of an underfunded state and a political system captured by elites for decades, but not in nearly a century had so many people felt the failure of government and indifference of the bosses so quickly and so deeply, on a scale and with an intensity that was difficult to ignore.

At first many workers went into survival mode. During 2020 nearly 20 percent of the labor force was laid off. The response of the federal government—though far less comprehensive than the interventions made by other capitalist democracies—offered some respite, but uncertainty and insecurity continued into 2021 even as the economic and health outlook improved. As the pandemic began to recede, albeit unevenly, and bosses called people back to work, many workers found that traditional labor arrangements, and their corresponding commutes, no longer appealed. Millions of workers left their jobs during 2021, with most moving to other positions as they sought improved pay, safer working conditions, and a work-life balance that met their needs.

If individual choices drove this "Great Resignation," the broad experience of the pandemic—an economic disaster followed by an uneven boom, unsafe working conditions, and a tight labor market—led thousands of workers to strike, threaten to strike, or otherwise take action on the job site. Anticipated by the educators' strike wave of 2018–2019, and bolstered by rising public support for unions (over 70 percent as of this writing, according to Gallup polling), this militancy began just weeks into the pandemic. By May 2020, workers at Amazon, Target, and Whole Foods had struck across the country over safety, pay, and benefits. Transportation, meatpacking, restaurant, healthcare, and other workers all held wildcat strikes to protect their health and to demand necessary equipment and hazard pay commensurate with their new status as "essential" workers.

This trend accelerated as the economy continued to grow and labor markets tightened in 2021. When ten thousand John Deere workers went on strike, October 2021 became known as "Striketober," with private sector workers striking with a fervor not seen in a generation during the last months of the year. This movement was not simply, or even primarily, the work of specific unions; rather, it spilled over into a broad working-class refusal to "return to normal." Renters, prisoners, and students all declared "strikes" in one form or another, particularly as paltry government assistance programs were left to expire by both parties.

This wave of working-class organizing sparked new unionization efforts. Close to one thousand union elections were held in the private sector in 2021, with around six hundred new unions achieving certification. Public approval of unions had prominent politicians tripping over themselves to join workers on the picket lines. All of this bolstered organizing and strike support, often in sectors of the economy with little previous union presence, including high-profile campaigns at Starbucks and Amazon. This, in turn, laid the groundwork for the large—and quite militant—strikes and strike threats that took place in 2023 within some of the country's largest companies and industries, starting with actors and writers and followed by the Teamsters and the United Auto Workers.

• • •

The Pandemic and the Working Class explores all of this and more. It seeks to provide a sense of how working people survived and experienced the pandemic, how and why this highly visible upsurge in working-class organizing took place, and what it all means in both the short term and long term. It does so in five parts.

The first part—three chapters—explores the pandemic and its impact on working people in broad strokes. Chapter 1 provides a general overview of how working people fared and responded during the pandemic, focusing in particular on (1) how the pandemic impacted different groups and categories of working people and (2) how various groups were and were not able to respond politically both within and outside of the workplace. Chapter 2 examines the relationship between the pandemic and its most grievous impact on working people: death. The chapter pays special attention to the variation in mortality from industry to industry, challenging public health frameworks that classify workers with simple demographic data rather than exploring the relationship between toil and its toll on human beings. Chapter 3 looks at the "inflation debate" that began in earnest by the end of 2020 as supply chains snarled and consumer prices rose at their fastest pace in a decade. Although the debate itself seems to hinge on a series of technical economic questions, the core of the discussion is a political one with great stakes for working people. How will the state intervene—and with whose interests in mind—in rescuing and restructuring an economy thrown into chaos by a pandemic?

The next three parts examine the pandemic and the working class through the lens of particular industries. Part II explores the industry that was perhaps most dramatically upended by the pandemic: food and hospitality. Chapter 4 examines the impact of the pandemic on farm labor and the production of food in the United States. It illuminates how farmworkers responded to new challenges and what this meant for food production and availability. Chapter 5 explores how unionized hospitality workers navigated the near-complete closure of the industry, from the initial emergency, through the shutdown, and then into the recovery. It examines how the hotel industry attempted to take advantage of the crisis to permanently alter the nature of work within the sector and how one union mobilized against these changes.

Part III explores the impact of the pandemic on the educational sector and on the most densely unionized and most regularly vilified workforce in the nation. Chapter 6 looks at university-level organizing in response to safety concerns around campus reopenings, with a particular focus on the explosive graduate worker strike at the University of Michigan. Chapter 7 turns to public schools and the struggle by a teachers union to fight for the needs of disabled students and workers during the pandemic. Finally, chapter 8 focuses on archival labor, exploring how the pandemic worked to reorient the relationship between historians, archivists, the archives, and the labor movement.

Part IV examines the front lines of the pandemic in public health. Chapter 9 explores the lived experience of nurses during the pandemic in order to understand their struggles, the broader crisis of healthcare, and the evolving conflicts between healthcare workers and hospital management. Chapter 10 turns to healthcare social workers in New York City to illuminate not only how they responded to the demands of COVID but also how marginalized people in their care struggled to navigate the added pressures brought on by the pandemic.

The final part of the book looks at the emergence of innovative forms of organizing during the pandemic. Chapter 11 explores an attempt by unions, community organizations, and faith congregations to put together an effective statewide coalition in Connecticut to address inequality during the pandemic. Chapter 12 examines the Emergency Workplace Organizing Committee, an attempt by the United Electrical, Radio, and Machine Workers of America and the Democratic Socialists of America to create a nationwide organizing strategy. Chapter 13 examines "union style" movements of immigrant small business owners and those classified as independent contractors to forge new alliances with the traditional labor movement and other organizations as they navigated the pandemic. Finally, chapter 14 explores COVID-era worker organizing within the growing cannabis industry and the broader fight for economic and racial justice.

Overall, *The Pandemic and the Working Class* presents a portrait of the pandemic and the working class that is at once dynamic, inspirational, and sobering. The political and economic forces arrayed against workers and their organizations were powerful and well organized prior to the pandemic, and they remain so. The ensuing crisis rarely improved conditions for working people, and in some cases it provided industry and its allies an opportunity to seize even more power. But workers continued to struggle, fight back, and build organizations, often in remarkably innovative ways. The lessons learned and solidarities formed in these remarkable moments of collective survival and resistance continue to inform and can help us illuminate the trajectory of the labor movement today.

Note

1. Jamie McCallum, *Essential: How the Pandemic Transformed the Long Fight for Worker Justice* (New York: Basic Books, 2022).

PART I

Opening Interventions

1

Work and the Labor Movement during the Pandemic

NICK JURAVICH and
STEVE STRIFFLER

No disaster is natural, and the COVID-19 pandemic in the United States was no exception. As disasters do, the disease threw our political, economic, social, and spatial inequalities into high relief. COVID-19 disproportionately sickened and killed people at the deadly intersections of capitalism, racism, and patriarchy in the United States, a process that played out in many ways and contexts: through our punitive immigration and criminal legal systems, as well as our unequal and insufficient systems of housing, healthcare, and social welfare. Untangling how COVID-19 became a greater disaster for some Americans is complex. Still, from the first infections and lockdowns, it was clear that one key site—perhaps *the* key site—of infection, impact, and struggle over the virus, and what it has revealed about our society, was the workplace.

The pandemic transformed the nature of work for nearly every working person, albeit in vastly different ways. The cumulative consequence of these transformations pushed the "labor question"—Who will do the work and under what conditions?—to the center of public debate in politics and media in ways not seen in decades. Even more significantly, the transformation of work generated new responses from workers themselves: new workplace actions, new solidarities, and new organizing efforts and tactics. Some scholars and organizers even argue that new forms of class consciousness have emerged from these years.

This sense of transformation and possibility animated much research, including our own. Yet, looking back, the overall trajectory and meaning of the three crucial years from the start of the pandemic in 2020 through the major labor disruptions of 2023 proves elusive. Each year produced head-spinning developments within months, many with contradictory implications, and the same was true of the whole period. In 2020, lockdowns and the largest spike in unemployment since the Great Depression gave way to a summer of mass protest after the murder of George Floyd. By the fall, a Republican president was eagerly signing his name to the checks flowing from a once-in-a-generation expansion of social welfare, and his Democratic opponent was promising to be the most pro-union chief executive in history.

The year 2021 began with the rollout of vaccines and the promise of a "return to normal," but it quickly appeared that many workers did not seek normalcy. By summer, news outlets were breathlessly reporting on a "Great Resignation" of workers and a tight labor market, measured in one-off bonuses for service workers and hand-scrawled signs from business owners decrying workers' unwillingness to return to their minimum-wage jobs. A series of contract campaigns and strikes won the moniker "Striketober" that fall, and in December the first stores in a new campaign to organize Starbucks filed their cards with the National Labor Relations Board (NLRB), even as the annual report from the Bureau of Labor Statistics (BLS) revealed another year of declining union density in the United States.

The first months of 2022 generated tremendous hope for labor, with hundreds of Starbucks stores winning NLRB elections and the independent Amazon Labor Union (ALU) shocking everyone from Jeff Bezos to seasoned labor organizers with their victory on Staten Island. The ALU's campaign, in particular, seemed to suggest possibility emerging from pandemic suffering; organizer Chris Smalls made headlines after leading a protest against unsafe working conditions at the facility in spring 2020, for which he was promptly fired. The grassroots militancy of these campaigns carried over to organized labor's established unions. In fall 2022 the largest higher education strike in US history, involving close to fifty thousand graduate students and other academic employees in the University of California system, opened a new phase in the academic labor movement, putting strike action more firmly on the table while winning impressive gains.

At around the same time, two of the largest and best-known private sector unions in the country underwent dramatic transformations that demonstrated the degree of workers' unwillingness to "return to normal" in their unions as well as on the job. Sean O'Brien was elected as Teamsters president in late 2021 with the support of a coalition of rank-and-file reformers, and the United Auto Workers' (UAW) overhaul of its elections process—ordered by a federal judge to make the union more accountable to its members in the wake of a series of corruption scandals—made possible the election of Shawn Fain in 2023. This would prove key in 2023 as both unions publicly prepared for battle and then achieved bold demands by threatening to strike, in the case of the Teamsters, and actually striking, in the case of the UAW.

As the year 2022 drew to a close, however, neither Starbucks nor Amazon had signed a contract, nor even begun to bargain in good faith, revealing once again the limits of US labor law (as of summer 2024, Starbucks has come to the table, while Amazon remains obdurate). The "most pro-union president" in history failed to win any reforms to these laws from a Democratic Congress, including the Protecting the Right to Organize, or PRO, Act, and also failed to preserve the modest but lifesaving gains that had been created in our social welfare programs.[1] Instead, President Joe Biden used his bully pulpit to end a contract dispute in the freight rail industry before a strike, despite four railroad unions voting down the contract that Congress ultimately imposed. The Federal Reserve spent the fall ratcheting up interest rates, effectively reasserting the "normal" balance of class power in the United States by privileging inflation reduction at the expense of unemployment (see chapter 3 for a much deeper discussion of the battle and debate around inflation). Gallup polling released on the eve of Labor Day 2022 revealed that 71 percent of Americans approved of unions, the highest level since 1965. Yet, BLS data from January 2023 showed that just 10.1 percent of workers were union members, the lowest level since the 1920s.[2] The task of addressing this gulf between US workers' enthusiasm for the labor movement and their participation in it would be picked up in 2023 by unions new and old, as discussed in the epilogue to this book.

In this chapter we do not offer any simple takeaways or assessments of our recent past. Rather, our purpose is to chart and untangle these many developments as best we can, both to set the stage for the more detailed research in this volume and to make the overall stakes of this research clear. Crisis, and even disaster, in the United States has sometimes opened up space for new forms of solidarity and organizing to take shape; the rise of the Congress of Industrial Organizations—itself building on militant, independent industrial organizing in the early 1930s—is the archetypical example.[3] In recent years, however, labor studies scholars have more often observed the process Naomi Klein described as the "shock doctrine" at work, as capital takes advantage of misery to make sure no crisis goes to waste.[4]

The pandemic has not—at least not yet—proven a transformational moment for class consciousness or worker organizing. Nor, however, have these years been dominated or defined by the unimpeded march of capital, try as some bosses have. This is why we believe research on the pandemic and the working class remains necessary. Despite promises of normalcy, the pandemic has not simply ended, and neither have workers' efforts to respond to, and make meaning of, the tremendous upheavals COVID-19 has wrought in their working lives. For all that has happened, the future of working-class organizing remains, as ever, unwritten.

2020: The New "Labor Question"—
Can You Work from Home?

In our home state of Massachusetts, the events that led to the uncontrollable community transmission of the COVID-19 virus, and to the effective start of the pandemic in the commonwealth, illustrate both the genuine novelty, confusion, and danger for people of all classes in the early days of the pandemic and the ways in which the virus quickly laid bare our economic and social inequalities. Biogen, one of the state's many vaunted biotech corporations, hosted a February conference for top executives from all over the world at a nonunion hotel on Boston Harbor (one of the few in the city's well-organized sector, as discussed in chapter 5). It became the nation's first "superspreader event," eventually infecting over three hundred thousand people.[5] Some Biogen executives did, indeed, get sick and even die, but most others quickly retreated to the relative safety of remote work. The hospitality workers whom Biogen's festivities unknowingly infected got sick and died, too; then, like nearly everyone else in the hospitality industry, they lost their jobs, while the disease they brought home tore far more quickly through their dense, urban, working-class communities than it did through the leafy suburbs where Biogen's top executives reside.

Virtually no one was left unaffected by the pandemic during the first weeks and months of the outbreak. Diverse groups of people faced a set of broadly shared events, experiences, and circumstances. The disease itself killed or debilitated enough healthy people to scare everyone as the government's inability to handle the crisis became readily apparent. Lack of knowledge about modes of transmission, symptoms, treatment, and possible vaccines left most people fearful and grasping for answers. The resulting economic disruption, and especially the uncertainty, also left few untouched. People scrambled to navigate jobs, businesses, schools, hospitals, and state bureaucracies, all the while trying to keep themselves and their families safe. The unprecedented and universal quality of the crisis contributed to the sense that, initially, we were all in this together and partially explains why even a polarized government was compelled to intervene on a massive scale.

And yet the crisis did what crises do. It exposed and exacerbated existing inequalities in ways that were at once predictable and surprising. The uberrich used their wealth to insulate and protect themselves. Many had been advocating for, and benefiting from, limited government for decades and were accustomed to using private wealth to reduce dependence on a public sector they had helped dismantle, and that most people rely on, whether in healthcare, transportation, or schooling. The pandemic proved no different. Billionaires booked private jets and island villas as they scampered to locales where the spread of the disease remained limited, while travel was broadly shut down for the rest of us. Some hopped onto yachts. Most learned to keep quiet about their cushy COVID "pivots," but some of the more insensitive or thoughtless periodically reminded us how they truly live in different worlds.[6]

Once safe, the rich quickly got down to business, quite literally. The pandemic was very good for the world's billionaires, an opportunity for the wealthy to advance their class war in "shock doctrine" style. So, too, was the recovery. Corporations and the super-wealthy scooped up billions in federal support while their wealth and profits soared. Globally, the wealth of billionaires grew by $4.4 trillion between 2020 and 2021 alone.[7] In the United States, where the three richest Americans held more wealth than the bottom 50 percent of the population before the pandemic, the country's billionaires increased their wealth by more than $2 trillion, or a gain of more than 70 percent as of October 2021. By May 2022, 745 US billionaires collectively held $5 trillion in wealth, or two-thirds more than the wealth of the bottom 50 percent of US households.[8] Prior to the pandemic, there was one American worth $100 billion. There would be nine by early 2021.[9]

The pandemic experience not only exposed the vast gap between billionaires and the rest of us. It also highlighted a range of less stark, though perhaps more felt, inequalities among those who work for a living. The most conspicuous work-based divisions emerged almost immediately around a simple question: Could your job be done remotely? Those who could work remotely—primarily college-educated professionals whose work could be done on networked computers, along with those educators, service providers, and culture workers who could perform their labor online—saw their living and working lives and spaces collapse into one another. This presented a whole host of new challenges but kept these workers and their families relatively safe from both the rampaging pandemic and financial ruin.

Those who could not work from home faced one of two terrible options: unemployment, which occurred in the spring of 2020 on a massive scale not seen in the United States since the Great Depression, or dangerous, and often deadly, in-person work. Almost everyone in the service economy faced one of these options, with nearly all hospitality workers laid off while those in retail, warehouses, deliveries, and healthcare went off to work with makeshift personal protective equipment. The resulting economy of the early pandemic thus took on a novel, three-part structure, mapped unevenly onto preexisting class and occupational divides: (1) the unemployed, (2) "essential" or "frontline" workers, and (3) those working from home. Some people, of course, experienced all three dimensions at different moments, and work itself was complicated by increased levels of family and self-care, which were in turn shaped by a woefully inadequate healthcare system.

The Unemployed

The importance of where one worked, and under what conditions, became immediately apparent when the outbreak first wreaked havoc on the US economy and labor market beginning in February 2020. As dramatic as the overall rise in (official) unemployment was during the first months of the pandemic, going from less than 4 percent in February to close to 15 percent by April, aggregate numbers fail to capture the extent of the pandemic's impact on total job losses or the variation across sectors. While the official unemployment rate stood at 14.4 percent in April 2020, the adjusted rate—which includes workers who left the labor force but are not counted as unemployed—was at an astounding 22.7 percent.[10]

Over 20 million people joined the unemployed in the first two months of the pandemic, with massive unemployment characterizing much of 2020. Many of these workers were not only left destitute and facing eviction, but found themselves in deadly situations as they lost the healthcare that came with their jobs in the midst of a global pandemic. This was exacerbated by the fact that so many Americans—especially since the Great Recession of 2007–2009—were working in low-wage service sector jobs. They had long been on the brink of disaster and unable to establish any sort of personal safety net.

Even detailed aggregate estimates miss the wide variation across the labor market. Workers in low-wage jobs were hit the hardest in the first months, and first year, of the pandemic because so many of their jobs were in the service sector, portions of which shut down almost completely at the start and then only slowly rebounded. In March 2020, leisure and hospitality companies quickly shed nearly five hundred thousand jobs, followed by the massive loss of almost 8 million jobs in that sector alone in April.[11] The losses in leisure and hospitality were particularly dramatic but broadly reflective of what was going on in the service sector as a whole. Perhaps most telling, "the job loss among low earners was so extreme that it actually pushed the median wage up a staggering 7 percent from 2019."[12] Wage rates appeared to improve statistically because the most poorly paid had simply lost their jobs.

The lowest-paying jobs accounted for nearly 60 percent of all job losses between February 2020 and October 2021 despite constituting only 30 percent of all jobs.[13] By contrast, employment among high-wage workers was left largely unchanged, with middle-wage workers falling in between (in contrast with the Great Recession, when middle-wage occupations lost jobs more rapidly than their low-wage counterparts). Women—particularly Black and Latina women—accounted for the majority of the decrease in the labor force, despite making up less than half of the workforce. This reflected their concentration in the service sector and the growing requirements of family care that came with the pandemic. Black and Hispanic workers overall were unemployed at higher rates, again largely tied to their prevalence in low-wage service sector jobs.[14] And, of course, those who worked outside the home and came into greater contact with other workers and the broader public got infected and died at higher rates.

Although unemployment remained high through 2020, the return of jobs combined with government relief reduced the high levels of hardship seen in the summer. Pandemic unemployment insurance, expanded child tax credits, and the paycheck protection program (though badly deployed and cynically exploited by bosses) generated life-sustaining income for millions. Millions of people nonetheless remained out of work and struggled to afford sufficient food or pay for housing through 2021.[15]

The Frontline Workers

By April 2020 about one-third of the labor force was classified "essential" or "frontline," meaning these workers had to work in-person during the pandemic. Most visible were the healthcare workers, cheered as heroes as they braved terrifying working conditions brought on by decades of privatization and disinvestment in public health: impossible staffing ratios, insufficient facilities, and a lack of basic equipment for their jobs and their own protection.[16] As sociologist Jamie McCallum notes, "Essential workers were called heroes when they left for work and treated as sacrificial lambs when they got there," becoming celebrated victims who had the impossible choice between risking their lives at work or risking their livelihoods by staying at home.[17] This had been true prior to the pandemic, of course. As historian William P. Jones explained in 2022, "It is the essential nature of these jobs that has made it so critical, in the view of many, to reduce the wages and protections of the workers who fill them." Jones dates this practice to the early twentieth century and the emergence of the "municipal housekeeping" movement, which extended the racist, patriarchal ideology of domestic labor—essential and thus exploited—to a wide variety of collective care work.[18]

Under these incredibly adverse conditions, one major factor made a clear difference: union membership. Unsurprisingly, unionized workers fared far better in their efforts to secure personal protective equipment, hazard pay, necessary sick leave, and other basic protections. These workers and their workplaces also proved far better at protecting the general public: unionized hospitals and nursing homes had markedly lower mortality rates during the early stages of the pandemic, a feature that extended to many other workplaces (see chapter 5 for a compelling look at the importance of unions during the pandemic). With union density at just below 11 percent at the start of the pandemic, however, the protection of union membership extended to only a minority of essential workers and, by extension, those they served.

Beyond the third of the labor force officially classed as "essential" were millions of other workers in retail and restaurants who were not technically "essential" but effectively remained on the front lines because their employers insisted on keeping their businesses open.[19] These essential workers—most of whom were among the working poor—quite literally made it possible for everyone else, particularly the professional middle class, to live. Low-wage workers had long produced, transported, stocked, and served food; kept hospitals and schools running; provided child and elder care; and cleaned and built virtually everything. But the reality of their essential roles became more visible and, at times, awkward and perverse during the pandemic, as the survival of remote workers required putting millions of low-wage workers in transparently unsafe working conditions. Delivery workers, paid shoppers, grocery store employees, retail workers, cleaners, and the like made it possible—and took on most of the associated risks—for professionals and their families to live in COVID bubbles.

These workers have received the most scholarly and journalistic attention as accounts of the pandemic have proliferated—and for good reason. Their labor was at once truly essential for the survival and functioning of society, but they quickly found themselves at the center of conflicts over what "essential" status meant when they demanded actual protections, compensation, and other measures for their own survival. As demonstrated by McCallum, whose book *Essential* is the most comprehensive overview of this labor to date, essential workers took the lead in organizing during the first year of the pandemic.

While BLS data showed a reduction in strikes and other actions during 2020—unsurprising, given that a third of the workforce was idled—"workers forced their managers, bosses, and corporate boards to provide lifesaving protocols, more paid sick days, raises, and better healthcare and other benefits. Were it not for workers blowing the whistle, we might never have known the hazards they faced or gotten the kind of improvements that saved lives."[20] Health and safety concerns shaped many of these workplace actions, including the one that led to Chris Smalls's firing from Amazon in Staten Island. In late March, as even pop star Britney Spears called for a general strike, unionized sanitation workers in Pittsburgh initiated an illegal wildcat strike to protest the lack of personal protection equipment and to demand hazard pay.[21] They were quickly followed by Teamsters at a large Kroger warehouse in Memphis who held a wildcat strike when one of the workers tested positive for COVID and the company had failed to implement protective measures or extend hazard pay.[22] Later in the week, poultry workers in Georgia followed suit, unhappy with the inadequate response by their employer, Perdue Farms. A week later, nearly one thousand meatpackers walked off the job in

Colorado, frustrated by the lack of safety gear, poor social distancing, and the fact that their employer would not extend sick pay to those who got COVID.

Essential workers tended to be in low-wage sectors, but they also included relatively well-paid professionals. Healthcare workers—an economically diverse sector—led half of all worker actions in 2020. Issues with staffing, working conditions, burnout, and pay had all been bubbling up as the industry became increasingly corporate during the past two decades. These came to a head during the pandemic as nurses and other healthcare workers not only burned out but also faced agonizingly difficult decisions (see chapter 9 for a powerful discussion of nursing during the pandemic). Walking out on dangerous jobs to protect themselves and demand better conditions for patients came up against the immediate urgency of saving people under chaotic conditions.[23] Many engaged in a range of creative workplace actions. Likewise, most of the issues that had led teachers to strike across the country in 2018–2019, including pay, working conditions, and burnout, intensified in 2020–2021. This not only led to increased political activity in the short term but also laid the foundation for subsequent militancy within the education sector during 2022 and 2023. Across industries, then, COVID intensified sources of worker discontent, often exacerbating existing issues in ways that could both unify and divide workers during and after the pandemic.

McCallum contends that a new class consciousness began to emerge among these workers in the course of 2020, along with several forms of concerted worker action. However, this solidarity began to run aground on the divisions that the pandemic's "labor question" created; specifically, whether campaigns for expanded social welfare and even organizing efforts themselves could, or should, allow workers to stay at home when others had to go to work. Those working from home, and even the unemployed, had come to rely on essential and frontline workers. What, then, were they owed?

Working from Home

Those working from home did experience very real hardships. Their families did not necessarily escape the disease, and they quickly realized that turning a home into a workplace, a makeshift school, or both brought with it a range of adverse effects. It was not simply that home suddenly became quite cramped but that the divide between work and home itself became blurrier and more arbitrary. This allowed employers to increase workloads at the same time as family (and self) care demands grew dramatically. The shift to working from home also badly exacerbated patriarchal systems of social reproduction; one study of academic labor showed that male economists saw their scholarly output spike during their time at home, while their female counterparts reported impossible schedules managing households now that all lived, worked, and went to school under one roof, swamping their ability to do their own research.[24]

And yet, professionals by and large kept their jobs, saw their incomes remain stable, and stayed relatively safe. They often had resources to move and work from safer and more comfortable locales. There was an imperfect—and, for some, tragic—period of adjustment, as well as a longer-term interrogation of the work-life balance more broadly, but most of this professional class was better positioned to navigate the changes brought about by the pandemic. Not surprisingly, then, the top quartile of earners had essentially recovered by the end of the summer and often saw their home values spike, even as the recovery remained slow for low-wage workers.

While early in the pandemic those working from home happily lent their voices to the chorus of cheers for essential workers, mutual dependence did not, by the fall, lead to solidarity among remote and essential workers. For a vocal elite—particularly a pundit class simultaneously frustrated by months of lockdowns and trying to triangulate between the COVID denialism of a growing swath of the Republican Party and the continued need for mitigation measures—the insistence on a return to normal grew to include attacks on workers taking action for their own safety. When educators, for instance, pointed out that public schools had seen nearly none of the necessary infrastructural or social investments to sustain safe work or learning, and pushed their districts to remain remote or take mitigation measures like masking in the fall of 2020, age-old canards about the selfishness of organized educators re-emerged with a vengeance (see chapters 6 and 7 for further discussions of educators' organizing).

2021: A Return to Normalcy?

Warren G. Harding is credited with coining the term "normalcy" in his 1920 presidential campaign as a vision for American voters believed to be weary of World War I, labor unrest, and, of course, a pandemic. The inauguration of Joe Biden and the rollout of the first COVID-19 vaccines in the early months of 2021 seemed to signal a similar return to many political observers. For working people, however, the promise of "normal" minimum-wage jobs coupled with rising rents, especially after so many had sacrificed so much, did not sit well.

Despite the cheers for essential workers in 2020, it was clear by 2021 that the bosses did not intend to actually reward these workers in any meaningful way. At Saint Vincent Hospital in Worcester, Massachusetts, nurses sought living wages, safe staffing ratios, and other basic improvements to their working conditions. Coming a year into the pandemic, a casual observer could have been forgiven for thinking it unlikely that these heroes would be denied at the bargaining table, and yet Dallas-based Tenet Healthcare Corporation signaled their "return to normal" by standing pat in their refusal of the nurses, who walked out on strike in March 2021 in what turned out to be an eight-month battle.[25]

As the economy reopened and bosses around the country sought a return to normal on terms similar to those of Tenet Healthcare, workers quit in record numbers. In 2021 nearly 50 million workers voluntarily left their jobs, according to the US Bureau of Labor Statistics—a process that continued into 2022.[26] Although the numbers were unprecedented, this mass exodus was in fact part of a broader quitting trend dating back more than a decade. Workers had been realizing for some time that their jobs had been degraded to the point of parody. The pandemic intensified the process as people left jobs due to a variety of interrelated factors, including retirement, fear, burnout, family obligations, lack of respect, limited opportunities for advancement, and a reconsideration of work-life balance. Much of this was less a mass resignation in the sense of people permanently abandoning the labor force—though this happened, especially for older workers—than it was a great reshuffling, whereby workers moved from one job to another as the pandemic led/forced people to rethink and reprioritize working conditions within a tightening labor market. As the economy heated up in 2021, demand for labor increased and gave (some) workers leverage at a time when people were questioning their relationship to work and quitting in larger numbers (which only further served to shrink the labor market and give workers a bit of bargaining power).[27]

Many workers simply sought better jobs, looking for safer, more flexible, and more decent working conditions, as well as improved pay and increased benefits. This process was uneven across sectors and shaped by race, gender, occupation, citizenship status, and other factors in occupational segregation. Hospitality and food services experienced the highest quit rates, but manufacturing saw rates increase as well, as did professional and business services. This was driven in part by a tight labor market, which gave many workers more options, but also by changing working conditions, which allowed some people to work from almost anywhere while leading others to opt out of dangerous working conditions. The process was also shaped by the responses of employers, some of whom moved fairly quickly to improve pay, benefits, and conditions, while others stayed the course and lost workers.[28]

Employers were faced with an unfamiliar problem: they suddenly lacked access to an unlimited supply of cheap labor. This, in turn, led to complaints from the business class that people were not working because they were living large off extended unemployment benefits, an argument that proved specious once benefits ended and unemployment numbers remained largely unchanged. The labor shortage and quitting were concentrated heavily in the service sector, especially hospitality and restaurants, as well as in healthcare. These industries had worked for decades to keep wages low, and in 2021 their corporate leaders refused to raise wages high enough to attract workers. According to US Census surveys, the labor shortage was the product of lousy, unattractive jobs combined with a series of factors that made it hard for many people to work.[29] More businesses were reopening or expanding, but conditions were such that many people could not return to work, or had found better work, especially in the service sector. In the case of nursing, for example, there wasn't so much a nursing shortage as the fact that many nursing jobs had become horrible and people were quitting—a long-standing problem but one made worse by the pandemic.

"Striketober" and the Rise of a New Militant Minority?

Workers walked out collectively as well as individually in 2021. "By the end of the year," McCallum notes, "there had been 250 strikes, far more than in any year since before the Great Recession."[30] Only seventeen of these, however, cleared the thousand-worker threshold that the Bureau of Labor Statistics employs in counting strikes, prompting Cornell University's School of Industrial and Labor Relations to create a new tracking system to catalog these smaller actions.[31]

Major strikes, when they did occur, generated significant enthusiasm among workers and suggested a transformation taking place even within unionized workplaces. Ten thousand John Deere workers went on strike in October 2021, the leading event in what became popularly known as "Striketober," with workers striking at, or near, levels not seen in a generation (at least in the private sector) during the last months of the year. Rank-and-file workers in the UAW's John Deere plants rejected the first contract their union sent them, pushing hard to eliminate the tiered structures that have come to dominate post-1981 industrial contracts and setting a tone for the contract battles to come at United Parcel Service and the Big Three automakers two years later.[32] Similar rank-and-file restiveness resulted in a close vote for the ratification of the International Alliance of Theatrical Stage Employees' contract for thirteen thousand workers in the film industry.[33]

Indeed, what stood out about these large strikes was not so much their numbers as their diversity. Joining some 10,000 workers at John Deere were thousands more in healthcare, food sales and processing, universities, construction, mining, and technology. Some 140,000 workers walked out and went on strike in more than 250 work stoppages in 2021, and about a third of these came from nonunionized workers. This breadth was due in part to the heightened concern about health and safety issues in virtually all workplaces, and the fact that workers were fed up. They wanted to be safer at work, and if they were going to be put at risk, they demanded better pay. In turn, such demands became easier to make as the labor market tightened and worker militancy encouraged others to act.[34]

Beyond strikes, close to one thousand union elections were held in the private sector in 2021, with around six hundred new unions achieving certification, often in sectors of the economy with little previous union presence (all trends that would continue through 2022). While the BLS data showed 241,000 union jobs lost in 2021—likely still a product of the pandemic's impact on certain sectors of the economy—hope for the future of the labor movement persisted into the new year, buoyed by the announcement of union elections at three Starbucks stores in and around Buffalo, New York.

2022: Hope and Reaction

Exactly two years after the pandemic began, in March 2022 the US economy was said to have four million more jobs than workers, companies were struggling with staffing, and wages were rising at an annual average of 5 percent. This recovery was nothing short of historic. Within two short years, after nearly unprecedented job losses, the official unemployment rate returned to roughly pre-pandemic levels.[35] And although low-wage jobs came back more slowly, by the middle of 2021 there were signs that the bottom end of the labor market had improved as well. Pay and working conditions may not have improved dramatically, but the increased demand for labor gave even low-wage workers some leverage, allowed them to switch jobs more easily, and did result in slightly improved pay.[36]

The month ended with a thunderclap: as ballots began being counted in the union election at Amazon's JFK8 facility in Staten Island on Thursday, March 31, the independent union was in the lead. The following day, the Amazon Labor Union's victory became official, a stunning blow to the heart of a corporation with enormous sectoral and market-setting power and one whose business model had become emblematic of the pandemic's class divides, in which working-class warehouse and delivery workers sustained the at-home economy of the remote-work sector.

Coupled with the wave of successful union elections at Starbucks, another longtime emblem of the post-industrial, post-union corporate landscape, and the rise of other independent or largely grassroots organizing efforts at workplaces large (Trader Joe's) and small (coffee shops and restaurants in many cities), 2022 seemed to augur a new chapter for the labor movement. At its summer convention, the AFL-CIO (American Federation of Labor–Congress of Industrial Organizations) promised a reinvestment in new organizing; not enough to stem the tide of union decline, as many observers were quick to note, but a welcome commitment nonetheless. Labor leaders Sara Nelson of the Association of Flight Attendants and Sean O'Brien of the Teamsters toured the country with socialist senator and former presidential candidate Bernie Sanders in August and September, joining picket lines and rallying with thousands of workers in US cities under the simple banner "The Working Class."[37]

Capital, however, stood poised to strike back, deploying a battery of tried-and-true tactics that have sustained the one-sided class war since at least the 1980s. Jeff Bezos and Howard Schultz quickly shed any lingering "nice guy" posturing they had cultivated toward their workers and deployed the full range of classic union-busting tactics. Neither corporation seemed to have any intention of bargaining in good faith, and nothing the National Labor Relations Board has done or is able to do, under its current construction, seemed likely to compel them (Starbucks has since come to the table). The Federal Reserve moved to raise interest rates, undercutting what little power workers had amassed in favor of bringing inflation down for creditors.

And when railway workers moved to fight the brutal conditions imposed on their workplaces by private equity—including a shameful lack of basic protections such as sick days—they quickly ran up against the limits of President Biden's pro-labor posturing. As at John Deere, a restive rank and file proved willing to vote down a negotiated contract, one Biden and his labor secretary, Marty Walsh, prematurely celebrated as a settlement. However, this did not stop Congress from imposing it anyway, at the president's urging.[38] While furious railway workers did not go so far as to strike, one union has since deposed its longtime leader in favor of a rank-and-file radical who challenged him.

Pandemic Contradictions: Where Do We Go from Here?

In 2022 public approval of unions reached its highest level since the mid-1960s. To be sure, this shift in public opinion had been happening for some time as more and more people confronted growing inequality and recognized that unions were key to slowing down the upward distribution of wealth. Still, it is clear that this pro-union mood was given an added jolt by the pandemic. Inequality was laid bare, and it was in the workplace where it was felt most intimately. It was at work where it became clear to so many that neither government nor business had the best interests of working people in mind and that many companies were not at all concerned about their employees' well-being. Workers had to defend themselves, and unions remain a crucial means for doing so.

It was not simply that the broader public came to appreciate frontline workers, recognizing that they were experiencing the brunt of the pandemic and that too many employers did not care. It was that along the way many working people seemed to develop a nothing-left-to-lose kind of assertiveness that resulted in the array of actions discussed throughout this book, ranging from strikes, walkouts, and unionization efforts to large-scale resignations and workplace protests. It became more acceptable and felt more possible to push back, and working people did just that, regardless of whether they had the protection of a union or not.

And yet a routine report in January 2023 from the Bureau of Labor Statistics provided sobering news. It revealed—with a painful predictability—that for all of this newfound energy, the labor movement had not yet been able to reverse the tide of union decline. Union density is certainly not the only way to measure the health of the labor movement, but the same forces that have made it so difficult to translate increased public approval of unions into greater numbers of unionized workers inevitably plague any organizing model that tries to advance the interests of working people. Out-of-control inequality, concentrated corporate power, and the ascendancy of the right have created, and were made possible by, a political system that is stacked against working people on every level from electoral politics and tax policy to labor law, the regulatory system, and the entire legal apparatus. The complete absence of anything resembling economic democracy produces a corrupt political system, and that political system ensures that gross inequality will flourish. It is this perverse political-economic amalgamation that makes organizing for structural change so difficult, even as it also exposes how broken the system is.

In this sense, the fact that workers in the United States have lost the meaningful right to organize during the exact same period when wealth has become increasingly concentrated should be of no surprise. Employers face little in the way of penalties when they violate workers' basic rights around work, organizing efforts, union formation, and contract negotiation and enforcement. When faced with recent efforts to unionize, companies like Whole Foods, Amazon, and Trader Joe's followed what is now a well-worn (and illegal) anti-union playbook: shutting down entire stores when workers move to unionize, firing troublemakers, reducing hours and cutting benefits, and holding captive audience meetings. They do this with legal impunity and with relatively little fear that it will hurt their public image or bottom line. To the contrary, it is what allows them to grow their wealth. Workers, by contrast, know (or quickly learn) that simply asserting their basic rights in the workplace, let alone organizing with coworkers, often leads to job loss or worse. These broad obstacles challenge any model of organizing, whether through unions or in some other form.

It was also the case that although the pandemic served to intensify a growing public awareness about class inequality within the United States, it revealed some very real divisions among working people that may make us rethink how we understand the "working class." Low-wage "essential" workers and professional middle classes were all failed by the US government during the pandemic. These groups share quite real interests that are opposed to the very wealthy who control our economy and political system. But the pandemic demonstrated how different their lived experiences are, how perverse their own class relationship can be, and how difficult it is to build solidarity among working people when their interests are often in conflict; when, for example, parents want schools reopened, patients want healthcare, or consumers want new products in ways that risk the safety of workers providing those goods and services. This class tension has long been present, but the pandemic brought it into sharp relief.

It is precisely this complex relationship between "the pandemic" and "the working class" that this book explores. How did the "pandemic experience" vary across the working class? To what extent did the pandemic remake the working class both economically and politically, by creating or exposing political divisions among working people?

This project began with the acknowledgment that labor is having a bit of a moment. A combination of factors—including heightened demand for labor that gives workers leverage; a series of high-profile victories that put winning on the table; and a growing consciousness that work, the economy, and the political system simply do not function for working people—have created an opening. How significant this moment is, how long it will last, or what political formations it will generate remain uncertain. But what is clear is that the experience of the pandemic has workers demanding more, rethinking work itself, and recognizing that organizing may quite literally be a matter of life and death.

Notes

1. Megan A. Curran, "Research Roundup of the Expanded Child Tax Credit: One Year On," Center on Poverty and Social Policy at Columbia University, Policy Report, vol. 6, no. 9, November 15, 2022, https://www.povertycenter.columbia.edu/publication/2022/child-tax-credit/research-roundup-one-year-on/.

2. Justin McCarthy, "U.S. Approval of Labor Unions at Highest Point since 1965," *Gallup*, August 30, 2022, https://news.gallup.com/poll/398303/approval-labor-unions-highest-point-1965.aspx; "Union Members 2022," news release, Bureau of Labor Statistics, January 19, 2023, https://www.bls.gov/news.release/pdf/union2.pdf/.

3. Robert Zieger, *The CIO, 1935–1955* (Chapel Hill: University of North Carolina Press, 1997).

4. Naomi Klein, *The Shock Doctrine: The Rise of Disaster Capitalism* (Toronto: Knopf Canada, 2007).

5. Michael Wines and Amy Harmon, "What Happens When a Super-spreader Event Keeps Spreading," December 11, 2020, https://www.nytimes.com/2020/12/11/us/biogen-conference-covid-spread.html/.

6. Perhaps most infamously, billionaire music and film mogul David Geffen felt the need to inform us that he had "isolated" to the Grenadines on his yacht in order to avoid the virus and hoped we all found ways to stay safe. Michele Robson, "How the Rich and Famous Escape the Pandemic," *Forbes*, December 27, 2020, https://www.forbes.com/sites/michelerobson/2021/12/27/how-the-rich—famous-escape-the-pandemic/?sh=3898d7c85521/.

7. Joseph E. Stiglitz, "COVID Has Made Global Inequality Much Worse," *Scientific American*, March 1, 2022, https://www.scientificamerican.com/article/covid-has-made-global-inequality-much-worse/.

8. Chuck Collins, "Billionaire Wealth, U.S. Job Losses, and Pandemic Profiteers," May 6, 2022, https://inequality.org/great-divide/updates-billionaire-pandemic/.

9. Jamie K. McCallum, *Essential: How the Pandemic Transformed the Long Fight for Worker Justice* (New York: Basic Books, 2022), 44.

10. Rakesh Kochar and Jesse Bennett, "U.S. Labor Market Inches Back from the COVID-19 Shock, but Recovery Is Far from Complete," Pew Research Report, April 14, 2021, https://www.pewresearch.org/fact-tank/2021/04/14/u-s-labor-market-inches-back-from-the-covid-19-shock-but-recovery-is-far-from-complete/.

11. McCallum, *Essential*, 30–31.

12. McCallum, *Essential*, 32.

13. Center on Budget and Policy Priorities, "The COVID-19 Economy's Effects on Food, Housing, and Employment Hardships," https://www.cbpp.org/sites/default/files/8-13-20pov.pdf/.

14. Kochar and Bennett, "U.S. Labor Market Inches Back."

15. Center on Budget and Policy Priorities, "COVID-19 Economy's Effects on Food, Housing, and Employment Hardships."

16. More than thirty-six hundred healthcare workers died from COVID-19 during the first year of the pandemic. "Lost on the Frontline," *The Guardian* and Kaiser Health News, https://www.theguardian.com/us-news/ng-interactive/2020/aug/11/lost-on-the-frontline-covid-19-coronavirus-us-healthcare-workers-deaths-database/.

17. McCallum, *Essential*, 5. See also Steven Thrasher, *The Viral Underclass: The Human Toll When Inequality and Disease Collide* (New York: Celadon Books, 2022).

18. William P. Jones, Labor and Working-Class History Association Presidential Address, OAH Conference, Boston, MA, April 1, 2022, https://youtu.be/KVicEvEpYxI/.

19. McCallum, *Essential*, 10. As Jamie McCallum points out, who got designated "essential" was often tied to the power of particular employers or industries who advocated for the classification. Hence, Walmart greeters were deemed essential.

20. McCallum, *Essential*, 12.

21. Mike Elk, "Black Garbage Workers Go on Wildcat Strike in Pittsburgh as General Strike Wave Spreads," *Payday Report*, March 25, 2020, https://paydayreport.com/black-garbage-workers-go-on-wildcat-strike-in-pittsburgh-as-general-strike-wave-spreads/.

22. Mike Elk, "Memphis Teamsters Wildcat Strike at Kroger's Crucial Southern Warehouse," *Payday Report*, March 27, 2020, https://paydayreport.com/memphis-teamsters-wildcat-strike-at-krogers-massive-southern-warehouse/.

23. Clarissa A. Leon and Mike Elk, "The Bureau of Labor Statistics Counted Only Eight Strikes in 2020, Payday Report Counted 1200," *Institute for New Economic Thinking*, July 13, 2021, https://www.ineteconomics.org/perspectives/blog/the-bureau-of-labor-statistics-counted-only-eight-strikes-in-2020-payday-report-counted-1-200/.

24. Zeina Hasna, Elisa Faraglia, Chryssi Giannitsarou, and Noriko Amano-Patiño, "Who Is Doing New Research in the Time of COVID-19? Not the Female Economists," Centre for Economic Policy Research/*VoxEU*, May 2, 2020, https://cepr.org/voxeu/columns/who-doing-new-research-time-covid-19-not-female-economists/. See also Hasna, Faraglia, Giannitsarou, and Amano-Patiño, "The Unequal Effects of COVID-19 on Economists' Research Productivity," November 17, 2021, https://iceanet.org/wp-content/uploads/2021/11/Amano-Patino.pdf/; and Ruomeng Cui, Hao Ding, and Feng Zhu, "Gender Inequality in Research Productivity during the COVID-19 Pandemic," Harvard Business School, 2020, https://www.hbs.edu/ris/Publication%20Files/Gender_Inequality_Accepted_Version_a47ba989-3951-43b7-aa34-b9537954bea9.pdf/.

25. Esteban Bustillos, "St. Vincent Nurses Ratify Contract after Months-Long Strike," WGBH, January 4, 2022, https://www.wgbh.org/news/local/2022-01-03/st-vincent-nurses-ratify-contract-after-months-long-strike/.

26. David Miller and Haley Yamada, "The Great Resignation: Its Origins and What It Means for Future Business," *ABC News*, May 2, 2022, https://www.whio.com/news/business/great-resignation/A6WKLWQGOLUUQCRF4PAOIMDH7M/.

27. Joseph Fuller and William Kerr, "The Great Resignation Didn't Start with the Pandemic," *Harvard Business Review,* March 23, 2022, https://www.hbs.edu/faculty/Pages/item.aspx?num=62290#:~:text=Abstract,more%20than%20a%20decade%20ago/.

28. McDonald's, for example, increased pay and improved benefits, offering emergency childcare, paid time off, and tuition reimbursement, while Walmart also made moves to attract workers and improve retention. And they were not alone. Fuller and Kerr, "Great Resignation Didn't Start with the Pandemic."

29. McCallum, *Essential*, 152.

30. McCallum, *Essential*, 163.

31. Kathryn Ritchie, Johnnie Kallas, and Deepa Kylasam Iyer, "Labor Action Tracker 2023," Cornell University, ILR School, https://www.ilr.cornell.edu/faculty-and-research/labor-action-tracker/annual-report-2023.

32. Noam Scheiber, "Striking Deere Workers Approve a New Contract on

the Third Try," *New York Times*, November 17, 2021, https://www.nytimes.com/2021/11/17/business/john-deere-strike-uaw-union-contract.html/.

33. Gene Maddus, "IATSE Contract Ratification Decided by Razor-Thin Vote Margins in Two Guilds," *Variety*, November 15, 2021, https://variety.com/2021/film/news/iatse-contract-vote-razor-thin-margins-1235112711/.

34. Juliana Kaplan and Madison Hoff, "140,000 Americans Walked out of Work Last Year to Strike for Higher Pay and Safer Workplaces—and Thousands Got What They Wanted," *Business Insider*, February 22, 2022, https://www.businessinsider.com/how-many-workers-strike-unions-2021-labor-shortage-wage-shortage-2022-2/.

35. With one caveat. Although jobs were going unfilled by 2022, there were 3 million fewer people employed than before the pandemic, meaning some people never returned to work. Center on Budget and Policy Priorities, "COVID-19 Economy's Effects on Food, Housing, and Employment Hardships."

36. Tim Smart, "COVID-19 Did a Number on the Workforce—and the Workplace," *U.S. News and World Report*, March 17, 2022, https://www.usnews.com/news/economy/articles/2022-03-17/covid-19-did-a-number-on-the-workforce-and-the-workplace/.

37. Tori Bedford, "Sanders Joins Rally for Worker's Rights," *Bay State Banner*, August 24, 2022, https://www.baystatebanner.com/2022/08/24/sanders-joins-rally-for-workers-rights/.

38. Ross Grooters, "What Would It Take for Rail Workers to Win?" *Labor Notes*, December 2, 2022, https://labornotes.org/2022/12/what-would-it-take-rail-workers-win/.

2

The Diseases Are the Symptoms
Working-Class Plagues—COVID-19 and Deaths of Despair

DEVAN HAWKINS

Massachusetts has been collecting data about mortality going back to the 1840s. The Massachusetts Department of Public Health uses this data to publish a figure showing the annual percentage of deaths attributable to four broad causes: infectious disease, heart disease, cancer, and injuries since 1843 (fig. 2.1).[1] Although this data deals with only one relatively small state, in the movement of the lines representing those causes of death you can see some of the most important trends and public health events of the past three centuries.

Looking at figure 2.1, almost everyone notices the rapid increase in infectious disease deaths that occurred in the period between 1918 to 1920. This spike in mortality is the 1918–1919 influenza pandemic, a pandemic that is often mislabeled as the Spanish flu, during which it has been estimated that as many as 500 million people, one-third of the global population, was infected and that between 50 and 100 million people died from the illness.[2] The 1918 influenza pandemic can be compared with other historic incidences of rapid increases in mortality, such as the precipitous decline in life expectancy in Russia following the collapse of the Soviet Union,[3] as well as the HIV pandemic, where in some parts of sub-Saharan Africa the disease was estimated to have reduced life expectancy by more than ten years.[4]

While figure 2.1 shows only its beginning, we have now lived through the largest and most deadly pandemic of an infectious disease in a century. As I write this chapter in the summer of 2023, COVID-19 has been estimated to have taken nearly 7 million lives globally,[5] of which more than 1 million occurred in the United States.[6] Global excessive deaths from the pandemic, which includes both deaths from COVID-19 directly and other health problems potentially exacerbated by the pandemic through 2021, were estimated to be 14.9 million.[7]

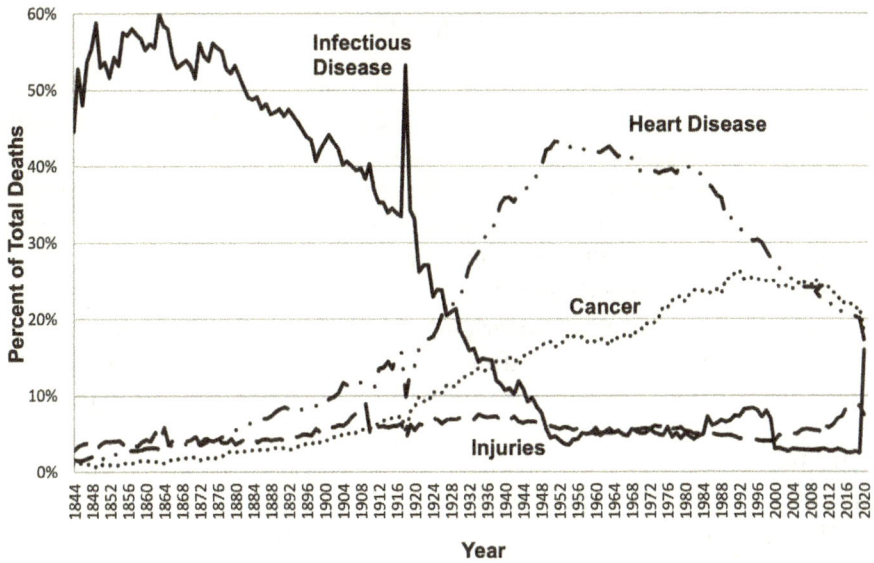

Figure 2.1. Deaths from selected causes, Massachusetts: 1844–2020. Source: Department of Public Health. "Massachusetts Deaths 2020." Mass.gov, January 2023. https://www.mass.gov/lists/annual-massachusetts-death-reports.

It is significant to note that as important and impactful as the pandemic has been for global health, mortality, and life expectancy, we had in fact begun to see increases in mortality in the United States long before the first cases of COVID-19 emerged. This meant that, although not as stark as deaths from the COVID-19 pandemic, tens of thousands of *more* people were dying every year than would be expected if these increases had not occurred.[8] These increases in mortality were so extreme that between 2016 and 2018, life expectancy actually declined in the United States.[9] These pre-COVID increases in mortality were driven by deaths from drug overdoses, suicides, and alcohol-related causes and are often referred to as *deaths of despair*.

What connects all of these historic health events in which mortality rates rapidly increase? Simply put, it is that the most socioeconomically vulnerable people typically face the harshest effects and that a key contributor to this vulnerability is people's work environments. Health challenges almost always tend to fall on workers employed in low-wage, dangerous, and insecure jobs.

In this chapter, I describe how this historic trend in workplace vulnerability to health challenges can be seen in deaths from COVID-19 and deaths of despair. I ask how work-related factors contributed to the risk for contracting and dying from these causes and explore how the COVID-19 pandemic exacerbated the risk for deaths of despair among workers.

COVID-19

Early in the COVID-19 pandemic, many cases of the disease were related to workplace transmission of the SARS-CoV-2 virus.[10] One of the first studies to examine the role that workplace transmission played in the initial stages of the pandemic looked at cases in six different regions of East Asia during the first forty days after local transmission of the virus began. The study found that 103 of the 690 locally transmitted cases initially identified were likely tied to workplace transmission. As expected, healthcare workers comprised a large share of these cases—over one-fifth. However, when looking at the earliest period—the ten days after local transmission began—it was shop salespeople, drivers, and construction laborers who made up the greatest share of cases. Vulnerability to work-related COVID-19 was not just confined to healthcare workers dealing with sick patients. It also included a wide range of workers interacting with the public.

The nature of work, then, put some workers at a higher risk for COVID-19 than others. Quantifying and understanding that risk was therefore an important part of the response to the pandemic. In mid-March of 2020, the *New York Times* published an article that used data from O*Net, a database that contains information about the characteristics of hundreds of occupations, to categorize occupations according to their risk of exposure to coronavirus. Occupational risk was quantified on two axes: physical proximity to others and frequent exposure to infectious diseases. The idea was that because the disease is passed through a respiratory mechanism, those people who frequently work close to others (whether the public or coworkers) will be at an elevated risk and that working with people who are frequently sick with infectious diseases will further increase their risk. The highest-risk jobs were those at the uppermost levels of both axes, a position that was dominated by healthcare occupations but also first responders. When considering those whose work was primarily defined by close contact with others, a wide variety of occupations were at a high risk, including personal care aides, hairdressers, food service workers, and cashiers.[11] Researchers found that over 14 million workers faced exposure to infections at least once a week, representing 10 percent of the workforce.[12] Additional work went into documenting workers employed in "essential industries"—those industries that were deemed so vital that they needed to maintain in-person work even when stay-at-home orders were being issued. The Brookings Institute used a list of essential industries created by the Department of Homeland Security to estimate the number of workers employed in these industries to be between 49 million and 62 million—34 to 43 percent of the workforce.[13]

Healthcare Workers

Throughout the pandemic it has been clear that healthcare workers have been at particularly high risk for infection.[14] Unfortunately, the administration of healthcare institutions seemed to disregard the vulnerability of their workers. As reported by the *Boston Globe*, in the first months of the pandemic in Massachusetts, some of these administrators downplayed the risks faced by their workers, stating the following:

> "We aren't seeing clusters . . . We still think a lot of it is coming from the community spread."
> "We simply can't tell where that person was infected."
> "While health care workers may be protected by PPE [personal protective equipment] during the work day . . . we are all potentially bumping up against this virus in our daily lives."[15]

When hospital administrations were making these claims, there were about 130 cases of COVID-19 per 100,000 residents of the Commonwealth of Massachusetts. At the same time, there were 534 and 658 cases per 100,000 workers at two of the leading Boston area hospitals. These rates were more than double those in surrounding Suffolk County, which had rates higher than the rest of the state (fig. 2.2). It was naïve to assume that a substantial amount of this increased risk was not due to working in a high-risk industry.

The denial of the role of workplace transmission in infecting healthcare workers meant that appropriate methods to protect healthcare workers were often not taken. In the early stages of the pandemic, there was a focus on methods like handwashing and disinfecting surfaces and less of a focus on ventilation, which is a more effective method to control the spread of a respiratory virus. There were also many shortages of personal protective equipment.[16]

Workplace Outbreaks

Throughout the pandemic, there were reports about workplace outbreaks of COVID-19. California, for example, had nearly twenty thousand such outbreaks between January 2020 and August 2021.[17] More than three hundred thousand cases of the disease were associated with these outbreaks. Close to half of these outbreaks occurred in the healthcare and social assistance industry. At a particularly high risk were workers in skilled nursing facilities, where there was an average of more than one outbreak per establishment. While it has been well known that residents of nursing facilities had a high risk of mortality during the pandemic, less attention has been given to the safety of workers in these facilities. Residential care facilities and community food and housing, emergency services, and hospitals also had high risks

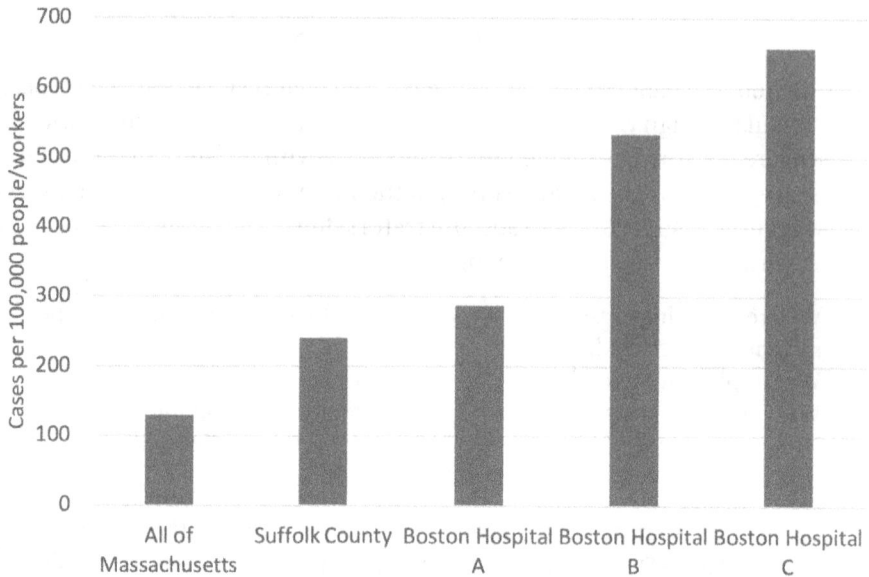

Figure 2.2. Rate of COVID-19 in Massachusetts, Suffolk County, and three Boston area hospitals as of April 3, 2020. Source: Author's analysis of data from P. D. McCluskey and T. Andersen, "Near Tripling of Employee Coronavirus Infections in Largest Massachusetts Hospitals in Past Week," *Boston Globe*, April 3, 2020; and Massachusetts Department of Public Health, April 2, 2024, "Coronavirus Disease 2019 (COVID-19) Cases in MA As of April 2, 2020," https://www.mass .gov/doc/covid-19-cases-in-massachusetts-as-of-april-2-2020/download.

of outbreaks. Outside of the healthcare industry, the food, education, retail (especially grocery stores), and construction industries also had high rates of outbreaks.

To focus on one of these vulnerable industries, 115 meat processing plants in nineteen states were affected by outbreaks in the month of April alone. These outbreaks resulted in nearly five thousand infections among workers.[18] The nature of the work itself made transmission likely because of the requirement to work in close proximity to others. The cool, dry work environment also created a setting for the virus to spread more easily. This risk, and the inaction of management to protect workers, prompted walkouts among meat processing workers, such as those at a Perdue plant in Georgia.[19] Management at one Tyson Foods plant was even reported to have bet on how many workers at the plant would be infected.[20]

In many cases, these studies underestimate the reported number of infected workers. Different jurisdictions have different requirements with respect to reporting workplace outbreaks. Furthermore, even when there are reporting requirements, these events often go underreported, which is a common challenge for occupational health surveillance in general. This underreporting can be due to ignorance about reporting requirements or can be done intentionally with the goal of concealing workplace outbreaks. It is also important to keep in mind that the cases represented by these reports of outbreaks represent only infected workers and not the family members and other household members they may have infected.

Workplace and Racial Ethnic Disparities in COVID-19

Workplace exposure proved an important contributor to the racial and ethnic differences in the risk for COVID-19. Throughout the pandemic, Black, Hispanic, and Native people in the United States had elevated rates of infection, hospitalization, and death from COVID-19 compared to white people, reflecting in part their location within the labor market.[21] Black workers are more likely to be employed in essential industries, and Black and Asian workers are the most likely to be employed in hospitals and other healthcare settings. Additionally, Black and Hispanic workers were more than twice as likely to be employed in meat processing compared to white workers (table 2.1).[22]

The differential racial and ethnic risk for COVID-19 was reflected in outbreak studies. In the California study discussed above, many of the essential industries with high rates of outbreaks employed workers of color disproportionately. For example, Latino workers comprised 50 percent of outbreak-associated cases in manufacturing, retail, accommodation and food services, and transportation and warehousing industries despite comprising only 40 percent of the population of California.[23] Similarly, in Utah, where Hispanic workers comprise 24 percent of the workforce, they represented 73 percent of COVID cases acquired during workplace outbreaks.[24] Unfortunately, workers of color also had less access to resources to protect themselves, such as paid sick leave.[25]

Work and Geographic Disparities

Work-related factors were also important contributors to geographic differences in the spread of COVID-19. In the early months of the pandemic, throughout the country at the county level, the proportion of workers employed in healthcare occupations was a significant predictor of the overall burden of COVID-19 in those counties.[26] This finding is supported by the fact that during the same period, even with many unreported cases, healthcare personnel comprised nearly one-fifth of all cases in the United States.[27]

In Massachusetts, cities and towns with more workers employed in the healthcare and social assistance and transportation industries and in service

Table 2.1. Percent employment by essential industries, occupations with frequent exposure to infection, and proximity to others, according to race/ethnicity, based on 2019 employment data.

Variable	White (%)	Black or African American (%)	Asian (%)	Hispanic (%)
Likely employed in essential industry	26.89	37.75	26.16	27.20
Healthcare and social assistance	12.76	19.82	14.62	11.11
Hospital	4.36	6.13	6.45	2.89
Animal slaughtering and processing	0.32	0.66	0.32	0.75
Likely and possibly employed in essential industry	35.41	44.64	35.16	33.00
Employed in occupations with frequent exposure to infections	11.28	14.73	13.02	11.37
Respiratory therapist	0.08	0.17	0.13	0.04
Respiratory nurse	2.60	2.60	3.98	1.06
Licensed practical or vocational nurse	0.49	1.20	0.30	0.43
Employed in occupations with frequent close proximity to others	25.10	29.03	24.26	25.81
Physical therapists	0.25	0.12	0.57	0.06
Personal care aids	0.93	2.37	1.63	1.44
Medical assistants	0.47	0.59	0.38	0.79
Employed in occupations with frequent exposure to infections and close proximity to others	8.12	10.75	9.95	6.23
Bus drivers	0.39	0.96	0.23	0.37
Flight attendants	0.09	0.12	0.08	0.08

Source: D. Hawkins, "Differential Occupational Risk for COVID-19 and Other Infection Exposure According to Race and Ethnicity," American Journal of Industrial Medicine 63, no. 9 (2020): 817–820.

and healthcare support occupations also tended to have higher rates of COVID-19 and higher COVID-19 positivity rates.[28] Similarly, in North Carolina, rural communities with more workers employed in meat processing and agricultural work tended to have higher rates of COVID-19.[29] Likewise, New York City neighborhoods that had a higher percentage of workers employed in essential industries and a lower percentage of workers working from home had higher rates of COVID-19.[30]

Challenging the Data

Even as studies documented the elevated rates of COVID-19 among high-risk workers, a frequent criticism has been that it is impossible to prove that the workers acquired COVID-19 at the workplace. One article about healthcare worker infections published in the *Boston Globe* in late March 2020 took on the framing of many hospital representatives (as discussed previously), with a subtitle stating that many of the infections were due to "community spread, as opposed to contact with infected patients."[31] Such a framing was often generalized to other workplaces.

Due to data limitations, many of the studies examining the relationship between work-related factors and COVID-19 outcomes were not able to isolate the role of work. A study published in 2023, however, using data from the 2020 National Health Interview Survey was able to control for a number of these confounding factors—in particular, age, gender, household size, and family income. After controlling for these variables, workers in the healthcare and social assistance industry—as well as healthcare practitioners and technicians, healthcare support personnel, and workers in protective services occupations—had rates of COVID-19 that were significantly elevated compared to other workers. This important paper also showed that work-related transmissions are not just relevant for the workers themselves but for those in their household as well. The authors found that compared to individuals in households without any workers, individuals in one-worker households had a 26 percent increased risk for COVID-19, households with two workers had a 41 percent increased risk, and households with three or more workers had a 70 percent increased risk.[32] A commentary on this article estimated a population attributable fraction of 24.6 percent, meaning that nearly one-fourth of cases of COVID-19 in 2020 among those eighteen or older could be attributable to work.[33]

Work and Mortality

Numerous studies showed how, among working-age people, the risk of COVID-19 mortality was strongly related to occupation. A study using Massachusetts death certificates found that those working in a variety of occupations, including healthcare support, transportation and material moving, food preparation and serving, building and grounds cleaning, production, construction, installation, maintenance, protective service, personal care, arts, and community and social service had an elevated risk of dying from COVID-19 compared to the average for all workers (fig. 2.3).[34]

In this Massachusetts study, the mortality rate among Hispanic and Black workers was over four times higher than the mortality rate for white workers. Furthermore, for most occupation groups with data available, the mortality rates among Hispanic and Black workers were higher than for white workers in the same occupation group. For the occupation groups with the five highest mortality rates, the mortality rate for Hispanic and Black workers was elevated compared to that of white workers. The mortality rate for Black healthcare support workers was close to three times higher than the mortality rate for white healthcare support workers. The mortality rate for Hispanic

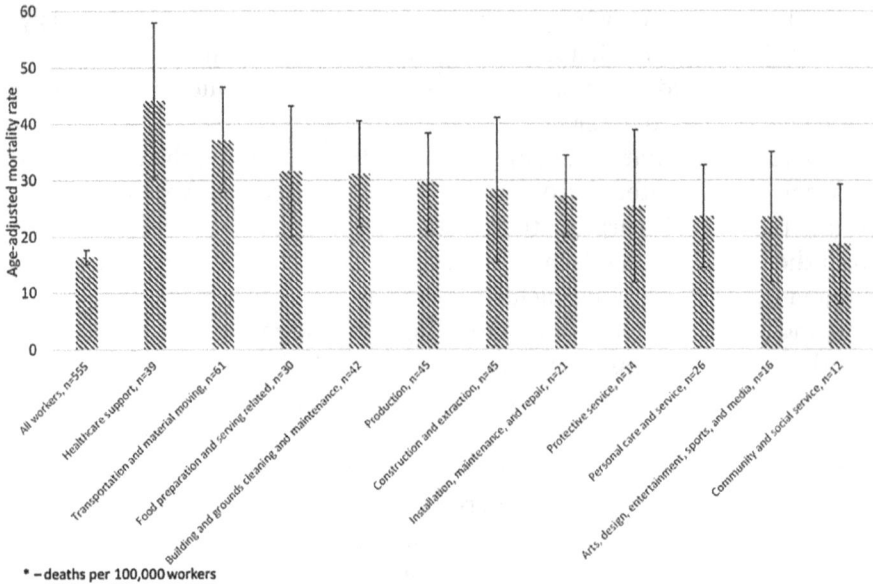

Figure 2.3. Age-adjusted COVID-19 mortality rates among workers ages 18–64 by occupation groups with elevated rates, Massachusetts, March 1–July 31, 2020. Source: D. Hawkins, L. Davis, and D. Kriebel, "COVID-19 Deaths by Occupation, Massachusetts, March 1–July 31, 2020," *American Journal of Industrial Medicine* 64, no. 4 (2021): 238–244.

food preparation and serving workers was eight times higher than the rate for white food preparation and serving workers. These findings indicate that work-related risk likely increased the risk of COVID-19 mortality for everyone, but these effects were more pronounced among workers of color. Quite clearly, there may be compounding disadvantages for workers of color. Not only were they facing higher risk of contracting COVID-19 at the workplace, but they also faced higher risk of severe outcomes possibly due to different factors, including lower access to testing/treatment and mistreatment in the healthcare system.

With respect to industry, the industries with the five highest rates of COVID-19 included department stores and discount stores, crop production, truck transportation, nursing care facilities, and taxi and limousine services. The highest number of deaths occurred in the construction, restaurant and other food services, and nursing care facilities industries. Additionally, although hospitals did not have an elevated rate, there was a relatively high number of deaths in that industry. Notably, the majority of the industries with elevated rates are industries where work cannot generally be completed remotely (fig. 2.4).

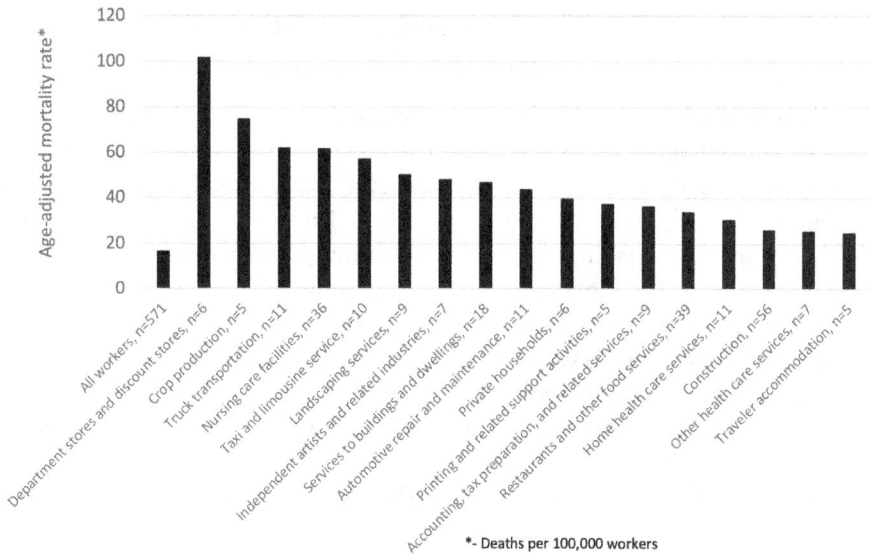

Figure 2.4. Age-adjusted COVID-19 mortality rates among workers ages 18–64 by industries with elevated rates, Massachusetts, March 1–October 31, 2020. Source: Author's analysis of data from the Massachusetts Registry of Vital Records and Statistics.

A key point is that during the pandemic, mortality increased not just due to COVID-19 itself but also from a variety of other causes of death that may have been exacerbated by the pandemic. Excess mortality, which refers to increased mortality compared to previous years, is a method for quantifying this increased risk of mortality. In California several occupational sectors were found to have elevated excess mortality rates: food/agriculture, transportation/logistics, manufacturing, facilities, retail, government/community, and health/emergency.[35]

A large study with data from forty-seven states later confirmed many of these state-level findings. Researchers found that workers in essential industries had mortality rates nearly two times higher than workers in other industries. Workers in industries including hospitality and food services, transportation and warehousing, agriculture, forestry, fishing and hunting, mining, construction, waste management, and remediation services had rates more than two times higher than workers in nonessential industries. With respect to occupation, the highest rates were observed among construction laborers, chefs and head cooks, sewing-machine operators, security guards and gaming surveillance officers, and roofers.[36]

COVID-19 Exacerbating Other
Workplace Health Problems

The health problems brought about by the pandemic are not just those directly caused by the virus itself. We are only now beginning to understand how the COVID-19 pandemic has exacerbated many already existing health challenges, including those impacting workers. During the pandemic, the rate of certain occupational injuries increased among some workers. For health-care practitioners, the rate of musculoskeletal injuries increased by more than 18 percent. For healthcare support workers, these injuries increased by over 14 percent. This increase was even greater for nurses, who saw their rate of musculoskeletal disorders increase by over 20 percent.[37] These increases are likely due to the increased physical work demands on healthcare workers during the pandemic.

Even before the COVID-19 pandemic there were concerns about increases in work-related violence in the healthcare industry, especially for workers of color. The pandemic likely exacerbated existing trends. Using data from the Bureau of Labor Statistics Survey of Occupational Injuries and Illnesses, which likely undercounts occupational injuries and illnesses,[38] there was an increase in the rate of violent injuries in the healthcare and social assistance industry between 2019 and 2020 when the rate of violent injuries increased by over 40 percent in hospitals.[39] The causative role played by the pandemic itself in these increases is supported by a study finding that among the more than 40 percent of nurses who experienced physical violence during the pandemic, the risk was higher among nurses who provided direct care to COVID-19 patients.[40] Another study that focused on a single hospital found that the rate of violent workplace incidents increased significantly during the pandemic and that the rates of violence were higher when the rates of COVID-19 were higher.[41] As the authors of this study point out, there was a certain irony—at the same time that praise was being heaped on healthcare workers, there was also a lack of attention to preventing violence and other injuries to these very same workers. Many other industries also experienced surges in violence during the pandemic, including retail, the airline industry, the restaurant industry, and other workplaces where some customers became more aggressive and resistant to masking and other COVID-19 safety rules and restrictions.[42, 43]

The pandemic also had contributed to mental health strain among workers. A survey among healthcare workers early in the pandemic found that these workers were stressed due to both the fear of contracting COVID-19 and changes in clinical activities brought about by the pandemic.[44] A survey in Massachusetts found that over a third of healthcare workers reported fifteen or more days with poor mental health in 2020.[45] These mental health stressors can contribute to burnout, referring to a feeling of exhaustion and depletion associated with work. Such burnout may further increase the likelihood of healthcare workers leaving the profession, contributing to shortages. Healthcare workers were not alone. One study found that compared to other workers, essential workers experienced higher rates of anxiety, depression, and substance use to cope with stress, and suicide ideation compared to other workers.[46] The temporary increase in unemployment during the pandemic likely increased mental and behavior health challenges for many workers.

The Pandemic and Life Expectancy

The pandemic in many ways accelerated changes in health that were already occurring. One of the best ways of comprehensively trying to understand the full impact of a shock like the pandemic is to look at life expectancy. Life expectancy at birth is a broad population health measure that represents the number of years someone can expect to live. At the time of this writing, we now have life expectancy data for the first three years of the pandemic in the United States. The pandemic had a massive impact on life expectancy for people in the United States, with life expectancy declining by 1.5 years from 78.8 in 2019 to 77.3 in 2020.[47] This decline continued with a further drop to 76.1 in 2021.[48] The burden of this decline in life expectancy has not been borne equally. While the overall decline was felt across all racial and ethnic groups, some groups experienced much more dramatic declines. Between 2019 and 2021, life expectancy for Native Americans declined by an astonishing 6.6 years, from an already low number of 71.8 to 65.2. Life expectancy for Hispanics declined by 4.2 years, from 81.9 to 77.7. Life expectancy for Black Americans declined by 4 years, from 74.8 to 70.8.

The annual average decline in life expectancy overall in the United States between 2019 and 2021 was about 1.4 years. For Native Americans, the racial/ethnic group with the largest decline in life expectancy, the average annual decline was 3.3 years. It is important to point out that while life expectancy has declined in other countries, the decline in the United States has been greater than in other comparable countries,[49] and in 2021 life expectancy began to increase in many countries while the decline continued in the United States.[50] While life expectancy did begin to recover in 2022, it did not reach its pre-pandemic levels and these racial/ethnic disparities persisted.[51]

What is perhaps most surprising about the data is that much of the decline in life expectancy during the pandemic is not due directly to deaths from COVID-19. In 2020 deaths from COVID-19 accounted for 73.8 percent of the decline in life expectancy, and in 2021 COVID-19 accounted for 50.0 percent of the decline. What other factors contributed to the decline? In both 2020 and 2021 the second-largest contributor to the decline was unintentional injuries, a category mostly comprised of drug overdoses. In 2021 alcoholic liver disease was the fourth-largest contributor while suicides were the fifth-largest contributor. Other important factors contributing to the decline were homicides, diabetes, and heart disease. This is why understanding increases in mortality from these causes—and, in particular, these increases among workers—is so crucial for understanding the full impact of the pandemic.

Deaths of Despair

Three of the causes of death already mentioned—unintentional injuries (predominantly drug overdoses), suicides, and alcoholic liver disease—have previously been identified as important factors contributing to declining life expectancy in the United States even before the COVID-19 pandemic. The factors contributing to increases in these causes of death are controversial, complex, and related to a mix of factors,[52] but studies have consistently shown that these increases in mortality have primarily been observed among people in their mid-years of life—often referred to as "working years"—and are primarily driven by increases in mortality from drug overdoses, especially those related to opioids, suicides, and, to a lesser extent, alcoholic liver disease. Based on the groundbreaking research into this topic by Anne Case and Angus Deaton, these causes of death have been collectively referred to as "deaths of despair."[53]

Beginning in the late 1990s, mortality from deaths of despair increased rapidly. Drug overdoses, for example, increased from 6.1 deaths per 100,000 people in 1999 to 28.3 deaths per 100,000 people in 2020. Most of these increases were related to increases in opioid-related overdose deaths, but other drugs like psychostimulants were also important contributors. Increases in suicide mortality, although not as drastic as drug overdoses, also increased from 10.4 deaths per 100,000 people in 2000 to a high of 14.2 deaths per 100,000 people in 2020.[54]

Scholars have been particularly interested in determining which populations were most vulnerable. Case and Deaton drew particular attention to how increases in mortality from these causes were so acute among middle-age white Americans that there was a substantial flattening in mortality trends, which contrasted with declining trends seen in other countries and among other racial and ethnic groups in the United States. Nevertheless, it is important to note that deaths of despair have been increasing across race and ethnic groups. Overall, mortality still remains much higher among other racial/ethnic groups compared to white people in the United States. Even before the pandemic, age-adjusted mortality rates were over 40 percent higher among both non-Hispanic Blacks and Native Americans in the United States. Other factors are associated with these increases in mortality. Mortality among those with lower levels of educational attainment is, for example, elevated and, in some cases, increasing. But occupation remains key.

During the pandemic, many industries experienced increases in occupational injuries, particularly related to increased violence in the workplace. While a concern in their own right, these injuries are also important because of the contribution they may have had to changes in the risk for drug overdoses during the pandemic. A variety of studies have identified occupational injuries as being a key component in the risk for opioid-related deaths. A Massachusetts study found that workers in a variety of blue-collar jobs had elevated mortality rates, including construction and extraction; farming, fishing, and forestry; material moving; installation, maintenance, and repair; transportation; production; food preparation and serving related; building and grounds cleaning and maintenance; and healthcare support (table 2.2).

It is not just the physical aspects of work that contribute to the risk for deaths of despair but also its psychosocial aspects. As we have seen, workers across industries experienced increases in psychosocial strain during the pandemic. One source of such strain was job security due to the rapid increases in unemployment during the early months of the pandemic and financial precarity throughout the pandemic. Occupations where workers are more likely to report job insecurity have higher rates of deaths of despair, especially opioid-related deaths. This association may exist because workers with less job security may feel more compelled to work even when injured or in pain, and opioids can be a tool to hide this pain. An association between job insecurity and opioid-related overdoses and other deaths of despair is particularly concerning because of evidence that job insecurity is increasing. In addition to increasing the risk for drug overdoses, job insecurity may also increase the risk for suicide. In the Massachusetts study, workers in occupations with elevated levels of job insecurity had more than a 30 percent higher risk of suicide compared to workers in occupations with lower levels of job insecurity.[55] Other studies have found that low levels of support at work, low levels of job control, and workplace bullying are associated with self-harm, suicide ideation, and suicide attempts.[56]

Protecting Workers

When considering both pandemics of infectious disease and deaths of despair, there are many policies that can be introduced to protect workers. Unfortunately, during the pandemic, efforts to address the role of work in the spread of COVID-19 were often too slow and did not go far enough. Even among frontline healthcare workers, many reported not having access to personal protective equipment in the early months of the pandemic. The Occupational Safety and Health Administration (OSHA), the main federal organization

Table 2.2. Rate, number, and percent of opioid-related overdose deaths by occupation group, overall and by gender, Massachusetts workers, 2011–2015, n=4,302.

Occupation	Rate of opioid-related overdose deaths/100,000 workers Mean (95% CI)			Opioid-related overdose deaths N (%)		
	Overall	Males	Females	Total	Males	Females
Construction and extraction	150.6 (146.0–155.1)[1]	152.3 (132.1–172.6)[1]	73.5 (0–166.6)[2]	1,096 (24.8)	1,084 (32.6)	12 (1.2)
Farming, fishing, and forestry	143.9 (125.4–162.3)[1]	205.9 (89.4–322.5)[1]	—[2]	61 (1.4)	—[2]	—[2]
Material moving	59.1 (54.4–63.7)[1]	71.9 (46.7–97.0)[1]	14.4 (0–35.5)	167 (3.9)	158 (4.8)	9 (0.9)
Installation, maintenance, and repair	54.0 (50.4–57.6)[1]	54.3 (38.0–70.6)	47.7 (0–121.9)	221 (5.1)	213 (6.4)	8 (0.8)
Transportation	42.6 (39.6–45.6)[1]	46.1 (31.3–60.9)	22.4 (0–47.0)	203 (4.7)	187 (5.6)	16 (1.6)
Production	42.1 (39.7–44.5)[1]	53.1 (39.0–67.2)	17.0 (4.9–29.0)	312 (7.3)	274 (8.2)	38 (3.9)
Food preparation and serving related	39.5 (37.5–41.6)[1]	51.6 (36.6–66.6)	28.9 (18.4–39.4)[1]	372 (8.6)	227 (6.8)	145 (14.8)
Building/grounds cleaning and maintenance	38.3 (35.8–40.9)[1]	54.2 (37.7–70.7)	10.2 (0.7–19.8)	230 (5.3)	207 (6.2)	23 (2.4)
Healthcare support	31.8 (29.2–34.5)[1]	43.1 (6.7–79.5)	30.1 (18–42.1)[1]	146 (3.4)	27 (0.8)	119 (12.2)
Personal care and service	23.7 (21.8–25.6)	43.1 (20.0–66.2)	17.5 (9.2–25.8)	153 (3.6)	67 (2.0)	86 (8.8)
Sales and related	20.0 (18.9–21.1)	26.2 (18.6–33.8)	13.5 (7.9–19.1)	342 (7.9)	230 (6.9)	112 (11.5)
Arts, design, entertainment, sports, and media	19.5 (17.2–21.8)	31.5 (13.2–49.8)	8.6 (0–17.7)	74 (1.7)	57 (1.7)	17 (1.7)
Community and social services	16.6 (14.3–18.8)	28.5 (5.3–51.7)	11.4 (1.8–21.0)	56 (1.3)	29 (0.9)	27 (.8)
Protective service	15.4 (13.3–17.4)	16.1 (6.0–26.2)	12.1 (0–30.8)	58 (1.3)	50 (1.5)	8 (0.8)
Architecture and engineering	12.5 (10.6–14.3)	12.0 (3.5–20.5)	15.1 (0–37.1)	47 (1.1)	38 (1.1)	9 (0.9)
Office and administrative support	11.7 (10.9–12.4)	15.9 (8.9–22.9)	9.9 (6.4–13.5)	248 (5.8)	98 (2.9)	150 (15.3)
Healthcare practitioner and technical	11.1 (10.1–12.1)	11.5 (2.1–20.8)	11.0 (6.0–16.0)	122 (2.8)	29 (0.9)	93 (9.5)
Management	8.6 (7.9–9.3)	12.5 (7.8–17.2)	3.5 (0.7–6.4)	164 (3.8)	135 (4.1)	29 (3.0)
Legal	7.9 (6.1–9.8)	8.9 (0–20.7)	6.9 (0–17.6)	19 (0.4)	11 (0.3)	8 (0.8)
Business and financial operations	7.4 (6.6–8.3)	11.2 (4.6–17.9)	4.0 (0.2–7.7)	76 (1.8)	55 (1.7)	21 (2.1)
Life, physical, and social science	6.5 (5.0–7.9)	9.8 (0–20.9)	—[2]	20 (0.5)	—[2]	—[2]
Computer and mathematical	5.6 (4.6–6.5)	6.5 (1.4–11.6)	—[2]	36 (0.8)	—[2]	—[2]
Education, training, and library	4.0 (3.4–4.5)	4.4 (0–9.2)	3.8 (0.9–6.7)	49 (1.1)	16 (0.5)	33 (3.4)
Military specific	—[3]	—[3]	—[2]	12 (0.3)	—[2]	—[2]
Unknown	—[3]	—[3]	—[2]	18 (0.4)	—[2]	—[2]
All Occupations	25.1 (23.4–26.8)	38.2 (35.3–41.2)	11.6 (10.0–13.2)	4,302 (100)	3,324 (100)	978 (100)

[1] Rate significantly higher than rate for all industry categories
[2] Suppressed due to cell size restriction
[3] Unable to calculate rate due to lack of denominator
Numerator source: Occupational Health Surveillance Program, 2011–2015

tasked with protecting the health and safety of workers, drew criticism for not taking enough action to protect workers during the pandemic. Due to a number of issues, including understaffing, OSHA was not able to do inspections into the large number of complaints about unsafe workplaces that were received during the pandemic. OSHA has fewer than two thousand inspectors, who are tasked with enforcing standards for 130 million workers at over 8 million worksites across the country.[57] A calculation from the AFL-CIO (American Federation of Labor and Congress of Industrial Organizations) estimated that with these numbers, OSHA can cover each workplace once every 129 years.[58] OSHA has the power to introduce standards to protect workers; however, the organization has frequently been slow to introduce new standards, often due to industry pressure. OSHA did introduce a temporary standard for COVID-19 protection in 2021, more than a year after the pandemic began, but it was only for healthcare workers.

Additionally, worker organizations also criticized federal organizations like the Centers for Disease Control and Prevention for their slow recognition of the aerosolized transmission of the SARS-CoV-2 virus. The seemingly esoteric debate about whether COVID-19 can be spread through aerosols (small specks of fluid produced when breathing) rather than solely through droplets (large amounts of fluid produced when coughing, sneezing, or speaking) had important relevance for infection control and preventing worker infections. With aerosol transmission, increasing importance is put on ventilation and air purification to prevent the spread of the virus.[59]

For a brief period, the United States did join most of the rest of the world by making it possible for sick workers to stay home and not lose their pay with the provision of temporary paid sick leave through the Families First Coronavirus Response Act, but even this intervention expired. There is evidence that the introduction of paid sick leave in states that did not already have access to paid sick leave substantially lowered the spread of COVID-19 in those states.[60] Unfortunately, many workers were left behind by these protections. A worker needed to be classified as an employee to have access to paid sick leave. Many gig workers, like those doing shopping through apps like Instacart, who have been denied employee classification, did not have paid sick leave provisions made available to them. Although the Families First Coronavirus Response Act mandated that paid sick leave be provided for most workers, through 2020 many workers did not report access to paid sick leave. Data from the 2020 National Health Interview Survey showed just a slight increase in the proportion of workers who said they had paid sick leave following the passage of the act. Using this same data, it was found that there was variability in the percentage of workers with access to paid sick leave according to occupation. For example, workers in essential occupations, including farming, construction, food preparation, building cleaning,

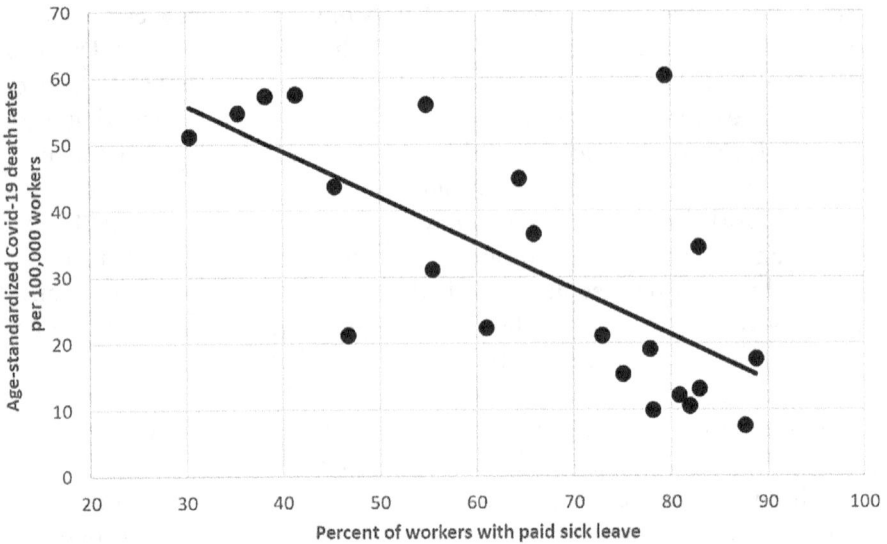

Figure 2.5. Association between access to paid sick leave and COVID-19 mortality rates by occupation, United States, 2020. Source: D. Hawkins, "Paid Sick Leave Is Good for Workers—and U.S. Public Health," July 25, 2023, STAT, https://www.statnews.com/2022/12/14/paid-sick-leave-workers-public-health/.

transportation, and healthcare support, had lower percentages of workers with paid sick leave compared to the overall access.[61] Workers in these high-risk occupations also tended to have higher rates of COVID-19 mortality (fig. 2.5).[62] Furthermore, Hispanic workers, workers with less than a high school education, and workers without health insurance coverage were also less likely to report having paid sick leave.[63]

Some states provided worker's compensation to workers with COVID-19 with the presumption that it was work-related, but the patchwork workers' compensation system throughout the country meant workers were not always aware of whether they qualified and how to access the benefits to which they were entitled. The presumption of the work-relatedness of COVID-19 among workers was also often challenged by businesses.

Confronting occupational factors that contribute to deaths of despair requires a wide variety of strategies. Treatment guidelines exist describing how opioids can be more safely prescribed to injured workers. A program known as Opioid Alternative Treatment Pathway has been piloted in Massachusetts. The program seeks to make alternative pain treatment available to injured workers in the workers' compensation system.[64] While it does not address the fundamental factors contributing to opioid use, some workplaces have made the anti-opioid drug Naloxone available to prevent overdoses at work, which is a growing problem.[65] These programs also require adequate training for workers about how to administer the drug.

Further upstream, interventions can focus on preventing injuries among workers. Evidence-based methods for preventing occupational injuries include health and safety regulations, inspections, engineering controls, personal protective equipment, and safety education. The Ergonomic Standard—which was introduced by Congress in 2000 before being quickly repealed following industry pressure—was designed to prevent the development of musculoskeletal disorders, one of the most common sources of pain in the workplace. If the standard had not been repealed and had been enforced, many cases of opioid use and overdose may have been prevented.

A frequent challenge when dealing with deaths of despair, COVID-19, and other health outcomes impacted by work is the increased fragmentation and insecurity of work. Policy proposals to protect workers from precarious work can include laws that disallow workers from being classified as contractors when they should be considered employees. Efforts in this direction have faced stiff industry opposition. The most famous example was the strong campaign for Proposition 22 in California, which exempted app-based driving companies from classifying their workers as employees, thereby excluding these workers from employee benefits and protections.

The long-term decline in unions and the associated health impacts of deunionization pose a particular challenge for protecting workers. Unions also help to protect the health of the community. A study found that COVID-19 infection rates were lower in unionized nursing homes.[66] Preventing the introduction of "right-to-work legislation" can be a way to prevent further decimation in unionization in the country. In some cases, we are seeing working people begin to fight back against employers and unionize. Large corporations such as Amazon and Starbucks have faced more forceful unionization campaigns, many of which have been successful.

In order to understand the role that work has on health, it is essential to have accurate data in health databases about, at the very least, the industry and occupation of workers. This data forms the foundation for many of the studies documenting the impact of deaths of despair and COVID-19 on workers discussed in this chapter. Unfortunately, too many health databases do not have this information. Including such data will make it easier to further document the impacts of work on health.

Conclusion

In this chapter I have focused on providing quantitative evidence of the disproportionate effects that COVID-19, drug overdoses, and suicides have had on vulnerable workers. This is what I and other epidemiologists do.

Epidemiologists also seek to understand the fundamental reasons behind these issues, their root causes. In the movements of the lines representing leading causes of death in Massachusetts since the mid-1800s, discussed in the beginning of this chapter, we see many instances where deaths have declined. These declines are not just historic accidents but are due to the efforts to understand what causes these deaths and the subsequent attempts to prevent them. Infectious diseases declined as sanitization, especially water sanitation, was introduced and as technologies like vaccines and antibiotics provided effective means to prevent and treat diseases. Injury deaths declined as road safety standards and seat belts were mandated. Lung cancer deaths declined with increased recognition of the role that smoking played in these deaths. Epidemiologically understanding the factors causing deaths is the first step in preventing them.

In a similar way, it is necessary to understand the role that work plays in the increases in mortality that we have witnessed in recent history. Whether considering COVID-19, drug overdoses, suicides, or the countless health problems that disproportionately impact vulnerable workers, ranging from fatalities, violence, heart disease, and cancers, these diseases are fundamentally symptoms—symptoms of a system that treats workers solely as a means for increasing profit; a system that has caused the fragmentation of work, weakening workers' ability to organize and collectively bargain for their own safety and fair wages; a system that has reduced employment security, pushing workers into increasing precarious forms of employment. There are steps that can and should be taken to protect workers without changing this system. Vaccines can be prioritized for workers in high-risk jobs. Drug treatment can be offered to workers without stigmatization. Paid sick and maternity leave can be mandated. Unfortunately, without fundamentally changing this system, the epidemics and pandemics we are currently living through and any that come in the future will continue to fall disproportionately on vulnerable workers.

Notes

1. "Massachusetts Deaths 2017," Boston, Massachusetts: Office of Population Health, Registry of Vital Records and Statistics, Massachusetts Department of Public Health, October 2019, https://www.mass.gov/doc/2017-death-report/download/.

2. J. K. Taubenberger and D. M. Morens, "1918 Influenza: The Mother of All Pandemics," *Revista Biomedica* 17, no. 1 (2006): 69–79; N. P. Johnson and J. Mueller, "Updating the Accounts: Global Mortality of the 1918–1920 'Spanish' Influenza Pandemic," *Bulletin of the History of Medicine* (2002): 105–115.

3. E. Brainerd, "Mortality in Russia since the Fall of the Soviet Union," *Comparative Economic Studies* 63, no. 4 (2021): 557–576.

4. E.O.O. Ile-Ife, "HIV/AIDS Situation in Africa," *International Dental Journal* 54(S6) (2004): 352–360.

5. World Health Organization, *"WHO Coronavirus (COVID-19) Dashboard,"* World Health Organization (2022), https://covid19.who.int/.

6. Centers for Disease Control and Prevention, "CDC Covid Data Tracker," Centers for Disease Control and Prevention (2022), https://covid.cdc.gov/covid-data-tracker/#datatracker-home/.

7. World Health Organization, "14.9 Million Excess Deaths Associated with the COVID-19 Pandemic in 2020 and 2021," World Health Organization, May 5, 2022, https://www.who.int/news/item/05-05-2022-14.9-million-excess-deaths-were-associated-with-the-covid-19-pandemic-in-2020-and-2021/.

8. J. Q. Xu, S. L. Murphy, K. D. Kochanek, E. Arias, "Mortality in the United States, 2018. NCHS Data Brief, no 355," Hyattsville, MD: National Center for Health Statistics, 2020, https://www.cdc.gov/nchs/products/databriefs/db355.htm/.

9. K. D. Kochanek, R. N. Anderson, E. Arias, "Changes in Life Expectancy at Birth, 2010–2018," NCHS Health E-Stat, 2020, https://www.cdc.gov/nchs/data/hestat/life-expectancy/life-expectancy-2018.htm.

10. F. Y. Lan, C. F. Wei, Y. T. Hsu, D. C. Christiani, and S. N. Kales, "Work-Related COVID-19 Transmission in Six Asian Countries/Areas: A Follow-Up Study," *PloS One* 15, no. 55 (2020): e0233588.

11. Lazaro Gamio, "The Workers Who Face the Greatest Coronavirus Risk," *New York Times*, March 15, 2020.

12. M. G. Baker, T. K. Peckham, and N. S. Seixas, "Estimating the Burden of United States Workers Exposed to Infection or Disease: A Key Factor in Containing Risk of COVID-19 Infection." *PloS One* 15, no. 4 (2020): e0232452.

13. A. Tomer and J. W. Kane, "How to Protect Essential Workers during COVID-19," March 31, 2020, *Brookings Report*, Brookings Institute (2020), https://www.brookings.edu/articles/how-to-protect-essential-workers-during-covid-19/.

14. D. Le and D. Hawkins, "Variation in Employment in Healthcare Occupations and County-Level Differences in COVID-19 Cases in the United States of America," *Journal of Occupational and Environmental Medicine* 63, no. 7 (2021): 629; M. M. Hughes, M. R. Groenewold, S. E. Lessem, K. Xu, E. N. Ussery, R. E. Wiegand, and M. J. Stuckey, "Update: Characteristics of Health Care Personnel with COVID-19—United States, February 12–July 16, 2020," *Morbidity and Mortality Weekly Report* 69, no. 38 (2020): 1364.

15. P. D. McCluskey and T. Andersen, "Near Tripling of Employee Coronavirus Infections in Largest Massachusetts Hospitals in Past Week," *Boston Globe*, April 3, 2020, https://www.bostonglobe.com/2020/04/02/metro/employee-infections-largest-massachusetts-hospitals-nearly-triple-week/.

16. E. J. Emanuel, G. Persad, R. Upshur, B. Thome, M. Parker, A. Glickman, and J. P. Phillips, "Fair Allocation of Scarce Medical Resources in the Time of Covid-19," *New England Journal of Medicine* 382, no. 21 (2020): 2049–2055.

17. Amy Heinzerling et al. "Workplaces Most Affected by COVID-19 Outbreaks in California, January 2020–August 2021." *American Journal of Public Health* 112, no. 8 (2022): 1180–1190.

18. J. W. Dyal et al., "COVID-19 among Workers in Meat and Poultry Processing Facilities—19 States, April 2020," *Morbidity and Mortality Weekly Report* 69, no. 18 (2020).

19. S. Hammond, "'This is not a game': Perdue Plant Employees Walk Out over COVID-19 Concerns," WMAZ, March 24, 2020, https://www.13wmaz .com/article/news/local/perdue-employees-walk-out-as-coronavirus-concerns -grow/93-7c7bdcbb-f3ec-439b-b541-9070e758b5cb/.

20. NPR, "Lawsuit Reveals Tyson Managers Took Bets on How Many Workers Would Get COVID-19," NPR, November 20, 2020, https://www.npr .org/2020/11/20/936973322/lawsuit-reveals-tyson-managers-took-bets-on-how -many-workers-would-get-covid-19/.

21. Centers for Disease Control and Prevention, "Risk for COVID-19 Infection, Hospitalization, and Death by Race/Ethnicity," https://www.cdc.gov/ coronavirus/2019-ncov/covid-data/investigations-discovery/hospitalization -death-by-race-ethnicity.html/.

22. D. Hawkins, "Differential Occupational Risk for COVID-19 and Other Infection Exposure According to Race and Ethnicity," *American Journal of Industrial Medicine* 63, no. 9 (2020): 817–820.

23. Heinzerling et al., "Workplaces Most Affected by COVID-19 Outbreaks in California."

24. D. P. Bui, K. McCaffrey, M. Friedrichs, N. LaCross, N. M. Lewis, K. Sage, and A. Dunn, "Racial and Ethnic Disparities among COVID-19 Cases in Workplace Outbreaks by Industry Sector—Utah, March 6–June 5, 2020," *Morbidity and Mortality Weekly Report* 69, no. 33 (2020): 1133.

25. A. P. Bartel, S. Kim, and J. Nam, "Racial and Ethnic Disparities in Access to and Use of Paid Family and Medical Leave: Evidence from Four Nationally Representative Datasets," *Monthly Labor Review* 142 (2019): 1.

26. D. Le and D. Hawkins, "Variation in Employment in Healthcare Occupations and County-Level Differences in COVID-19 Cases in the United States of America," *Journal of Occupational and Environmental Medicine* 63, no. 7 (2021): 629.

27. Hughes et al., "Update: Characteristics of Health Care Personnel with COVID-19—United States, February 12–July 16, 2020."

28. D. Hawkins, "Social Determinants of COVID-19 in Massachusetts, United States: An Ecological Study," *Journal of Preventive Medicine and Public Health* 53, no. 4 (2020): 220.

29. D. Carrión, E. Colicino, N. F. Pedretti, K. B. Arfer, J. Rush, N. DeFelice, and A. C. Just, "Assessing Capacity to Social Distance and Neighborhood-Level Health Disparities during the COVID-19 Pandemic," *MedRxiv*. 2020.

30. D. Carrión, E. Colicino, N. F. Pedretti, K. B. Arfer, J. Rush, N. DeFelice, and A. C. Just, "Neighborhood-Level Disparities and Subway Utilization during the COVID-19 Pandemic in New York City," *Nature Communications* 12, no. 1 (2021): 1–10; T. C. Yang, S. Kim, Y. Zhao, and S.W.E. Choi, "Examining Spatial Inequality in COVID-19 Positivity Rates across New York City ZIP Codes," *Health & Place* 69 (2021): 102574.

31. Priyanka Dayal McCluskey, "More Than 160 Boston Hospital Workers Test Positive for Coronavirus," *Boston Globe*, March 27, 2020, https://www.bostonglobe.com/2020/03/26/metro/dozens-boston-hospital-staffers-have-contracted-coronavirus/.

32. A. Gaffney, D. U. Himmelstein, D. McCormick, and S. Woolhandler, "COVID-19 Risk by Workers' Occupation and Industry in the United States, 2020–2021," *American Journal of Public Health* 113, no. 6 (2023): 647–656.

33. J. Paul Leigh, "COVID-19 May Have Been Job Related for One Fourth of Diagnosed Adults," *American Journal of Public Health* 113, no. 6 (2023): 634–636.

34. D. Hawkins, L. Davis, and D. Kriebel, "COVID-19 Deaths by Occupation, Massachusetts, March 1–July 31, 2020," *American Journal of Industrial Medicine* 64, no. 4 (2021): 238–244.

35. Y. H. Chen, M. Glymour, A. Riley, J. Balmes, K. Duchowny, R. Harrison, and K. Bibbins-Domingo, "Excess Mortality Associated with the COVID-19 Pandemic among Californians 18–65 Years of Age, by Occupational Sector and Occupation, March through November 2020," *PLoS One* 16, no. 6 (2021): e0252454.

36. Y. H. Chen, R. Chen, M. L. Charpignon, M. V. Kiang, A. R. Riley, M. M. Glymour, and A. C. Stokes, "COVID-19 Mortality among Working-Age Americans in 46 States, by Industry and Occupation," *MedRxiv* (2022).

37. Bureau of Labor Statistics, "Survey of Occupational Injuries and Illnesses (SOII)," Bureau of Labor Statistics, December 22, 2022, https://www.bls.gov/respondents/iif/.

38. E. A. Spieler, and G. R. Wagner, "Counting Matters: Implications of Undercounting in the BLS Survey of Occupational Injuries and Illnesses," *American Journal of Industrial Medicine* 57, no. 10 (2014): 1077–1084.

39. Bureau of Labor Statistics, "Survey of Occupational Injuries and Illnesses (SOII)," December 22, 2022.

40. H. D. Byon, K. Sagherian, Y. Kim, J. Lipscomb, M. Crandall, and L. Steege, "Nurses' Experience with Type II Workplace Violence and Underreporting during the COVID-19 Pandemic," *Workplace Health & Safety* (2021): 21650799211031233.

41. S. S. McGuire, B. Gazley, A. C. Majerus, A. F. Mullan, and C. M. Clements, "Impact of the COVID-19 Pandemic on Workplace Violence at an Academic Emergency Department," *American Journal of Emergency Medicine* 53 (2022): 285-e1.

42. H. Tiesman, S. Marsh, S. Konda, S. Tomasi, D. Wiegand, T. Hales, and S. Webb, "Workplace Violence during the COVID-19 Pandemic: March–October, 2020, United States," *Journal of Safety Research* 82 (2022): 376–384.

43. J. Anderson, "COVID-19 in the Airline Industry: The Good, the Bad, and the Necessary," *NEW SOLUTIONS: A Journal of Environmental and Occupational Health Policy* 32, no. 2 (2022): 92–99.

44. J. Coto, A. Restrepo, I. Cejas, and S. Prentiss, "The Impact of COVID-19 on Allied Health Professions," *PLoS One* 15, no. 10 (2020): e0241328.

45. Massachusetts Department of Public Health, "COVID-19 Frontline Healthcare Worker Study: Legislative Report," Massachusetts Department of

Public Health, January 2023, https://www.mass.gov/doc/covid-19-frontline
-healthcare-worker-study-0/download/.

46. M. É. Czeisler, R. I. Lane, E. Petrosky, J. F. Wiley, A. Christensen, A. R.
Njai, S. M. Rajaratnam, "Mental Health, Substance Use, and Suicidal Ideation
during the COVID-19 Pandemic—United States, June 24–30, 2020," *Morbidity
and Mortality Weekly Report* 69, no. 32 (2020): 1049; K. Gibb, D. P. Bui, and X. P.
Vergara, "Increases in Prevalent Depressed Mood and Suicidal Ideation among
Workers during the COVID-19 Pandemic—Findings from the California Health
Interview Survey," *International Journal of Environmental Research and Public
Health* 20, no. 2 (2023): 1253.

47. E. Arias, B. Tejada-Vera, F. Ahmad, and K. D. Kochanek, "Provisional Life
Expectancy Estimates for 2020," Vital Statistics Rapid Release, no. 015 (July
2021), https://www.cdc.gov/nchs/data/vsrr/vsrr015-508.pdf/.

48. E. Arias, B. Tejada-Vera, K. D. Kochanek, and F. B. Ahmad. "Provisional Life
Expectancy Estimates for 2021," Vital Statistics Rapid Release, no. 23 (August
2022), https://stacks.cdc.gov/view/cdc/118999/.

49. G. Huang, F. Guo, K. F. Zimmermann, L. Liu, L. Taksa, Z. Cheng, M. Tani,
and M. Franklin, "The Effect of the COVID-19 Pandemic on Life Expectancy in
27 Countries," *Scientific Reports* 13, no. 1 (2023): 8911.

50. S. Rakshit, M. McGough, K. Amin, and C. Cox, "How Does U.S. Life Expectancy Compare to Other Countries?" Peterson-KFF Health System Tracker,
December 6, 2022, https://www.healthsystemtracker.org/chart-collection/
u-s-life-expectancy-compare-countries/.

51. E. Arias, K. D. Kochanek, J. Q. Xu, and B. Tejada-Vera, "Provisional Life
Expectancy Estimates for 2022," Vital Statistics Rapid Release, no. 31, National
Center for Health Statistics. (November 2023), https://dx.doi.org/10.15620/
cdc:133703.

52. K. M. Harris, M. K. Majmundar, and T. Becker, eds., *High and Rising Mortality Rates among Working-Age Adults* (Washington, DC: National Academies
Press, 2021).

53. A. Case and A. Deaton, "Rising Morbidity and Mortality in Midlife among
White Non-Hispanic Americans in the 21st Century," *Proceedings of the National
Academy of Sciences* 112, no. 49 (2015): 15078–15083; A. Case and A. Deaton,
"Mortality and Morbidity in the 21st Century," *Brookings Papers on Economic
Activity* (2017): 397.

54. M. F. Garnett, S. C. Curtin, and D. M. Stone, "Suicide Mortality in the United
States, 2000–2020," *NCHS Data Brief* (433) (2022): 1–8.

55. D. Hawkins, L. Punnett, L. Davis, and D. Kriebel, "The Contribution of
Occupation-Specific Factors to the Deaths of Despair, Massachusetts, 2005–
2015," *Annals of Work Exposures and Health* 65, no. 7 (2021): 819–832.

56. A. Milner, K. Witt, A. D. LaMontagne, and I. Niedhammer, "Psychosocial
Job Stressors and Suicidality: A Meta-Analysis and Systematic Review," *Occupational and Environmental Medicine* 75, no. 4 (2018): 245–253.

57. Bureau of Labor Statistics (n.d.), U.S. Department of Labor, Commonly Used
Statistics, Occupational Safety and Health Administration, https://www.osha.gov/

data/commonstats#:~:text=Federal%20OSHA%20is%20a%20small,officer%20
for%20every%2070%2C000%20workers/.

58. AFL-CIO, "Death on the Job: The Toll of Neglect, 2011," April 28, 2011, https://aflcio.org/reports/death-job-2011/.

59. Dyani Lewis, "Why the WHO Took Two Years to Say COVID Is Airborne," *Nature* 604(7904), (April 6, 2022): 26–31.

60. S. Pichler, K. Wen, and N. R. Ziebarth, "COVID-19 Emergency Sick Leave Has Helped Flatten the Curve in the United States: Study Examines the Impact of Emergency Sick Leave on the Spread of COVID-19," *Health Affairs* 39, no. 12 (2020): 2197–2204.

61. D. Hawkins, "Disparities in Access to Paid Sick Leave during the First Year of the COVID-19 Pandemic," *Journal of Occupational and Environmental Medicine* 65, no. 5 (2023): 370.

62. D. Hawkins, "Paid Sick Leave Is Good for Workers—and U.S. Public Health," STAT, July 25, 2023, https://www.statnews.com/2022/12/14/paid-sick
-leave-workers-public-health/.

63. Hawkins, "Disparities in Access to Paid Sick Leave," 370.

64. MA Department of Industrial Accidents (MA DIA), "Opioid Alternative Treatment Pathway Announcement," June 12, 2017, https://www.mass.gov/news/
opioid-alternative-treatment-pathway-announcement/.

65. Bureau of Labor Statistics, "Deaths from Unintentional Overdoses in the Workplace Continued to Rise in 2019," Bureau of Labor Statistics, July 29, 2021, https://www.bls.gov/opub/ted/2021/deaths-from-unintentional-overdoses-in
-the-workplace-continued-to-rise-in-2019.htm/.

66. A. Dean, J. McCallum, S. D. Kimmel, and A. S. Venkataramani, "Resident Mortality and Worker Infection Rates from COVID-19 Lower in Union Than Nonunion US Nursing Homes, 2020–21: Study Examines Resident Mortality and Worker Infection Rates from COVID-19 in US Unionized Nursing Homes, 2020–21," *Health Affairs* 41, no. 5 (2022): 751–759.

3

Sorting Out the Politics of Inflation, Past and Present

SAMIR SONTI

In December 2020, the cover of the *Economist* broadcast a question haunting its readership: "Will inflation return?" Over the two years that followed, the fear was more than confirmed. As prices rose at the fastest pace in a generation, inflation moved to the center of national debate and became the most significant political economic legacy of the pandemic. Republicans as well as moderate Democrats seized upon the issue, expressing their opposition to the size and scope of the Biden administration's economic agenda in the technical language of inflation expectations. The pandemic stimulus had unleashed too much demand, they held, and—even worse—it padded workers' pocketbooks, forcing employers to bid up wages at alarming rates. Progressives, for their part, countered with arguments about bottlenecks and corporate power. The authors of the Inflation Reduction Act drew in part on this interpretation in promoting the expansion of productive capacity as the optimal way to rebalance supply and demand over the long run. In the short run, however, the institution most preoccupied with the return of inflation was the Federal Reserve (often referred to as "the Fed"). Together with central bankers around the world, Fed officials responded with that most orthodox of anti-inflation measures: interest rate hikes intended to cool demand. While insisting that they hoped to achieve a "soft landing," or a reduction of inflation without any adverse effect on the labor market, individuals like Federal Reserve chair Jerome Powell nevertheless expressed a willingness to do whatever it took to get prices under control.[1]

What Powell and his colleagues feared above all else was a return to the 1970s, when inflation climbed to well above 10 percent even as economic growth slowed. As central bankers and most academic economists have come to see it, that Great Inflation occurred for a simple reason: because liberals let it happen. A mistaken belief in the attainability of "full employment" led policymakers in the 1960s and 1970s to tolerate inflation—and in giving an inch, they relinquished a mile, seeding the expectation that inflation would forever continue. The crisis was resolved, in this view, thanks only to heroic action by Federal Reserve chair Paul Volcker, who in 1979 broke with Keynesian practice and dramatically raised interest rates—stabilizing prices at the cost of the steepest downturn since the Great Depression. This "Volcker Shock" has ever since served as a cautionary tale of what must be done if inflation gets out of hand. In short, the lesson of the 1970s is this: we must never again attempt to live beyond our means.[2]

But what if the scale of the economic action required to meet the ongoing socioeconomic and planetary crises confronting the United States and the world comes with some degree of inflation? What if, in other words, conservative critics are right to suggest that an ambitious policy vision could be inflationary? And what if those planetary crises—or future pandemics, or geopolitical tensions, or an aging population—introduce new, supply-side inflationary risks? Is the danger of inflation really so great that it should take priority over the urgent need to invest in a more equitable and green future? Can inflation be avoided only through austerity—some combination of higher interest rates and lower public expenditures? Is it possible to save the planet under such macroeconomic conditions? Or might there be other ways of interpreting the problem of inflation and different means for managing it?[3]

The inflation that accompanied the COVID pandemic threw these issues into sharp relief, and the experience therefore provides an occasion to reflect on how the politics of inflation control bear on working-class struggle. Whereas Federal Reserve monetary policy is designed to address an inflation resulting from excess demand, the price increases that began in 2021 and continued through much of 2022 were mainly due to pandemic-related supply disruptions. Indeed, research from the Federal Reserve Bank of San Francisco found that "almost the entire run-up in inflation in the post-2021 period is due to Covid-sensitive inflation."[4] Never before had the global economy been intentionally shut down as it was during the peak of the crisis, and the process of restarting it was bound to be accompanied by various frictions that led to the shortages and bottlenecks that cascaded along the intricate supply chains spanning the entire world. If the pandemic stimulus programs (both the CARES Act and the American Rescue Plan) did inject substantial spending power into the economy by the early months of the Biden administration's tenure, the crucial fact is that this demand collided with a severely restricted supply of key goods—most famously, at first, semiconductors, a necessary input into all manner of electronic devices. Higher interest rates geared toward cooling demand would be little match for these underlying problems of supply. And, as it happened, by the end of 2023, researchers were concluding that the slowdown in inflation ("disinflation") that had begun a year earlier had been the result not of monetary policy but of supply-side expansion generated by strong economic growth.[5]

Going forward, however, central bankers' commitment to tight monetary policy as a means of combating inflation threatens to make sustained investment into necessary areas like renewable energy and green infrastructure, care work, and housing more difficult to undertake. Paradoxically, this may leave the economy vulnerable to even graver supply-side inflationary risks over the longer term. In recognition of this problem, activists and scholars have begun to suggest alternatives to the orthodox anti-inflation tool kit. In particular, organizers with the Groundwork Collaborative and economists like Isabella Weber and Evan Wasner have pointed to the causal role played by firms with substantial market power in exacerbating an inflation that began with pandemic-related disruptions to global supply chains.[6] Their arguments represent a renewal of an older tradition in the politics of inflation that dates to World War II and its aftermath, which I call the "structural view." Emerging intellectually out of the institutional tradition in the US economics profession, and gaining political force from the industrial union movement, the structural view was one that saw an inflationary tendency in an economy marked by a high degree of corporate power over prices, production, and investment. Firms in concentrated industries retained the ability to drive prices upward in excess of costs and to do so whether demand was strong or sluggish. General monetary policy would not be effective against such market power inflation and indeed may worsen the situation by preventing necessary investment in sectors where shortages prevailed—for instance, housing and energy. As the economists and unionists who advanced the structural view saw it, the variety of inflation that existed in the postwar United States called for democratic oversight of income determination—that is, prices, profits, and wages—and credit allocation. Taken together, these represented pillars of a democratic economic planning regime that could enable simultaneous pursuit of full employment with management of inflationary pressure when and where it emerged. These policy instruments may once again be of interest as progressives reckon with how to manage inflation while making needed social, environmental, and public health–related investments over the years to come.

This chapter proceeds in three parts. First, it locates the origins of the structural view in debates over how to control inflation during World War II. Over the course of the conflict, the Office of Price Administration (OPA) succeeded in containing inflation even as the economy expanded at unprecedented rates—an expansion promoted in no small part by Federal Reserve policy. The OPA and wartime Federal Reserve represented the structural view in action, and the model thus established may be a useful one for progressives to consider today. Second, the chapter briefly charts the career of the

structural view during the decades after World War II. Business conservatives strongly opposed the planning agenda implicit in the structural view
and waged a successful mobilization in the early postwar years to dismantle
the OPA and establish an "independent" central bank. Well into the 1970s,
however, the economists and unionists who were committed to the structural
view articulated a critique of general monetary policy and campaigned for
a return to some form of incomes policy and selective credit policy. Their
arguments exerted real influence over inflation policy up until the final defeat
of the Volcker Shock. Finally, the chapter considers the legacy of the Volcker
Shock and reflects on what a renewal of the structural view could mean for
working-class politics today.

Origin of the Structural View

Political concern about the pricing power of big business goes far back indeed.
In its modern form, one might start with the antimonopolist struggles to
regulate the rates set by the railroads and public utilities in the late nineteenth
century.[7] A structural view of inflation, however, took shape only in the years
around World War II as economists in the Franklin D. Roosevelt administration struggled to devise a scheme for controlling inflation while sustaining a
robust defense mobilization. Before the 1930s, prices in the United States fell
as often as they rose, and deflation loomed as a problem of equal significance
to inflation.[8] During the First World War, consumer prices soared, becoming one of the most intractable issues confronting wartime officials, but this
great inflation was followed in 1920 by an equally disastrous deflation. The
Great Depression, too, was marked above all by a steep collapse in prices, and
a central goal of many New Deal measures was achievement of a reflation
of the general price level.[9] But by 1940, as military preparedness displaced
domestic reform as the overriding economic priority, all sights shifted to the
problem of inflation. How to prevent a repeat of the World War I experience
animated this debate and brought forth a set of competing perspectives on
what caused inflation in the first place—perspectives that would remain at
the center of the politics of inflation over the following decades.[10]

One such analysis came from John Maynard Keynes, most notably through
a 1940 pamphlet titled *How to Pay for the War*, in which the Cambridge
economist inverted the theory he had made famous a few years before by
applying it to the new conditions of wartime expansion. During the Depression, Keynes began, "we have been accustomed to a level of production which
has been below capacity," and under "such circumstances, if we have more
to spend, more will be produced and there will be more to buy." "But in wartime," he noted, "the size of the cake is fixed." Once everything is running at
maximum capacity, production reaches its limit—and there is no additional

buying to be done. What's more, thanks to the high level of wartime employment, household incomes rise, and the result is that an "increased quantity of money available to be spent in the pockets of consumers will meet a quantity of [consumer] goods which is not increased" as more and more resources are diverted away from civilian and into military sectors of the economy.[11] Without a corrective policy of some sort, Keynes said, the inevitable result would be a steady increase in the level of consumer prices.

"If we work harder," he thus concluded, "we can fight better." "But we must not consume more." Seen this way, preventing inflation during the wartime mobilization involved *limiting demand*—that is, "to restrict spending power to the suitable figure and then allow as much consumer's choice as possible [as to] how it shall be spent." This Keynes proposed to achieve through a plan of "deferred earnings," whereby workers would receive some amount of their pay after the war. Together with high taxation, such deferral of earnings would in theory soak up much of the excess demand and thereby alleviate the inflationary pressure. To be sure, Keynes did acknowledge that demand restraint on its own may not do the whole job. Thus, "some measure of rationing and price control should play a part in our general scheme," in particular when the supply of a specific good is "restricted for special reasons." But these interventions, he insisted, should be "adjunct to our main proposal," which was to manage general inflation by limiting overall spending.[12] In short, this was a macroeconomic theory of inflation that located the cause as excessive demand.

An alternative viewpoint came from John Kenneth Galbraith, an economist who had been influenced by the older institutional tradition in the discipline—one attuned to the structural unevenness of the economy and less concerned with economic aggregates. As Galbraith saw things, inflation was more complicated than Keynes's demand-centric theory suggested. In particular, Galbraith argued that it was a mistake to separate between, first, what he called a "bottleneck inflation," or price increases that resulted from supply issues in specific industries and sectors, and, second, a "general inflation," or the sort stoked by excess total demand. Indeed, he added, "I am not sure that complete rejection of the distinction would not be wise."[13] For better or worse, as Galbraith later explained in his memoirs, "there would be no nice point at which demand in general would exceed supply in general"—the national economy could not be reduced to those sorts of textbook curves. Instead, after a decade of depression, everything was "askew," with "surplus capacity here" and "shortages there," all of which could bear on price interactions and movements of the overall price level in unpredictable ways.[14]

It was well within reason, indeed, to anticipate a scenario in which "unemployed or redundant labor" prevailed over a chunk of the economy while, elsewhere, still "fifty percent of our industrial production may be 'bottle-necked'" due to specific supply constraints. Under such circumstances, prices of all sorts might start rising in a manner "wholly indistinguishable" from a so-called general inflation, even though the economy as a whole was operating nowhere near capacity. And by the time the original bottlenecks were broken, those first price increases would have transmitted in innumerable directions and set the stage for another round of problems—and then another and another. "Full employment," therefore, "will have little or no relation to the appearance of inflation" and "important decisions in price policy and fiscal policy will have to be made long before fiscal policy is reached."[15]

Two takeaways could be derived immediately from Galbraith's analysis. First was that an exclusive focus on aggregate demand would lead to the wrong policy response. While "inflation can be checked by a sufficient overall reduction of expenditures," he warned, "this measure has the crudity in application of any general or blanket measure." Addressing an inflation that began with, say, an increase in the "price of aluminum scrap" by suppressing household income to the point that "purchase of pots, pans, and other items would be checked" might make sense in the abstract. But this would have the adverse effect of sapping demand for a host of goods where no comparable problem existed. Meanwhile, it would "remove a very desirable pressure for expansion of capacity" that may in time yield more aluminum scrap—or whatever else had been in short supply to begin with. And if demand restraint was not the optimal way of dealing with the wartime inflation, the second takeaway was that additional targeted interventions, like price controls and rationing, may well be necessary. "To control any considerable number of prices in all of their dimensions is a Gargantuan task," Galbraith admitted, but that might just be what it took to "check inflation without hampering expansion or curbing the consumption of commodities or the use of services which are plentiful."[16]

During World War II, the Roosevelt administration undertook this "Gargantuan task" of price control by establishing the Office of Price Administration, an agency that Galbraith helped to lead and that continues to stand as the best example of successful inflation control without demand restraint.[17] Initially composed of a modest staff charged with stabilizing the prices of a select number of goods vital to national defense, the OPA developed into the largest and perhaps most iconic of the wartime agencies with passage of the Emergency Price Control Act just after the attack on Pearl Harbor. In April 1942, when Franklin Roosevelt issued the General Maximum Price Regulation (GMPR)—"the most important date in the history of wartime economic policy," in Galbraith's view—the OPA gained the authority to regulate the price of every good and service in the United States with the exception of agricultural products.[18] And when the Stabilization Act became law that October, most food products too were brought within the OPA's jurisdiction. The next year, FDR pushed the price control program even further with a "Hold the Line" order, which effectively prohibited any price increases whatsoever for the duration of the conflict. Taken together, these policies resulted in a period of four years during which the OPA oversaw across-the-board price controls, which as of 1944 covered some eight million prices and the rents paid by forty-five million tenants across the country.[19]

Running such an operation—in an era before serious computing power and barcodes, no less—required substantial people power. At its peak, the OPA full-time staff exceeded sixty-four thousand, ranking second in size within the federal government only to the US Postal Service. Assisting this army of public employees were nearly eighty thousand volunteers, mostly women, who monitored compliance across the country.[20] As for enforcement, the OPA relied on some fifty-five hundred War Price and Rationing Boards in local communities. In 1944 alone, authorities issued more than sixteen thousand injunctions and undertook twenty-three thousand damage suits and nine thousand prosecutions.[21] Disputes were handled through a special Emergency Court of Appeals, which ensured that endless litigation through the federal courts would not disrupt the OPA's urgent work.[22] Indeed, as historian Meg Jacobs has observed, this was a "radical model of state management: a popular government agency working in alliance with a coalition of labor, consumers, and social liberals that challenged the right of private industries to set their own prices and sell their items freely."[23]

In so challenging the right of private industries, the OPA invariably raised the question of how profits are to be determined, and this perhaps was where the agency took its most radical stance. OPA officials refused to set prices based on the business-preferred "cost-plus" basis, which called for prices to be maintained a certain percentage above cost so as to guarantee firms a given rate of profit on each product. Instead, throughout the war, the OPA expected industries to keep prices stable while absorbing new cost increases—even if this meant witnessing some downward pressure on the rate of return. Under this "overall earnings standard," as long as the industry on average would not be forced into the red by the OPA's decisions, the price they ordered would be there to stay. In practice, given the high volume of sales occurring under the maximum production wartime economy, there was still plenty of absolute profit to be made. As OPA director Leon Henderson put it, "Consideration of profits makes it clear that industries can well afford to absorb even substantial cost increases and by doing so make a contribution to the stabilization of the price level."[24] Nevertheless, this was a tough pill for businessmen to swallow, one they only begrudgingly tolerated during the wartime emergency.

In any case, the OPA worked very well. Between 1941 and 1946, the annualized rate of consumer price inflation averaged approximately 5 percent; after the GMPR went into effect, that figure was 3.6 percent; during the period of

Hold the Line, it was 1.6 percent.[25] "That so much could be accomplished with the market, totem of totems, in partial suspense," Galbraith later commented, "was deeply damaging to the established faith."[26] But that did not bother the public—popular support for the OPA only grew as the war progressed, with opinion polls conducted in the spring of 1946 finding more than 70 percent of respondents in favor of the continuation of controls into peacetime.[27] And, notably, with respect to Keynes's argument in *How to Pay for the War*, all of this was accomplished without a steep reduction in the level of consumption. Indeed, despite the rationing of various products, households consumed greater quantities of nondurable goods throughout the war and, by every measure, enjoyed improvements in nutritional intake.[28] Moreover, while wages were also placed under control from mid-1942 through V-J Day, the tight labor market that prevailed led to a meaningful compression of the income distribution, with the share of income going to the top 10 percent of earners falling by 13 percent between 1939 and 1944. The increase in union membership accomplished through the war, moreover, ensured that this downward redistribution would not easily be reversed.[29]

Finally, it is worth drawing attention to one entity that played little role in preventing inflation during the war: the Federal Reserve. In fact, far from implementing a tight monetary policy, the central bank throughout the conflict and into the postwar years worked closely with the Treasury Department to facilitate the federal government's war finance program. Federal Reserve chair Marriner Eccles (1934–1948) described his job as "a routine administrative job" that simply "executed Treasury decisions."[30] Specifically, this involved fixing short- and long-term government debt at low rates—a monetary policy of "pegs" upon which the fiscal mobilization was built. In practice, this involved a Federal Reserve commitment to purchase Treasury securities as needed to guarantee that the government's borrowing costs remained at the targeted levels. To ensure that this policy of monetary ease would not permit the speculative use of cheap credit, the central bank implemented a variety of *selective* credit controls. Household borrowing for purchases of durable goods—automobiles, refrigerators, and the like—was restricted even before Pearl Harbor, and in 1942 that list of products grew to include nondurables like clothing, hats, and footwear. By the end of the war, the Federal Reserve was also regulating the use of credit for purchases of real estate, stocks, and traded commodities to prevent asset speculation.[31] The idea was that instead of relying on one broad lever, that of general monetary policy, the central bank could manage the flow of credit for different purposes—plentiful for necessary wartime public expenditure, limited for less urgent consumption and speculative activity.

An important economic lesson of the World War II experience was thus that maximum production, full employment, and inflation control could all be achieved in practice. In this sense, the OPA and wartime Federal Reserve continue to stand as the clearest example of the structural view in action. But, of course, these were emergency conditions that would not persist for long. In the aftermath of V-J Day, the political challenges associated with such a structural approach would erupt in full force. The manner in which those politics were negotiated would set the terms of debate over inflation and economic policy more generally over the decades to come.

"Planning for Peace" or "Planned Stagnation"?

The fate of the OPA and the wartime Federal Reserve–Treasury arrangement is instructive for thinking through the dilemma facing progressives today. Coming out of the war, industrial unionists and New Dealers saw in the wartime economic policy institutions the outlines of a social democratic governance regime that could be carried into the future. As the CIO political action committee put it in *The People's Program for 1944*, with the federation's election manifesto and vision for the postwar political economy, "There is no line of demarcation between planning for war and planning for peace."[32] Or as civil rights and labor leader A. Philip Randolph argued, "If full employment can be maintained in war for destruction, it can also be maintained in peace for construction."[33] The Employment Act of 1946, which took the teeth out of the originally proposed full employment legislation, no doubt represented a setback for the forces in this camp. Still, by explicitly committing the federal government to the pursuit of "maximum employment, production, and purchasing power," the bill did mark something of a milestone. The extent to which these goals could be achieved, however, hinged on how the problem of inflation would be managed: by building on the precedent established during the war or by a turn toward demand restraining fiscal and monetary policy? On this crucial question, the structural view suffered two important defeats in the immediate postwar years.

The first involved the OPA. Into the spring of 1946, anywhere between two-thirds and three-quarters of those surveyed expressed support for the maintenance of price controls over food, clothing, and various durable goods.[34] The Truman administration itself pressed for extension of the OPA, at least until the process of reconversion to peacetime production had been completed, and the labor movement made this a top political demand. Moreover, the months after the war witnessed the largest US strike wave in terms of person-hours idled as unions seeking to maintain workers' real purchasing power—in the face of reduced production and the loss of overtime pay—put forth demands for hefty pay increases. Most iconic was the United Auto Workers' (UAW) campaign to force General Motors (GM) to provide autoworkers with a 30 percent wage increase while committing to refrain from increasing the price of an automobile. Denouncing GM's counter that they would meet the pay request but refuse to discuss prices as a "bribe offer," UAW president Walter Reuther insisted that the union would "not be a party to sand-bagging the American customer."[35] Under the banner of "Purchasing Power for Prosperity," the UAW stayed out for nearly four months in a walkout that was as much about the shape of the postwar political economy as it was about industry-specific concerns.[36]

But if the US labor movement emerged from World War II at the peak of its power and ambition, the business community was even more emboldened.[37] And corporate leaders were most concerned to ensure that the high degree of public intervention into their affairs would not extend beyond the emergency period. GM refused at all points to consider "ability to pay" with the UAW, maintaining that price setting was a managerial prerogative into which neither union nor state ought to encroach. The turning point came when the OPA consented to an increase in steel prices after US Steel and the United Steel Workers settled on a substantial wage hike, as from then it was only a matter of time before the UAW was forced to accept similar terms. This also marked the end of the OPA's Hold the Line period, and between that point and the July 1, 1946, expiration of the OPA's statutory authorization, business organizations led by the National Association of Manufacturers waged a relentless drive to gut the price control program once and for all.[38] After the meat industry effectively waged a capital strike in response to Truman's attempt to continue even modest controls—halting production and depriving consumers of beef and pork—the administration backed down. By the fall, all controls had been lifted and prices soared—climbing by some 20 percent over the latter half of the year and putting business interests in the position to advance what proved to be a persuasive case that allegedly irresponsible unions had unleashed a dangerous wage-price spiral. This argument contributed in no small part to a conservative landslide in the congressional midterm elections that November—and Republicans and Southern Democrats used their resulting supermajority to pass the Taft-Hartley Act over Truman's veto the following year.[39] As UAW strategist Donald Montgomery presciently commented to Reuther in mid-1946, "Labor has been made the scapegoat of this inflation."[40]

Although it took somewhat longer, adherents of the structural view suffered a similar defeat with respect to the Federal Reserve. After the war, the main question concerning the central bank was whether it would continue its cooperation with the Treasury Department in maintaining low rates for government debt. As the CIO Full Employment Policy Committee put it in a statement to the Congressional Joint Economic Committee, "There is no more important single area for bold Government action than in the fields of credit, fiscal, and monetary policy."[41] Truman Council of Economic Advisers chair, Leon Keyserling, elaborated upon this theme the next year: "Low inter-est rates are always desirable. In periods of inflation they have the undesirable collateral consequence of contributing to inflationary forces, but even then they have the economic advantage of facilitating the expansion of produc-tive capacity which is the best road to stability." Rather than "abandon the advantages of cheap money," the government should instead "adopt other measures to curb the inflationary forces." This could be accomplished, for instance, by strictly regulating what banks were able to do with the capital they held in reserve, effectively placing higher interest charges on banks' speculative borrowing but keeping those "within narrow limits."[42] In short, Keyserling was calling for a policy of selective allocation of credit—keeping money cheap for needed investments and dear for those investors who would play with it in dangerous ways. This would have transformed the financial system into something like a public utility, with a progressive central bank sitting at its apex.

Then–Federal Reserve chair Marriner Eccles had been an ardent New Dealer who in 1933 went so far as to insist before the Senate Finance Com-mittee, "You have got to take care of the unemployed or we will have a revo-lution in this country."[43] In the immediate aftermath of the war, moreover, he had supported the extension of price controls and an excess profits tax as the cornerstones of a reconversion anti-inflation program. By the latter 1940s, however, in the wake of those defeats, Eccles became an increasingly outspoken critic of the system of interest rate pegs that had carried over from the war. As he put it, these had made the Federal Reserve an "engine of inflation."[44] With the support of financial sector leaders like Russell C. Leffingwell of J. P. Morgan and Co., Eccles and other Federal Reserve officials mounted a campaign for central bank "independence"—that is, the indepen-dence to use general monetary policy to combat inflation without regard for the fiscal policy objectives pursued by the government's executive and legislative branches. As a group of University of Chicago economists put it in a letter defending the campaign for central bank independence, "Monetary policy cannot serve two masters."[45] After the mobilization for the Korean War touched off another round of inflationary pressure, Federal Reserve officials informed the Truman administration that they would no longer support the peg—a declaration of independence that came to be known as the Federal Reserve–Treasury Accord of 1951. The UAW's Donald Montgomery once again cut to the heart of the matter, posing the question before a congres-sional committee the year after the accord of whether the Federal Reserve would be "a part of government or a government apart."[46]

Thereafter, the independent Federal Reserve emerged as an institutional adversary of working-class politics. As scholars Gerald Epstein and Juliet Schor have observed, "By freeing monetary policy from governmental control, [the accord] played a major role in establishing the terms on which capital would score a significant victory against labor."[47] Indeed, in contrast to the orthodox view, holding that liberal monetary policy by a politicized Federal Reserve permitted inflation to take off in the 1960s and 1970s, the road to the Volcker Shock very much began in the 1950s. It was then that what political economists Benjamin Braun and Leah Downing have called the "holy trinity" of modern central banking—the independence to control inflation by means of short-term interest rate hikes—became something of a gospel for Federal Reserve officials like Chair William McChesney Martin (1951–1970).[48]

At no point in the quarter century after the accord, however, did the central bank's use of general monetary policy to combat inflation go uncontested. By the late 1950s, when the Martin Federal Reserve insisted upon raising interest rates to combat moderate inflation even as unemployment failed to dip below 5 percent, and hovered much higher in certain regions, adherents of the structural view put forward an analysis they would repeat into the 1970s: that monetary policy would not work to address the "new inflation" of the postwar era. Between 1957 and 1960, no fewer than four congressional probes inquired into the dilemma of creeping inflation in the face of sluggish economic performance—an early instance of what would later erupt as "stag-flation."[49] The culprit, they held, was corporate power. Speaking before the Senate Subcommittee on Antitrust and Monopoly, which conducted a multi-year investigation into the problem, institutional economist Gardiner Means identified an "administrative inflation," or one that resulted from the ability of firms with substantial market power—for instance, steel corporations—to meet profit targets by way of administered prices.[50] When "market structure has a bearing on inflationary price behavior," John Kenneth Galbraith added, "the further question arises whether it bears also on the effectiveness of [monetary] controls."[51] Both answered that question in the negative: "There is nothing in this theory," Means elaborated, "which indicates that monetary measures can control an administrative inflation without creating excessive unemployment."[52] Industrial unions seized upon this analysis, bringing it to the center of collective bargaining disputes—including the 1959 steel strike, the largest work stoppage in US history—and using it to argue for measures like advance price notification by firms in concentrated industries.[53]

Against this backdrop, policymakers in the 1960s and into the 1970s did indeed explore alternative forms of managing inflation. The Kennedy administration, preoccupied with maintaining the integrity of the dollar in the face of mounting deficits in the balance of international payments, made inflation control a priority but hoped to achieve this end not by austerity but through an "incomes policy." The wage-price guideposts they devised sought to peg workers' pay to the rate of productivity growth, thereby stabilizing unit labor costs and preventing businesses from feeling the need to raise prices. The Johnson administration struggled to continue with this policy even as Vietnam spending introduced a different inflationary pressure, and in 1971 the Nixon administration went so far as to experiment with outright wage and price controls.[54] Meanwhile, congressional Democrats reacted to the independent Federal Reserve's ongoing reliance on tight monetary policy in the latter 1960s with the Credit Control Act of 1969, which authorized the regulation of specific forms of credit. The central bank now had a statutory basis to do just what Leon Keyserling had called for years earlier—to determine to whom and for what ends credit would be allocated.[55] Later, in 1977, Congress amended the Federal Reserve Act to require that the body manage the financial system in a manner "commensurate with the economy's long run potential to increase production," while the Full Employment and Balanced Growth Act of 1978 stated that "coordinated use of fiscal and monetary policies in conjunction with specific targeted policies are necessary to combat inflation."[56] Here were the beginnings of a program of selective credit policy whereby the central bank acquired the ability to utilize surgical methods—rather than just the blunt instrument of general monetary policy—to manage inflation while pursuing broader economic objectives.[57] All of this testifies to the durability of the structural view throughout the postwar period.

The way in which such alternatives are implemented, however, is nothing if not political. The idea of incomes policy begs the question, Which incomes will be subject to the greatest control—those accruing to labor or to capital? Throughout these years the labor movement protested what they felt was the unfair burden that incomes policies placed on workers' wages as opposed to profits. As early as 1965, Nat Weinberg of the UAW declared the Kennedy-Johnson guideposts "dead" because of the "rigid and inequitable manner in which they were applied."[58] In a 1979 statement calling for "comprehensive mandatory controls," the AFL-CIO highlighted the need for "equity and fairness and equal sacrifice by all members of American society" in contrast to the "one-sided impact" of past incomes policies.[59] Rectifying this one-sided impact would have required a direct confrontation with capital and challenge to existing profit levels. Together with the disruption of the price signal that stricter controls would involve, such intervention into corporate incomes may well have adverse implications for private investment that would have to be overcome by the public sector. Similarly, effective implementation of selective credit policy could not be conceived apart from more thoroughgoing control of the entire financial system. As the opponents of the Credit Control Act put it in the minority report on that bill, taken to its logical conclusion the statute could "establish a complete credit police state."[60] The ominous language notwithstanding, the point that the effectiveness of such measures would depend on a high degree of financial repression was valid indeed. Taken together, equitable implementation of structural alternatives like incomes and credit policy required nothing less than democratic economic planning—with workers' organizations playing an active role in the guidance of investment and determination of wages, prices, and profits. In short, this meant class politics at the highest levels.

A far more straightforward way of dealing with the inflation that erupted in the 1970s was what Gardiner Means called "planned stagnation."[61] If Federal Reserve policy had been consistently challenged over the years since the accord, for all practical purposes its "independence" remained intact. Indeed, through the decade, Federal Reserve chair Arthur Burns (1970–1978) oversaw a steep tightening of monetary policy that in no small part inspired the reforms of 1977 and 1978. Beginning in 1979, the Jimmy Carter–appointed head of the central bank, Paul Volcker (1979–1987), took things further in imposing an unprecedentedly draconian monetary policy that choked the money supply and took short-term interest rates to upward of 20 percent. The impact of this "Volcker Shock" has been well documented by scholars; it triggered the steepest recession since the Great Depression, sending unemployment into the double digits, and set off a debt crisis that cut across the Third World. Perhaps its most significant effect, however, was how it served as what political economists Leo Panitch and Sam Gindin called a "path to discipline" of the working class. This was no accident: Volcker saw inflation and union power as two sides of the same coin, and the technical dimension of the monetary policy he implemented should not obscure his larger ambition of decisively weakening the ability of organized workers to compete for a larger share of income; this was its own type of incomes policy. More than willing to share the glory, Volcker later repeatedly acknowledged that the Reagan administration's attack on the Professional Air Traffic Controllers Organization played just as important a role in finally conquering the problem of inflation.[62] The terminal decline into which the US labor movement entered in the years after are the lasting legacy of this coup.

The Return of Inflation

Over the four decades following that Volcker Shock, consumer price inflation was not a serious problem, and the politics of inflation receded in turn. But, of course, that period was also marked by rising inequality, public sector retrenchment, and financialization. This correlation is not coincidental. The Federal Reserve campaign against inflation was, again, an offensive against the US labor movement, which central bankers and conservative officials understood as the institutional driver of inflation expectations. Neoliberal policy at home, together with trade liberalization and the resultant internationalization of manufacturing, consolidated the victories achieved by Volcker and then Ronald Reagan, and the economic insecurity these victories produced deserves most of the credit for the stability in the consumer price level over the past generation.

Paradoxically, this working-class defeat created the conditions for both the growth of a speculative asset economy and for the Biden administration's embrace of a more expansive fiscal policy in 2021 and 2022. Once inflation had been vanquished, interest rates began a historic, secular decline that may only now be reversing direction. Indeed, the trajectory of interest rates over the past seventy-five years reads something like an index of working-class power. To put it bluntly, monetary authorities concluded that in the absence of a credible working-class threat, inflation was less of a danger and policy could adjust accordingly. As Alan Greenspan put it in explaining why inflation failed to materialize during the late 1990s economic boom, "Atypical restraint on compensation increases has been evident for a few years now and appears to be mainly the consequence of greater worker insecurity."[63] Hindsight affords the benefit of understanding that what then seemed like "atypical restraint"—in comparison to the wage militancy of a couple decades prior—was actually the new normal.

Of course, not everyone exhibited restraint. As capital became cheaper to access, an increasingly unregulated financial sector pushed asset prices to dangerously high levels, a dynamic that contributed to the Great Financial Crisis in 2008. In the wake of the crash, the Federal Reserve under Ben Bernanke (2006–2014) adopted what was then an unprecedented monetary policy of ultra-low short-term interest rates and "quantitative easing," or monthly purchases of bonds intended to bring down long-term borrowing costs and encourage investment. If these measures helped to avert a depression, they also provided the fuel for an incredible asset price boom, one that yet again accrued most of all to the wealthy. In addition, it facilitated the emergence of what political scientist Benjamin Braun has called "asset manager capitalism," in which colossal firms like BlackRock sit at the apex of the global economy.[64] Notably, though, even as the total monetary base of the national economy swelled almost fivefold between 2010 and 2014, inflation stubbornly refused to budge, averaging less than the Federal Reserve's conservative 2 percent target over the decade as a whole. This experience suggested that the danger of recession accompanied by deflation was, in fact, of greater concern than renewed inflation.

If this monetary regime of low wages, low interest rates, and low consumer price inflation was a boon to the financial sector, it also created the conditions for a more progressive fiscal policy. Specifically, deficits no longer appeared to be a barrier to public investment, as low borrowing costs promised to enable the federal government to easily finance expenditures over the long term. This was the context in which the Biden administration formulated its ambitious physical and social infrastructure program in early 2021. While

Federal Funds Rate, 1954-2023

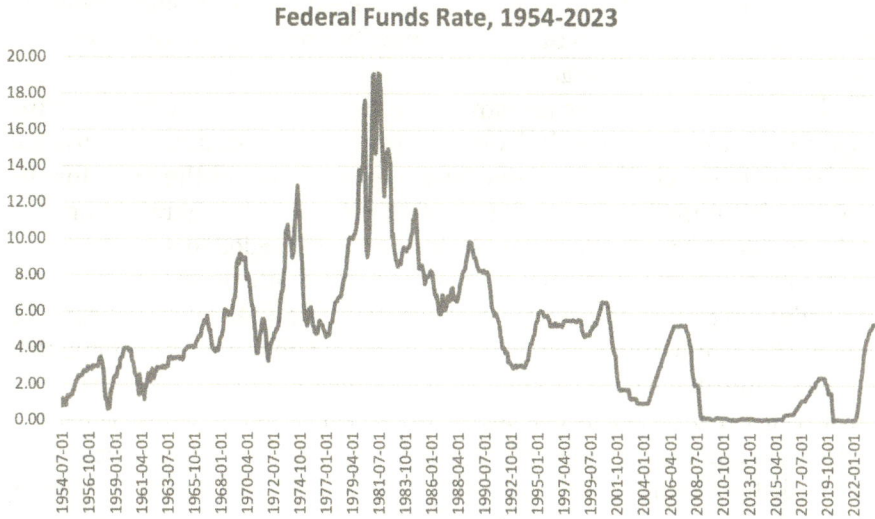

Figure 3.1. Federal Funds Rate, 1954–2023. Source: Board of Governors of the Federal Reserve System [US], Federal Funds Effective Rate [FEDFUNDS], retrieved from FRED, Federal Reserve Bank of St. Louis; https://fred.stlouisfed.org/series/FEDFUNDS/, November 3, 2023.

the fiscally conservative ideological climate still required the administration to demonstrate on paper how the proposed Build Back Better plan would pay for itself in time, in truth there seemed to be no structural obstacle to relying on debt to make it possible. The line separating monetary and fiscal policy had been blurred thanks to the Federal Reserve's new posture, and this held the promise of a definitive break from the discipline demanded through the neoliberal era. Or as proponents of Modern Monetary Theory put it, the only limits on federal spending were political will and the objective physical capacity of the economy.[65] Technically speaking, jobs for all and a Green New Deal were within reach.

The return of inflation turned all of this on its head. After concluding that the pandemic inflation would not prove "transitory," the Federal Reserve, together with central bankers around the world, began the most severe exercise in monetary tightening in decades. While Federal Reserve chair Jerome Powell (2022–present) expressed the hope that the institution would be able to engineer a "soft landing" of cooling inflation without adversely affecting the labor market, he was resolute in proclaiming his willingness to tolerate any negative consequences that may accompany the pursuit of price stability. Progressive forces justly criticized this continued use of an anti-inflation tool that works by means of economic contraction, not least because the price pressures that touched off the current inflation experience resulted from the exceptional circumstances of the pandemic. But perhaps of greater histori-cal significance may be what this new monetary regime portends for efforts to achieve continued public investment in climate and social infrastructure. As of this writing, the possibility of fiscal-monetary coordination directed toward socially necessary expenditure appears to be off the table for the foreseeable future. In short, the hope that there may be a straightforward and painless path to the robust public investments needed to meet the crises of climate and social reproduction has been called into question.

Yet despite the fact that central bank interest rate adjustments remain the principal anti-inflation policy tool in the immediate term, it is notable that the pandemic experience witnessed the return of the old structural view in mainstream debate. For one, again, the Biden administration's signature legislative achievement, the Inflation Reduction Act (IRA), was conceptual-ized as distinct from, if not in opposition to, the demand-centric orthodoxy of the period since the Volcker Shock. The notion that the best long-term safeguard against inflationary pressure is an expansion of productive capac-ity—above all in green infrastructure and transportation—exemplifies what some commentators have characterized as a novel kind of "supply-side lib-eralism."[66] The IRA also included a provision granting Centers for Medicare and Medicaid Services officials the authority to leverage their bargaining power with pharmaceutical companies in the interest of reducing the prices of prescription drugs. Meanwhile, New York attorney general Letitia James has proposed state-level rules to prohibit price gouging, defined as sudden increases of greater than 10 percent.[67] Outside of the United States, govern-ments have implemented measures designed to stabilize specific prices—those of energy, above all—and thereby circumvent the need to resort to generalized contractionary policy. In Spain, for instance, policymakers have relied on gas and electricity price caps together with housing and public tran-sit subsidies—the latter financed through progressive taxation—to provide relief to working-class households burdened by the increasing cost of living.[68] Similarly, the German government introduced energy price regulations in response to the shocks resulting from the Russian invasion of Ukraine, and European Union energy ministers followed by endorsing a broader stabiliza-tion measure in December 2022.[69] All of this flies in the face of decades of neoliberal market idolatry.

New scholarship has added force to this policymaking trend. Economist Isabella Weber, for example, has been perhaps the highest-profile propo-nent of alternative ways of thinking about the causes and potential cures of the pandemic inflation.[70] Among the central contributions offered by Weber and her coauthors has been a rigorous treatment of the concept of "sellers' inflation," which they define as "the ability of firms with market power to hike prices." The contention that well-situated corporations exploited the pandemic environment of snarled supply chains by raising prices above and beyond their heightened costs circulated widely in the early stages of the pandemic. Critics countered that corporate concentration had increased for decades while prices on average had remained stable as evidence in favor of exonerating big business from the charge. But in an important study examining firm-level pricing decisions and the transmission of price increases from systemically important industries, Weber and economist Evan Wasner provided extensive empirical data to substantiate the claim previously intuited by observers: pandemic conditions were different, and they induced corporate pricing behavior to change. Specifically, they found that sector-wide cost increases and bottlenecks—in short, supply shocks—resulted in "temporary monopoly power" of a sort that enabled powerful firms "to hike prices not only to protect but to increase profits." Elsewhere, Weber and her coauthors have begun to identify those industries most systemically important to inflation through their direct (e.g., housing) and indirect (e.g., energy) impacts on the general price level. In the face of such sector-specific inflationary drivers, they note, "It is not sufficient for monetary stabilization to rely on purely macroeconomic means designed to respond to demand-pull inflation."[71] Neither Gardiner Means nor John Kenneth Galbraith could have put it better.

What's more, even before the pandemic, economists Mike Konzcal and J. W. Mason had begun to elaborate a case for the Federal Reserve to distinguish between monetary policy and credit policy. "The central bank," they argued in 2017, "needs to accept its responsibility for actively directing credit to particular end uses" and to dispense with the idea that "macroeconomic management can be carried out by setting one interest rate."[72] They point to the long history of debates over the range of tools available to central bankers to regulate credit with an eye toward both encouraging productive investment and preventing speculative activity. More recently, legal scholar Lev Menand has offered a pathbreaking analysis of the real statutory mandate imposed on the Federal Reserve. The institution's sole and exclusive purpose, as stipulated by Congress from the 1913 Federal Reserve Act through the reforms of the 1970s, is to "administer the banking system" so as "to ensure that [banks] create enough money to keep the economy growing at its full potential."[73] Compelling central bankers to adhere to that objective, in short, does not require radical legislative solutions but, rather, concerted political pressure to enforce existing law. During the financial crisis and again in the early days of the pandemic, the Federal Reserve demonstrated a jaw-dropping capacity to influence global economic conditions. There is no reason why that power cannot be used in more creative and humane ways when it comes to the challenge of reconciling inflation management with socially necessary investment.[74]

Conclusion

The pandemic inflation reintroduced a dilemma that has historically confronted working-class social forces: how to reconcile the goals of relative price stability and economic justice for all. The orthodox approach to inflation control—namely, the Federal Reserve's reliance on demand restraining general monetary policy—has long been understood to be adverse to the interests of working people. Not only does it function by raising unemployment and obstructing socially necessary investment, but also it simply may not work to address the underlying causes of upward price pressure. The pandemic experience has thrown this into sharp relief, as monetary policy is no match for an inflation that originates in disrupted global supply chains. To the extent that climate crises, geopolitical tensions, demographic shifts, housing shortages, and still further public health disasters might generate ongoing shocks that result in specific types of inflation, it is incumbent upon progressives to offer clear analyses and alternative policy solutions.

Between World War II and the 1970s, institutional economists and union officials provided just that—a structural view on inflation that located its causes in the configuration of postwar capitalism and suggested targeted measures for dealing with it. Proponents of the structural view stressed in particular the need for public intervention into the determination of income shares—at the broadest level, between workers' wages and capital's returns—and purposeful regulation of the flows of credit. Ultimately, realization of this structural view called for a sort of democratic economic planning that could challenge the prerogatives of corporate executives and private investors. These politics were fraught, and in the end, the inflation that erupted in the 1970s was resolved not along lines of social justice as envisioned by those committed to the structural view but by means of austerity imposed by an "independent" central bank. The neoliberal order was built upon the wreckage that ensued.

The recent crisis, however, has created the space once more for ideas that recall the old structural view to circulate. Scholars have begun elaborating compelling explanations of the causes of price pressure—highlighting the role of concentrated economic power, for instance—and challenging the orthodox approach of the Federal Reserve. Public policy in the United States and elsewhere has to some extent incorporated these ideas, if only in halting ways. Nevertheless, the terms of debate on inflation have shifted, and it will be the task of progressives to build the power required to turn these concepts into meaningful programs. The stakes could not be higher.

Notes

1. Jerome Powell, "Transcript of Chair Powell's Press Conference," September 20, 2023, https://www.federalreserve.gov/mediacenter/files/FOMCpresconf 20230920.pdf/.

2. For an important corrective to the interpretation that places the blame for the 1970s inflation on Keynesians' misguided tolerance of inflation, see James Forder, *Macroeconomics and the Phillips Curve Myth* (Cambridge: Cambridge University Press, 2014).

3. Even before the onset of the pandemic and Ukraine war–related inflation, observers had drawn attention to the potential inflationary implications of an aging global population. See Charles Goodhart and Manoj Pradhan, *The Great Demographic Reversal: Ageing Societies, Waning Inequality, and an Inflation Revival* (London: Palgrave Macmillan, 2020).

4. Adam Hale Shapiro, "A Simple Framework to Monitor Inflation," Federal Reserve Bank of San Francisco Working Paper 2020-29, 14, https://www.frbsf.org/ wp-content/uploads/sites/4/wp2020-29.pdf/.

5. Mike Konzcal, "Supply-Side Expansion Has Driven the Decline in Inflation," Roosevelt Institute, September 8, 2023, https://rooseveltinstitute.org/ wp-content/uploads/2023/09/Supply-Side-Expansion-Has-Driven-the -Decline-in-Inflation-202309.pdf/. See also, for instance, James Mackintosh, "Why the Fed Shouldn't Get Credit for the Fall in Inflation," *Wall Street Journal*, November 8, 2023.

6. See especially Isabella Weber and Evan Wasner, "Sellers' Inflation, Profits, and Conflict: Why Can Large Firms Hike Prices in an Emergency?" *Review of Keynesian Economics* 11, no. 2 (2023): 183–213.

7. The US Supreme Court's 1876 *Munn v. Illinois* decision deemed constitutional legislation seeking to regulate the prices set by businesses "affected with a public interest," thus initiating a long debate that would stretch into the New Deal over how to define the public interest. See, for example, William Novak, *New Democracy: The Creation of the Modern American State* (Cambridge: Harvard University Press, 2022), 180–217.

8. According to calculations by the Federal Reserve Bank of Minneapolis, over the century before Roosevelt's presidency, there were thirty-four years during which prices on average fell, thirty-five years during which they remained unchanged, and thirty-one years during which they rose. "Consumer Price Index, 1800-," Federal Reserve Bank of Minneapolis, October 31, 2023, https:// www.minneapolisfed.org/about-us/monetary-policy/inflation-calculator/ consumer-price-index-1800-/. See also Seth Ackerman, "How Inflation Became a Fact of Life," February 22, 2023, *Jacobin*, https://jacobin.com/2023/02/ inflation-wwii-uk-us-1950s-normal-prices/.

9. David M. Kennedy, *Freedom from Fear: The American People in Depression and War, 1929–1945* (New York: Oxford University Press, 1999), 157.

10. On this World War II debate, see, for example, Isabella Weber, *How China Escaped Shock Therapy: The Market Reform Debate* (London: Routledge, 2021),

42–68; Wesley W. Widmaier, *Economic Ideas in Political Time: The Rise and Fall of Economic Orders from the Progressive Era to the Global Financial Crisis* (Cambridge: Cambridge University Press, 2016), 51–76; Stephanie Laguerodie and Francisco Vergara, "The Theory of Price Controls: John Kenneth Galbraith Contribution," *Review of Political Economy* 20, no. 4 (2008): 569–593.

11. John Maynard Keynes, *How to Pay for the War: A Radical Plan for the Chancellor of the Exchequer* (London: Macmillan, 1940), 4–5, 8.

12. Keynes, *How to Pay for the War*, vi, 4–6, 51–53.

13. John Kenneth Galbraith, "The Selection and Timing of Inflation Controls," *Review of Economics and Statistics* 23, no. 2 (1941): 82.

14. John Kenneth Galbraith, *A Life in Our Times* (Boston: Houghton Mifflin, 1981), 129.

15. Galbraith, "Selection and Timing of Inflation Controls," 83.

16. Galbraith, "Selection and Timing of Inflation Controls," 83–84.

17. The OPA dates to Roosevelt's May 29, 1940, establishment of a Price Stabilization Division of the National Defense Advisory Council. This was converted to the Office of Price Administration and Civilian Supply before taking its final form as the OPA with the passage of the Emergency Price Control Act in late 1941. See Hugh Rockoff, *Drastic Measures: A History of Wage and Price Controls in the United States* (Cambridge: Cambridge University Press, 1984), 86–92. Of everything Galbraith wrote over a long career, he later noted "none had such an effect on national policy or my own life" as his 1941 *Review of Economics and Statistics* essay. Galbraith, *Life in Our Times*, 129.

18. Galbraith, *Life in Our Times*, 165. Galbraith had initially advocated for the OPA to confine itself to selective controls, while the businessman and head of the World War I–era War Industries Board, Bernard Baruch, had pushed the administration to impose a comprehensive controls program.

19. Rockoff, *Drastic Measures*, 93; Meg Jacobs, *Pocketbook Politics: Economic Citizenship in Twentieth-Century America* (Princeton: Princeton University Press, 2004), 200 and 179–220.

20. Rockoff, *Drastic Measures*, 123.

21. Andrew H. Bartels, "The Office of Price Administration and the Legacy of the New Deal, 1939–1946," *Public Historian* 5, no. 3 (1983): 21–22; Rockoff, *Drastic Measures*, 143.

22. "Price and Sovereignty," *Harvard Law Review* 135, no. 2 (2021): 759.

23. Jacobs, *Pocketbook Politics*, 180.

24. Discussion of GMPR profit rules in Jacobs, *Pocketbook Politics*, 192–193. Henderson quoted in Jacobs, *Pocketbook Politics*, 193.

25. Rockoff, *Drastic Measures*, 109. For a comparison of different estimates on the OPA's effectiveness, see J. W. Mason and Andrew Bossie, "Public Spending as an Engine of Growth and Equality: Lessons from World War II," Roosevelt Institute, September 2020, https://rooseveltinstitute.org/wp-content/uploads/2020/09/RI_LessonsfromWWIIPart2_WorkingPaper_202009.pdf/, 23.

26. Galbraith, *Life in Our Times*, 171.

27. Rockoff, *Drastic Measures*, 101.

28. Rockoff, *Drastic Measures*, 128–130.

29. Mason and Bossie, "Public Spending as an Engine of Growth and Equality," 29–46.

30. Quoted in Allan Meltzer, *A History of the Federal Reserve*, vol. 1: *1913–1951* (Chicago: University of Chicago Press, 2003), 579.

31. Meltzer, *History of the Federal Reserve*, 604.

32. *The People's Program of 1944* (Washington, DC: CIO PAC, 1944), reprinted in Joseph Gaer, *The First Round: The Story of the CIO Political Action Committee* (New York: Duell, Sloan, and Pearce, 1944).

33. Quoted in Katherine Lee Rader, "Tangled Fates: Casting Racial and Economic Equality in Twentieth Century America," PhD diss., University of Pennsylvania, 2021, 279.

34. Rockoff, *Drastic Measures*, 101.

35. Quoted in Nelson Lichtenstein, *Most Dangerous Man in Detroit: Walter Reuther and the Fate of American Labor* (New York: Basic Books, 1995), 232.

36. Nelson Lichtenstein, "From Corporatism to Collective Bargaining: Organized Labor and the Eclipse of Social Democracy in the Postwar Era," in *The Rise and Fall of the New Deal Order, 1930–1980*, ed. Steve Fraser and Gary Gerstle, 122–152 (Princeton: Princeton University Press, 1989).

37. On organized business after the war, see Howell Harris, *The Right to Manage: Industrial Relations Policies of American Business in the 1940s* (Madison: University of Wisconsin Press, 1982).

38. Barton Bernstein, "The Truman Administration and the Steel Strike of 1946," *Journal of American History* 52, no. 4 (1966): 791–803.

39. Jacobs, *Pocketbook Politics*, 221–231.

40. Donald Montgomery, "Memo on Inflation," July 2, 1946, box 378, folder 11, Donald E. Montgomery Papers, Walter P. Reuther Library of Labor and Urban Affairs, Wayne State University, Detroit, Michigan.

41. US Congress, Joint Economic Committee, Subcommittee on Monetary, Credit, and Fiscal Policies, *Monetary, Credit, and Fiscal Policies: Hearings before the Subcommittee on Monetary, Credit, and Fiscal Policies*, 81st Cong., 1st sess., 1949, 299.

42. Council of Economic Advisers to Harry S. Truman, February 2, 1950, box 2, SR, Leon H. Keyserling Papers, Harry S. Truman Presidential Library, Independence, Missouri.

43. Quoted in Dwight L. Israelsen, "The Economic Thought of Marriner S. Eccles," *Economic Research Institute Study Papers*, 94-11, May 1994, https://core .ac.uk/download/pdf/19985214.pdf/.

44. Marriner S. Eccles with Sidney Hyman, *Beckoning Frontiers: Public and Personal Recollections* (New York: Knopf, 1966), 398–433.

45. Theodore Schultz et al., "The Failure of Present Monetary Policy," January 30, 1951, box 61, folder 2, item 1, Marriner S. Eccles Papers, https://fraser.stlouisfed .org/archival-collection/marriner-s-eccles-papers-1343/letter-mr-marriner -s-eccles-466559/.

46. US Congress, Joint Committee of the Economic Report, Monetary Policy

and the Management of the Public Debt: Hearings before the Subcommittee on General Credit Control and Debt Management, 82nd Cong., 2nd sess., 1952, 818.

47. Gerald A. Epstein and Juliet B. Schor, "The Federal Reserve–Treasury Accord and the Construction of the Postwar Monetary Regime in the United States," *Social Concept* 7, no. 1 (1995): 7–48.

48. Robert L. Hetzel, *The Monetary Policy of the Federal Reserve: A History* (Cambridge: Cambridge University Press, 2008), 49–59; Benjamin Braun and Leah Downy, "Against Amnesia: Re-Imagining Central Banking," Council on Economic Policies Discussion Note, January 2020, https://www.cepweb.org/wp-content/uploads/2020/01/CEP-DN-Against-Amnesia.-Re-Imagining-Central-Banking.pdf/. See also Robert M. Bremner, *Chairman of the Fed: William McChesney Martin Jr. and the Creation of the Modern American Financial System* (New Haven: Yale University Press, 2004).

49. Norikazu Takami, "The Baffling New Inflation: How Cost-Push Theories Influenced Policy Debate in the Late 1950s United States," *History of Political Economy* 47, no. 4 (2105): 605–629.

50. Gardiner C. Means, *Administrative Inflation and Public Policy* (Washington, DC: Anderson Kramer Associates, 1959).

51. John Kenneth Galbraith, "Market Structure and Stabilization Policy," *Review of Economics and Statistics* 39, no. 2 (1957): 124–133.

52. Means, *Administrative Inflation and Public Policy*, 32–33.

53. Kristoffer Smemo, Samir Sonti, and Gabriel Winant, "Conflict or Consensus: The Steel Strike of 1959 and the Anatomy of the New Deal Order," *Critical Historical Studies* 4, no. 1 (2017): 39–73; Nat Weinberg, "The Death of the United States Guideposts," in Anthony D. Smith, ed., *The Labor Market and Inflation: The Proceedings of a Symposium Held at the International Institute for Labour Studies in Geneva, 24–26 October 1966, under the Chairmanship of Pierre Massé* (New York: St. Martin's Press, 1968), 44.

54. On incomes policies, see Craufurd D. Goodwin, ed., *Exhortations and Controls: The Search for a Wage-Price Policy, 1945–1971* (Washington, DC: Brookings, 1975); and Andrew Y. Elrod, "Stabilization Politics in the Twentieth Century United States: Corporatism, Democracy, and Economic Planning, 1945–1980," PhD diss., University of California, Santa Barbara, 2021.

55. Stacey L. Schreft, "Credit Controls: 1980," *Federal Reserve Bank of Richmond Economic Review* (1990), 26–28.

56. Lev Menand, *The Fed Unbound: Central Banking in a Time of Crisis* (New York: Columbia Global Reports, 2023).

57. On the idea of selective credit policy in the postwar period, see Eric Monnet, *Controlling Credit: Central Banking and the Planned Economy in Postwar France, 1948–1973* (Cambridge: Cambridge University Press, 2018). See also US Congress, House of Representatives, *Activities by Various Central Banks to Promote Economic and Social Welfare Programs: Staff Report*, 91st Cong., 2nd sess., 1970, Committee Print 53-679 O.

58. Weinberg, "Death of the United States Guideposts," 24.

59. AFL-CIO Research Department, *Inflation, 1979: An Analysis with Suggested Solutions* (Washington, DC: AFL-CIO, 1979).

60. US Congress, House of Representatives, Committee on Banking and Currency, Lowering Interests, Fight Inflation, Help Housing, Small Business, and Employment: Report Together with Minority and Additional Views, 91st Cong., 1st sess., 1969, No. 91-755, 66. See also Douglas J. Elliott et al., "The History of Cyclical Macroprudential Policy in the United States," Finance and Economics Discussion Series, Division of Research & Statistics and Monetary Affairs, Federal Reserve Board, 2013-29, https://www.federalreserve.gov/pubs/feds/2013/201329/201329pap.pdf/.

61. Gardiner Means, "How to Control Inflation in the United States: An Alternative to Planned Stagnation," *Wage-Price Law & Economics Review* 1, no. 1 (1975): 47–74. Exploration of the causes of the 1970s inflation is beyond the scope of this chapter. For an insightful analysis of changes in how the economics profession made sense of the "great inflation" in the 1970s and after, see Aurélien Goutsmedt, "From the Stagflation to the Great Inflation: Explaining the US Economy of the 1970s," *Revue d'Économie Politique* 131, no. 3 (2021): 557–582.

62. See, for example, Leo Panitch and Sam Gindin, *The Making of Global Capitalism: The Political Economy of U.S. Empire* (New York: Verso, 2012), 164–172. See also Tim Barker, "Other People's Blood," *n+1* 34 (2019), https://www.nplusone mag.com/issue-34/reviews/other-peoples-blood-2/.

63. "Testimony of Chairman Alan Greenspan," The Federal Reserve's Semiannual Monetary Policy Report before the Committee on Banking, Housing, and Urban Affairs, US Senate, February 26, 1997, https://www.federalreserve.gov/boarddocs/hh/1997/february/testimony.htm/.

64. Benjamin Braun, "Asset Manager Capitalism as a Corporate Governance Regime," in *The American Political Economy: Politics, Markets, and Power*, ed. Jacob S. Hacker et al., 270–294 (Cambridge: Cambridge University Press, 2021).

65. See, for example, Stephanie Kelton, *The Deficit Myth: Modern Monetary Theory and the Birth of the People's Economy* (New York: Public Affairs, 2020).

66. Whether "supply-side liberalism" deserves to be called new is an open question. See Brent Cebul, *Illusions of Progress: Business, Poverty, and Liberalism in the American Century* (Philadelphia: University of Pennsylvania Press, 2023).

67. "Attorney General James Announces Price Gouging Rules," Office of the New York State Attorney General, March 2, 2023, https://ag.ny.gov/press -release/2023/attorney-general-james-announces-price-gouging-rules-protect -consumers-and-small/.

68. Jorge Uxó, "Inflation and Counter-Inflationary Policy Measures: The Case of Spain," Hans-Böckler-Stiftung, No. 83-5, December 2022, https://www .boeckler.de/en/faust-detail.htm?sync_id=HBS-008483/.

69. Tom Fairless, "Germany to Cap Energy Prices as Industry Is Pushed to the Brink," *Wall Street Journal*, September 29, 2022.

70. Zachary Carter, "What If We're Thinking about Inflation All Wrong?" *New Yorker*, June 6, 2023.

71. Isabella M. Weber and Evan Wasner, "Sellers' Inflation, Profits, and Conflict." See also Isabella Weber et al., "Inflation in Times of Overlapping Emergencies: Systemically Significant Prices from an Input-Output Perspective," January 1, 2022, University of Massachusetts Economics Department Working Paper Series, https://scholarworks.umass.edu/econ_workingpaper/340/.

72. Mike Konzcal and J. W. Mason, "A New Direction for the Federal Reserve: Expanding the Monetary Policy Toolkit," Roosevelt Institute, December 2017, https://rooseveltinstitute.org/wp-content/uploads/2020/07/RI-Monetary-Policy-Toolkit-201711.pdf/.

73. Menand, *Fed Unbound*, 24.

74. For an authoritative account of the Federal Reserve since the financial crisis, see Adam Tooze, *Crashed: How a Decade of Financial Crisis Changed the World* (New York: Viking, 2018).

PART II

Food, Labor, and Hospitality

4

Crises and Essential Workers

The Impact of COVID-19 on Farmworkers and Guest Worker Programs

ISMAEL GARCÍA-COLÓN

As COVID-19 took hold in the United States in the spring of 2020, the initial problems of overburdened health facilities caused by the inability and refusal of governments to prepare for a pandemic led to important transformations in labor relations. The measures to contain COVID-19 also created food supply problems that persisted in early 2022. The closing of workplaces left many workers throughout the North Atlantic countries, but particularly in the United States, without access to a safety net capable of sustaining their livelihoods. Food insecurity loomed as soon as early disruptions in the production and circulation of food occurred. In places like New York City, many families without access to government help began to form long lines of people requesting food assistance from the pantries of religious organizations and nonprofit groups. Sonny Perdue, the US Secretary of Agriculture under the Trump administration, who had previously lobbied the federal government on behalf of agribusinesses and food processing industries, attempted to lower wages and extended temporary work visas. At the same time, lockdowns, mask mandates, and other measures to contain COVID-19 changed the way that workers performed their tasks.

Despite these new challenges, the ensuing so-called food crisis, and the responses to it, were not something new in the history of US agricultural production. When government officials, agribusinesses, and food processing firms engage in a discourse of crisis, one must ask who and what is in crisis and for what purposes capital mobilizes labor to avert and resolve crises. Attention to labor relations and how state actors and economic interests seek to structure unequal access to power and wealth are key to understanding the deeper meanings of crises. In this chapter, I explore the impact of COVID-19 policies on labor relations in agriculture and those policies, linkages to previous crises that shaped the construction of farm labor forces in US agriculture.

Understanding the effects of COVID-19 on the production and distribution of food requires examining how pandemics and crises in the history of guest worker programs have shaped the paths through which government officials and employers mobilize and allocate labor. Securing guest workers and migrant farm labor requires that governments maintain open borders; for their part, employers need to sustain and expand their profits by lowering their labor costs and keeping workers disorganized. These policies not only have revealed the contradictions within anti-immigrant policies, they also have impeded the containment of COVID-19 by allowing travel and crowded living and working conditions.

Studies that attempt to theorize the construction of crises are anchored in symbolic anthropology. In the first year of the pandemic, an article by Cora Hirst attempted to reconcile the historical sociology of Pierre Bourdieu and the ahistorical structuralism of Claude Lévi-Strauss in the understanding of COVID-19 as a crisis that entails the articulation of unprecedented phenomena with recurring phenomena.[1] However, symbolic meanings and discourse analysis yield an incomplete understanding of the complexity of COVID-19 as a crisis because they do not consider political economy and, therefore, social differentiation and subject formation. If part of the COVID-19 crisis was supposedly a labor shortage, one cannot think of crises as simply unprecedented phenomena and the responses to them but, rather, as part of deeper strategies of power and the actions of social actors to structure class inequality.

It is also important to highlight the political context in which COVID-19 emerged and in which farm labor developed in the immediate years before the pandemic. In the United States as well as in Western Europe, a wave of right-wing governments and elected officials began to transform policies and institutions. The Trump administration sought to deepen the liberalization of farm labor and guest work. The nativism of this right-wing wave revived guest worker programs as the solution to the increasing immigration and refugee crisis. In 2018, as a response to the right-wing resurgence, social democrat–elected officials increased their visibility in the United States and initiated a push for reforms of labor laws. In New York state, elected officials led the enactment of labor reforms in the agricultural sector. In 2019 these reforms included the expansion of collective bargaining and overtime laws in agriculture. The new labor rules encountered stiff opposition from farmers, who were not successful in blocking their final implementation.[2] Unfortunately, farmworker activists, supportive policymakers, and pro-labor elected officials have not been able to transform the increased visibility of farmworkers into essential workers deserving additional labor rights and greater political clout at the national level. The federal government is still dominated by conservative and pro-business immigration policymakers and elected officials, impeding possibilities for effective change.

The study of the impact of COVID-19 on guest worker programs and migrant farm labor migration requires an anthropology of capitalism to illuminate how contingencies shape the paths through which labor is deployed and allocated, which in turn determine how subjects maneuver within fields of force as they are conceptualized and categorized in state formations. As scholars, we need to pay attention to how the impact of COVID-19 shaped not only the biopolitics of agricultural production and migration but also how policies to contain the pandemic were imposed, transforming labor relations across the globe. The dynamics surrounding the development of guest worker programs are one important example of the multiple processes constituting and constituted by labor relations.[3]

By characterizing the processes that shape guest worker programs simply as part of neoliberalism, scholars obscure the ways those processes are "unfolding, intertwining, spreading out, and dissipating over time" during so-called crises.[4] In this chapter, I argue that elected officials, farmers, and agribusinesses mobilize a language of crises, food security, and essential workers in order to secure the exploitation of a deportable and racialized immigrant labor force. The COVID-19 pandemic represented a new opportunity for these sectors to activate this language. During the pandemic, the development of food production revealed the contradictions between global capitalism, the political economy of agriculture, and public health. In what follows, I briefly examine the history of guest worker programs and the initial impact of COVID-19 on farm labor.

During the early twentieth century, emergent guest worker programs met with a strong nativist response in places like Germany, South Africa, and the United States. Although labor unions challenged employers who sought to use new immigrant groups as strikebreakers, employers' constant efforts to lower labor costs and discipline workers entrenched their dependence on immigrant labor, helped by dispossession, ethnic segmentation, and racism. From the 1870s to the 1920s, governments restricted immigration with racial and nativist policies, such as the Chinese Exclusion Act of 1882 and the Foran Act of 1885 in the United States, while extending and increasing safety net and welfare services for citizens. Temporary migration of workers was offered as an alternative for meeting labor shortages.[5] Guest work became an alternative that calmed anti-immigrant sectors as the government implemented deportation and gatekeeping practices in order to impose limits on immigration. Thus, employers could expand their profits by using temporary migrant workers while governments protected the jobs and safety nets of their citizens. In the United States, the first Bracero Program began during the First World War with the recruitment of Mexican workers. Government officials and farmers claimed that labor shortages resulting from the war justified the creation of a guest worker program.[6]

When World War II broke out, the US federal government instituted an emergency guest worker program with migrant workers from Mexico, Canada, and the British Caribbean colonies. Government officials and growers argued that maintaining food production in the face of war-related labor shortages was a matter of national security. In reality most of these shortages were the result of the labor demands of war-related industries *and* the reluctance of growers to pay higher salaries. After the war, the US government continued the Mexican Bracero Program, and the Immigration and Nationality Act of 1952 expanded considerably the use of guest workers under the H-2 visa program. The history of guest worker programs underscores the permanent use of labor-busting and deportation practices to maintain a docile, low-wage labor force. Capital is always looking to preserve these conditions, no matter how, when, or where they can find the labor power needed.[7]

The contradictions of using guest worker programs again became visible when governments attempted to control the spread of COVID-19. The arrival of COVID-19 to the United States and Western Europe coincided with preparations for and the beginning of agricultural work in the fields. As Germany began to close its borders, the harvest of early vegetables was interrupted by an insufficient labor supply, risking the rotting of asparagus in the ground. In the United Kingdom, farmers had trouble hiring farmworkers for raspberry picking and harvesting potatoes. Italy needed migrant workers to harvest more than a quarter of the strawberry, bean, and lettuce crops. The initial lockdowns kept 150,000 guest farmworkers from Romania, Poland, India, and elsewhere from entering the country. Growers and small farmers began to raise their voices, arguing that labor shortages in agriculture constituted a threat to food security. In fact, the United States and European governments declared food to be an issue of national security as millions of their citizens stockpiled food and other household supplies during the lockdowns.[8] Governments began to open borders for migrant farmworkers and to designate their jobs as essential.

The argument from many government officials, growers, and labor advocates was that the need for guest workers resulted from the local population's unwillingness to work under the arduous labor conditions of agriculture— long, often backbreaking hours for low wages.[9] Relatively few local workers applied for agricultural jobs. In France some people signed up on a website that matched workers with farms, and major supermarket chains pledged to buy from French farms.[10] Some Italians working in restaurants, bakeries, and cafés turned to farm labor after they lost their jobs, preferring outdoor work, which they considered to be safer.[11] These were exceptions, however, to a general lack of domestic workers willing to take agricultural jobs during the pandemic at the wages and under the conditions being offered.

In areas of the US Southwest and Midwest, low wages and the displacement of domestic workers by guest worker programs continued while anti-immigrant sentiments prevailed. As governments began to implement measures to contain COVID-19, the closing of businesses and government services created problems for the production, processing, and circulation of food. The reliance on deportable, low-wage, and immigrant workers in US agriculture prompted large agribusiness interests and their allied government officials to promote policies facilitating labor control and availability.

As the Trump administration increasingly used nativism and the pandemic to implement aggressive immigration bans, arguing that these policies reduced job competition from immigrants, the US State Department, citing growers' concerns about pandemic-related labor shortages, encouraged agricultural employers to hire guest farmworkers by waiving interview requirements for H-2A workers and making it easier for employers to rehire current H-2A workers.[12] However, guest farmworkers with H-2A visas can lose their jobs at any time for complaining about their working and living conditions or for becoming sick. As in the past, because employers have the power to force guest workers to leave the United States immediately, workers' fear of losing their livelihoods made them unlikely to confront and protest abuses.

On April 20, 2020, the US Citizenship and Immigration Services (USCIS), under the US Department of Homeland and Security, extended H-2A workers' stay in the United States beyond the three-year maximum allowed under a prior regulation. USCIS issued this temporary rule in order to "provide agricultural employers with an orderly and timely flow of legal foreign workers, thereby protecting the integrity of the nation's food supply chain and decreasing possible reliance on unauthorized aliens." Officials argued that the disruptions and uncertainty caused by COVID-19 created a public health emergency in the US agriculture sector during the 2020 summer harvest season.[13] Iman Haqiqi and Marziyeh Bahalou Horeh found that the impact of COVID-19 on agricultural production was 2.63 percent, or approximately $10 billion worth of crops and livestock. Small farms were more vulnerable than larger farms, though larger farms represent a bigger share of agricultural production.[14]

US agricultural businesses expect approximately 200,000 seasonal guest workers from Mexico and Central America to enter the country with H-2A visas each year.[15] H-2A guest workers account for nearly 10 percent of the more than 2 million farmworkers in the country, but they are a minority among US farmworkers, and half of all US farmworkers are undocumented.[16] In March 2020 the US Department of State experienced a 20 percent increase in processed H-2A visas compared to the previous year (from 22,374 to 26,957 visas). This number of H-2A visas issued was surpassed in April 2020, with 313,030 issued, a record for H-2A visas issued in a single month. In fact, the H-2A visa program has no caps on the number of visas that can be issued annually: the total number of H-2A visas granted was 204,801 in 2019; 213,394 in 2020; 258,000 in 2021; and 298,336 in 2022.[17] The expansion of the H-2A program during the Trump administration was also linked to the increase in the number of brokers who hire and transport H-2A workers. Even in Puerto Rico, a US territory that sends migrant farmworkers stateside, farmers are hiring H-2A workers for local agriculture. These trends demonstrate US agriculture's dependence on one of the most exploited groups of workers.

The situation in the United States regarding guest work during COVID-19 was not unique. European countries and Canada also experienced problems with the hiring and transportation of guest workers. As the pandemic wore on in 2020, European countries recruited three hundred thousand migrant workers from Eastern Europe to harvest asparagus, pick strawberries, and plant late-season crops. The German government allowed farmers to airlift migrant workers from Romania and Bulgaria to ease labor shortages, and German farmers organized flights to transport twenty-eight thousand guest workers in April and May. Florian Bogensberger, a farmer in Bavaria, paid approximately eleven thousand dollars to fly in twenty-three Romanian guest workers. However, these measures did not solve the labor shortage problem, and they also created concerns about the possibility of importing new COVID-19 infections. Friedrich Ostendorff, a member of the German Green Party, denounced the importation of guest farmworkers as exploitation of people desperate to make a living during COVID-19.[18] In Italy, unemployment pushed citizens to find jobs in agriculture, but their numbers were insufficient for a labor regime characterized by the mobilization of a temporary and mostly immigrant labor force. Even during a pandemic, agricultural employers relied on lowering labor costs in order to increase profits.[19]

When government officials and growers refer to labor shortages as a problem, they are talking about their inability to attract workers who will accept low wages just to be able to eke out a living and sustain their families. Even before the increase in COVID-19 infections among the non-guest workers, US agriculture was experiencing a shortage of workers, causing harvesting problems and raising labor costs and crop prices. In 2019 workers in the dairy industry in New York state received wage increases as a result of so-called labor shortages.[20] By May 2020, grocery stores were selling two pounds of strawberries for 17 percent more than the previous year, and a pint of cherry tomatoes sold for 52 percent more.[21]

Labor shortages and dependence on guest workers are also the result of working conditions in agriculture. Workers toil the fields under the sun with high temperatures, soaking with sweat for more than eight hours a day. They commonly experience violation of their rights, including subpar wages, unsafe housing, coercion, and sexual harassment. Moreover, most farmworkers are undocumented and thus vulnerable to abuse and deportation, while guest workers tend to be isolated from the communities surrounding their labor camps. The inequities embedded in their contracts are not the outcome of negotiations but, rather, an official expression of their unequal status. For example, recruiters in countries like Mexico often extort high fees from guest workers, who then arrive indebted in the United States. Workers often are not paid the Adverse Effect Wage Rate—that is, the minimum wage required for domestic and guest agricultural workers by the US Department of Labor— because employers subtract transportation, housing, and other costs from their pay. Would-be guest workers, who generally come from rural areas with high unemployment, continue applying for H-2A jobs, however, because of the opportunity they offer to support their families. In addition, hiring H-2A workers has the effect of depressing wages and pressuring other farmworkers to work faster and thus endanger their well-being. It also increases the problems with housing for all rural workers.[22]

In extreme cases, migrant farmworkers became victims of human trafficking through the H-2A program. In June 2021 a contractor transported a farmworker from Monterrey, Mexico, to a corn farm in Georgia. He worked twelve hours a day with fifteen-minute lunch breaks, earning only $225 for fifteen days of work. He escaped eventually and returned to Mexico. The federal government indicted his contractor on charges of forced labor, mail fraud, witness tampering, and conspiracy to commit money laundering, human smuggling, and labor trafficking. The employer had threatened workers with deportation or violence.[23]

Work in agriculture has always been "essential work" however invisible it might be to most people. Labor advocates tried to make sure that the public was aware that farmworkers were needed to resolve the food shortages caused by the COVID-19 crisis, even if they came from other countries.[24] But designating guest farmworkers as essential workers did not stop some farmers and federal officials from reducing their wages. Many employers continued lobbying against the H-2A pay rule requiring guest workers to be paid the highest prevailing wage in an agricultural region.[25] Despite this rule, farmworkers were paid about half the wages of comparable workers in other industries.[26] Under the Trump administration, efforts to lower agricultural wages were led by former White House chief of staff Mark Meadows and Agriculture Secretary Sonny Perdue, both friends of big agribusinesses.[27]

In California the prevailing wage was $14.77 per hour, higher than the state minimum of between $12 and $13 per hour, depending on the size of the employer. The Trump administration's proposal was to lower H-2A wages to $8.34 per hour. Even as the American Farm Bureau supported the Trump administration's reduction of wages, the California Farm Bureau Federation opposed it. As demands from restaurants and wholesalers decreased, the federation preferred an expansion in government paycheck protections and assistance in the delivery of foods to community pantries and food banks. This stance reflected the trouble California growers have attracting farmworkers in areas where the high cost of living makes it impossible for them to find housing and to pay for other living expenses. Federal efforts to reduce wages were mostly intended to benefit employers in the Southeast, where tobacco growers could save $5.42 an hour in North Carolina and $3.15 an hour in Florida.[28]

In addition, Secretary Perdue lobbied intensively for the US Department of Agriculture to take over the administration of the H-2A visa program, currently under the US Department of Labor. A takeover of the H-2A visa program by the Department of Agriculture would dramatically increase agricultural employers' influence over the program. In a further show of his lack of support for farmworkers, Perdue did not earmark any of the money from the Coronavirus Aid, Relief, and Economic Security Act (CARES) for farmworkers and instead provided farmers $16 billion in direct aid and $3 billion for food programs to purchase agricultural products.[29] Perdue also emphasized the need to favor the H-2A program over any attempt to enact comprehensive immigration reform and to unify immigrant families. He pointed out that "[The H-2A program] doesn't offend people who are anti-immigrant because they don't want more immigrant citizens here. We need people who can help U.S. agriculture meet the production."[30] Farmworker advocacy organizations challenged these new regulations in court and delayed their implementation until the Biden administration took office.[31]

Notably, one of the first measures taken by the Biden administration was to overturn the new H-2A regulations enacted by the Trump administration. Its official policy of a "fair, orderly and humane immigration system" includes the expansion of number of H-2A visas issued per year.[32] In November 2022 and February 2023, the Biden administration issued new regulations upholding the highest prevailing wage and making changes to how the Adverse Effect Wages Rate is calculated. Farmers and their lobby organizations filed federal suits attempting to stop the enforcement of the new rules, but thus far their lawsuits have not prevailed in court.[33]

COVID-19 social distancing also represented a problem for food production. Employers typically transport farmworkers in crowded buses and trucks. Worker housing tends to be crowded, too, in barracks with bunk beds. Such working conditions made it difficult for farmworkers to hand-wash regularly, and protective gear, when available, is often uncomfortable to wear during hot weather. Moreover, many agricultural employers did not make changes to comply with social distancing recommendations or provide personal protective equipment and information about COVID-19. Making this situation worse, in the United States most farmworkers lack health insurance and paid sick leave, so skipping a day of work because of illness was not an option.[34] In Canada the situation was similar, with reports of employers prioritizing production at the expense of workers' physical and mental health.[35] On April 16, 2020, the disregard for protections for farmworkers led Familias Unidas por la Justicia and the United Farm Workers to file a lawsuit asking the Washington State Department of Health and Department of Labor and Industries to begin health and safety standards protections for farmworkers.[36]

The lack of information in Spanish also makes it difficult to provide adequate information to workers. In 2020 a Facebook Live event sponsored by the United Farm Workers attracted more than eighteen thousand farmworkers, with most indicating that their employers had not provided information about COVID-19.[37] Some workers even heard from employers, "There's no such thing as COVID-19. It's an invention of the government."[38]

As a result of the working and living conditions, COVID-19 tended to be more prevalent in counties with larger concentrations of farmworkers. In a study of the incidence of COVID-19 among workers in related agricultural activities, Jayson L. Lusk and Ranveer Chandra found that 9.31 percent of hired workers (170,137) and 9.01 percent of migrant workers (27,223) had contracted COVID-19 as of March 31, 2021. In terms of deaths, there were 2,969 (0.16 percent) among hired workers and 459 (0.152 percent) among migrant workers.[39]

Many of the working and living conditions in US agriculture are not new under COVID-19, but the pandemic made them more visible and increased the probability of their becoming worse as time passed,[40] as reports about COVID-19 spreading among the farmworkers suggest: 29 guest workers infected on a farm in North Carolina and 36 farmworkers, including guest workers, in Washington state.[41] In Tennessee, 200 workers on a farm were infected. New Jersey reported 110 farmworkers ill, and 170 cases were confirmed in one greenhouse in New York. In Florida 91 H-2A migrants tested positive for COVID-19 out of a crew of approximately 120 workers.[42] Crowded housing is one of the principal causes of outbreaks. Rooms with bunk beds, housing in some cases from 9 to 15 workers, facilitate outbreaks. In California 25 percent of farmworkers living in a housing facility tested positive for COVID.[43]

Many undocumented farmworkers in the United States continued working in the fields because of their ineligibility to apply for unemployment and their fear of being deported if they used public services. The situation is very similar in Europe, where a guest farmworker on a German farm remarked, "Everybody feels a bit scared, but we also need to work."[44] A farmworker advocate in the state of Florida said, "When there is an economic reality that you need to work to feed your family, then you're going to be more likely to take a risk and not speak up about unsafe conditions, because you feel like you don't have a choice."[45] One employer in Virginia kept workers under lockdown, ordering them to remain in the camps and fields. Although they were successful in containing the virus, workers complained that their worksite had become a prison, that they had lost their freedom and were practically slaves.[46] Other employers told workers not to get tested for COVID-19 because they would be fired if they tested positive and not be paid if required to quarantine. These actions effectively forced many farmworkers to continue working in the fields while sick.[47] Employers' strategies at the expense of workers resulted in employment in agricultural production not being impacted as strongly by the pandemic as were other sectors of the US economy. By August 2020 the unemployment rate in agricultural production was only 5.6 percent, even though workers in agriculture were some of the most affected by COVID-19.[48]

Despite these hurdles, workers registered their opposition and resisted these dangerous working and living conditions. Fifty workers at a California pistachio farm went on strike against their employer after a COVID outbreak in June 2020. One of their main complaints was the lack of personal protective equipment. These nonunionized workers forced their employers to clean the processing plant and hire a mobile testing facility. Even as the employer was trying to hide information about the outbreak from current workers, it was not informing new workers of the outbreak.[49]

Mobilizing workers across long distances to produce food is worth the trouble as long as it keeps labor costs down for farmers and agribusinesses, as the ongoing history of farm labor migration and guest worker programs in the United States, Western Europe, and other developed countries indicates. However, the language of crises and the political ecology of COVID-19 challenge us to rethink contemporary labor relations in agriculture. Securing temporary and readily available migrant farmworkers whom the government and employers can mobilize quickly requires immigration regulations that maintain open borders. The extension of visas and lowering of guest workers' wages and the opening of borders and airlifting of thousands of guest workers are examples of the gambles that governments and growers took to build a migratory infrastructure and secure their profits. These policies reveal the contradictions within anti-immigrant and deportation policies, not least the haphazard barriers to the spread of COVID-19 exemplified by allowing international and domestic travel for migrant workers who were then exposed to crowded living and working conditions. As if lowering farmworkers' standard of living were not sufficient for large agribusinesses who seem to care only about profits at any cost, governments continue to acquiesce to growers' preferences for controlling labor policies.

Pandemic events like COVID-19 affect government policies and their close relationships with capital. Farmers and agribusinesses use their influence in political campaigns and with elected officials to take advantage of and transform existing labor relations. As anthropologist Eric Wolf points out, the power to mobilize and supply labor renders some behaviors possible, less possible, or impossible.[50] The policies intended to contain COVID-19 created labor shortages that could not be resolved by hiring local workers because government officials rendered them undesirable for agriculture a long time ago.[51] The separation of the local population from agricultural work implied the elimination of a particular way of life with complex skills and knowledge. Meanwhile, the need for temporary migrant farmworkers continues, constituting guest farmworkers as racialized subjects who are available to fulfill the demands of capital. Regardless of being considered essential workers, US farm labor is mostly constituted by undocumented workers, permanent authorized immigrants, colonial subjects, people of color, and guest workers. During COVID-19 times, guest workers and other farmworkers became briefly visible as essential workers, but they continue to be expendable and disposable during times of crisis. A solution to their plight involves transforming the balance of power between employers, government officials, and workers based on labor, immigrant, and civil rights.[52]

Following the easing of the federal government's mandate on COVID-19, climate change seems to be the next looming crisis that will affect agriculture. Rising temperatures are already having major effects on crop cultivation and harvests throughout the world. High temperatures and the overuse of water resources are resulting in droughts. At the same time, higher levels of heat affect the health of farmworkers. There is ample evidence of how heat exposure causes health risks to farmworkers—for example, there is a link between chronic kidney disease and heat stress among agricultural workers. In the future, employers will have to reschedule work shifts to prioritize work in the shade or at night. Otherwise, they will be risking not only low productivity but the physical well-being of workers as well.[53] In addition, many H-2A guest workers are already climate refugees escaping drought and harsh labor conditions under rising temperatures in the Global South. What the COVID-19 crisis teaches us as we face the climate change crisis is that food security entails more than mere access to its distribution.

As government officials and employers keep fostering migration and encroaching on migrants' rights, in the process cheapening the farm labor force and deforesting and polluting large areas for agriculture, ravaging epidemics and climate change will worsen the conditions that continue destroying food sovereignty and the production of an adequate food supply. The COVID-19 moment presented us with another opportunity to reveal the inequalities and arbitrariness of labor rights in agriculture. The COVID-19 crisis made visible to all the continuous ruptures and unevenness of global capitalism, which include food scarcity and massive unemployment. Many people experience these conditions on a daily basis outside of the United States and Western Europe. By deploying a discourse of crisis, elected and government officials, farmers, lobbyists, and agribusinesses engage in the politics of fear to advance their agendas. Crises can have multiple meanings, but the world is real and the power to allocate labor structures how thousands of people make their livelihood as guest workers and migrant farmworkers.

Notes

An earlier version of this chapter appeared in Ismael García-Colón, "The COVID-19 Spring and the Expendability of Guestworkers," *Dialectical Anthropology* 44 (September 2020): 257–264.

1. Cora Hirst, "A State of Emergency, a State of Transition: How the Covid-19 Pandemic May Help Reconcile Historicism and the Anthropology of Crisis," *Student Anthropologist* 7, no. 1 (2020): 88–93.

2. Amir Khafagy, "A Year Later, New York's First Farm Workers Union Struggles to Secure Its First Contract," *Documented*, December 12, 2022, https://documentedny.com/2022/12/12/new-york-farmworkers-farm-workers-union/#:~:text=Farm%20workers%20on%20Long%20Island,struggle%3A%20winning%20a%20fair%20contract/; Rachel Wharton, "Food Is Not a Prop for Senator Jessica Ramos. It's a Platform," *New York Times*, April 29, 2021, https://www.nytimes.com/2021/04/29/dining/jessica-ramos-food.html/.

3. Sharryn Kasmir and August Carbonella, Introduction to *Blood and Fire: Toward a Global Anthropology of Labor* (New York: Berghahn Press, 2014), 23.

4. Eric R. Wolf, *Pathways of Power: Building an Anthropology of the Modern World* (Berkeley: University of California Press, 2001), 390.

5. Rick Baldoz, *The Third Asiatic Invasion: Empire and Migration in Filipino America, 1898–1946* (New York: New York University Press, 2011); Andreas Fahrmeir, *Citizenship: The Rise and Fall of a Modern Concept* (New Haven: Yale University Press, 2007); Cindy Hahamovitch, "Creating Perfect Immigrants: Guestworkers of the World in Historical Perspective," Labor History 44, no. 1 (2003): 69–94; Cindy Hahamovitch, *No Man's Land: Jamaican Guestworkers in America and the Global History of Deportable Labor* (Princeton: Princeton University Press, 2011).

6. Nicholas De Genova and Nathalie Peutz, *The Deportation Regime: Sovereignty, Space and the Freedom of Movement* (Durham, NC: Duke University Press, 2010); Gilbert G. Gonzalez, *Guest Workers or Colonized Labor? Mexican Labor Migration to the United States* (Boulder, CO: Paradigm Publishers, 2006); Hahamovitch, No Man's Land; Moon-Ho Jung, *Coolies and Cane: Race, Labor, and Sugar in the Age of Emancipation* (Baltimore: Johns Hopkins University Press, 2006); Erika Lee, *At America's Gate: Chinese Immigration during the Exclusion Era, 1882–1943* (Chapel Hill: University of North Carolina Press, 2003); Mae M. Ngai, *Impossible Subjects: Illegal Aliens and the Making of Modern America*

(Princeton, NJ: Princeton University Press, 2004); Eric R. Wolf, *Europe and the People without History* (Berkeley: University of California Press, 1982).

7. Wolf, *Europe and the People without History,* 361.

8. Liz Alderman, Melissa Eddy, and Amie Tsang, "Migrant Farmworkers Whose Harvests Feed Europe Are Blocked at Borders," *New York Times,* March 27, 2020, https://www.nytimes.com/2020/03/27/business/coronavirus-farm-labor-europe.html/; Melissa Eddy, "Farm Workers Airlifted into Germany Provide Solutions and Pose New Risks," *New York Times,* May 18, 2020, https://www.nytimes.com/2020/05/18/world/europe/coronavirus-german-farms-migrant-workers-airlift.html/; Jason Horowitz, "For Some Italians, the Future of Work Looks Like the Past," *New York Times,* May 24, 2020, https://www.nytimes.com/2020/05/24/world/europe/italy-farms-coronavirus.html?referringSource=articleShare/.

9. Gabriel Thompson, "'The Sun Is Hot and You Can't Breathe in a Mask'—Life as an Undocumented Farmworker," *The Guardian,* May 28, 2020, https://www.theguardian.com/us-news/2020/may/28/undocumented-farmworker-us-immigration-california/.

10. Alderman, Eddy, and Tsang, "Migrant Farmworkers Whose Harvests Feed Europe"; Eddy, "Farm Workers Airlifted."

11. Horowitz, "For Some Italians."

12. Madeline Leung Coleman, "As the Trump Administration Restricts Legal Immigration, It's Expanding a Class of Vulnerable Guest Workers," *The Appeal,* June 10, 2020, https://theappeal.org/trump-immigration-policyh-2a-visa-expansion-guestworkers/.

13. US Department of Homeland Security, "Temporary Changes to Requirements Affecting H-2A Nonimmigrants Due to the COVID-19 National Emergency," *Federal Register* 8, CFR Parts 214 and 274a (CIS No. 2667-20; DHS Docket No. USCIS-2020-0008), RIM 1615-AC55, Document No. 2020-08356.

14. Iman Haqiqi and Marziyeh Bahalou Horeh, "Assessment of COVID-19 Impacts on U.S. Counties Using the Immediate Impact Model of Local Agricultural Production (IMLAP)," *Agricultural Systems* 190 (2021): 103132.

15. Jacques Leslie, "The White House Wants to Give Farmworkers Who Put Food on Your Table a Dire Pay Cut," *Los Angeles Times,* May 21, 2020, https://www.latimes.com/opinion/story/2020-05-21/farmworkers-h2a-visas-sonny-perdue-united-farmworkers-minimum-wage/.

16. Coleman, "As the Trump Administration Restricts Legal Immigration"; Mike Dorning and Jen Skerritt, "Every Single Worker Has Covid at One U.S. Farm on Eve of Harvest," *Bloomberg,* May 30, 2020, https://www.bloomberg.com/news/articles/2020-05-29/every-single-worker-has-covid-at-one-u-s-farm-on-eve-of-harvest/.

17. Andrea Hsu and Ximena Bustillo, "America's Farms Are Desperate for Labor. Foreign Workers Bring Relief and Controversy," NPR, WNYC, July 27, 2023, https://www.npr.org/2023/07/27/1187682674/farm-workers-guest-workers-h-2a-visa-agricultural-harvest-farm-labor/; Philip Martin, "A Look at H-2A Growth and Reform in 2021 and 2022," *Insight & Analysis,* Mexico Institute,

Wilson Center, January 3, 2022, https://www.wilsoncenter.org/article/look-h-2a
-growth-and-reform-2021-and-2022/; "Temporary Agricultural Visas Increase in
2020, Despite Pandemic," *USA Facts*, April 23 and 29, 2021, https://usafacts.org/
articles/temporary-h2a-agricultural-visas-increase-in-2020-despite-pandemic/.

18. Eddy, "Farm Workers Airlifted."

19. Horowitz, "For Some Italians."

20. Christina Goldbaum, "Trump Crackdown Unnerves Immigrants, and the
Farmers Who Rely on Them," *New York Times*, March 18, 2019, https://www
.nytimes.com/2019/03/18/nyregion/ny-farmers-undocumented-workers-trump
-immigration.html/.

21. Dorning and Skerritt, "Every Single Worker."

22. David Bacon, "Biden's Immigration Reform Should Roll Back Exploitative
'Guest Worker' Programs," *People's World*, May 13, 2021, www.peoplesworld.org/.

23. Michael Sainato, "'A Lot of Abuse for Little Pay': How US Farming Profits
from Exploitation and Brutality," *The Guardian*, December 25, 2021.

24. Coleman, "As the Trump Administration Restricts Legal Immigration";
Thompson, "The Sun Is Hot."

25. The US Department of Labor determines the prevailing wage from four
different sources: the state or federal minimum wage rates; wages agreed by collective bargaining; the Adverse Effect Wage Rate based on surveys conducted
by the US Department of Agriculture and US Bureau of Labor Statistics; and
the applicable prevailing wage based on surveys carried out by the US Department of Labor. Farmworker Justice, "Prevailing Wage Determinations under
the 2022 H-2A Rule," Farmworker Justice Fact Sheet, October 2022, https://
www.farmworkerjustice.org/wp-content/uploads/2022/10/2022-H-2A-Rule
-Prevailing-Wage-Standards.pdf/.

26. Leslie, "The White House."

27. Bacon, "Biden's Immigration Reform."

28. Coleman, "As the Trump Administration Restricts Legal Immigration";
Leslie, "The White House."

29. Coleman, "As the Trump Administration Restricts Legal Immigration."

30. Bacon, "Biden's Immigration Reform."

31. Farmworker Justice, "Farmworker Groups File Federal Lawsuit Against U.S.
Department of Labor's Decision to Freeze Wages under the H-2A Agricultural
Guestworker Program," November 30, 2020, https://www.farmworkerjustice.org/
news-article/farmworker-groups-file-federal-lawsuit-against-u-s-department
-of-labors-decision-to-freeze-wages-under-the-h-2a-agricultural-guestworker
-program/.

32. The White House, "Fact Sheet: The Biden Administration Blueprint for
a Fair, Orderly and Humane Immigration System," July 27, 2021, https://www
.whitehouse.gov/briefing-room/statements-releases/2021/07/27/fact-sheet-the
-biden-administration-blueprint-for-a-fair-orderly-and-humane-immigration
-system/.

33. Andrew Kreighbaum, "H-2A Guestworker Wages Get Overhaul in
Labor Department Rule (1)," *Bloomberg Law*, February 27, 2023, https://news

.bloomberglaw.com/daily-labor-report/h-2a-guestworker-wages-get-overhaul-under-labor-department-rule/; Vegetable Growers News, "Ag Labor Group Sues to Halt H-2A Changes," November 28, 2022, https://vegetablegrowersnews.com/news/ag-labor-group-sues-to-halt-h-2a-changes/.

34. Dorning and Skerritt, "Every Single Worker"; Leslie, "The White House."

35. Megan Kinch, "Covid-19 Makes a Bad Situation Worse for Agricultural Migrant Workers in Canada," *Equal Times*, April 23, 2021, https://www.equaltimes.org/covid-19-makes-a-bad-situation?lang=en/.

36. Jocelyn Sherman, "Farm Worker Unions File Emergency Petition for Judicial Review, Citing Urgent Need for 'Clear and Decisive Action' to protect WA Farm Workers," *United Farm Workers*, April 16, 2020, https://ufw.org/lnicividwa/.

37. Lindsay Campbell, "More COVID-19 Outbreaks Are Hitting Farmworkers: It's Not Just the Meat Plants That We Need to Worry about," *Modern Farmer*, June 10, 2020, https://modernfarmer.com/2020/06/more-covid-19-outbreaks-are-hitting-farmworkers/; Coleman, "As the Trump Administration Restricts Legal Immigration."

38. Coleman, "As the Trump Administration Restricts Legal Immigration."

39. Jayson L. Lusk and Ranveer Chandra, "Farmer and Farm Worker Illnesses and Deaths from COVID-19 and Impacts on Agricultural Output," *PLoS One* 16, no. 4 (2021): 6, doi.org/10.1371/journal.pone.0250621/.

40. Campbell, "More COVID-19 Outbreaks"; Coleman, "As the Trump Administration Restricts Legal Immigration."

41. Coleman, "As the Trump Administration Restricts Legal Immigration."

42. Michael Lauzardo, Nadia Kovacevich, Anthony Dennis, Paul Myers, Joan Flocks, and J. Glenn Morris, "An Outbreak of COVID-19 among H-2A Temporary Agricultural Workers," *American Journal of Public Health* 111, no. 4 (2021): 571–573.

43. Danielle Echeverria, "Farmworker Cases Spike in Tight Housing," *San Francisco Chronicle*, July 16, 2020; Nezahualcoyotl Xiuhtecutli and Annie Shattuck, "Crisis Politics and US Farm Labor: Health Justice and Florida Farmworkers amid a Pandemic," *Journal of Peasant Studies* 48, no.1 (2021): 77; Kristi Sturgill, "At Least 176 Test Positive for Coronavirus at Ventura County Farmworker Housing Complex," *Los Angeles Times*, June 30, 2020, https://www.latimes.com/california/story/2020-06-30/at-least-176-positive-coronavirus-tests-at-ventura-county-farmworker-housing-complex/.

44. Eddy, "Farm Workers Airlifted."

45. Campbell, "More COVID-19 Outbreaks."

46. Miriam Jordan, "Migrant Workers Restricted to Farms under One Grower's Virus Lockdown," *New York Times*, October 19, 2020, https://www.nytimes.com/2020/10/19/us/coronavirus-tomato-migrant-farm-workers.html/.

47. Campbell, "More COVID-19 Outbreaks."

48. Derek Farnsworth, "U.S. COVID-19 Policy Affecting Agricultural Labor," *Choices* 35, no. 3 (2020): 1–6; Daniel A. Sumner, "Impact of COVID-19 and the Lockdowns on Labor-Intensive Produce Markets, with Implication for Hired Farm Labor," *Choices* 36, no. 3 (2021): 3.

49. Associated Press, "Farmworkers at Central California Pistachio Farm Strike after Dozens Test Positive for the Coronavirus," *Los Angeles Times*, June 25, 2020, https://www.latimes.com/california/story/2020-06-25/farmworkers-at-central-california-pistachio-strike-after-dozens-test-positive-for-the-coronavirus/.

50. Wolf, *Pathways of Power*, 385.

51. Ismael García-Colón, *Colonial Migrants at the Heart of Empire: Puerto Rican Workers on U.S. Farms* (Oakland: University of California Press, 2020).

52. Bacon, "Biden's Immigration Reform."

53. Moussa El Khayat, et al., "Impacts of Climate Change and Heat Stress on Farmworkers' Health: A Scoping Review," *Front Public Health* 10 (2022): 782811, doi:10.3389/fpubh.2022.782811/. PMID: 35211437; PMCID: PMC8861180; Fabiana B. Nerbass, et al., "Occupational Heat Stress and Kidney Health: From Farms to Factories," *Kidney International Reports* 2, no. 6 (2017): 998–1008, doi: 10.1016/j.ekir.2017.08.012/ PMID: 29270511; PMCID: PMC5733743; Qianyao Pan, et al., "Compensation Incentives and Heat Exposure Affect Farm Worker Effort," *PLoS One* 16, no. 11 (2021): e0259459, https://doi.org/10.1371/journal.pone.0259459/.

5

The Battle of the Shutdown

How Hospitality Workers Confronted Disaster Capitalism during the COVID-19 Pandemic

CARLOS ARAMAYO

In March 2020 the Biogen corporation held an international conference at the Marriott Long Wharf Hotel in Boston. Unbeknownst to the scientists and executives in attendance, one or more participants came to the meeting infected with the COVID-19 virus. Over the next several days, the virus circulated among those in attendance in crowded meeting rooms and as they ate in banquet halls. When the conference ended, the meeting attendees boarded planes at Logan Airport traveling to destinations around the globe. It is now estimated that this conference, the United States' first documented superspreader event, led to tens of thousands of people contracting COVID-19.[1]

Within weeks, the country's hospitality industry was shut down. Hotels either closed entirely or limited their services to essential medical personnel working to contain the virus. Restaurants ended indoor dining and focused on delivering food to the sheltering public as states enacted stay-at-home orders. Casinos, cruise ships, and theme parks closed entirely. Millions of workers were laid off overnight—the largest mass layoff in the nation's history. They faced enormous insecurity as they had to navigate overwhelmed unemployment systems, the loss of employer-provided healthcare during a pandemic, and the uncertainty of when, if ever, they would return to their jobs.

To make matters worse, the hospitality industry did little to assist its laid-off workforce during the pandemic. Instead, after the initial shock of the shutdown faded, many hotel management companies and ownership groups saw unprecedented opportunities in the crisis. Seeing closures as a once-in-a-lifetime tabula rasa, hoteliers and real estate moguls launched an explicit and comprehensive campaign to "reimagine" the hotel experience.

Employers fired longtime employees, brought in technology to eliminate positions, and cut back on guest amenities, including daily room cleaning. As the pandemic waned during 2021 and most hotels reopened their doors, many of these changes became permanent.

Most hospitality workers faced these challenges alone. Unionized workers, however, faced them collectively. Unionized hotel workers across the country organized aggressively to help one another and to combat the hotel industry's cynical attempts to take advantage of the pandemic. In collaboration with their union, workers set up networks to navigate the unemployment systems, extend health benefits, run food banks, and raise donations from the public. They challenged municipal, state, and federal politicians to intervene to protect their jobs during government-mandated shutdowns. And as the industry reopened, they directly confronted hotel companies and owners by demanding that employers bring every worker back to their pre-pandemic positions.

This chapter tells a story in two parts. First, using evidence from hotel owners' earnings calls and the lived experience of hotel workers, it shows how quickly and explicitly capitalists tried to take advantage of the disruptions caused by the pandemic. Using the hotel industry in Boston as a case study, the chapter reveals how badly the industry failed in protecting and assisting workers at the onset of the pandemic. It shows how, instead, hotel management made drastic changes to their operating models, including several mass firings, that would lead to significant reductions in labor costs.

Second, this chapter tells the story of how the twelve thousand members of Boston's UNITE HERE Local 26 worked together to navigate the pandemic and fought back against changes the hotel industry tried to implement during the crisis. As president of the local, I rely on my own personal notes and recollections as well as the materials our organization produced during this time to outline the challenges we confronted, the successful campaigns we ran, and the lessons we learned from facing this unprecedented crisis. I show how, by focusing on our members' needs, our union not only survived but also thrived, organized, and won important victories during the tragedy of COVID-19. We accomplished all of this by maintaining an open and democratic engagement with our membership and by taking decisive action.

This story shows how an industry used the crisis created by COVID-19 to increase profit margins by permanently reducing labor costs and how workers organized and mobilized to fight these changes. It also dramatically illustrates the union difference. While nonunion workers faced the pandemic and the onslaught of changes the hotel industry implemented alone, unionized workers met them together. And together they were able to survive and thrive even in a time of profound crisis.

The Hotel Industry and COVID-19

THE ONSET OF THE VIRUS

Beginning in the middle of March 2020 the COVID-19 pandemic devastated the hotel industry in Boston. Hotel occupancy rates declined dramatically as it became clear that the Biogen conference had resulted in a significant outbreak. When Utah Jazz center Rudy Gobert, who had been staying at the Ritz-Carlton, tested positive for COVID on March 11 after playing at Boston's TD Garden, the NBA suspended its 2019–2020 season and the decline in hotel occupancy rates accelerated even more. By the end of March, Massachusetts governor Charlie Baker had issued a statewide stay-at-home order, and most hotels had either closed or were housing only essential medical staff.[2]

According to the American Hotel and Lodging Association, the Boston hotel market was profoundly disrupted by the pandemic. By August 2020 hotel occupancy had fallen to 33 percent, compared to 86 percent occupancy in August 2019.[3] Only two other markets—Hawaii and Orlando—fared worse than Boston during the early months of the pandemic. Thousands of workers in the hotel industry were laid off as bookings were canceled and properties temporarily shuttered. Many of these workers expected their employers to help them during this unprecedented crisis. Unfortunately, the hotel industry turned a blind eye to its workforce, choosing profits over people.

Initially, the industry downplayed the severity of the virus. At the nonunion Marriott Long Wharf, site of the Biogen conference, the hotel continued with business as usual, reassuring the public that they had increased the frequency and intensity of cleaning at the property.[4] For three weeks after the conference, the hotel kept its doors open and required employees to come to work. More broadly, the hotel industry desperately tried to deny the reality of the COVID-19 crisis during the early days of the pandemic despite evidence that hotels were a site of transmission for the virus. Concerns about workplace safety and worker health were either dismissed or downplayed as manageable if suitable cleaning precautions were followed. Profits trumped health concerns even in the face of a deadly virus.

Governor Baker's stay-at-home order, issued on March 23, 2020, ultimately forced the hotel industry to take the pandemic seriously. As travel ground to a halt, properties either closed or stayed open only to house essential workers. Thousands of hotel employees were laid off overnight and told to apply for unemployment assistance to make ends meet. Many hotel employees had limited experience with the unemployment assistance system and found the state's confusing bureaucracy difficult to navigate. This problem was compounded by the Department of Unemployment Assistance being overwhelmed by a deluge of new applications from tens of thousands of workers left without jobs because of the pandemic. Understaffed and using borderline-obsolete online technology, a backlog of applications quickly built up, leaving workers and their families desperate.

For hotel workers, the challenges of navigating the unemployment system were compounded by hotel management's failure to assist their laid-off employees. Many workers reached out to their human resource departments—who traditionally handle unemployment questions—to have pay rate information verified or to get help uploading documents to the state.[5] Instead of finding help, workers either received no reply or were told to wait for a solution. Working from home due to the government-imposed shutdowns, human resource managers were totally unprepared for a problem of this magnitude. Many simply threw up their hands and told their employees to keep calling the Department of Unemployment Assistance hotline. Rather than step up and take care of their employees, human resource departments across the industry abandoned workers. With hotels closed, workers' labor was unnecessary, and the industry treated its employees and their families as disposable.

The hotel industry's disregard for its employees was underscored by the ending of employer-provided benefits, in particular health insurance, within a month of the onset of the pandemic. Citing policies that tied eligibility for healthcare benefits to hours worked, most hotel companies ended coverage for their employees by May 2020. Cynically pointing to Massachusetts' relatively affordable public healthcare options, hotel employers chose to end employer-provided coverage in the middle of a global health crisis.[6] As the pandemic slowed down the industry, hotel owners and managers decided to protect their assets at the expense of the health and well-being of their employees. James F. Risoleo, the president, CEO, and director of the largest hotel real estate investment trust (REIT), Host Hotels & Resorts, neatly summed up this strategy in its second quarter 2020 earnings call: "As lodging demand plummeted to record lows in April," he said, "we worked with our operators . . . and reduced overall hotel operating costs by 72% year-over-year. Cost savings were primarily driven by steep reductions in wage and benefit expenses."[7]

MASS FIRINGS

As pandemic-related closures continued into the summer and fall of 2020, the hotel industry saw an opportunity to permanently lower labor costs by terminating large numbers of employees. Large-scale firings are difficult when hotels are open and operating. The constant churn of guests needing service makes it difficult to downsize the workforce quickly, and even seasonal variations in the industry are too uneven to allow employers to make bold moves. Because events and surges in travel can happen at almost any time, hotels need to keep staff on the payroll even if their schedules vacillate with the ebbs and flows of the business. The almost total halt to travel and events during the pandemic provided a unique opportunity to, as one REIT CEO put it, "never waste a crisis."[8]

In Boston, mass firings happened exclusively in the nonunion segment of the hotel industry. This is because, as I discuss below, Local 26's contracts guaranteed a year of job security for laid-off employees. However, not being represented by Local 26 did not prevent hundreds of fired nonunion workers from organizing to fight back against their former employers with the assistance of the union. After several mass firings, large numbers of workers approached the union and began campaigns to demand their employers reverse their decisions to terminate them. The first—and most successful—of these campaigns started when the Four Seasons Boston fired 192 workers at the beginning of June 2020.

The Four Seasons is an iconic Boston hotel. Located on Boylston Street, its rooms overlook the public garden. Well-heeled guests and elite Bostonians frequented the Bristol Lounge, where the daily afternoon high tea service would often spill over to an evening of martinis and hors d'oeuvres. Workers at the hotel were not represented by Local 26, but the property matched the wages and benefits of the surrounding union-represented competition. The hotel even had a supposedly independent complaint adjudication process meant to mimic the union's grievance procedure. Workers at the Four Seasons were constantly reminded by management that they were chosen to be the best ambassadors of the city; they were told they were family, not employees.

Given this, it came as a shock when hotel management sent a letter to nearly half of its workforce saying, "The extreme loss of revenues has forced us to make some difficult decisions to reduce costs while managing the short- and long-term business realities. This includes permanent layoffs."[9] Isolated at home three months after the onset of the pandemic, Four Seasons workers received this letter informing them that they had lost their jobs—jobs that many of them had held for decades. Adding insult to injury, the letter explained that, due to the company's financial challenges, workers would be paid only half of the severance payments promised in their employee handbook. As Ricardo Mathelus, a server at the Bristol Lounge who had worked for the hotel for twenty-one years, summed it up, "I feel embarrassed. I feel insulted. I feel disrespected. I feel unwanted. I feel used, actually."[10]

As nonunion workers, the Four Seasons employees had no contract and no recourse to a grievance process to force the company to pay them the severance they had been promised. They also did not enjoy the contractual job security provisions that UNITE HERE Local 26 had negotiated with dozens of Boston hotels. These protections guaranteed that workers would maintain their seniority for a year while on layoff. Instead, the employee handbook that laid out the employment policies at the Four Seasons—and in many cases mimicked Local 26 contracts—was not enforceable in court because it contained a disclaimer that granted management the right to change the terms of employment at will and without notice. Without a union, the Four Seasons workers had no recourse other than to refuse the severance offer from their employer and try their luck telling their story to the public.

Shortly after being fired, a group of Four Seasons workers reached out to Local 26 to see if the union could provide them with assistance getting their jobs back or, at least, receiving their full severance. Union organizers met with the group over Zoom along with a labor attorney who reviewed screenshots of both the letters they had received and their employee handbook. It quickly became clear that, with few legal options, the workers needed to launch a public campaign demanding the hotel reinstate them to their positions. For this to be successful, the several dozen former employees who gathered for this first Zoom meeting needed to build a majority consensus among the fired workers. Typically, this would be done through in-person meetings and house calls followed up by large delegations to management and public protests. However, with pandemic restrictions still in effect, workers had to find novel ways to organize and confront management.

Four Seasons workers, in consultation with Local 26 staff, decided to demonstrate majority opposition to the hotel's actions by constructing a "selfie petition." They called, texted, and emailed their coworkers asking them to take a selfie and then e-sign a petition that declined the hotel's severance offer and demanded the reinstatement of their jobs. In less than a week, 120 workers (over 60 percent of those who had been fired) signed the petition, and after another Zoom with all the signatories, they decided to email the petition along with all of their photos to hotel management and to contact the press. They hoped that when Boston's elite heard about how the hotel had mistreated them, the public furor would bring Four Seasons management to its senses. Their hopes were answered.

Starting with a *Boston Globe* front-page feature article on the mass firings, the story exploded. Local television crews visited fired workers at their homes and tried to get into the hotel to find a management representative. Encouraged by *Boston Globe* columnist Shirley Leung's call for a boycott of the property, Boston socialites and politicians, including Joseph Kennedy III and prominent businessman Larry Moulter, declared they would stop patronizing the hotel and its restaurants.[11] Senator Ed Markey held a televised (and socially distanced) meet-and-greet with fired workers at his Malden residence, declaring, "The Four Seasons promises top of the line service for its guests, but is providing bottom of the barrel protections for its workers."[12] Under this barrage of public disdain, the Four Seasons realized that it had made a mistake. On June 16, 2020, the hotel informed the workers they would receive their full severance package and that if their positions were restored when the hotel reopened, they would get their jobs back. Most important, the hotel put all of this in an enforceable, written settlement.[13]

The unique profile of the Four Seasons helped the fired workers win their full severance package and at least a chance to get their jobs back. Unfortunately, hundreds of other nonunion Boston hotel workers who were fired during the pandemic did not have this advantage. Nowhere was this more evident than at the Host Hotels–owned Marriott Copley Place.

Although the Marriott Copley is a large hotel that is connected to the Hynes Convention Center, its history and clientele paled in comparison to the Four Seasons. Instead of a well-appointed tearoom and cocktail lounge, it had a sports bar with walls of televisions. Instead of foreign dignitaries and celebrities, its rooms were filled with conference attendees and tourists. Equally important, the hotel is owned by the largest hotel REIT, Host Hotels, while the Four Seasons is owned by a Bill Gates–associated private equity investor. REITs, more than any other hotel ownership vehicles, saw the pandemic disruption as an opportunity to permanently reduce labor costs and increase their margins going forward. This was of value to REITs because their special tax status is tied to passing on a fixed percentage of returns to investors—and returns at a hotel are driven by keeping daily room rates high and labor costs low. Every penny saved by reducing labor costs during the pandemic would come back a hundredfold in the years to come. As Host Hotels president and CEO Mark Risoleo said on an earnings call shortly after the firings at the Marriott Copley Place, "From redefining our operating model with our managers, we expect to generate $100 million to $150 million of potential long-term cost savings based on 2019 revenues."[14]

Two weeks before Thanksgiving 2020, the Marriott Copley Place fired half of its staff. Like the Four Seasons, the hotel's general manager, Alan Smith, blamed the pandemic economy. "Our hotel has experienced unprecedented business impact due to the pandemic," he wrote to the *Boston Globe*. "We have maintained open communications with our valued employees. Many are now reviewing severance offers, which are competitive within the industry."[15] These severance packages were based on years of service at the hotel, with one week of wages being paid out for every year an employee worked at the property. However, unlike previous severance packages at the hotel, these offers were capped at ten years of service. This meant that no matter how long an employee had worked at the property, the maximum severance they could receive was ten weeks of pay. Additionally, shortly after the firings, a rumor (later confirmed) began to spread that the entire restaurant and bar staff had been fired because the hotel planned to subcontract all of the food and beverage services after the pandemic. The hotel also planned to replace phone operators with technology, to permanently close and outsource the laundry department, and to reconcept the club lounge with fewer staff. Host and Marriott used the pandemic closure to significantly reduce labor costs at the hotel.

Some of the workers at the Marriott Copley had been part of an unsuccessful campaign to organize the hotel with Local 26 in the mid-2010s. Having seen the success of the Four Seasons campaign, they asked the union to help them launch a similar campaign. Like their counterparts across the city, the Marriott workers organized a majority selfie petition and delegated management over Zoom, demanding they be reinstated. They also told their story to the press, which again jumped to cover the story of a large hotel treating its workers unfairly. The *Boston Globe* ran a feature story with photos of the workers, several workers appeared on local television stations to tell their stories, and local pundits called for a boycott of the Marriott Copley. Politicians also rallied to support the workers: the Boston City Council passed a resolution condemning the firings, Mayor Marty Walsh called on the hotel to reverse its decision, and senators Elizabeth Warren and Ed Markey met with groups of former Marriott employees. As social distancing restrictions had been relaxed in Massachusetts, the fired workers escalated the campaign by taking to the streets, picketing and leafleting in front of the hotel.

For months Marriott workers protested their employer's decision to fire them in the middle of a pandemic. As of 2024, none of these workers have been given their full severance package or returned to their prior positions, although a few were offered entry-level jobs after reapplying. Food and beverage at the hotel are now subcontracted to third-party operators, new labor-saving technology has been introduced at the front desk, and the laundry has been outsourced. Most of the workers who were fired have found other hospitality jobs, many of them in the newly opened, unionized, Omni Seaport Hotel that anchors Boston's other convention center, the Boston Convention and Exhibition Center.

PERMANENT RESTRUCTURING

The hotel industry was not satisfied with the labor savings created by mass firings and outsourcing. Seeking more ways to permanently increase revenues, the industry reexamined every aspect of a hotel stay to find ways to cut costs. All the major hotel brands looked at every service and amenity provided to hotel guests and asked if that service was necessary. While mass firings lowered labor costs by reducing staff, combining jobs, and outsourcing whole departments, reimagining the hotel stay created savings by eliminating or altering the services provided to the guest. As Mark Brugger, the president and CEO of DiamondRock Hospitality, succinctly put it:

> We are doing things that we've never done before. We've combined jobs we've never combined before. We're running at efficiency levels on low occupancy we've never done before. I think the brands are testing new models for distribution of allocated cost. Do we need all these cluster people? Can technology replace what we had before? It's a once in a generation opportunity to reinvent a lot of their programs, right, because if you've furloughed or laid off people, you can really then restaff and rethink the whole model, which I know they are doing on a number of fronts.[16]

By examining every aspect of a hotel stay and experimenting with guests' tolerance to reduced services and amenities, the hotel industry found extraordinary ways to cut costs, particularly in housekeeping departments.

Early in the pandemic, the few hotels that remained open intensified cleaning procedures between different guests checking in to a room but eliminated stay-over cleaning for customers residing in a hotel for more than one night. The logic was simple: at the time, health experts believed COVID-19 was transmitted by droplets that might be left on surfaces, and most guests did not want a stranger in their room during a pandemic. Quickly, hotels noticed the obvious: if daily room cleaning could be eliminated entirely, the cost savings from the reduction in the housekeeping workforce would be significant. The challenge was how to convince guests that the end of daily room cleaning enhanced the quality of their stay at a property after the pandemic waned.

Hilton Hotels pioneered a radical approach to eliminating daily room cleaning. In 2020 they launched Hilton CleanStay, a system-wide program that ended daily room cleaning in all but the most exclusive of the chain's properties.[17] Partnering with the makers of Lysol, Hilton published elaborate protocols for how their properties would be cleaned, focusing on the disinfection of "high touch" areas, increased frequency of cleaning of public areas, and the introduction of touchless technology throughout their properties.[18] Hilton assured its customers that "the Hilton CleanStay program delivers an industry-defining standard of cleanliness across Hilton's family of brands globally to give our guests peace of mind from check-in to check-out."[19] Hilton's argument was a corporate doublespeak gem: guest rooms would be cleaner even though they were cleaned less.

This bold move was unanimously applauded by hotel ownership groups. As Thomas Baltimore, CEO of Park Hotels (owner of a large Hilton portfolio), said, "I am thrilled with Hilton's recent announcement for opt-in housekeeping at the majority of its hotels. We believe that measures like these will push the industry in the right direction, not only from a profitability standpoint but also from an environmental standpoint."[20] Housekeeping had been a notoriously difficult place to cut labor costs in hotels. Room cleaning is labor intensive, demanding workers perform repetitive and physically stressing tasks daily. For hotels to retain workers and avoid workplace injury, workloads must be adjusted to the strains on room attendants' bodies. At union hotels, the contract places strict limits on the number of rooms a housekeeper can attend to in a day and provides reductions in that quota for excess checkouts, travel time from floor to floor, and rooms with multiple beds. Although these protections do not exist at nonunion hotels and the workload is generally greater, there are limits governed by the physical nature of the job. Also, attempts to introduce robots or other technology to room cleaning in hotels have failed because of the idiosyncrasies of room design and how guests leave rooms in different states each day. The only precedent for eliminating daily cleaning had been Marriott's "Make a Green Choice" program, where customers received incentives, usually in the form of loyalty points, to turn down cleaning. Because customers had to choose to be in this program, it had only a modest impact on labor costs at Marriott hotels. Hilton's total elimination of daily cleaning was unheard of and revolutionary.

The potential for cost savings by ending daily cleaning was extraordinary. Cost savings came from reducing expenditures on cleaning products and amenities (like towels) that were refreshed on a daily basis. But most dramatically, savings came from permanently eliminating room attendant positions. With fewer rooms to clean every day, fewer room attendants were necessary. Responding to a question about how significant these savings might be, Thomas Baltimore from Park responded, "If you take our portfolio, and if you assume we get 100 basis points or if we're lucky to [get] 300 basis points, you're looking at probably $30 million to $90 million a year in sort of operational savings when you look at a pre-COVID environment."[21] Translating this to jobs lost, Local 26's International Union, UNITE HERE, estimated that if all hotels in the United States ended daily cleaning, 40 percent of room attendant jobs would disappear overnight.[22]

After Hilton moved aggressively to eliminate daily room cleaning, the other two major brands, Marriott and Hyatt, were forced to act. Both brands were skeptical about how guests would respond to the elimination of daily housekeeping service but knew that in order to stay competitive and please their owners they needed to do something. At the lower end of the market, both hotel brands followed Hilton's lead by ending daily cleaning at limited-service brands.[23] At their mid-range brands, Hyatt decided to go to an opt-in model where guests were informed at the front desk or on the Hyatt app that they needed to specifically ask for housekeeping service at the time of check-in. As of the writing of this chapter, Marriott hasn't settled on a standard practice, with some mid-range hotels reintroducing the "Make a

Green Choice" program but providing automatic daily cleaning, and other properties following Hyatt's opt-in model.

While the end of daily room cleaning was the most dramatic service change in the industry during the pandemic, other services and amenities were also ended or radically changed. Citing the rise in popularity of gig-based food delivery companies like Uber Eats and DoorDash, many hotels eliminated or greatly reduced in-room dining service.[24] Where room service did survive the pandemic, it was transformed into a door-drop model where bags of food are left outside guests' doors. In many nonunion hotels, dedicated room service staff were replaced by restaurant workers and supplemented by housekeeping staff who ran deliveries and collected trash from outside of rooms. Bell staff and door staff were also in the "right-sizing" crosshairs as the industry reopened. These jobs had historically served very different purposes: door staff welcomed guests to the hotel, held cars at the curb, and hailed cabs, while bell staff delivered luggage and other amenities to rooms. Coming out of the pandemic closures, many hotels decided to combine these jobs into one classification, reducing staff and adding duties without adjusting pay. At the front desk, hotel management companies installed new labor-saving technologies. All the major hotel brands introduced revamped mobile applications that allowed guests to check in to their room online, with some of these apps also using Bluetooth technology to convert a mobile phone into a mobile key, allowing guests to bypass the front desk entirely. Apps could also be used to order room service and other amenities directly, in many cases eliminating the need for an on-site phone operator.

The pandemic closures were a once-in-a-generation opportunity for the hotel industry to overhaul every aspect of the hotel guest stay with an eye to efficiency and labor savings. From the elimination of daily room cleaning to the introduction of new technologies, the industry cynically used the COVID-19 crisis to eliminate jobs and extract more value from the workers who remained. Nonunion workers tried, with limited success, to protest mass firings and resist industrial change. Meanwhile, in Boston and across the United States and Canada, UNITE HERE mounted a comprehensive defense against the disaster capitalism of the hospitality industry.

The Union's Emergency Response

COVID PROTOCOLS

In the wake of the Biogen conference, it became clear that health and safety protocols in the hospitality industry were grossly inadequate to protect workers and guests from the spread of COVID-19. This was amplified for UNITE

HERE Local 26 members and leaders when a Ritz-Carlton Hotel housekeeper became ill after cleaning basketball player Rudy Gobert's room while he was infected with the virus. Despite multiple interventions from the union shop stewards, the Ritz continued to operate normally for a week after the Utah Jazz basketball players stayed at the property.[25] In addition to the housekeeper who had cleaned Mr. Gobert's room, several other workers also began to experience COVID-19 symptoms.[26] Without clear guidelines from the CDC, state, or city, the hotel continued to downplay concerns about the spread of the virus. The situation came to a head on March 15, 2020, when union members confronted management declaring they would not come to work unless their health and safety concerns were addressed. Local 26 actively intervened to back this action, writing to management, "The Ritz's obligation to keep the workplace safe in this extraordinary emergency goes beyond the normal operation of sick leave. The Ritz is obligated to protect both those employees who may already be infected and those who may become infected if their infected co-workers are forced to work while exposed."[27] Two days later, the hotel closed.

These early COVID experiences underscored the need for comprehensive health and safety protocols in the hospitality industry. Facing a novel and highly transmissible coronavirus, hotel workers found themselves risking their lives simply while doing their jobs. Although many workers were laid off as the pandemic took hold, some were deemed essential workers and had to continue working, particularly at hotels that stayed open to house medical professionals and flight crews. Workers at these properties were scared. They faced the uncertainty of going to work knowing they might bring a potentially fatal virus home to their families.

Given these circumstances, Local 26 members who were still working demanded comprehensive health and safety protocols to deal with COVID-19. Workers, backed by union leadership, petitioned their employers on measures designed to protect employees. These included making work voluntary, adequate employer-provided personal protective equipment (PPE), enhanced sanitizing protocols, regular testing for workers, and up to ten additional sick days for COVID-related illness or quarantine. The union, working with health and safety experts from Yale University, synthesized these demands into a ten-page Memorandum of Understanding (MOU), one of the longest and most comprehensive ever drafted. With this MOU in hand, shop stewards called for Zoom meetings with hotel managers at properties across the city. The stewards then encouraged their coworkers to join the meeting (often assisted on the technical front by their children) to demand that management sign the MOU. The stewards, with the help of union staff, screen-shared with managers and walked them through each section of the agreement, asking coworkers to comment on why each piece of the document was important to them. These e-delegations implicitly (and sometimes explicitly) relayed the message that Local 26 workers would not go to work unless management agreed to the protocols outlined in the MOU.

To build broad support for hotel workers' demands, Local 26 leadership engaged state and municipal politicians and media outlets in asserting that hospitality workers needed to be included in decision making regarding COVID-19 health and safety protocols. Working with then-mayor Marty Walsh's administration and Governor Baker's COVID advisory board, the union emphasized that hotels and restaurants needed enforceable rules to operate as safely as possible in the uncertain early COVID environment.[28] Union leaders testified at hearings held by the city of Boston and the Massachusetts State Senate emphasizing the need for the municipal and state authorities to implement rules to hold the hotel industry to high safety standards. This message was reiterated in an opinion piece I published in the *Boston Globe* laying out Local 26's best thinking on how to open hotels during the COVID pandemic, in which I wrote, "We cannot put profits before the health and safety of hotel workers and the traveling public."[29]

Facing pressure from members and politicians, all of Local 26's worksites adopted the union's proposed protocols. Later, the state's taskforce published their own protocols for reopening the hospitality industry, which largely echoed the practices developed by Local 26.[30] In the early days of COVID-19, union hotel workers in Boston fought for a healthy and safe workplace for all hotel workers in Massachusetts. Their successes made the whole industry safer and undoubtedly saved lives.

UNEMPLOYMENT ASSISTANCE

By the end of March 2020, thousands of Local 26 members had been laid off. Without income from their employers, workers had to turn to unemployment assistance to make ends meet. While some banquet workers had previous experience with unemployment, most union members had stable jobs with regular schedules and had never had to apply for public assistance. As discussed above, they found an antiquated, underfunded system that was ill-equipped to deal with the volume of claims being made at the beginning of the pandemic. The Department of Unemployment's website failed on a regular basis, and call center wait times ballooned to over five hours. Added to this, many non-native English speakers who were new to the unemployment system struggled to understand how to apply for and, more importantly, how to stay on benefits.

During the first week of the shutdown, shop stewards across the city reported to union leadership that members were having serious problems accessing unemployment benefits. Without a steady income, they faced missing rent or mortgage payments, mounting utility bills, and potential food insecurity. Seeing the scale of the problem, the union realized it needed to do more than triage individual cases that had been brought to the attention of stewards and union staff. Instead, Local 26 decided to call every member of the union to check if they were having problems with the unemployment system, determine what those problems were, and make a plan to address them. To ensure these calls were as useful as possible, union staff and shop steward volunteers received training on how Massachusetts unemployment assistance worked and how to escalate problems effectively within the system. This approach enabled the union to both identify general, systemic problems with unemployment assistance and to help individuals who were struggling to get benefits because they were frustrated and overwhelmed by the process.

For larger systemic problems, the union used its political influence to obtain more resources for the Department of Unemployment and to streamline the application process for first-time applicants. Union leadership reached out to state legislators to alert them to the problems workers were facing with the unemployment system and to urge quick fixes. The state AFL-CIO also played an invaluable role in advocating for overall fixes to the unemployment system, particularly for workers in industries that had been closed due to the pandemic.[31]

On an individual level, union staff and volunteers took down the details of members' cases and worked to resolve them as quickly as possible. Using digital phone technology while working from home, they made multiple calls simultaneously to the Department of Unemployment Assistance. To navigate long wait times, union staff and volunteers prepared multiple cases for a single call to the department. Once on the line, they dialed in multiple unemployed workers to resolve their cases quickly. As it became clear there were different types of problems that needed to be resolved, staff and volunteers organized calls to deal with one class of problem at a time. This not only helped members get much-needed benefits quickly, but it also helped the Department of Unemployment clear multiple backlogged problems simultaneously.

To supplement unemployment assistance, the union began an aggressive fund-raising campaign. Since the mid-2010s, Local 26 had campaigned aggressively to improve contract standards for its members. This led to three prolonged strikes at Harvard University, all seven union-represented Marriott hotels, and the Battery Wharf Hotel. During these campaigns, the union aggressively reached out to students, faculty, meeting planners, and guests to build customer support and raise donations for striking workers. As the pandemic shut down the hospitality industry, the union reached out to every individual and organization that had given money during the strikes to ask for financial assistance. The local also partnered with the city's chapter of the United Way to amplify this call for donations. In all, the union raised over half a million dollars to be distributed directly to its members.

Local 26's program to assist members with unemployment continued for months after the start of the pandemic. By helping more than twelve hundred members to access benefits that allowed them to make ends meet, this program demonstrated the union difference during the early months of the pandemic. While human resource departments were closed and unavailable to workers, the union's rank-and-file leadership took care of Local 26 members early in the crisis. As the entire industry faced mass layoffs, the union leadership and shop stewards stepped up to meet the challenge of keeping money in members' pockets when it mattered most.

The Prolonged Shutdown

HEALTH BENEFIT EXTENSIONS

As the pandemic shutdown dragged on, Local 26's focus shifted from the immediate challenge of mass layoffs and dangerous working conditions to the long-term goal of preserving good, unionized jobs with excellent wages and benefits for hotel workers. Many rank-and-file leaders of Local 26 had been through prior crises in the industry. The September 11th attacks and the 2008 financial crisis led to serious reductions in business and leisure travel. In both cases, hotel companies tried to use these business downturns to make permanent changes to the workforce through hour cuts, benefit reductions, and departmental closures. Union members successfully fought back against wage and benefit cuts, but some positions, particularly in food and beverage, were eliminated. Having been active in these battles against austerity over the prior two decades, Local 26 workers knew that the COVID-19 pandemic gave the industry an unprecedented opportunity to try to undermine the wage and benefit standards they had struggled for decades to create. After both September 11th and the 2008 financial crisis, hotels remained open, albeit with fewer guests. The total shutdown caused by the pandemic opened the door to radical efforts by the hotel industry to cut labor costs. Local 26 members knew they needed to rally and fight to maintain their livelihoods.

The first benefit to come under threat was health insurance. Almost all Local 26 members received employer-provided health insurance where eligibility for coverage was pegged to hours worked. With nearly every worker in the hospitality industry laid off, thousands of employees and their family members faced the threat of losing their health insurance during a global health crisis. While Massachusetts offers healthcare benefits to individuals who lose employer-provided healthcare, transitioning to the state system is complicated and potentially costly. In a global pandemic, continuity of care was essential not only to keep union members physically healthy but also to reduce mental stress. If payments were not made to maintain hotel workers' healthcare, they faced the loss of coverage for themselves and their families.

Initially, the members and leaders of the union decided to approach employers directly to extend healthcare benefits. Given the sudden nature of the COVID-19 crisis, they reasoned, employers should at the very least continue benefits until there was more clarity on when the industry shutdown might end. This demand seemed especially straightforward as the hospitality industry, in particular the hotel sector, was coming off years of record profits. Certainly, workers believed, their employers would reward their years of dedicated service in the wake of an unprecedented and unforeseen disaster. Workers signed Action Network e-petitions to their employers asking for a six-month extension of benefits. When hotels failed to respond to these petitions, workers organized virtual and (a few socially distanced) outdoor delegations to management at dozens of unionized hotels in Boston. However, with few exceptions, they were met with a deafening silence from management representatives.[32]

Faced with this indifference from employers, the union decided to use reserve funds from their Taft-Hartley health plan to extend worker benefits. In Boston most hotel workers were insured by Local 26's Taft-Hartley health plan, UNITE HERE Health. After decades of building and improving the plan, it provided effectively free family healthcare for thousands of hospitality workers. During the mid-2010s, the union led an aggressive campaign to restructure the health plan and build a significant funding reserve by voting to kick high-cost providers out of the plan. The logic was that by eliminating expensive doctors and hospitals, workers could preserve excellent, affordable healthcare, build a substantial reserve fund, and put more money into wages. What the members and leadership of Local 26 did not foresee was that the accumulated reserve funds would now save their healthcare coverage during the pandemic.

By March 2020 the Local 26 health fund had built up almost a year of reserve funding, meaning that health benefits could be paid for a year without any additional contributions from employers. Realizing that the hospitality industry was not going to fund the extension of health benefits for laid-off hotel workers, the union leadership began advocating the use of reserves to pay for continuing members' insurance. Initially, many employer trustees blocked any significant use of reserve funding. Representatives from hotel management argued that the reserve needed to be preserved to offset the losses the industry suffered due to the pandemic. The union leadership argued that, while some reserves need to be maintained for the long-term health of the fund, union membership had bargained the buildup reserved—at the expense of raises or other benefits—precisely for situations like the COVID-19 pandemic. Eventually, after members began to raise the question of continued coverage with local human resource departments, union leadership convinced some of the employer trustees of the fund to release assets from the reserve. This enabled Local 26 members to keep their health benefits until the beginning of 2021.[33] Unlike nonunion hospitality workers, who lost employer-provided coverage as soon as they were laid off, union members kept their medical coverage during the global health emergency.

RECALL EXTENSION

By the summer of 2020 some hospitality employers began to see the pandemic as an opportunity to permanently change the composition of their labor force. As discussed previously, nonunion hotels in Boston, like the Marriott Copley, Four Seasons, Revere, and Marriott Cambridge, unilaterally fired hundreds of their workers to both reduce the overall workforce and to open the door for subcontracting. Management was prohibited from taking this type of draconian action at union hotels because Local 26's contract protected workers' jobs and seniority for twelve months during a layoff. This safety net had been bargained to protect members' jobs against the seasonality of the travel and tourism industry and to allow workers some flexibility in employment to attend to family matters or to pursue other opportunities. It was not intended to deal with long-term closures of properties. In fact, when hotels closed for renovations, the union typically negotiated a separate agreement to address the dislocations caused by management-directed closures. The pandemic created an unprecedented situation where a *force majeure* of unknown duration forced hotels to either close or operate with limited staff. As the COVID-19 crisis dragged on, Local 26 members and leadership realized that the layoff protection enshrined in the contract was insufficient; if the layoffs lasted for over a year, members faced the real possibility of being fired. But since the pandemic closures were a natural and governmental phenomenon, rather than imposed by management, the union had no legal right to bargain over their effects. Understanding this threat, Local 26 members and leaders began a comprehensive campaign to extend recall rights for all hotel workers, union and nonunion. This fight included worker mobilization, political advocacy, media campaigning, and high-profile public actions.

Local 26 members and leadership drafted a Memorandum of Agreement extending recall protections for thirty months. With this in hand, they delegated management demanding expanded recall rights. At hotels that were open, members also appealed directly to guests by distributing handbills at entrances. To support these actions, the union launched a website featuring a list of Boston-area hotels that had made the commitment to rehire their workers after the pandemic and shaming those that hadn't.[34] Local 26 members also lobbied municipal and state politicians to enact legislation to protect hotel workers' jobs during the pandemic. In Providence, Rhode Island, following a large rally at city hall, the city passed a law guaranteeing the right of hotel workers to return to their previous positions after the pandemic.[35] In Massachusetts over three thousand hotel workers attended an online listening session with state legislators urging them to protect these good hospitality jobs. This led to State Representative Marjorie Decker introducing legislation to force hotels to extend recall rights to all of their employees after the pandemic subsided. Although this legislation did not pass, it helped elevate the dispute over hotel workers' fate during the pandemic in the state and national media.[36] This debate focused on how hospitality jobs, particularly good union hotel jobs, provided a pathway for Black and brown communities to access the middle class. These high-paying jobs (a hotel housekeeper earns over twenty-eight dollars an hour in a Local 26–represented hotel) with excellent benefits historically transferred wealth from the lucrative tourism and travel industry to the working-class neighborhoods of Boston. Hotel workers, primarily women and people of color, helped build the first generation of wealth in their communities; they bought houses, sent their children to college, and participated in community life. If these jobs disappeared after the pandemic, Black and brown neighborhoods stood to lose one of only a few pathways to access wealth in the postindustrial economy.[37]

This public and comprehensive campaign led to every union hotel in Boston and Rhode Island signing the Memorandum of Agreement extending recall rights and protecting workers' jobs by April 2021. In the nonunion sector of the industry, workers did not fare as well. Although the Four Seasons workers and some Marriott Copley workers succeeded in getting their jobs back, hundreds of other fired workers have never been offered the chance to return to their positions. The fight for recall rights clearly demonstrated the difference a union makes for working people.

The Return to Work

The hospitality industry in Boston slowly began to reopen in the spring of 2021. As workers returned to their jobs as housekeepers, servers, and door staff, they found an industry intent on using the pandemic closures to eliminate jobs and create new efficiencies. Labor-saving trends that began before COVID-19, such as the introduction of new technologies, accelerated as hotels reopened. In addition, many hotel companies used the shutdowns to completely reassess their products and the amenities they offered to guests. Most dramatically, the Hilton Corporation, as discussed previously, announced that it would be ending automatic daily room cleaning in all its non-luxury hotels.

Nonunion hotel workers had no choice but to accept these changes. Unionized workers, however, decided to fight back. As they returned to work, the members of Local 26 rallied to oppose these threats. Using the slogan "When the guests come back, we come back," over a thousand union members—the largest meeting in Local 26 history—gathered at the Boston Park Plaza in July 2021 to plan their response to the industry's desire to eliminate their jobs. Boston's acting mayor, Kim Janey, attended the meeting and pledged the city's support for their efforts. The mayor and many members of the city council then led a march past some of the city's biggest hotels, insisting that their workers' jobs be restored as hotels reopened.[38]

Following this event, the members of Local 26 escalated their campaign, demanding the restoration of all amenities, such as room service, breakfast restaurants, and bell service, and insisting that all Boston-area hotels guarantee daily room cleaning. Workers leafleted guests over the summer advising them to request housekeeping service and alerting them to continued closures of various departments. Workers also used the grievance and arbitration procedure to force management to reopen entire hotels. When properties tried to offer grab-and-go from restaurants, shop stewards claimed that this violated the collective bargaining agreement because it displaced room service jobs. A similar argument was made about door staff being asked to take luggage or make other deliveries to guest rooms. These grievances successfully restored hundreds of hospitality jobs across the city.

In addition to continuous leafleting of customers, union shop stewards and leadership looked for potentially significant liabilities to leverage employers to guarantee room cleaning. For example, the union filed grievances to arbitration at multiple Boston hotels demanding workers be paid for vacation hours they were contractually due to accrue during the extended COVID-19 layoffs. Facing significant liability, many hotels traded the curing of this arbitration for a contractual guarantee to clean rooms daily. Local 26 also worked with UNITE HERE to make the elimination of daily room cleaning a national story. Housekeepers across the country interviewed with dozens of local and national press outlets, arguing that the end of daily cleaning was simply a labor-cutting measure to eliminate a service that all hotel guests expected to be included with their stay. They emphasized that not cleaning rooms daily did more than just eliminate jobs; it also made the work much more difficult and less safe. As one room attendant, Brenda Holland, told the *Wall Street Journal*, "It's backbreaking work. . . . Before we were tired, but not like this."[39]

The campaign to restore daily room cleaning succeeded at all of Boston's unionized hotels. In addition, Local 26 members worked together with their counterparts in fourteen other cities in the United States and Canada to reach a global agreement on daily housekeeping with Hilton, Marriott, and Hyatt as part of contract negotiations in 2022. This accord not only guarantees daily cleaning but also provides for escalating financial penalties if a property fails to comply with the terms of the agreement. Nonunion hotel workers have fared far worse—many hotels have eliminated daily cleaning, laying off hundreds of room attendants and making working conditions significantly more difficult for employees who now clean only rooms where the guests have checked out. Although the union has reached an agreement on daily room cleaning with the major player in the industry, the campaign to secure a better workplace for all housekeepers continues.

Conclusions

COVID-19 was the most profound crisis hospitality workers in Boston have ever faced. Most hotels and restaurants closed for months, and thousands of workers were laid off. Those who still reported to their jobs faced life-threatening conditions as an unknown virus spread through the community. Workers lived through extraordinary uncertainty and disorientation.

In this maelstrom, Local 26 members found solid ground in their union. Working together they mobilized to help one another work in the safest conditions possible, obtain unemployment benefits, keep their health insurance, and preserve their good jobs. As a union, hospitality workers carried themselves and their families through the crisis. They did this with little or no help from their employers, who ignored their demands for assistance and embraced disaster capitalism, cynically using the pandemic to eliminate jobs, cut back on services, and permanently worsen working conditions. The COVID-19 pandemic and its fallout in the hospitality industry clearly demonstrated the union difference in the most tangible ways. Union workers kept their jobs, their benefits, and their lives; nonunion workers were fired, lost benefits, and, sadly, sometimes died.

Going forward, it remains to be seen if this experience will inspire more hospitality workers to join unions. Clearly the harsh and disparate experience of COVID-19 and the continuing labor shortage in the service industry has led some workers to organize, but the many obstacles to unionizing in the United States remain. Nationally, Starbucks Workers United and the Amazon Labor Union have succeeded at winning high-profile, fiercely contested National Labor Relation's Board representation elections, only to see these companies use tried-and-true legal strategies to stall contract negotiations. In Boston, Local 26 successfully organized hundreds of concessions workers at Logan Airport during the pandemic, including prevailing in one campaign where a prominent worker leader was fired, but there has not been an avalanche of new organizing in the hotel industry.[40] Workers at major hotels who participated in collective campaigns to fight mass firings during the pandemic at the Marriott Copley Place and Four Seasons Boston remain nonunion. Some of these workers are still in touch with leaders of Local 26 and are interested in the protections that come with a union contract, but they report that many of their coworkers suffer from a helplessness typical of survivor syndrome. They are certain that, despite the labor shortage, if they begin an organizing campaign, history will repeat itself and they will all be fired. Maybe with time these fears will fade and the anger and shock many nonunion workers felt toward their employers at the height of the pandemic will return and drive a new wave of organizing.

At hotels that did not face mass firings, the ground for organizing may be more fertile. Local 26 has received calls from workers at several nonunion hotels that rehired their incumbent workforce asking about how to begin an organizing campaign, including the Hyatt Regency Boston and Seaport Hotel, where workers have recently won union recognition campaigns.[41] These workers did not live through the trauma of arbitrary firings but are experiencing difficult working conditions caused by the hotel industry's drive to maximize profits as the pandemic has slowed. With daily room cleaning eliminated and many jobs combined, workers at these hotels report taxing and unsafe working conditions. The labor shortage has exacerbated the problem of overwork with many workers being forced to work six or seven days a week, leading to an increase in workplace injuries. Workers at these properties also know about how Local 26 helped its members during the pandemic, having heard about the union's campaigns either in the media or from family and friends in the industry. These nonunion workers are also less afraid of being fired for union activity because the labor shortage makes it easier to find another job—although this has also made organizing challenging because some of these workers have chosen to leave their jobs rather than fight to improve working conditions at the hotel. Hopefully, this interest in unionizing will lead to several new organizing drives in Boston's hotel industry in the coming years.

To take full advantage of this rekindled interest, Local 26 has permanently dedicated staff resources to hotel organizing. The union has also begun a program to engage its existing membership on the importance of organizing new hotels. During the pandemic, the union difference in the hotel industry was clearer than it has ever been before. In the face of disaster capitalism, the union fought back and won. Now the challenge is to build on this success by organizing the unorganized and become a bigger, bolder, and more powerful union. I hope we can meet the challenge head-on.

Notes

1. Carl Zimmer, "One Meeting in Boston Seeded Tens of Thousands of Infections, Study Finds," *New York Times*, August 26, 2020, https://www.nytimes.com/2020/08/26/health/covid-19-superspreaders-boston.html/.

2. Tim Logan, "In a Matter of Days, Coronavirus Has Devastated Boston's Hotel Industry," *Boston Globe*, March 25, 2020, https://www.bostonglobe.com/2020/03/25/business/matter-days-coronavirus-devastated-bostons-hotel-industry/.

3. American Hotel and Lodging Association, *State of the Hotel Industry Analysis: Covid-19 Six Months Later* (Washington, DC: AHLA, August 2020), 8.

4. Felice J. Freyer, Andy Rosen, and Katie Johnston, "Coronavirus Outbreak at Biogen Meeting in Boston Shows Widening Impact of Illness," *Boston Globe*, March 6, 2020, https://www.bostonglobe.com/2020/03/06/metro/seven-total-presumptive-coronavirus-cases-mass/.

5. Pay rate verification information is particularly important for events-based workers like banquet servers, the bulk of whose income is both seasonal and gratuity based.

6. For a good discussion of how employers rationalized ending coverage, see Josh Bivens and Ben Zipperer, "Health Insurance and the COVID-19 Shock: What We Know So Far about Health Insurance Losses and What It Means for Policy," *Economic Policy Institute*, August 26, 2020, https://www.epi.org/publication/health-insurance-and-the-covid-19-shock/.

7. Host Hotels & Resorts Inc. (HST), "Q2 2020 Results—Earnings Call Transcript," July 31, 2020, *Seeking Alpha*, https://seekingalpha.com/article/4363160-host-hotels-and-resorts-inc-hst-ceo-jim-risoleo-on-q2-2020-results-earnings-call-transcript/.

8. Park Hotels & Resorts Inc. "Q2 2021 Earnings Call Transcript," *Motley Fool*, August 6, 2021, https://www.fool.com/earnings/call-transcripts/2021/08/06/park-hotels-resorts-inc-pk-q2-2021-earnings-call-t/.

9. The hotel's letter about the firings was excerpted in Katie Johnston, "Four Seasons Hotel Fires Nearly Half Its Staff," *Boston Globe*, June 10, 2020, https://www.bostonglobe.com/2020/06/10/nation/four-seasons-hotel-fires-nearly-half-its-staff/.

10. Johnston, "Four Seasons Hotel Fires."

11. Shirley Leung, "Making Four Seasons Pay for Its Treatment of Workers," *Boston Globe*, June 11, 2020, https://www.bostonglobe.com/2020/06/11/business/making-four-seasons-pay-its-treatment-workers/.

12. Nichole Berlie, "Senator Markey Calls for More Hotel Worker Protections Following Mass Layoffs," WCVB5, June 14, 2020, https://www.wcvb.com/article/sen-ed-markey-calls-for-more-hotel-worker-protections-following-mass-layoffs/32861879/.

13. Katie Johnston and Shirley Leung, "Four Seasons Reverses Course on Severance Pay, Promises Full Package to Laid-Off Workers," *Boston Globe*,

June 17, 2020, https://www.bostonglobe.com/2020/06/17/nation/four-seasons
-reverses-course-severance-pay-promises-full-package-laid-off-workers/.

14. RevPAR is an acronym for Revenue per Available Room, a standard metric
for hotel profitability. Host Hotels & Resorts Inc., "Q4 2020 Results—Earnings
Call Transcript," *Seeking Alpha*, February 19, 2021, https://seekingalpha.com/
article/4407586-host-hotels-resorts-inc-s-hst-ceo-jim-risoleo-on-q4-2020
-results-earnings-call-transcript/.

15. Katie Johnston, "'I am left with nothing': Marriott Copley Terminates Half
Its Staff, Adding to the Thousands of Hotel Workers Unemployed around Boston,"
Boston Globe, November 15, 2020, https://www.bostonglobe.com/2020/11/15/
nation/marriott-copley-terminates-half-its-staff-thousands-hotel-workers
-unemployed-around-boston/.

16. DiamondRock Hospitality Company, "Q3 2020 Results—Earnings Call
Transcript," *Seeking Alpha*, November 8, 2020, https://seekingalpha.com/
article/4386659-diamondrock-hospitality-company-drh-ceo-mark-brugger
-on-q3-2020-results-earnings-call.

17. The irony that wealthy customers staying at Waldorf Astorias somehow
were not worthy of this change to cleaning protocols was not lost on many
commentators.

18. See "Hilton CleanStay," Press Release, July 5, 2021, https://stories.hilton
.com/releases/hilton-cleanstay-from-checkin-to-checkout.

19. "Hilton CleanStay," Press Release, July 5, 2021.

20. Park Hotels & Resorts Inc. "Q2 2021 Results—Earnings Call Transcript," *Motley Fool*, August 6, 2021, https://www.fool.com/earnings/call-
transcripts/2021/08/06/park-hotels-resorts-inc-pk-q2-2021-earnings-call-t/.
Claims about the positive environmental impacts of eliminating daily cleaning are suspect; see Chloe Zilliac, "Are Hotel Greening Programs Hurting
Housekeepers?" *Sierra*, January 12, 2020, https://www.sierraclub.org/sierra/
are-hotel-greening-programs-hurting-housekeepers/.

21. Park Hotels & Resorts Inc., "Q2 2020 Earnings Call Transcript," *Motley Fool*,
August 7, 2020, https://www.fool.com/earnings/call-transcripts/2020/08/07/
park-hotels-resorts-inc-pk-q2-2020-earnings-call-t.aspx/.

22. *UNITE HERE, Playing Dirty: The Hotel Industry's Plan to End Daily Room
Cleaning Would Cost Women of Color Billions* (New York: UNITE HERE, 2021).
Available at https://unitehere.org/wp-content/uploads/Playing-Dirty-Report
-FINAL.pdf/.

23. Typical limited-service brands are Hyatt Place and Courtyard by Marriott.

24. Room service had traditionally been a "loss leader" in the hotel industry
because it required dedicated staff that had to work full shifts no matter how
many orders were made during a given meal period.

25. Katie Johnston and Evan Allen, "As Coronavirus Spreads, Workers Say
Employers Are Putting Them at Risk," *Boston Globe*, March 20, 2020, https://
www.bostonglobe.com/2020/03/21/nation/coronavirus-spreads-workers-say
-employers-are-putting-them-risk/.

26. The union was never able to confirm if these members had COVID-19, as testing was still largely unavailable in Massachusetts at this time.

27. Carlos Aramayo to Eric Carrey, March 16, 2020.

28. See Jon Chesto, "Mayor Marty Walsh Appoints Group of Advisers to Help Boston Reopen Its Economy," *Boston Globe*, May 26, 2020, https://www.boston globe.com/2020/05/26/business/mayor-marty-walsh-appoints-group-advisors -help-city-reopen-its-economy/; Karen Spilka, "Senate to Host Listening Session on Economic Recovery, Reinvestment, and Workforce amid COVID-19," Press Release, June 11, 2020, https://karenspilka.com/updates/2020/6/11/senate-to -host-listening-session-on-economic-recovery-reinvestment-and-workforce/.

29. Carlos Aramayo, "How Massachusetts Can Protect Hospitality Workers and Tourism," *Boston Globe*, May 19, 2020, https://www.bostonglobe.com/2020/05/19/ opinion/how-massachusetts-can-protect-hospitality-workers-tourism/.

30. See Commonwealth of Massachusetts, "Operators of Lodgings MA Safety Standards," https://www.mass.gov/doc/operators-of-lodgings-protocol -summary-english/download/.

31. For a good summary of the legislative debate and actions around unemployment assistance, see The Commonwealth of Massachusetts, *Report of the SENATE COMMITTEE ON POST AUDIT AND OVERSIGHT entitled Concerning a Review of the Performance of the Commonwealth's Unemployment Insurance System and Related Programs during the COVID-19 Pandemic*, August 18, 2022, https://malegislature.gov/Bills/192/S3108.pdf/.

32. The only employers that agreed to extend health benefits were university cafeterias. Harvard and MIT both agreed to continue all employee benefits for the remainder of the spring semester. Later, they extended these benefits to cover the remainder of the year.

33. Health coverage for Local 26 members was eventually extended until June 2021 due to the passage of the American Rescue Plan Act (ARPA) in March 2021. This legislation, lobbied for by many unions including UNITE HERE, included 100 percent subsidized continuation of health coverage (COBRA) coverage. The UNITE HERE Health plan actively assisted members in signing up for COBRA and bore the immediate financial costs of extending coverage and the bureaucratic burden of applying for and receiving reimbursement from the federal government. For a summary of this legislation, see Thomas Kaplan, "What's in the Stimulus Bill? A Guide to Where the $1.9 Trillion Is Going," *New York Times*, March 30, 2021, https://www.nytimes.com/2021/03/07/us/politics/whats-in -the-stimulus-bill.html/.

34. See Katie Johnston, "Union Calls Out Hotels That Haven't Committed to Rehiring Workers," *Boston Globe*, March 17, 2021, https://www.boston globe.com/2021/03/17/business/union-calls-out-hotels-that-havent-committed -rehiring-workers/.

35. Providence City Council, "Providence City Council Says 'Yes' to the Hospitality Worker Comeback Legislation," *City Council: Recent News*, November 5, 2020, https://council.providenceri.gov/2020/11/05/providence-city-council -says-yes-to-the-hospitality-worker-comeback-legislation/.

36. The hearing regarding this legislation covers the broader economic and policy issues that were at stake. It can be watched at Joint Committee on Labor and Workforce Development, Hearing, May 11, 2021, https://malegislature.gov/ Events/Hearings/Detail/3710/.

37. The fight to have hotel workers recalled after the pandemic was also a national campaign of Local 26's parent union, UNITE HERE. For a good summary, see Michael Sainato, "Furloughed US Workers Fight to Return to Their Jobs after a Year on Pause," *The Guardian*, April 21, 2021, https://www.theguardian .com/business/2021/apr/21/us-workers-unite-here-furlough-coronavirus/.

38. See Shira Laucharoen, "Kim Janey and Hospitality Workers Call for Back to Work Initiative," *Dig Boston*, July 7, 2021, https://digboston.com/ kim-janey-and-hospitality-workers-call-for-back-to-work-initiative/.

39. Kate King, "Housekeepers, Hotel Owners Square Off over Daily Service," *Wall Street Journal*, November 2, 2021, https://www.wsj.com/articles/ housekeepers-hotel-owners-square-off-over-daily-service-11635854400/.

40. Katie Johnston, "Worker Who Fought for Union at Logan Airport Restaurants Is Fired after Union Win," *Boston Globe*, March 3, 2022, https://www .bostonglobe.com/2022/03/03/business/worker-who-fought-union-logan -airport-restaurants-is-fired-after-union-win/.

41. Katie Johnston, "Workers at Hyatt Regency Vote to Join Union," *Boston Globe*, June 19, 2022, https://www.bostonglobe.com/2024/06/18/business/ hyatt-regency-boston-local-26-union-talking-points.

PART III

The Education Industry

PART II

6

No Cuts—No Cops—No COVID

The Graduate Employees' Pandemic Strike at the University of Michigan–Ann Arbor

KATHLEEN BROWN

This chapter considers the graduate workers' strike for a "Safe and Just Campus" at the University of Michigan–Ann Arbor between September 8 and 16, 2020. Led by the Graduate Employees' Organization (GEO) AFT Local 3550, representing over two thousand graduate workers in Ann Arbor, the strike was the culmination of months of organizing against the University of Michigan's opaque reopening plans during the early months of the COVID-19 pandemic. At the time, the 2020 work stoppage was only the second open-ended strike by GEO since the union's four-week recognition strike in 1974 and the first time graduate student instructors had struck while a collective bargaining agreement was in effect. Unable to make progress at the bargaining table, and excluded from fall reopening decisions, graduate workers engaged in a defensive work stoppage for nine days. Coming at the end of summer, traditionally a low point in the rhythm of campus organizing, the strike reflected the urgency and fear many workers felt at the threat of COVID-19 given that vaccines, testing, and adequate personal protection equipment were unavailable. This existential urgency impelled graduate workers to break the law to secure their demands, as the strike violated both a no-strike clause in the collective bargaining agreement and Michigan's Public Employment Relations Act, which prohibits public employees from engaging in work stoppages.[1] As the strike continued, its effects rippled outward, spreading to residential advisors who were fearful of catching COVID in the dorms, and influenced the first-ever faculty vote of no confidence in the university president.

As workers experienced viscerally, the pandemic exposed the profit-making motive that compelled them to work, risking illness and death so that profit would not be disrupted. This was most evident in so-called essential industries, where workers were publicly lauded for their labor, despite little material aid or protection against the virus. Spurred by the life-and-death threat posed by COVID, workers across "essential" industries took defensive action to protect their health and the health of their loved ones. Graduate workers drew inspiration from bus drivers in Detroit, Amazon warehouse workers on Long Island, and meatpackers in the Midwest who walked off the job demanding safer working conditions.[2] When the virus did not abate over the summer of 2020, higher education workers attempted to influence administrators' reopening plans. At the University of North Carolina, faculty, staff, and unionized service workers sued the University of North Carolina System over unsafe working conditions,[3] while faculty at scores of universities circulated petitions and open letters critiquing lack of transparency and safety in university operations. Higher education labor also attempted to defend themselves from COVID-related austerity measures pushed through with little oversight. At Rutgers University, a coalition of unions negotiated cost-sharing measures to lessen the pandemic's effects on the lowest-paid.[4] Organized graduate workers at University of Michigan–Ann Arbor responded to both challenges: administrators' failure to engage in meaningful reopening decision making and the university's top-down COVID-related austerity measures.

The 2020 strike was not simply about safety in the narrow, epidemiological sense, however. Inspired by the 2020 summertime Black Lives Matter uprising after the police murders of George Floyd and Breonna Taylor, rank-and-file graduate workers also resisted the expansion of campus policing. In addition to their COVID safety strike platform, GEO members called for a reduction in campus police funding by 50 percent; disarming campus police officers; and cutting ties with Immigration, Customs, and Enforcement and the Ann Arbor Police Department. The connection between health and public safety was concretized by the university's decision to deploy campus and city police alongside work-study students to police social events as a condition of reopening campus. More broadly, GEO members used the strike to call into question campus police funding, a challenge that had not been made since the U-M student movement against deputization of campus police in 1990.[5] Thus, in striking to reduce funding for campus police and expand funding for graduate students and campus social services, union members embraced explicitly abolitionist thinking nurtured by the summer's uprising.[6]

While the material outcomes of GEO's strike were mixed, the explosive nine-day strike demonstrated that rank-and-file graduate workers were willing to break the law to force their employer to implement health and safety measures. In addition, by demanding the defunding and demilitarization of campus police, graduate workers sought to exert labor's power over "violence workers" during a national reckoning with police violence.[7] Fundamentally, the 2020 strike was an exercise in collective action and collective care that solidified a core of rank-and-file activists committed to class struggle union-ism. The 2020 strike was an important training ground for graduate workers, who again broke state law by striking for six weeks in 2023. The 2023 strike was the longest GEO strike to date, and graduate workers successfully faced down an injunction—the same legal tactic that had ended the 2020 strike—to win a living wage for most of the bargaining unit.

Background

The University of Michigan is a leading R1 (research 1) public university that employs over thirty-five thousand individuals as one of the largest employers in the state of Michigan. Each semester approximately two thousand graduate student instructors are hired by the university as the second-largest teaching cohort after tenure track faculty. The university estimates that 90 percent of undergraduate students will be taught by graduate student instructors at some point in their college career,[8] and financial analysis shows that the combination of high tuition and low labor costs means that graduate labor created approximately $200 million in surplus for the university in 2022.[9] The university has three campuses: the Ann Arbor campus is the largest, with a total student body (undergraduate and graduate) of over fifty thousand; Dearborn has over eight thousand,[10] and Flint has approximately sixty-five hundred.[11] U-M's endowment is the ninth largest in the country and grew from $12 billion in 2019 to over $17 billion in 2022, increasingly allocated toward venture capital and private equity.[12] Even as the endowment has bal-looned, the university's board of regents constrains the percentage of the endowment used for operating costs, reducing it from 5.5 percent in 1995 to 4.5 percent in 2010, where it remains today.[13] Despite the university's wealth, educational resources remain lopsided in favor of the wealthier Ann Arbor campus; Flint and Dearborn students and instructors continue to struggle for equitable funding and workloads.[14]

Faced with a rapidly spreading pandemic in the early spring of 2020, the University of Michigan, like many higher education institutions, passed along pandemic-related financial losses to workers and students.[15] In an industry shaped by high tuition fees and high institutional debt, there was much to be lost in empty dorms and classrooms and canceled football games. Given the unprecedented upheaval of shuttered businesses and immediate layoffs in the early months of the pandemic, GEO members anticipated a veritable "shock doctrine" of austerity by their employer. In early April, U-M's Office of Human Resources used the threat of future austerity to pressure GEO mem-bers to accept a three-year contract with lower-than-inflation wage increases. On April 20, 2020, then-president Mark Schlissel announced a plethora of financial cuts, warning that the university faced a financial shortfall ranging from $400 million to $1 billion.[16] At an April meeting with the All Campus Labor Council, a coalition of campus unions, Democratic regent Paul Brown reeled off a list of financial losses: empty dorms, the cancelation of the NCAA playoffs, canceled spring and summer programming, delayed elective medical procedures, and no fall football. Subsequently, the university announced that all discretionary spending was paused, hiring and salaries for nonunion workers were frozen, and retirement matching was suspended. Layoffs quickly followed: at the university's Flint campus, over 41 percent of non–tenure track faculty were laid off.[17] Michigan Medicine, the medical arm of the University of Michigan, laid off more than seven hundred medical workers, including thirty-eight emergency medical technicians, citing COVID-related disruptions.[18] In June the board of regents, initially unhappy with President Schlissel's proposed budget, ultimately voted to increase tuition, housing, and healthcare costs and levy an additional "COVID fee" on Ann Arbor students.[19] From this signaling, the university communicated that it had deep financial motivations to return to regular operations as quickly as possible, despite ongoing COVID infections and deaths. Thus began the administration's insistence on a "public health informed" residential semester for fall 2020.

Suspicious of this dire financial picture, University of Michigan and Michigan Medicine labor unions called for the university to "open the books" to demonstrate proof of the institution's financial woes.[20] When administrators failed to respond, campus unions hired accounting professor and former American Association of University Professors treasurer Dr. Howard Bunsis to audit the university's publicly available finances. Instead of scarcity, Bunsis found "abundant financial resources," evident in Moody's AAA bond rating of U-M and $6.7 billion of unrestricted reserves—over half of the University of Michigan's then–$12.4 billion endowment.[21] Bunsis concluded that if the pandemic was a storm, the university certainly had the means to weather it, whereas low-paid workers did not.[22] In other words, this was the "rainy day" that Michigan's endowment could guard against.

As fall neared, communication from the University of Michigan rhetorically gestured toward health and safety in email announcements and webinars yet failed to acknowledge how inviting tens of thousands of students and workers back to campus, with no vaccine and with no real possibility of social distancing, would result in mass contagion. If illness did occur, students, hale and hearty, would recover. No mention was made of older faculty and staff members or immunocompromised or disabled students. The unarticulated assumption was that death would happen elsewhere to someone else but not to U-M Wolverines. This is, of course, an ableist fallacy. One of the first workers to die of COVID was African American bus driver and AFSCME Local 1583 member Troy Dixon, age forty-eight.[23] To date, the University of Michigan has never publicly acknowledged his or other employees' COVID deaths.

COVID Spring: Shared Sacrifice?

As COVID disruptions multiplied, graduate workers struggled to absorb the impact of the pandemic. Union-wide phone banking revealed the difficulties graduate workers faced: interrupted research, canceled paid internships and jobs, and increased caretaking work, which would make progress toward a degree difficult, if not impossible. Graduate workers with children and international graduates were particularly burdened, struggling under increased caregiving responsibilities and buffeted by a hostile political environment. Others encountered shuttered libraries and closed borders; some encountered illness and relatives' deaths. Work disruptions created a chain effect that graduates scrambled to respond to. In one case, a graduate worker who gave voice lessons to supplement a small teaching salary had to immediately apply for food stamps when their freelance voice instruction ended abruptly. In another, a parent struggled with caring for children at home and was unable to make progress on their dissertation, despite the program clock ticking. Another student was forced to end twelve months of research overnight and move in with friends; yet another needed to care for ailing parents and was unable to return to research. Gender, race, and class cut across these experiences. Those with more resources—mainly white, upper-middle-class graduates—were able to weather COVID-related disruptions; first-generation and working-class students—especially women and students of color—had less ability to do so.

After recording graduate workers' difficulties in navigating the pandemic, GEO members proposed collective solutions. Rank-and-file GEO members took inspiration from the Chicago Teachers Union's (CTU) and the United Teachers of Los Angeles's (UTLA) willingness to fight for their students' communities, especially CTU's call for rent and mortgage relief for Chicago families in the early months of the pandemic. Graduate workers saw U-M's vast resources and called for their redistribution to ease workers' financial strain under an emergency "COVID Caucus," which had the explicit goals of securing safer working conditions for the community and financial relief for graduates. In just one week in May 2020, the caucus collected over eighteen hundred signatures in an open letter that called on the board of regents and President Mark Schlissel to deliver emergency grants, an additional year of graduate funding, increased support for international students whose travel was disrupted, flexible childcare funding, and, most critically, a seat at the table in deciding on fall working conditions.[24] These demands went on to form the basis of GEO's fall strike platform.

In response to the COVID Caucus's open letter, university spokesperson Rick Fitzgerald repeated blandishments that U-M "remains committed to providing a safe campus environment for all students and employees . . . as we explore how we will return to in-person classes, teaching and research for the fall semester" but that many of the financial demands, such as child-care subsidies, extended funding, and help for international students, were not "financially feasible."[25] In a reply-all email, billionaire Republican regent Ron Weiser dryly asked, "Where is the money supposed to come from for your monetary demands[?]"[26] Declining to meet with GEO members, administrators referred the COVID Caucus to Academic Human Resources for "any and all employment-related matters."[27] Yet Academic Human Resources refused to speak about "student"-related matters such as timeline extensions and additional funding. Throughout the summer, university administrators shuffled graduate students between human resources and the graduate school while refusing to talk—let alone negotiate—over the demands outlined in GEO's open letter. If graduate workers could not bargain with human resources over what they needed, and if the university administrators refused to meet with GEO, what options did graduate students have to meaningfully influence their working conditions?

Finding little recourse through impact bargaining, and denied meetings with university administrators, graduate workers began an agitational campaign, preparing for a work stoppage. As the COVID Caucus wrote in June 2020:

> While we are strategically omnivorous and want to continue to use all tools in our toolkit, our experience from the past and in this struggle so far suggests that the administration is not going to listen to us unless we make it so they have no other choice, which means a major action. The administration's secretive approach means that members do not have access to information about the university's intentions, reasoning, or plans, but we have every reason to think the university's moves will not be in our best interests. We cannot wait until a majority of members come knocking at GEO's door to ask if something will be done, because by then it will be too late. We need to take the opposite approach: organize them into the anti-austerity struggle so that we are prepared to respond adequately. Therefore, we have to actively build toward a Fall major action.[28]

The university's lack of transparency in fall preparations became a major target of organizing among faculty, students, and staff. At a time when vaccines did not exist, COVID tests were rare, and contact tracing was the main tool to identify contagion, the fear of a massive outbreak stemming from in-person university operations was very real. In late July more than fifteen hundred University of Michigan faculty and staff signed an open letter calling for the university to disclose autumn COVID screening, tracing, and isolation plans as well as contingency plans "for what will be done if an outbreak exceeds control."[29] When university administrators failed to adequately provide this, a second letter, signed by seven hundred university members, insisted that "in the absence of a clear plan based on science, we should not be reopening in person, but asking the students to stay home, in accordance with the recent call from Governor [Gretchen] Whitmer to all state universities."[30] This concern was underscored by the university's own COVID-19 Ethics and Privacy Committee, which advised U-M president Mark Schlissel on July 31, 2020: "Our main point here is . . . to underscore, with urgency, our concern that current plans for Fall 2020 will not meet the reasonable standard for safety recommended by our report, that good alternatives exist, and that it is not too late to pursue them." Further, the Ethics and Privacy Committee maintained that the university's fall plans risked inflicting "grave harm" on the university and surrounding communities.[31] Students with disabilities petitioned for remote study and work accommodations, arguing that "although many students will desire and benefit from at least some face-to-face instruction, those benefits will not outweigh the risks to others who are more vulnerable to COVID-19 or who want to protect vulnerable loved ones."[32] Close to fifteen hundred parents, faculty, and undergraduates signed a Change.org petition calling for university-wide surveillance testing, citing numerous universities that had developed their own testing services and protocols.[33]

Despite the flurry of open letters and petitions, the university continued to move ahead with plans for an in-person semester without widespread testing, tracing, or quarantine capacity. U-M's insistence on a residential semester contrasted sharply with the views of Governor Whitmer, who called for a remote semester within the state; the plans of Eastern Michigan University, located in nearby Ypsilanti, which delayed the start of the fall semester for three weeks; and the intentions of Michigan State University, which preemptively moved to remote instruction for the fall of 2020. Similarly, Ann Arbor Public Schools maintained remote instruction during the fall. In relation to its close neighbors, the University of Michigan's in-person semester was an outlier.

Unheard through open letters, GEO members escalated actions to draw attention to their demands. Graduate workers commented at regents' meetings; mobilized car caravans; hosted socially distanced protests outside the president's mansion; staged speak-outs; collected major actions pledges; and, on the eve of the start of fall classes, held a die-in at the center of campus complete with a coffin, a trumpeter playing "Taps," and mock gravestones to make visible the human consequences of the university's reopening plans.[34] Simultaneously, faculty organized demonstrations demanding better testing and tracing protocols and put forth multiple resolutions in the Senate Advisory Committee on University Affairs calling for a vote of no confidence in the university's reopening plans and a vote of no confidence in President Schlissel,[35] maintaining that the "University of Michigan leadership has consistently refused to be moved by countless concerns expressed by faculty, staff, students, and local residents through formal communications, petitions, and protests with respect to its Fall 2020 re-opening plans."[36] As the first day of classes, August 31, drew near, GEO members prepared to confront university intransigence through the strike weapon.

An Abolitionist Strike

Concurrently, it became impossible to talk about health and safety without engaging with the threat that police violence posed to certain members of the community, dramatized in the nationwide uprising for Black Lives. Spurred by the widely publicized police murders of African Americans George Floyd, Tony McDade, Breonna Taylor, and others throughout the spring of 2020, the uprising brought unprecedented numbers of people into action. Studies estimate that between 15 million and 26 million people in the United States participated in actions against police violence and ongoing police immunity.[37] The uprising catapulted calls for defunding police and police abolition into mainstream discourse. These demands, long championed by feminist abolitionists such as Angela Davis and Ruth Wilson Gilmore, reimagine safety pursued not through violence work and mass incarceration but by investing in infrastructures of care: healthcare, housing, education, jobs, mental health, and substance abuse support. The pandemic exposed the brittleness of the infrastructure of care in the United States as millions struggled with unemployment and food scarcity while policing budgets remained unaffected. GEO members connected COVID safety demands and police defunding through this lens, which, according to members, "also serve[d] as a practice in building community power."[38] By late August, GEO members voted overwhelmingly to add police disarmament; defunding of campus police by 50 percent; and a university commitment to cut ties with Immigration, Customs, and Enforcement to their slate of strike demands.[39] The decision, made only days before the strike began, reflected the ideological impact of the summer's uprising on a layer of membership who sought to use the work stoppage to contest funding priorities at the University of Michigan.

The "defund" or "abolitionist" demands, as they became to be known, were both a reflection of the particularities of the summer uprising and indicative of longer-standing abolitionist praxis by GEO members, including a history of activism against police violence in Ann Arbor. This history goes back at least to November 2014, when white Ann Arbor police officer David Ried shot and killed forty-year-old African American Ann Arbor resident Aura Rosser in her home. GEO members helped form the coalition From Ann Arbor to Ferguson, which called for justice for Rosser by bringing charges against Ried. The chief of police, John Seto, declined to charge Ried, and in the years since has been employed as the University of Michigan's director of housing security, demonstrating the porous relationships between local and campus police. In 2019–2020 contract negotiations, GEO's racial justice working group proposed disarming and demilitarizing campus police in the contract platform. U-M deemed proposed contract language to be "permissive," or outside the scope of negotiable issues. Failing to garner the leverage needed to make meaningful progress on these demands, members voted to drop them prior to contract ratification. Yet only a few months later, demands to disarm and defund campus police were revived by GEO's policing working group and put in front of the membership for a vote on August 25, 2020, where they were overwhelmingly approved.

The call for the University of Michigan to divest from policing and invest in the needs of the community and students is part of a larger reckoning with campus policing across the United States. As historians Yalile Suriel, Grace Watkins, and their colleagues show, following the massacres of student activists at Jackson State and Kent State in 1970, universities hired police to protect university interests against internal and external threats in a (potentially) less lethal manner than municipal police or the National Guard. Disciplining students, especially rebellious ones, became a major focus of campus police operations post-1970.[40] This function is evident today in higher-profile cases of police repression against students, such as campus police pepper-spraying Occupy activists at UC Davis in 2011,[41] the arrest of climate activists at the University of Michigan in 2018,[42] and police attacks and military-grade surveillance of wildcat strikers at UC Santa Cruz in 2020.[43] Nor is "campus" policing limited to the confines of university grounds. Many university police forces' jurisdiction has expanded off-campus to police poorer and Blacker neighborhoods on the periphery of wealthy and majority-white campuses. This has led to criminalization and brutalization of local populations at the hands of campus officers, who often work in tandem with municipal police.[44]

While critics of the strike sought to characterize GEO's COVID and abolitionist demands as unrelated, the university linked these issues directly by relying on the police to secure a "public-health-informed residential semester." In July 2020 university officials announced the "UM Ambassadors Program," which paired federal work-study students with city and campus police officers to patrol social gatherings on and off-campus.[45] Heavily criticized by undergraduate coalitions like the Students of Color Liberation Front, the Ambassadors Program demonstrated the university's reliance on coercion to secure its reopening, a task that would disproportionately harm Black and brown campus and community members.[46] As GEO argued, "Policing and surveillance are not 'public health-informed'; they are harmful to physical and mental health. Increased police presence on campus and in the wider community will further jeopardize the safety of Black and brown graduate workers, students, faculty, staff, and community members amid a pandemic that is already disproportionately ravaging Black and brown communities."[47]

The demands to defund campus police ("no cops") called into question university funding priorities ("no cuts") in the face of COVID. Union activists asked why, in one of the wealthiest universities in the country, on-campus security received over $30 million in funding each year while researchers were told to tighten their belts and staff were furloughed, while mental health service providers labored under long waiting lists and low pay, while the university maintained a full-time food pantry for hungry students, and while graduate workers often did not earn enough to afford to live in Ann Arbor. As recent research has shown, campus police activity at the University of Michigan over the past two decades, measured in the form of violations, has significantly decreased—yet police funding has not.[48]

Pulling the Emergency Brake

Despite the outbreak of protests over health concerns as the fall neared, the administration continued to move ahead with a residential semester. During impact bargaining, the university's Office of Human Resources revealed that the university was concerned that students would not pay full tuition for a remote semester. Instead, the university asked students to take the "Wolverine Culture of Care" pledge,[49] which transferred the responsibility of public health onto students who pledged to wear masks, wash hands, and socially distance themselves.

The university did make some adaptations as protesting voices grew louder. While refusing a universal right to remote work, departments were permitted to make their own decisions about teaching modality. This meant that in sympathetic departments, graduate student instructors had more autonomy over course instruction. On the other side, less-sympathetic departments did not make these accommodations. Other adaptations included lower density on-campus housing and dining options, the cancelation of fall break to minimize student travel, and an anticipated switch to remote instruction after the Thanksgiving holiday.[50] Football remained the one outlier. Initially canceled by Big Ten officials, the season was quickly rescheduled after an intense backlash by fans. Although the stadiums were empty for the season, football games would continue.[51] Indeed, even when on-campus COVID tests were unavailable to the general university population, the university ensured athletes' access to regular COVID testing to keep athletics going, an irony not lost on striking graduate students.[52]

Dissatisfied with the university's failure to seriously negotiate with graduate workers over most open letter demands, and with an increasing sense of urgency over campus conditions, GEO members voted to strike starting on September 8, 2020, Labor Day.[53] The strike authorization vote approved an initial four-day strike and then could be reauthorized, if necessary. Strike demands included:

- transparent and robust testing, contact tracing, and safety plans for campus;
- support for graduate student instructors working remotely and an option to switch to remote from hybrid/in-person;
- flexible childcare subsidies for parents and caregivers, including those with school-age children or care obligations for adults;
- improved International Center support for international students and the repealing of the discriminatory international student fee;
- unconditional support for all graduate students in the form of timeline and funding extensions, an emergency grant, and flexible leases and rent freezes at U-M housing;
- a demilitarized workplace;
- diversion of funds from campus police toward social services (involving a cut of 50 percent to DPSS [Department of Public Safety and Security] annual budget);
- and an ending of ties to local law enforcement (AAPD [Ann Arbor Police Department]) and other agencies (ICE [Immigration and Customs Enforcement]).

In the early morning of Tuesday, September 8, 2020, hundreds of graduate workers gathered in front of University of Michigan construction sites. Cognizant that some university operations had shifted online, and hoping to interrupt the university's ongoing capital outlay, GEO picketed the multimillion-dollar Ruthven Museum site, which was under renovation for administration offices. There, masked GEO members began picketing in the pouring rain, shouting, "Save our health, not your wealth!" and "U-M makes us sick!" Picket lines began at 5:00 a.m. to intercept construction workers and expanded to multiple high-visibility campus locations later in the day.

Coming after months of social distancing and online-only organizing, the atmosphere of the strike was ebullient and defiant: graduates expressed elation at seeing hundreds of people come together mixed with anger at the university. Support for the strike spread across campus: undergraduates posted images of President Schlissel depicted as the grim reaper, and chalked slogans of "U-M Makes Us Sick" appeared across the campus. Online, memes pilloried the university's "culture of care," offering buyers a U-M-branded coffin. The graduate a cappella group, GradTONES, produced a version of the Michigan fight song "Hail to the Victors" as "Hail to the vectors viral / Hail to the COVID spiral / Hail to ignoring science / Hail to public health defiance."[54] On the picket line, strikers took safety seriously: masks were obligatory and each picketer registered their picket location for contact tracing. Picket lines stretched as picketers attempted to stay six feet apart. For those who could not take part in in-person picketing, organizers hosted Zoom "pickets" where members called the board of regents, President Schlissel, and deans of colleges, urging them to make movement in negotiations. Throughout the strike, external support flowed in: GEO received seventy thousand dollars in strike funds through social media crowdsourcing, as well as food donations from other grad unions, local labor chapters, socialist groups, and local politicians.

As the strike continued, it acted as a lightning rod for broader campus discontent and contested reopening plans. Residential halls, filled with thousands of students, quickly became COVID hotspots, which in turn sparked undergraduate worker organizing. On September 9, residential staff, undergraduate residential advisors who lived and worked in the residence halls, voted overwhelmingly to strike by ending mail delivery and common area supervision.[55] Their decision to strike stemmed from University Housing's unresponsiveness to their calls for regular access to COVID testing; "sufficient, effective" personal protective equipment; and hazard pay. As they wrote, "The University has repeatedly referred to the Wolverine Culture of Care but has not extended this same care to us."[56]

Positioned at the front lines of COVID contagion, residential advisors watched student after student fall ill. The university moved sick students into isolation housing in a residential hall on North Campus that had been slated for demolition, where students waited the requisite ten days of quarantine before being able to return. Quarantined students took to social media to criticize poor conditions, including lack of toilet paper and microwaves in the isolation housing, while parents organized on Facebook to deliver lozenges, tea, and other supplies to ill students.[57] GEO members delivered leftover food from the picket lines to quarantined students. Once again, the care shown by grassroots activity contrasted strongly with perceived institutional disinterest.

On September 9 the university attempted to end the strike by producing an "exploding" offer that would be withdrawn if GEO members did not accept it. Management offered some concessions around flexible childcare subsidies and better COVID testing protocols but presented little to nothing on police funding, degree timelines, or extended degree funding. The university communicated that if GEO members did not accept the offer, the administration would request a court order to force graduate student instructors back to teaching. This spurred heated debate at that evening's general membership meeting as GEO leadership endorsed the offer. However, the university's failure to move on most demands, combined with the emergent strike of residential advisors, led 1,250 GEO members to reject the university's first offer. Participation and support for the strike among membership increased as the strike continued.[58]

By September 10, 2020, the strike spread further. Student workers from the dining halls and cafés staged a walkout over safety concerns, joining over one thousand in a march through campus. This illustrated what GEO members had anticipated: that GEO, as one of the most organized and active unions on campus, could act as an "emergency brake" on the university's reopening and amplify the demands of nonunion or less-organized workers.[59] Indeed, campus labor's response was uneven. The Lecturers' Employee Organization (AFT Local 6244), representing twelve hundred lecturers on the Ann Arbor campus, encouraged members to materially support the strike and attend pickets, although they did not engage in a work stoppage, citing their no-strike clause. A handful of individuals from AFSCME Local 1583, representing custodians, dining hall workers, and service workers on campus, participated in pickets but were hampered by very low levels of union activity and organization. MNA–UMNPC, [Michigan Nurses Association–University of Michigan Nurses Professional Council] the nurses union at Michigan Medicine, released statements of support but faced their own existential threat under the spread of the virus.

On Sunday, September 13, GEO members reauthorized the strike's continuation, while the university escalated legal proceedings against GEO by requesting a court injunction to "avert further irreparable harm to the university, its student body, their parents, and the general public."[60] The claim of "irreparable harm" was not lost on members concerned about possible life-and-death consequences of the fall's reopening. The university retained the legal services of Butzel Long, which represented corporate interests attempting to reverse Governor Whitmer's emergency COVID closures.[61] The law firm emphasized the strike's illegality throughout their motion paperwork. The Democratic Board of Regents' strategy of invoking anti-labor law to discipline graduate students fighting for public safety sparked outrage among university employees, many of whom voiced their disagreement in open letters and social media posts.

By Monday the strike became increasingly difficult as the administration ratcheted up pressure on graduate workers. Deans of colleges encouraged faculty to scab on the strike, while Provost Susan Collins described the strike as "disruptive, confusing and worrisome" for undergraduates and declared, "GEO's strike falls outside of that negotiation and is based on a number of issues, some of which have very little to do with the wages, hours, and working conditions of GSIs [graduate student instructors] and GSSAs [graduate student staff assistants]."[62] Of course, refusing the bounds of negotiable subjects was exactly the point, given the university's refusal to meet with graduate students on extended degree timelines and funding or to negotiate over workplace safety.

At the same time, GEO's decision to strike over campus police funding polarized the Ann Arbor campus and local labor community. While picketing construction sites in the early morning, most skilled trades workers turned around at the sight of a picket line. Yet a smaller number of skilled tradespeople, upset by GEO's demands to defund campus police and the banner reading "GEO Stands 4 Black Lives," initially threatened to cross, describing the line as a protest and not a picket. Only after intense debate between graduate and construction workers, as well as conversations between building managers and AFT Michigan representatives, did these trade workers turn around. Some undergraduate residential advisors communicated their initial discomfort with GEO's demand to defund DPSS, given their close relationship with security officers who respond to students in crisis, but collaboration increased as the strike continued. These experiences show both the power of labor solidarity but also the tensions that accompanied more-controversial demands.

The polarizing effect of the strike extended to students, parents, and tenure track faculty. A number of parents and undergraduate students took to social media to communicate their anger at disruption to in-person learning and in members' decision to call for defunding of police, which was seen as evidence of graduate student "wokeness."[63] Faculty, too, were split. Some faculty voiced their disagreement at department meetings and social media, while others supported the strike. Departments, particularly in the humanities, circulated public letters urging the university to negotiate. This polarization carried over into the faculty senate, where faculty members narrowly voted in favor of a vote of no confidence in Mark Schlissel and the university's reopening plan, the first vote of no confidence in the university's history.[64]

Following through on legal threats, the university filed for a temporary restraining order against GEO on September 14, and union members debated next steps.[65] Operating under the incorrect assumption that an injunction would immediately bankrupt or even destroy the union, on September 16, 2020, some 1,074 GEO members voted to accept the university's second offer, 239 members voted to reject, and 66 abstained. Debate at the general membership meeting identified dissatisfaction with the university's offer but an unwillingness, or an inability, to continue striking under the threat of a pending injunction. The university's second offer secured a commitment to more robust baseline COVID testing, permission to temporarily switch to remote work if individual workers could not resolve acceptable in-person work conditions, an additional staff hire at the International Center to support international graduate students, more flexible childcare subsidies for unlicensed care given childcare facility closures, and a recommendation by Rackham Graduate School to extend funding and program timeliness across departments.[66] By January 2021 Dean Mike Solomon of the graduate school instructed departments to offer additional funding and extended time-to-degree for affected PhD cohorts.[67]

The strike's abolitionist demands were less immediately successful, although their presence in the strike resolution was precedent-setting. No funds were diverted from campus police to social services and no commitment to disarmament was made. As an alternative, the university proposed a task force to study campus safety and, unwilling to continue the strike, membership voted to accept it. From the moment its work began, however, the university curtailed the task force's mission, shoehorning its timeline into four short months and narrowing its scope from a "holistic review and assessment" of public safety to an "initial comprehensive review." The results were somewhat predictable, as Sarah Brown of the *Chronicle of Higher Education* reported: "Instead of centering the voices of Black and brown people, [the task force] ended up serving largely as a sounding board for parents of undergraduates, most of them white, who opposed scaling back the university's police presence."[68]

Not all the university's concessions toward policing and racial justice were symbolic, however. A few weeks after the strike's end, the University of Michigan canceled the U-M Ambassadors Program, moving away from policing social distancing. In October the university created the George Floyd Memorial Scholarship to support students "who have demonstrated commitment to bettering their community through social justice," hired twenty new full-time faculty members with "scholarly expertise in racial inequality and structural racism," and launched "Anti-Racism Collaborative Awards" for graduate scholarship that advanced racial justice.[69]

As an outcome of their own strike, residential advisors were able to secure personal protection equipment in the residence halls; weekly meetings between residential hall representatives and University of Michigan Housing management and two hundred dollars in Blue Bucks, the campus currency, as hazard pay. The seed planted during the 2020 COVID strike came to fruition in August 2024, when residential advisors successfully voted to unionize.

Conclusion

Despite U-M administration's warning of dire financial straits in mid-2020, the fiscal crisis was averted through tens of millions of dollars in federal CARES Act funding,[70] cuts in salaries and benefits for workers, an increase in tuition, and construction postponement.[71] U-M President Mark Schlissel's projected financial cliff turned into a financial mountain as U-M's endowment grew from $12 billion to $17 billion in the post-pandemic boom, partially fueled by government money.[72] Financially, the University of Michigan system prospered during the pandemic. This bounty, however, has not been redistributed to workers, who have struggled in the years since under-increased inflation and cost of living.

By mid-semester of fall 2020, fears of widespread COVID infection had proven correct. On October 20 the Washtenaw County Health Department issued a two-week "stay in place" order for undergraduates, citing hundreds of cases traced back to undergraduates at the University of Michigan. As the *New York Times* reported, the University of Michigan was the site of numerous COVID-19 outbreaks, many radiating out from residence halls and fraternities and sororities.[73] By Thanksgiving break the university informed students that their winter 2021 housing contracts on campus would be canceled and that they should not return to campus. With a spate of outbreaks stemming from undergraduate residencies, the administration moved most winter 2021 instruction online.

Even into January 2022, faculty and graduate workers continued to respond to the threat of COVID. When the Omicron surge led to three hundred thousand infections per day and disrupted flights and closed workplaces, faculty and graduate instructors organized a mass, unsanctioned move to online instruction for the first two weeks of the 2022 winter semester. The "e-pivot" initiative was a response to U-M administrators' refusal to delay the start of the semester, as other universities had done, or to temporarily shift online, as the local school district had done. The e-pivot open letter garnered almost two thousand signatories who either moved to online instruction or pledged to support those who did.[74] This informal boycott of in-person instruction confirmed that even into 2022, instructors were still willing to take emergency action to protect their health and the health of the community, most certainly reflecting the impact of the 2020 strike.

Internally, the 2020 strike led to increased confidence in grad workers' ability to take collective action. When the Lecturers' Employees Organization (LEO), representing non–tenure track faculty at the University of Michigan, negotiated their contract in the summer and fall of 2021, hundreds of GEO members pledged to respect the picket line should LEO members strike. Perhaps fearing another work stoppage only one year after GEO's strike, the administration conceded to major LEO demands, resulting in a historic contract win for pay parity for lecturers across all three campuses, the culmination of a long campaign waged by LEO and the tri-campus One University Campaign.[75]

Beyond concrete concessions, the 2020 strike forced the university to negotiate over "permissive" subjects it had refused to discuss throughout the previous four months. The task force on policing, which, while limited, compelled the university to discuss the issue of police violence and safety in a public manner. The effort to further public safety continued during 2023 contract negotiations, where GEO members proposed that the university fund an unarmed, non-police emergency response team. While funding was not secured, negotiations committed U-M president Santa Ono to make a statement in support of a non-police response team as part of Ann Arbor and Ypsilanti's Care-Based Safety initiative, despite the subject's "permissive" nature.[76] This demonstrates that the differentiation between "permissive" and "mandatory" bargaining subjects is a question of power, not technicalities.

Graduate workers built on the 2020 strike experience during their contract campaign in 2023. After months of fruitless time at the negotiating table, GEO members went on strike on March 29, again violating the contract's no-strike clause and the Public Employment Relations Act of 1947. Once again, the university moved to enjoin the union. This time members were prepared for the threat of an injunction and voted to defy the court ruling, intentionally taking on the risk of fines and even possible arrest of officers. In her ruling on April 10, 2023, Washtenaw County judge Carol Kuhnke denied the university's temporary restraining order and injunction, arguing that the university had failed to prove that the strike had caused "irreparable harm."[77] With that, GEO members had successfully faced down the legal threat that had terminated the 2020 strike. To date, GEO's 2023 strike is the longest in GEO's history. For six weeks, graduate student instructors struck their labor until the end of the winter semester, while contract negotiations continued until August 25, 2023, under the threat of a renewed fall strike. The strike withstood intense strike-breaking tactics by administrators, including the university's lawsuit; withheld pay for striking instructors; and even falsified or invented grades when the strike extended past the end of the grading period.[78] Ultimately, the strike secured the largest wage increases in the union's history, bringing thousands of PhD students up to a living wage, among a host of other important contract gains.[79] The strength and tenacity of the 2023 strike would not have been possible without members' 2020 strike experience.

GEO's strike contributed to the post-pandemic upsurge in higher education labor struggles. Since 2020, academic workers at New York University, Rutgers University, University of California, Temple University, Columbia University, Harvard University, and other colleges have struck, challenging the neoliberal priorities of higher education of low-wage teaching forces coupled with ballooning administrators' salaries and undergraduate tuition rates. High-paid administrators are increasingly unilateral decision makers who prioritize the logic of profit over pedagogical needs, with little to no accountability to the wider campus workplace. Organized labor—specifically, graduate worker labor—has sought to alter this power imbalance.

The strike for a "Safe and Just Campus" was an attempt to wrest power from unresponsive administrators who prioritized university profit making over employee and student well-being, evident in imposed austerity, increased tuition rates, and the insistence on an in-person semester. In a desperate attempt to influence university reopening plans, graduate workers rebelled against Michigan's anti-union laws that prohibit public employees from striking. By withholding their labor, graduate workers forced the university to change course in COVID mitigation plans and bargain over "permissive" subjects, something university administrators had previously refused to do. Perhaps most important throughout the protracted, months-long struggle, many graduate workers were transformed by the experience of fighting an employer that, despite having a Democratic-majority board of regents and liberal rhetoric of "dialogue" and "care," steamrolled workers' concerns and reverted to anti-labor legal maneuverings to break a strike. Finding no solution from above, graduate workers turned toward one another, developing a rank-and-file "culture of care" to protect the community's health and safety amid a deadly pandemic.

Notes

1. The Public Employment Relations Act became law in 1947 amid a nationwide crackdown on organized labor that included the federal Taft-Hartley Act (1947). This barrage of anti-union legislation followed the largest strike wave in US history, in 1946. See, for example, Nelson Lichtenstein, *Labor's War at Home: The CIO in World War II* (Philadelphia: Temple University Press, 2003), 238–240.

2. "COVID-19 Strike Wave Interactive Map," *PayDay Report*, 2020. https://paydayreport.com/covid-19-strike-wave-interactive-map/.

3. Kate Murphy, "Campus Workers Sue UNC System, Claiming Unsafe Working Conditions during Pandemic," *News & Observer* (Raleigh, NC), August 11, 2020, https://www.newsobserver.com/news/local/education/article244858712.html/.

4. Emma Petit, "Will Covid-19 Revive Faculty Power?" *Chronicle of Higher Education*, August 26, 2020, https://www-chronicle-com.proxy.lib.umich.edu/article/will-covid-19-revive-faculty-power/.

5. Kathleen Brown, "No Guns, No Cops, No Code: The 1980s Anti-Deputization Movement at the University of Michigan," *The Abusable Past*, August 1, 2022, https://www.radicalhistoryreview.org/abusablepast/forum-6-3-no-guns-no-cops-no-code-the-1980s-anti-deputization-movement-at-the-university-of-michigan/.

6. These "abolitionist demands," as they became called, were the most polarizing and controversial of the strike, invoking sharp parental criticism and unease by some labor locals. For a short overview, see Alejo Stark, Jasmine Ehrhardt, Amir Fleischmann, "The University of Michigan Graduate Workers Are on Strike," *Jacobin Magazine*, September 11, 2020, https://www.jacobinmag.com/2020/09/university-michigan-graduate-workers-strike/.

7. Micol Seigel's *Violence Work* (Durham, NC: Duke University Press, 2018) illuminates the relationship between policing and militarization as manifestations of state violence and reification of policing in attempting reform.

8. Craig Schwartz, Butzel Long, and the board of regents of the University of Michigan, "Motion for Temporary Restraining Order and Preliminary Injunction with Brief," September 14, 2020, https://publicaffairs.vpcomm.umich.edu/wp-content/uploads/sites/19/2020/09/Motion-for-TRO-and-PI-with-Brief.pdf/.

9. Howard Bunsis, "Full Analysis of the Financial Condition of the University of Michigan," January 2023, https://drive.google.com/file/d/13UIyNwXt4bJNo7L8VkEZYy80s8gm25UZ/view/.

10. U-M Dearborn, "Facts and Figures," 2022, https://umdearborn.edu/about-um-dearborn/facts-figures/.

11. U-M Flint, "General Student Body," 2021, https://www.umflint.edu/ia/campus-statistics/general-student-body/.

12. According to university publications, the university's investment portfolio grew in venture capital and private equity from 36 percent to 41 percent in 2021. See U-M's "Report of Investment" (2021), 6. https://www.bf.umich.edu/wp-content/uploads/2021/12/2021.ROI_.Final_.12.6.2021.pdf/.

13. David Jesse, "U-M Socks away Millions in Endowment as Families Face Rising Tuition," *Detroit Free Press*, February 4, 2021, https://www.freep.com/story/news/local/michigan/2018/02/02/u-m-socks-away-millions-endowment-families-face-rising-tuition/875225001/.

14. The One University campaign, founded in 2018 by tri-campus undergrads and lecturers, has organized for equitable funding across all three campuses for years. See Grace Jensen, "The One University Campaign," *Ecurrent.com*, July 31, 2019, https://www.ecurrent.com/feature/the-one-university-campaign/.

15. Daniel McGraw, et al., "As the Virus Deepens Financial Trouble, Colleges Turn to Layoffs," *New York Times*, July 16, 2020, https://www.nytimes.com/2020/07/16/us/coronavirus-college-faculty-layoffs.html/.

16. Mark Schlissel, "A COVID-19 Update from President Mark S. Schlissel," University of Michigan Office of the President, April 20, 2020, https://president.umich.edu/news-communications/letters-to-the-community/a-covid-19-update-from-president-mark-s-schlissel/.

17. Samuel Zwickel, "U-M Flint Cuts 41% of Lecturers, Citing Dire Financial Outlook," *Detroit Free Press*, June 22, 2020, https://www.freep.com/story/news/local/michigan/2020/06/22/um-flint-layoffs-lecturers-leo-michigan/3232929001/.

18. Steve Marowski, "Michigan Medicine Nearly Cuts Layoffs in Half; 738 Employees to Be Cut by End of June," *MLive.com*, June 19, 2020, https://www.mlive.com/news/ann-arbor/2020/06/michigan-medicine-nearly-cuts-layoffs-in-half-738-employees-to-be-cut-by-end-of-june.html/.

19. Don Jordan, "U-M Regents Approve Budget Shaped by COVID-19 Challenges," Vice President of Communications, Michigan News, University of Michigan, June 29, 2020, https://news.umich.edu/u-m-regents-approve-budget-shaped-by-covid-19-challenges/; Minutes, Board of Regents Meeting, University

of Michigan, June 25, 2020, https://regents.umich.edu/meetings/agendas/
june-25-2020/.

20. "President Schlissel, Open the Books to UM Employees," Huron Valley
Area Labor Federation Online Petition, June 2020, https://actionnetwork.org/
petitions/president-schlissel-open-the-books-to-u-m-employees?clear_id=true/.

21. Howard Bunsis, "University of Michigan Has $6.7 Billion in Unrestricted
Reserves to Spend," Report for Lecturers' Employee Organization, June 23, 2020,
https://www.youtube.com/watch?v=QX_y8hej2QM/.

22. Paul Campos makes the case for wealthy universities like the University
of Michigan to tap their endowments in order to avoid layoffs and furloughs.
Paul Campos, "Rich Colleges Can Afford to Spend More," *New York Times*,
June 6, 2020, https://www.nytimes.com/2020/06/06/opinion/sunday/colleges
-endowments-covid.html/.

23. "In Memoriam," American Federation of State, County and Municipal
Employees (AFSCME), June 2020, https://afscme.org/covid-19/in-memoriam/;
and Kristin Haas, *Being Human during COVID*, e-book (Ann Arbor: University
of Michigan Press, 2021), 7.

24. GEO COVID Caucus, "UM Grad Student COVID Letter to UM Board of
Regents, President Schlissel, Provost Collins, and Deans," Submitted with over
1,800 signatures, May 8, 2020, https://docs.google.com/document/d/e/2PACX
-1vRKrII9UAlRF_glSNLhzzeQDQ_RTb3peAoogr4xWvX_K8UxnsShwL0hLA2
MOROJI3uPpiWJnKhOKl0e/pub/.

25. University spokesperson Rick Fitzgerald, "U-M Official Reply" to COVID
Caucus, May 15, 2020, https://docs.google.com/document/u/4/d/e/2PACX-1vQh
Db7wjwk7SjtmnZP0ZjBkTHOaYjWqTMVmXEo1TbUCE26o5hBY8myVcoTz9
l3ST_CtLMYZ54IjIZX4/pub/.

26. Email from Regent Ronald Weiser to GEO president Sumeet Patwardhan,
sent May 8, 2020.

27. University spokesperson Rick Fitzgerald, "U-M Official Reply" to COVID
Caucus, May 15, 2020.

28. COVID Caucus memo, GEO, June 4, 2020.

29. "Open Letter to the University of Michigan Administration on the Fall Re-
Opening," July 28, 2020, Signed by over 1,500 individuals, https://docs.google
.com/document/u/1/d/e/2PACX-1vRZk5mbS88Bua5FNfBRi0z2fveHlVy4hWz
kMV5hgvdeU10kv_hA0RQU6IiddXWliVt1qDbepwWY0TpW/pub/.

30. "Second Open Letter on the UM Reopening," August 7, 2020, Signed
by over 700 individuals, https://docs.google.com/document/u/3/d/e/
2PACX-1vSgP6b0ccY_QX6Y3r22xA3oxeKSPoJFRchUYS_0gxEysG9tM3J-55
ZfMO5611nzJAI2ZifYTEhhsOmV/pub?urp=gmail_link/.

31. Full excerpt from the Ethics Committee's July 31 letter: "The question
now is: Given the current incomplete control of the COVID-19 pandemic in the
US and globally, would concentrating some 45,000 students in Ann Arbor from
across the US and around the world run a significant risk of not meeting this
safety standard—and is there a way of avoiding this without compromising vital
academic and social interests? Accumulating evidence now suggests there is such

a risk of creating a new 'hot spot' of viral infection within the University and the surrounding community, which would inflict considerable—in some cases grave—harm." The COVID-19 Ethics and Privacy Committee, "Update on the Current Situation and Planning for the Fall Term," July 31, 2020, https://drive .google.com/file/d/1hcO4IuY9Rck3rXFojSUydgYD8YhMdRmy/view/.

32. Luke Kudryashov, Elizabeth McLain, and Ashley Wiseman, "Letter: Concerns about Equity and Safety in Fall Reopening Plans," June 25, 2020, Endorsed by GEO Local 3550, Disability Culture @UM, and hundreds of individuals, https://docs.google.com/document/d/15UY5G86Dpc R2PK6OTRHjO_DkitnqbVuNTTIzfE4Mzn0/edit/.

33. Holly LeCraw, "The University of Michigan Community Needs a Better Testing Plan," August 20, 2020, Signed by 1,414 individuals, https://www.change .org/p/university-of-michigan-the-university-of-michigan-community-needs -more-covid-testing/.

34. Dominic Coletti, "GEO Stages 'Die-In' to Protest Fall Reopening," *Michigan Daily*, August 31, 2020, https://www.michigandaily.com/news/academics/ geo-die/.

35. Caroline Llanes, "U of M Faculty, Staff Protest over COVID-19 Testing and In-Person Instruction," Michigan Radio, August 18, 2020, https://www.michigan radio.org/education/2020-08-18/u-of-m-faculty-staff-protest-over-covid-19 -testing-and-in-person-instruction/.

36. Agenda, "Motion 2 and Motion 6," UM Faculty Senate Meeting, September 16, 2020, https://facultysenate.umich.edu/wp-content/uploads/2020/09/9-16 -20-Agenda-for-the-Faculty-Senate-Meeting-with-motions.pdf/. An additional aspect in faculty's dissatisfaction of President Mark Schlissel was his poor handling of sexual abuse and harassment at the university, including his promotion of Provost Martin Philbert, who was fired in 2020 for decades of sexual harassment involving twenty women.

37. Larry Buchanan, Quoctrung Bui, and Jugal K. Patel, "Black Lives Matter May Be the Largest Movement in U.S. History," *New York Times*, July 3, 2020, https://www.nytimes.com/interactive/2020/07/03/us/george-floyd-protests -crowd-size.html/.

38. Roshan Krishnan and Matt Sehrsweeney, "GEO Members: 'We Are Striking as an Act of Community Care'," *Strikewave.com*, September 16, 2020, https://www.thestrikewave.com/original-content/geo-striking-as-an-act-of -community-care/.

39. Policing-related demands were adopted at the August 25, 2020, General Members Meeting. "GEO'S Demands for a Safe and Just Pandemic Response for All," Graduate Employees' Organization, September 4, 2020, https://www.geo3550 .org/2020/09/04/geos-demands-for-a-safe-and-just-pandemic-response-for -all/.

40. Yalile Suriel, Grace Watkins, Jude Paul Matias Dizon, and John Joseph Sloan III, eds., *Cops on Campus: Rethinking Safety and Confronting Police Violence* (Seattle: University of Washington Press, 2024).

41. CNN Wire Staff, "California Campus Police on Leave after Pepper-Spraying,"

CNN, November 21, 2011, https://www.cnn.com/2011/11/20/us/california-occupy
-pepperspray/index.html.

42. Nathan Clark, "Protesters Charged in UM Climate Strike Trespassing Case
Plead Responsible to Civil Infraction," *Mlive.com*, December 19, 2019, https://
www.mlive.com/news/ann-arbor/2019/12/protesters-charged-in-um-climate
-strike-trespassing-case-plead-responsible-to-civil-infraction.html/.

43. Lauren Kaori Gurley, "California Police Used Military Surveillance Tech at Grad
Student Strike," *Vice.com*, May 15, 2020, https://www.vice.com/en/article/7kppna/
california-police-used-military-surveillance-tech-at-grad-student-strike/.

44. Davarian L. Baldwin's *In the Shadow of the Ivory Tower: How Universities
Are Plundering Our Cities* (New York: Bold Type Books, 2020) investigates how
campus police play a pivotal role in making areas "safe" for university real estate
investment and expansion.

45. Ann Arbor Police Department, @A2Police, "Please see the below announcement regarding our partnership with @UMich to help keep everyone safe, on and
off campus," Tweet announcing partnership with University of Michigan Ambas-
sador Program, *Twitter.com*, August 20, 2020, https://twitter.com/A2Police/
status/1296421615186710528/.

46. Black Student Union, La Casa, et al., "Op-Ed: A Call to End the Michigan Ambassadors Program," *Michigan Daily*, September 7, 2020, https://www.michigandaily
.com/section/columns/op-ed-call-end-michigan-ambassadors-program/.

47. GEO Communications Chair, "GEO Statement Following Work Stoppage
Ballot Results: Membership Authorizes Walk-Out over Pandemic and Policing
Demands," Press Release, *GEO3550.org*, September 7, 2020, https://www.geo3550
.org/2020/09/07/geo-statement-following-work-stoppage-ballot-results-
membership-authorizes-walk-out-over-pandemic-and-policing-demands/.

48. "How does police activity change over time?" *AbolitionGEO.org*, August
1, 2020, http://abolitiongeo.org/.

49. "Our Community Has Shared Responsibility," Office of Student Life, University of Michigan, 2020, https://studentlife.umich.edu/parents/article/our
-community-has-shared-responsibility%C2%A0/.

50. "Announcing a Public-Health-Informed Fall Semester for the University
of Michigan," Office of the President, University of Michigan, June 22, 2020,
https://president.umich.edu/news-communications/letters-to-the-community/
announcing-a-public-health-informed-fall-semester-for-the-university-of
-michigan/.

51. Isaiah Hole, "Jim Harbaugh, Mark Schlissel Release Statements Re: Big Ten
Return," *USAToday.com*, September 16, 2020, https://wolverineswire.usatoday
.com/2020/09/16/michigan-football-jim-harbaugh-mark-schlissel-release
-statements-re-big-ten-return/.

52. Rainer Sabin, "Michigan Athletics COVID-19 Update: 9 More Test Positive
in Last Week," *Detroit Free Press*, July 31, 2020, https://www.freep.com/story/
sports/college/university-michigan/wolverines/2020/07/31/michigan-athletics
-covid-19-update/5557342002/.

53. GEO Communications Chair, "GEO Statement Following Work Stoppage

Ballot Results: Membership Authorizes Walk-Out over Pandemic and Policing Demands."

54. Rebecca Marks (@RebeccaAMarks), "In honor of @geo3550's historic collective action and the return of @UMichFootball, an update to the @UMich fight song #StrikeForSafeCampus," Twitter.com, September 17, 2020, https://twitter.com/RebeccaAMarks/status/1306660443398778881/.

55. Francesca Duong, et al., "Resident Advisers Announce Strike in Protest of U-M COVID-19 Response," *Michigan Daily*, September 9, 2020, https://www.michigan daily.com/campus-life/resident-advisers-announce-strike/.

56. "Umich ResStaff Striking, Submit COVID-19 Related Demands to the University of Michigan," Residential Staff Press Release, September 8, 2020, https://docs.google.com/document/d/1qbd-G8mnJfbj5HXq GDOXO08A2BqgGV_GVRVMJzD0kCA/edit/.

57. Steve Marowski, "Cold Eggs, No Microwaves: University of Michigan Students in Quarantine Housing Needed Help," *MLive.com*, September 17, 2020, https://www.mlive.com/news/ann-arbor/2020/09/cold-eggs-no-microwaves -university-of-michigan-students-in-quarantine-housing-needed-help.html/.

58. GEO Communications Chair, "GEO Membership Votes to Reject Offer, Continue Work Stoppage," Press Release, *GEO3550.org*, September 9, 2020, https://www.geo3550.org/2020/09/10/geo-membership-votes -to-reject-offer-continue-work-stoppage/.

59. Craig Schwartz, Butzel Long, and the Board of Regents of the University of Michigan, "Motion for Temporary Restraining Order and Preliminary Injunction with Brief," September 14, 2020, https://publicaffairs.vpcomm.umich.edu/ wp-content/uploads/sites/19/2020/09/Motion-for-TRO-and-PI-with-Brief .pdf/.

60. Leah Graham, "University Files Unfair Labor Practice Charge against Grad Student Union," *Michigan Daily*, September 12, 2020, https://www .michigandaily.com/news/administration/university-files-unfair-labor-practice -charge-against-grad-student-union/.

61. Graham, "University Files Unfair Labor Practice Charge against Grad Student Union."

62. Leah Graham and Alex Harring, "U-M Deans Push On with Classes as Graduate Students Strike," *Michigan Daily*, September 9, 2020, https://www.michigan daily.com/news/academics/deans-emails-strike/.

63. Many parents took to public commentary at the board of regents meeting to criticize GEO's strike and the university's pivot to online teaching, claiming they weren't paying for "Khan Academy" or the "University of Phoenix," revealing how the consumerist model of higher education framed education not as a public good but as a private commodity.

64. Leah Graham and Alex Harring, "Vote of No Confidence in U-M President Mark Schlissel Passes, Official Ruling Says," *Michigan Daily*, September 18, 2020, https://www.michigandaily.com/section/academics/schliss-no-confidence/.

65. It was not until September 16, 2020, that a Washtenaw County judge decided a hearing was necessary to consider the university's request for a

temporary restraining order, setting the date for September 24. Members did not know about the hearing date when they voted to end the strike on September 16. The implication from union leadership was that a court battle would immediately threaten the union's existence, an assessment that, in hindsight, proved to be incorrect.

66. GEO Communications Chair, "GEO Ends Historic Strike; Forces Progress on COVID, Policing Demands," Press Release, *GEO3550.org*, September 16, 2020, https://www.geo3550.org/2020/09/16/geo-ends-historic-strike/; and U-M Public Affairs, "Outline of U-M Proposal to GEO," September 22, 2020, https://publicaffairs.vpcomm.umich.edu/outline-of-u-m-proposal-to-geo/.

67. Rackham Graduate School, "Graduate Programs Step Forward with Plans for Doctoral Student Completion," University of Michigan, January 22, 2021, https://rackham.umich.edu/discover-rackham/graduate-programs-step-forward-with-plans-for-doctoral-student-completion/.

68. Sarah Brown, "Was This Antiracist Task Force Set Up to Fail?" *Chronicle of Higher Education*, June 4, 2021, https://www.chronicle.com/article/was-this-antiracist-task-force-set-up-to-fail/.

69. Lauren Love, "University to Launch Several New Anti-Racism Initiatives," *University Record*, October 20, 2020, https://record.umich.edu/articles/u-m-to-launch-several-new-anti-racism-initiatives/; Rackham Graduate School, "Anti-Racism Collaborative Awards Graduate Student Summer Research Grants," University of Michigan, June 20, 2021, https://rackham.umich.edu/discover-rackham/anti-racism-collaborative-awards-graduate-student-summer-research-grants/.

70. The Ann Arbor campus received $25,244,052 under the Higher Education Emergency Relief Fund, half of which was designated for emergency grants to students, although the total reporting may be incomplete. U-M Flint received approximately $27 million in federal CARES Act funds to split between payments released to students and the institution. Flint received approximately $571,000 for CARES Act Part 3 (Strengthening Institution Program [SIP]). These amounts do not include the tens of millions of CARES Act funding received by Michigan Medicine. "CARES Act Reporting," Office of Budget and Planning, University of Michigan Ann Arbor, September 30, 2020–June 22, 2022, https://obp.umich.edu/mandatory-reporting/cares-act-reporting/; "CARES Act," COVID-19 Federal CARES Act Utilization, University of Michigan Flint, https://www.umflint.edu/covid-19/cares-act/; "HEERF Reporting," CARES Act, Office of Financial Aid and Scholarships, University of Michigan Dearborn. https://umdearborn.edu/financial-aid/consumer-information/heerf-reporting/.

71. At the June 25, 2020, board of regents meeting, Dr. David Spahlinger, president of U-M Hospitals and Health Centers and University of Michigan Medical Group, outlined that Michigan Medicine had received $136 million of federal CARES aid, offsetting a projected loss of $139 million. For FY 2021, $70 million in salary and benefit cuts, in the form of frozen salaries and halted retirement contributions, translated into a projected surplus of $44 million for the hospital system; in other words, workers paid for Michigan Medicine's surplus out of their

own pockets. By the end of 2021, Michigan Medicine showed a profit of over $340 million, far above operating surpluses in the years immediately preceding the pandemic.

72. Kim Kozlowski, "University of Michigan's Endowment Grew 41% to $17 Billion during Pandemic," *Detroit News*, October 21, 2021, https://www.detroitnews.com/story/news/local/michigan/2021/10/21/university-of-michigan-endowment-17-billion-40-percent-growth-during-pandemic/6124618001/.

73. Shawn Hubler, "After a 'Covid Semester,' the University of Michigan Gets Tougher on the Virus," *New York Times*, November 20, 2020, https://www.nytimes.com/2020/11/20/us/coronavirus-colleges-michigan.html/.

74. "Letter of Support for E-Pivot," 1,948 signatories, January 3, 2022, https://docs.google.com/document/d/1DlGb5Ex-JKABvF—5mHzVB2npPij9Hb0xggaXI3Y6n4/edit/.

75. "Bargaining Update: Parity on Pay Minimums Won," *LEO2021.org*, September 11, 2021, https://www.leo2021.org/leo-bargaining-updates-2021/leo-update-911-parity-on-minimums-won-bargaining-tomorrow/.

76. Kayla Clarke, "University of Michigan President Agrees to Support Unarmed, Non-Police Emergency Response Program," *ClickOnDetroit.com*, August 23, 2023, https://www.clickondetroit.com/all-about-ann-arbor/2023/08/23/university-of-michigan-president-agrees-to-support-unarmed-non-police-emergency-response-program/.

77. Jordyn Pair, "University of Michigan Grad Union Strike Can Continue, Judge Rules," *MLive.com*, April 10, 2023, https://www.mlive.com/news/ann-arbor/2023/04/university-of-michigan-grad-union-strike-can-continue-judge-rules.html/.

78. Kathleen Brown, "GEO vs. the University of Michigan," September–October 2023, *Against the Current*, https://againstthecurrent.org/atc226/geo-vs-the-university-of-michigan/.

79. Riley Hodder, "GEO Accepts UMich Contract Offer, Ends Five-Month Strike," *Michigan Daily*, August 25, 2023, https://www.michigandaily.com/news/geo-accepts-umich-contract-offer-ends-five-month-strike/.

7

Disability Justice and the Education Labor Movement during the COVID-19 Pandemic

KATHRYN M. MEYER

> I want to say unequivocally that disabled people are everywhere. We are one of the largest oppressed groups on the planet. We are part of political movements, even if you don't know or don't acknowledge that we are. No matter what community you're working with, you are working with disabled people. (And given how violent and polluted our world is, those numbers will only continue to grow.)
>
> —Mia Mingus

In March 2020, no longer able to ignore or evade the COVID-19 pandemic that touched all corners of the globe, public schools in Massachusetts made the difficult decision to close.[1] Despite many education leaders' initial optimism that schools would return to in-person learning in a matter of weeks, COVID-19 would soon become a mass disabling event, effectively closing schools for the remainder of the academic year.[2] In fact, by May 2022—just over two years since the country's first confirmed COVID case—the United States had the highest number of COVID-19 deaths compared to any other wealthy nation.[3] Moreover, the deadly impact of COVID in the United States cannot be decontextualized from disabled, chronically ill, and immunocompromised people's experiences. While the Centers for Disease Control and Prevention reports that one in four people have a disability,[4] the number of disabled people is growing and will likely continue to grow with the prevalence of long COVID.[5] Therefore, this pandemic must be analyzed from a lens that centers on the disproportionate impact it has had on disabled people.

In this study I have focused on how schools responded to the pandemic because of their centrality in communities. Though schools are primarily sites of learning, they also provide essential material goods and services, such as special education services and recreational opportunities, which are often difficult to obtain through means-tested and bureaucratic social programs.[6] Yet, schools also reproduce and maintain capitalist culture and norms. Providing meals, childcare, mental health services, special education, and recreation, schools can enrich families' and communities' lives. At the same time, their provisioning of these services makes schools critical to ensuring that our economy runs the way it was intended in both the short and long term. Proximally, with children in school, families can go to work, do their job, and thus secure profits for their employers. Distally speaking, children go to school and then enter the workforce, thus maintaining a capitalist economic order where the many (workers) work for the few (owners).[7] The COVID-19 pandemic, however, not only disrupted the capitalist order but also amplified dark truths about the deep inequities in the US public education system.[8] Since public education's early days, educators, students, and families have been forced to navigate economic austerity that has resulted in underfunded schools, poorly ventilated and neglected facilities, large class sizes, and limited resources.[9]

Disastrous events, however, can be a mobilizing force.[10] For those with power and privilege, these events can raise their consciousness to injustices and harms that they previously evaded. In other words, while our public school systems' deep inequities might have been new to many who are white, wealthy, and nondisabled, these inequities were overly familiar for many disabled and multiply marginalized people.[11] Nonetheless, as their interests converged, education workers, students, and families across the country collectively asserted that schools were no longer safe during a global pandemic and, moreover, that allowing schools to operate as usual would have disastrous implications for the health, safety, and well-being of entire communities.

Historically, teachers unions have amplified the need for improved school facilities, smaller class sizes, and increased resources. Fed up with having to do more with less, unions' fight for improved working and learning conditions has surged in the last ten years. Moving beyond "bread-and-butter issues" like salaries and benefits, many of these campaigns have organized for racial and economic justice. The Chicago Teachers Union's campaign for the Schools Chicago's Students Deserve is a powerful example of teachers unions linking working and learning conditions with racial justice and equity for students, including those with disabilities. Their fight included enacting a more holistic education, expanding wraparound services, addressing segregation, and meeting the needs of multilingual and disabled students.[12] As extant literature shows, unions can be powerful levers for change when they engage in organizing that is rooted in community solidarity, rank-and-file democracy, and worker power. As we move forward in a pandemic that has magnified and exacerbated the deep inequities that continue to be reproduced along lines of race, class, and ability, it is critical to think about how the labor movement can dismantle ableism in schools and organize for justice-centered working and learning conditions for people with disabilities.

The pandemic's disproportionate impact on disabled and multiply marginalized workers has brought to the surface a need to examine how unions are fighting for their needs and those of disabled students, particularly in communities that are highly stratified across race, class, and disability. Therefore, using disability rights and disability justice as anchors for my analysis,[13] I examined how the Boston Teachers Union (BTU) responded to the needs of disabled workers, students, and their families during the first two years of the pandemic.

Analytic Anchors:
Disability Rights and Disability Justice

DISABILITY RIGHTS

Disabled people have fought for their rights to community inclusion, education, and a dignified life for as long as humans have been on this earth. That said, within a US context, the modern disability rights movement is often defined by the organizing and activism of disabled people and allies fighting for the passage and enforcement of Section 504 of the Rehabilitation Act of 1973, a law that prohibited federal and federally funded organizations, agencies, and institutions from discriminating on the basis of disability.[14] By providing legal protections, people with disabilities now had clear pathways to use the court system when their rights were being violated. Since the passage of the Rehabilitation Act of 1973, a series of other critically important laws protecting disabled people have passed, including the Education for All Handicapped Children Act in 1975 (later renamed the Individuals with Disabilities Education Act) and the Americans with Disabilities Act (ADA) in 1990. Together, these laws enshrined civil rights for people with disabilities.

Although codifying legal and civil rights for disabled people is essential, it is also necessary to consider how racism and ableism are embedded into all aspects of US life, including our court system.[15] More specifically, our court system privileges those who are closer to white, straight, cis, nondisabled, and wealthy markers, marginalizing those who deviate from them. As such, many Black, brown, and queer people with disabilities have organized outside of the legal system, building a movement that does not rely on an apparatus built by and for white, nondisabled, cis-hetero men.[16]

DISABILITY JUSTICE

Disability justice activists, through grassroots organizing and collective solidarity, fight for the liberation of all oppressed people. Sins Invalid, which identifies itself as "a disability justice based performance project that incubates and celebrates artists with disabilities," has identified ten principles that frame the disability justice movement (see table 7.1).[17] Together, these ten principles resist viewing disability as a single issue and instead embrace the wholeness and multiple identities of disabled people.

Table 7.1 Sins Invalid's Disability Justice Principles

Principle	Definition
Intersectionality	Founded by Black feminists, intersectionality examines how people are privileged, marginalized, and/or excluded, based on their positioning at the intersections of multiple axes of oppression.[A]
Leadership of the most impacted	Leaders should include those living at the nexus of systemic and structural oppressions.
Anti-capitalist politics	The resistance of practices that privilege productivity, efficiency, and ableist conceptions of normalcy.
Cross-movement solidarity	Partnership and coalition-building with other justice movements (e.g., racial justice and reproductive justice) while also pushing other movements to include anti-ableism in their work. This includes pushing white disability movements to fight against racism and ableism.
Recognizing wholeness	Disabled people have worthy experiences, histories, perspectives, insights, and feelings.
Sustainability	Disability justice is a long-term movement: "deep, slow, transformative, unstoppable wave of justice and liberation."[B]
Commitment to cross-disability solidarity	Disability is an expansive umbrella that includes people with physical, intellectual, and mental health disabilities, and those who are neurodivergent, chronically ill, D/deaf, blind, and more.
Interdependence	The commitment to work together to meet each other's needs.
Collective access	Everyone has access needs, and they can be communicated creatively and flexibly.
Collective liberation	Justice and liberation must include all oppressed people.

A. Kimberle Crenshaw, "Mapping the Margins: Identity Politics, Intersectionality, and Violence against Women," *Stanford Law Review* 43, no. 6 (1991): 1241–1299, https://doi.org/10.2307/1229039/.

B. Sins Invalid, *Skin, Tooth, and Bone: The Basis of Movement Is Our People*, 2nd ed. (Berkeley, CA: Sins Invalid, 2019), 25.

Procedures for Analysis

I searched for articles from March 2020 to March 2022 that covered BTU demands that protected disabled workers, students, and their families during the first two years of the COVID-19 pandemic. I chose to focus on the *Boston Globe* as my primary search source because it is the most-read newspaper in Massachusetts. I excluded opinion pieces and editorials, instead focusing on what the BTU demanded to protect their members, students, and families. Articles that reported actions, organizing, and advocacy from the BTU were included. After completing my search in the *Boston Globe*, I searched Google News for any demands that were not covered by the *Globe*. This resulted in finding two additional articles. One article covered a lawsuit filed by the BTU, and the second covered how BTU nurses responded to COVID testing failures.[18] The BTU actions were first descriptively and then critically examined to understand how their demands might align with disability rights or disability justice principles.

Results

This analysis demonstrates how the pandemic catalyzed the BTU to address issues that have long impacted disabled and multiply marginalized communities. More specifically, the BTU centered on these issues because they were no longer unique to those with disabilities and other marginalized identities. A strong example of interest convergence,[19] the BTU fought for protections that now overlapped with the needs of those from dominant and privileged identities (Finding 1). With converging interests, the BTU amplified the wholeness and humanity of workers, students, and families (Finding 2) and used legal frameworks (i.e., rights-based and legislative strategies) to meet the needs of disabled workers (Finding 3). Finally, this analysis also illustrates how the BTU worked outside of legal frameworks and aligned with grassroots approaches within the labor movement (e.g., rallies [Finding 4]).

Finding 1: The BTU's Demands Are a Form of Interest Convergence

The BTU was a central voice in pushing back on an insufficient state response to reopening schools. Yet, we cannot understand how the BTU protected disabled workers, students, and families without understanding nondisabled interest convergence.[20] More specifically, nondisabled people advocated for policies, measures, and practices that protected disabled people because doing so aligned with needs and interests of nondisabled people. For example, the BTU fought for high-quality ventilation and updated facilities through collective bargaining: "Teachers' struggles during the pandemic sharpened the focus on facilities. 'We knew what the issues were before that,' she [BTU president Jessica Tang] said, 'but the pandemic underscored the importance of deferred maintenance, which did inhibit efforts to get our students back into buildings more quickly.'"[21] While addressing poor air quality and ventilation has been a critical mitigation effort throughout the pandemic, it is also a long-standing climate justice issue that has disproportionately harmed Black and brown communities.[22] The pandemic surfaced this need, not because it was new but because it impacted many white and nondisabled people for the first time.

Two principles of disability justice are sustainability and anti-capitalist politics. Asserting that human worth is not defined by capital or profits, both principles call for communities to resist focusing on urgency and productivity, which further disables and harms everyone.[23] During fall 2020, when state leaders were pushing for schools to reopen, the BTU did not give in to a false sense of urgency to begin the school year during a deadly pandemic. Instead, the BTU pushed for slowing down as a means of ensuring that families, students, and workers were all fully equipped and supported to completely enact meaningful learning for students.[24] *Boston Globe* staffer Bianca Vázquez Toness reported:

> The union, along with two statewide teachers' unions, has called for devoting more time to professional development, learning health protocols, and planning. "The typical district professional development allotment at the start of the school year is wholly inadequate in the context of our current crisis," reads the proposal from the Boston Teachers' Union, Massachusetts Teachers' Association, and American Federation of Teachers Massachusetts.
>
> The union also wants time to meet with parents and students one-on-one before heading back to the classroom to prepare them for the new rules of social distancing and wearing masks and [to] check whether students need computers. Only after these two phases, should educators begin teaching.[25]

The BTU's emphasis on slowing down aligns with both sustainability and anti-capitalism. Again, we see the BTU responding to long-standing needs identified by disability justice organizers and framing it as a pandemic-specific issue when it is, in fact, something endemic to schools and society.

Finding 2: Humanizing Workers, Students, and Families and Their Right to Self-Determination

DEMANDING TEACHERS HAVE A SEAT AT THE TABLE

Throughout school closures, the BTU demanded worker autonomy and self-determination when deciding when to return to in-person schooling. Felicia Gans reported on how the BTU believed that a collaborative reopening plan "minimizes safety risk for students, educators, and community."[26] In their rejection, not only did they indicate the belief that including teachers' voices was essential in reopening but that their inclusion would protect students and community members—not just teachers. This is a powerful example of the BTU putting the idea that "teachers' working conditions are students' learning conditions" into practice.[27] In other words, the BTU was not just rejecting a reopening to meet their workforce's needs, but they were also rejecting it as a demonstration of care and solidarity with students they teach and the communities in which they work.

BTU members also emphasized how including teachers' voices and perspectives is more than just "good practice" or "the right thing to do." In fact, those most impacted by school closures can add wisdom and insights that are critical in any plan focused on a return to in-person learning. High school educator Matt Ruggiero told a *Boston Globe* reporter about how his classroom did not have a window, saying, "I'm deeply concerned that we're working from a [reopening schools] draft removed from the experience of people who work in school buildings."[28] Ruggiero was raising the importance of making sure those who are most affected by reopening (i.e., workers) were included in its planning. By sharing that his classroom lacks a window, he is also illustrating the important insights and understanding that teachers bring to the table about their school contexts.

The BTU's commitment to ensuring that teachers are meaningfully included in decision making, however, is complicated by the fact that the K–12 teacher workforce remains overwhelmingly white and nondisabled.[29] As such, it is important not to mistake the BTU's call for teachers to have a say in how and when schools reopen with disability justice's principle of including leadership of the most impacted. The founders of the disability justice movement were focusing on those at the center of interlocking oppressions (e.g., disabled people of color).[30] Therefore, with a teacher workforce that is predominantly white, cis, and nondisabled, Ruggiero's call to action—to include teachers in reopening plans—cannot fully align with disability justice. For the union's reopening demands to be more aligned with disability justice, more information is needed to understand how the BTU looked beyond professional identities and considered how those who are multiply marginalized across race, ethnicity, disability, and other minoritized identities are meaningfully included in the district's plans.

CENTERING AND AMPLIFYING TEACHERS' MULTIPLE IDENTITIES

Several articles, however, covered how the BTU made demands that centered members' broader lives, needs, and sociocultural identities. In a survey conducted before the 2020 school year, the BTU found that two-thirds of respondents were either at risk for serious COVID-19 or lived with someone who was.[31] More specifically, their results demonstrated that teachers are just as likely to be vulnerable to COVID-19 or live with someone who is. In the BTU leadership's response to Governor Charlie Baker's accusation that teachers were selfishly taking vaccines from other high-risk and vulnerable people, they amplified the fact that teachers' identities extend beyond their role as educators and workers. Presidents from the BTU, the American Federation of Teachers Massachusetts, the Massachusetts Teachers Association, and the Massachusetts American Federation of Labor and Congress of Industrial Organizations (AFL-CIO) released a statement condemning Baker's narrative:

> It is sad and, frankly, reckless that on the one-year anniversary of the COVID-19 pandemic shutting down our state, Governor Charlie Baker is pitting one vulnerable group against another. . . . The Baker administration's weaponization of the fact that most educators are under the age of 65 distorts several realities, including the presence of underlying health conditions. It ignores the fact that many educators live with and take care of sick or elderly family members, and worry about bringing the virus home with them.[32]

This quotation demonstrates how the BTU's leaders resisted attempts to reduce members down to a single identity. Through calling out Governor Baker's false narrative, the BTU's response makes clear the danger in failing to acknowledge the lived experiences of teachers, many of whom are disabled and chronically ill themselves or living with family members who are. Moreover, they also positioned this danger as one to not take lightly. Calling Baker's statements about teachers "reckless," they bring to light the significant health consequences of his words as they remind those reading their statement about the high risk that teachers carry of contracting COVID-19 and potentially transmitting it to others in their homes.

The disability justice movement is committed to recognizing the wholeness of every disabled person. Importantly, their experiences, needs, perspectives, and histories are considered and centered even when it might be at odds with societal pressures to produce and maintain the status quo.[33] In many ways the BTU committed to recognizing and honoring the wholeness of their members even when it meant going against powerful political leaders who were steadfast on moving forward without considering the needs and lived realities of the teacher workforce. There was also evidence that the BTU was demonstrating a commitment to collective access and liberation. Pushing back on a vaccine rollout that excluded disabled and immunocompromised people under the age of sixty-five, the BTU insisted that until educators, particularly those in households at high risk for serious COVID-19, were included, the public health and safety of those in the Boston school community would be in jeopardy.[34]

Centering the multiple identities of their members, particularly those who are racially marginalized, also shaped how the BTU responded to vaccine mandates. More specifically, they did not shy away from looking at how vaccine mandates intersected with race and the importance of maintaining and supporting a racially diverse workforce. In a January 2022 membership vote with 84 percent in favor, the BTU reached an agreement with Boston mayor Michelle Wu, allowing members who were unvaccinated to continue to report to work if transmission rates were low and if they met requirements to get tested for COVID-19 twice per week. During higher transmission periods, unvaccinated members were barred from entering their workplaces. BTU president Jessica Tang told reporters that this agreement was critical to maintaining a diverse teacher workforce, whereas enforcing a vaccine mandate could lead to the disproportionate dismissal of Black and Latine/x educators. Citing the Tuskegee syphilis experiment, the *Boston Globe* explained how violent racism in our medical system has led to distrust and apprehension for many people of color.[35]

Disability justice activists have also highlighted how mandates can be misaligned with disability justice. Citing long histories of medical trauma and surveillance, Mia Mingus advocates for collective care and solidarity: taking care of one another so that everyone gets what they need to feel safe and protected.[36] This could include, for example, providing safe spaces for workers to learn about vaccines from people they trust who share their sociocultural identities in their own communities. Tang also recognizes the limitations of a mandate that would result in an even whiter workforce, raising important questions about whether disability justice can be achieved without building trust and solidarity during a pandemic when educators of color are disproportionately harmed by vaccine enforcement.

Finding 3: Demanding BPS Uphold the Legal Rights of Disabled Members

In February 2022 the BTU filed a federal lawsuit against Boston Public Schools (BPS) for violating the ADA. In their suit, the union alleges that BPS ignored and discouraged accommodation requests for those who were at high risk for COVID-19. In other instances, members "received conflicting information."[37] The BTU, more specifically, cited cases where members with chronic illnesses and disabilities were denied accommodations and forced to take unpaid leave. Other members who were denied requests returned to work and experienced serious health consequences. For example, Arianna

MacNeill reported that a paraprofessional with hypertension and diabetes contracted COVID-19 upon returning to work and was out for one month as she recovered.

The BTU's lawsuit for violating the ADA was an act of solidarity with disabled workers and, importantly, centered those most affected by the pandemic. In this case, the BTU demanded that Boston schools comply with the ADA, calling out administration when they violated the rights of disabled workers. This is important because unions have their own internal grievance policies, which every worker can use when navigating an employer's contract violations. By choosing to report an ADA violation with the Equal Employment Opportunity Commission, the BTU leadership is looking beyond contract agreements and violations while advocating for the civil rights of its disabled members.

Although this study has mainly focused on the BTU's demands, given the differences between disability rights and disability justice, it is important to consider what it means to use litigation as a means for change. Relying on the courts to protect disabled people is firmly situated within a rights-based approach. Distinct from disability justice, securing protections for BTU members using legal frameworks places trust in the court system to uphold the civil rights of people with disabilities. Moreover, relying solely on government infrastructure is insufficient because disabled people, particularly those who are multiply marginalized, have not been able to depend on the law or government policy to protect them.[38] Therefore, protecting people and communities with disabilities also requires practicing community and collective solidarity outside of state apparatuses (e.g., the court system).[39] With a focus on community interdependence and collective liberation, disability justice operates outside of legal institutions that have failed to uphold the rights of those marginalized across race, class, ethnicity, gender, sexuality, religion, and more. In short, while the BTU has leveraged the law to advocate for the rights of disabled workers, disability justice animates a both/and approach to organizing that integrates government intervention with community and grassroots responses. In the following section, I will discuss how the BTU also enacted approaches centered on grassroots and community organizing.

Finding 4: The BTU Moves beyond Litigation and Union-Management Collaboration

Throughout school closures and the return to in-person learning, there were times when the BTU engaged in direct actions that deviated from the legal strategies I previously discussed. This is best illustrated by the BTU's pushing back on BPS administration's plan to return to in-person learning for eligible students with disabilities and disability labels. While the BTU was never in disagreement about prioritizing those who needed in-person instruction, they advocated for a return that concentrated on the safety and health of workers, students, and their families.[40]

To ensure their voices were heard, the BTU participated in rallies and protests that advocated for increasing safety and mitigation efforts for students and staff returning to in-person learning. For example, in August 2020 the BTU co-sponsored a protest with other community groups that were also concerned about reopening schools during a deadly pandemic. The BTU and their community partners rallied for assurances that would prioritize a safe return for educators and students. During the rally, BTU member Becca MacLean identified a need for the district to follow through on their promise to provide enhanced ventilation systems and for universal access to clean water and soap.[41] Advocating for the safety of students and staff continued with another rally organized by the BTU and other community organizations, including the Black Boston COVID-19 Coalition, BPS Families 4 COVID Safety, and the Boston Education Justice Alliance. Gathering outside the Massachusetts State House in December 2021, they called for robust contact tracing, improved ventilation systems, and higher vaccination rates at all schools.[42] More specifically, they spoke out against policies that protest organizers believed disproportionately impacted students of color, students with disabilities, and multilingual learners. These rallies and protests were happening at the same time the BTU was demanding to be meaningfully included in the development of the district's reopening plans. The BTU's willingness to embrace a both/and approach to institutional and grassroots strategies suggests they recognize the limitations of relying solely on legal, state, and institutional apparatuses.

The BTU's both/and approach to protecting workers and students did not just extend to rallies and protests. When CIC Health—a private agency hired to pool-test students—struggled to fulfill their obligations, Avery Bleichfeld reported that BTU nurses tested students themselves. One nurse said, "Of course, I wanted to test them right away because I do not want to expose more kids to somebody that is positive, maybe, in that pool, in the classroom. . . . So I went ahead and had to close my office to see regular incoming students, and I went out to test 19 students—two different pools—and I tested one that was positive."[43] While this placed extra labor and pressure on nurses, it also illustrates their refusal to wait for BPS central offices, the city, or the state to manage student testing challenges. Instead, BTU nurses took matters into their own hands when they felt that the health and safety of their community was at stake. Further, BTU members acted outside of a standing agreement and went beyond their job responsibilities to protect the school community when the plan in place failed to live up to its promise.

Discussion

The COVID-19 pandemic has illuminated many endemic inequities and injustices that are not new to disabled and multiply marginalized people.[44] Instead, those who can claim more privileged identities are becoming more aware of how our education system sustains practices that harm those who are marginalized across race, class, and ability. Further, since unions are made up of and run by educators—most of whom are white, cis, and nondisabled—they are not exempt from this pre-pandemic evasion.[45] In this study, I examined how one large union, the BTU, navigated a deadly pandemic that has disproportionately impacted those who are disabled and multiply marginalized. The findings can be interpreted as both promising and a call for further action.

First, the BTU pushed back on a district response that they found to be inadequate, especially given how deadly COVID-19 is and how many schools lacked the proper ventilation and infrastructure to protect workers and students from infection. Aligning with disability justice organizers' approaches,[46] the BTU did not wait for existing systems and institutions to reduce the threat of COVID-19 but, rather, chose to proactively fight for expanded protections for their workers. This is best demonstrated in the BTU's use of litigation to defend disabled members who were not provided the accommodations to which they were entitled under the ADA.[47]

Yet, Sins Invalid's principles for disability justice assert that relying solely on legal strategies and rights-based approaches is insufficient because it narrowly centers those with privileged identities who can benefit most from the US legal frameworks (e.g., white, nondisabled, cis men). Moreover, to be protected by the ADA, one needs to be able to navigate a system that requires not just disclosing disability but also obtaining an official diagnosis from a medical professional. This process is not just expensive and time-consuming, but it also privileges those who are white. Disabled people of color experience serious medical racism and ableism, making it difficult to obtain the medical documentation often required to be eligible for ADA protection.[48] As such, there are significant limitations to using a litigation strategy that often excludes disabled people of color.

Instead of relying on strategies that emphasize working within an existing institutional or legal system, the disability justice movement provides alternatives that are firmly established in collective solidarity and addressing root causes of oppression.[49] The BTU has shown some examples of this type of solidarity: nurses tested students for COVID-19 when the contracted testing agency failed to do so; they also organized a rally for safer working and learning conditions.[50] Neither strategy relied on the state; the BTU took matters into their own hands. Setting the stage for more expansive work that strives to protect disabled members, the BTU is well positioned to continue to animate the principles of disability justice, and there is no better time to do so. In fact, there have been increasing calls for the labor movement to center disability justice more intentionally in their organizing.[51] More specifically, *Labor Notes*, an organizing hub for rank-and-file union members, has recently partnered with People's Hub, an online training school rooted in justice and transformative movements, to build intentional bridges between labor and disability justice.[52] In sum, the BTU's work and the increasing intersection between disability and labor justice has the potential to transform how unions organize around issues directly impacting workers with disabilities.

Limitations

This study focused on how the BTU responded to the safety and health needs of disabled workers and students during the pandemic. However, the data set did not allow me to deeply explore how the union navigated tensions between the health and safety of the BPS community and the reality that many students with disabilities rely on schools for necessary services and supports. The BTU strongly advocated for the reopening of schools with strong infrastructure that would protect teachers, students, and families from infection, often reminding the larger community that they were not against in-person learning. Despite this, little is publicly known beyond the statements they provided to the press. Building on emerging research and investigative journalism,[53] there is a need for further work that analyzes how unions navigated this tension, especially those committed to dismantling systems of oppression.

This study critically examined how the BTU responded to the safety of workers and students during the COVID-19 pandemic. Documents gathered were all public-facing and accessed through the *Boston Globe* search feature. These findings speak specifically to the messages the BTU sent to the greater public about how they navigated a complex global public health crisis. As such, they do not necessarily give us a window into the decision-making process about their strategies and approaches.

Conclusion

As this analysis illustrates, disabled workers in public education have had to navigate their own health and safety at a time when federal, state, and local officials dismissed or ignored their needs. The BTU is a case study of how the labor movement can center on the needs of disabled members. While this study shows one union's promising commitment to protecting those most vulnerable to COVID-19, it reveals an opportunity for the larger labor movement to be in solidarity with disabled workers and community members. In the words of disabled activist, writer, and creator Alice Wong, "If there's anything to come out of this pandemic, I hope that people realize that, for many of us, we have always been here, we have always survived. And, in many cases we have the solutions."[54]

Notes

Epigraph from Mia Mingus, "Access Intimacy, Interdependence, and Disability Justice," *Leaving Evidence*, April 12, 2017, https://leavingevidence.wordpress.com/2017/04/12/access-intimacy-interdependence-and-disability-justice.

1. Felice Belman and John Hilliard, "Community Spread of Coronavirus Seen in 7 Mass. Counties; Baker Closes Schools, Restricts Restaurants, Bans Gatherings over 25," *Boston Globe*, March 15, 2020, https://www.bostonglobe.com/2020/03/15/nation/baker-closes-all-mass-schools-announces-restaurant-restrictions-bans-gatherings-over-25-people/.

2. Ainslie Cromar, "Charlie Baker Orders Schools to Stay Closed for the Rest of the Academic Year," *Boston.com*, April 21, 2020, https://www.boston.com/news/coronavirus/2020/04/21/massachusetts-schools-closed-coronavirus/.

3. Benjamin Mueller and Eleanor Lutz, "U.S. Has Far Higher Covid Death Rate Than Other Wealthy Countries," *New York Times*, February 1, 2022, https://www.nytimes.com/interactive/2022/02/01/science/covid-deaths-united-states.html/.

4. CDC, "1 in 4 US Adults Live with a Disability," *CDC Newsroom*, August 16, 2018, https://www.cdc.gov/media/releases/2018/p0816-disability.html/.

5. Lily Roberts, Rose Khattar, and Mia Ives-Rublee, "COVID-19 Likely Resulted in 1.2 Million More Disabled People by the End of 2021—Workplaces and Policy Will Need to Adapt," February 9, 2022, *Center for American Progress*, https://www.americanprogress.org/article/covid-19-likely-resulted-in-1-2-million-more-disabled-people-by-the-end-of-2021-workplaces-and-policy-will-need-to-adapt/.

6. Tina L. Cheng, Margaret Moon, and Michael Artman, "Shoring Up the Safety Net for Children in the COVID-19 Pandemic," *Pediatric Research* 88, no. 3 (2020): 349–351, https://doi.org/10.1038/s41390-020-1071-7/.

7. Jean Anyon, "Social Class and School Knowledge," *Curriculum Inquiry* 11, no 1 (1981): 3–42, https://doi.org/10.1080/03626784.1981.11075236.

8. Keeanga-Yamahtta Taylor, "Who's Left Out of the Learning-Loss Debate," *New Yorker*, October 17, 2022, https://www.newyorker.com/news/essay/whos-left-out-of-the-learning-loss-debate/.

9. Marjorie Murphy, *Blackboard Unions: The AFT and the NEA, 1900–1980* (Ithaca: Cornell University Press, 1992), 7–12.

10. Jane McAlevey, *No Shortcuts: Organizing for Power in the New Gilded Age* (New York: Oxford University Press), 111.

11. Mia Mingus, "You Are Not Entitled to Our Deaths: COVID, Abled Supremacy & Interdependence," *Leaving Evidence*, January 2016, 2022, https://leavingevidence

.wordpress.com/2022/01/16/you-are-not-entitled-to-our-deaths-covid-abled -supremacy-interdependence/.

12. McAlevey, *No Shortcuts*, 149.

13. Sins Invalid, *Skin, Tooth, and Bone: The Basis of Movement Is Our People*, 2nd ed., (Berkeley, CA: Sins Invalid, 2019).

14. Sami Schalk, *Black Disability Politics* (Durham, NC: Duke University Press, 2022), 28.

15. Subini Ancy Annamma, David Connor, and Beth Ferri, "Dis/Ability Critical Race Studies (Discrit): Theorizing at the Intersections of Race and Dis/Ability," *Race Ethnicity & Education* 16, no. 1 (2013): 1–31, https://doi.org/10.1080/136133 24.2012.730511/.

16. Sins Invalid, *Skin, Tooth, and Bone*, 10–20.

17. Sins Invalid, *Skin, Tooth, and Bone*, 22–27. Also see Sins Invalid website, "About Us," https://www.sinsinvalid.org/about-us/.

18. Arianna MacNeill, "Boston Teachers Union Sues District over Accommo-dations during Pandemic," *Boston.com*, February 9, 2022, https://www.boston. com/?post_type=post&p=24258989; Avery Blechfeld, "Mass Schools Face COVID Test Delays," *Bay State Banner* (Boston, MA), October 6, 2021, https://www .baystatebanner.com/2021/10/06/mass-schools-face-covid-test-delays/.

19. Derrick A. Bell Jr., "*Brown v. Board of Education* and the Interest Con-vergence Dilemma," *Harvard Law Review* 93, no. 3 (January 1980): 518–533; Annamma et al., "Dis/Ability Critical Race Studies," 17.

20. Bell, "*Brown v. Board of Education*"; Annamma et al., "Dis/Ability Critical Race Studies," 17.

21. Jenna Russell, "After a Year of Tensions with District Leaders, Boston Teach-ers Propose New Contract to Improve Working Conditions," *Boston Globe*, July 20, 2021, https://www.bostonglobe.com/2021/07/20/metro/after-year-tensions -with-district-leaders-boston-teachers-propose-new-contract-improve-working -conditions/.

22. Aspen Institute, *K12 Climate Action Plan*, 2021, https://www.thisisplaneted .org/img/K12-ClimateActionPlan-Complete-Screen.pdf/.

23. Talila "TL" Lewis, Working Definition of Ableism—January 2022 Update, *TL's Blog*, January 1, 2022, https://www.talilalewis.com/blog; Sins Invalid, *Skin, Tooth, and Bone*.

24. Katie Lannan, "Groups Urge Cancellation of Spring MCAS," *Boston Globe*, February 18, 2021, https://www.bostonglobe.com/2021/02/18/metro/ groups-urge-cancellation-spring-mcas/; James Vaznis, "For Many Mas-sachusetts Districts, School Year Might Start 2 Weeks Late," *Boston Globe*, July 27, 2020, https://www.bostonglobe.com/2020/07/27/metro/ many-massachusetts-districts-school-year-might-start-2-weeks-late/.

25. Bianca Vázquez Toness, "Boston Schools Tentatively Plan 'Hybrid' Approach for Fall," *Boston Globe*, July 22, 2020, https://www.bostonglobe .com/2020/07/22/metro/boston-tentatively-plans-hybrid-approach-fall/.

26. Felicia Gans, "Boston Delays Next Phase of In-Person School as Coro-navirus Positivity Rate Rises to 4.1 Percent," *Boston Globe*, October 7, 2020,

https://www.bostonglobe.com/2020/10/07/metro/boston-delays-next-phase
-in-person-school-coronavirus-positivity-rate-rises-41-percent/.

27. Eric Hirsch, Scott Emerick, Keri Church, and Ed Fuller, "Teacher Working Conditions Are Student Learning Conditions: A Report on the 2006 North Carolina Teacher Working Conditions Survey," Center for Teaching Quality, 2007, https://files.eric.ed.gov/fulltext/ED498770.pdf/.

28. Toness, "Boston Schools Tentatively Plan 'Hybrid' Approach for Fall."

29. Elizabeth Kozleski and William Proffitt, "A Journey toward Equity and Diversity in the Educator Workforce," *Teacher Education & Special Education* 43, no. 1 (2020): 63–84, https://doi.org/10.1177/0888406419882671/; Carlyn Mueller, "'I Didn't Know People with Disabilities Could Grow Up to Be Adults': Disability History, Curriculum, and Identity in Special Education," *Teacher Education and Special Education* 44, no. 3 (2021): 189–205, https://doi
.org/10.1177/0888406421996069/.

30. Sins Invalid, *Skin, Tooth, and Bone*, 10–20.

31. James Vaznis, "All Boston Public Schools to Start School Year Remotely," *Boston Globe*, August 21, 2020, https://www.bostonglobe.com/2020/08/21/metro/
all-boston-public-schools-start-school-year-remotely/.

32. Boston Globe, "Read the Full Statements from the Baker Administration and Teachers Unions," March 11, 2021, https://www.bostonglobe.com/2021/03/11/
metro/do-math-read-full-statement-baker-administration-criticizing-teachers
-vaccination-proposal/.

33. Sins Invalid, *Skin, Tooth, and Bone*, 10–20.

34. *Boston Globe*, "Read the Full Statements from the Baker Administration and Teachers Unions"; Adam Vaccaro, "Baker, Teachers Unions Trade Barbs as Educators Seek Quicker Vaccines or Delay to Full School Openings," *Boston Globe*, March 11, 2021, https://www.bostonglobe.com/2021/03/11/nation/stinging
-rebuke-baker-administration-denies-teachers-request-that-they-receive
-vaccinations-their-schools/.

35. Naomi Martin, "Mostly Educators of Color Could Face Termination Due to Vaccine Mandate, Boston Teachers Union Says," *Boston Globe*, January 26, 2022, https://www.bostonglobe.com/2022/01/26/metro/mostly-educators-color
-could-face-termination-due-vaccine-mandate-boston-teachers-union-says/.

36. Mingus, "You Are Not Entitled to Our Deaths."

37. MacNeill, "Boston Teachers Union Sues District over Accommodations."

38. Schalk, *Black Disability Politics*, 7.

39. Mingus, "You Are Not Entitled to Our Deaths."

40. Toness, "Boston Schools Tentatively Plan 'Hybrid' Approach for Fall"; Naomi Martin and James Vazniz, "Boston to Reopen 28 Schools for 1,700 More Students," *Boston Globe*, December 7, 2020, https://www.bostonglobe
.com/2020/12/07/metro/boston-reopen-28-schools-1700-more-students/; James Vaznis and Bianca Vázquez Toness, "Boston to Randomly Test Teachers and Other Educators Weekly for COVID-19," *Boston Globe*, April 27, 2021, https://www.bostonglobe.com/2020/09/10/metro/boston-schools
-teachers-union-reach-agreement-school-reopening/.

41. Deanna Pan, "Boston Housing Activists, Teachers, Parents Rally for Eviction Protections and Remote Learning," *Boston Globe*, August 19, 2020, https://www.bostonglobe.com/2020/08/19/metro/boston-housing-activists-teachers-parents-rally-eviction-protections-remote-learning/.

42. Jeremy C. Fox, "Families and School Nurses Rally at State House for Better COVID-19 Precautions in Schools," *Boston Globe*, December 15, 2021, https://www.bostonglobe.com/2021/12/15/metro/families-school-nurses-rally-state-house-better-covid-19-precautions-schools/.

43. Bleichfeld, "Mass Schools Face COVID Test Delays."

44. Mingus, "You Are Not Entitled to Our Deaths"; Alice Wong, *Year of the Tiger* (New York: Penguin Random House, 2022), 267.

45. Kozleski and Proffitt, "Equity and Diversity in the Educator Workforce"; Mueller, "Disability History, Curriculum, and Identity in Special Education."

46. Mingus, "You Are Not Entitled to Our Deaths."

47. MacNeill, "Boston Teachers Union Sues District over Accommodations."

48. Jamelia Morgan, "Toward a DisCrit Approach to American Law," in *DisCrit Expanded: Reverberations, Ruptures, and Inquiries*, eds. Subini A. Annamma, Beth A. Ferri, and David J. Connor (New York: Teachers College Press, 2022), 13–30.

49. Sins Invalid, *Skin, Tooth, and Bone*.

50. Bleichfeld, "Mass Schools Face COVID Test Delays"; Jeremy C. Fox, "State Lets Boston and Worcester Schools Delay Return to Full-Time Classroom Instruction," *Boston Globe*, March 24, 2021, https://www.bostonglobe.com/2021/03/24/metro/boston-worcester-schools-allowed-delay-return-full-time-classroom-instruction/.

51. Katie Meyer, "Building a Community of Disabled Workers Changed My Relationship with My Union," *The Jacobin*, April 10, 2023, https://jacobin.com/2023/04/disabled-workers-union-organizing-grad-students-university-solidarity/.

52. Labor Notes Staff, "Welcomes, Farewells, and New Projects at Labor Notes," June 22, 2023, https://labornotes.org/blogs/2023/06/welcomes-farewells-and-new-projects-labor-notes/.

53. On emerging research, see Rachel Elizabeth Fish, David Enrique Rangel, Nelly De Arcos, and Olivia Friend (2023), "Inequality in the Schooling Experiences of Disabled Children and Their Families during COVID-19," in *Disability in the Time of Pandemic*, ed. Allison C. Carey, Sara E. Green, and Laura Mauldin (UK: Emerald Publishing Limited), 135–153, https://doi.org/10.1108/S1479-354720230000013008/. On investigative journalism, see Sara Luterman, "'We Feel Like We Lost Two Years of Education': School Closings Are More Complicated for Parents of Children with Disabilities," *The 19th*, February 1, 2022, https://19thnews.org/2022/02/covid-school-closures-remote-learning-complicated-students-disabilities/.

54. Wong, *Year of the Tiger*, 335.

8

Archival Labor and Labor Power

Using COVID Collections to Rethink History Making and the Labor Movement

LIA WARNER

In April 2020, Manhattan borough historian Robert Snyder convened a meeting of New York–based historians to discuss how "we can study, document and analyze the pandemic going forward."[1] It was already clear that the COVID-19 pandemic was going to be a momentous historical event and that historians would have to think on their feet about how to understand this history and formulate research agendas. Over three years later, it is clear that the COVID-19 pandemic has incited a new type of history making that has inspired memory workers—namely, local and academic historians and archivists—to come together in a totally new configuration.

One of the dominant trends that emerged from conversations like these all over the world was a category of memory work I call COVID collections. COVID collections are archives or projects that document life during the pandemic. They were conducted by large research institutions and governments as well as community organizations and individuals. COVID collections sprang up around a variety of themes and deployed different research or artistic methods to explore specific questions or reach unique audiences. From web crawls, to oral histories, to social media accounts, these documentary resources captured the lived experience of millions of people worldwide, either through their own words or forms of expression or through the emerging media and information surrounding them during the pandemic.

COVID collections are united by a self-conscious historical attitude. Phrases such as "Witness to History," "Chronicling COVID," or "YOU are the Primary Source" recur in COVID collection titles and websites. COVID collections seem to spring from and tap in to a collective anxiety about living in unprecedented times; this existential crisis triggered a similarly unprecedented, widespread popular interest in history making and historicization.

Because the pandemic cast working-class struggles and inequality in high relief, many COVID collections explicitly and implicitly deal with work and workers. Collections like the "Work and COVID-19" web archive specifically investigate and document the activities of unions, government agencies, nonprofits, and industry consultants during the pandemic. But more general collections that seek to capture daily life or memorial practices also archive the multiple sites of pandemic labor performed by everyone from first responders to homemakers.

Contemporaneous collecting activity has been done before but certainly is not the norm for archivists or historians. During these exceptional times, the roles of the archivist, historian, and historical subject become blurred. Indeed, COVID collections upset the ordinary balance between these actors, opening up space for the responsibilities and opportunities of each role to be challenged or reoriented.

In this chapter, I specifically focus on the labor of archivists in the creation of COVID collections. Archival methodologies and archival labor provide support for COVID collecting efforts, and archival labor has become more visible and active during the pandemic. Significantly, the pandemic has instigated changes in archival labor that have positioned archivists to take on major strategic roles in building movements to combat inequality and exploitation.

Analyzing the pandemic through an archival lens reveals the ways that contemporary memory work and historical sense making expose underlying systems of power that affect people in their everyday life. Archives are defined by the functions of collecting, organizing, preserving, and disseminating information, both physically and digitally. The ways in which archivists go about performing these functions are not neutral or natural; they stem from the specific historical practices of individuals and institutions who sought to ensure that their activities would be available to certain future audiences. Francis X. Blouin Jr. and William G. Rosenberg trace the emergence of the concept of authority within archives in history, beginning by noting that "since antiquity, archives have been the place where socially important records have been housed." In addition to privileging records that reinforced the social order, "as notions of political authority migrated ideologically to other spheres, archives were increasingly regarded as locations of authentic records." Thus, "archives became privileged locations for determining historical truth."[2]

In the making of COVID collections, individuals with no credentials or qualifications nonetheless entered en masse into this authoritative record-keeping tradition. When archives are reimagined as a tool of democracy, the ability to share and recognize collective experiences, particularly in a time of intense isolation, contributes to the possibility of collective action and movement building. As such, the archival approach to the COVID-19 pandemic is a valuable conceptual tool for the labor movement. Furthermore, archivists themselves are an important group of workers who are uniquely positioned to help draw attention to the structural workings of capitalism, sexism, and racism, and to actively combat these forces in their work. They are worthy of closer examination in labor history and historiography.

This chapter is directly informed by my experience working in archives during the pandemic and on the COVID Collections Project.[3] The COVID Collections Project is a collaboration between the Initiative for Critical Disaster Studies and the Archives and Public History Program at New York University (NYU) and the E. L. Quarantelli Resource Collection at the University of Delaware (UD) Disaster Research Center. As of this writing, the team has identified and surveyed over one thousand collecting initiatives worldwide and received survey feedback from almost three hundred unique collectors or collecting institutions. To supplement this data, I conducted five semi-structured interviews with archivists, librarians, and historians who either run or use a COVID collection. I tie these sources together with contemporary literature on the impact of COVID-19 on archives, labor movements, and communities as well as theoretical texts on archives and public memory.

Although there were no respondents who focused exclusively on archival labor during the pandemic, labor and the labor movement was a thematic focus of more than 10 percent of collectors who responded to our survey. While this figure accounts only for collectors who used explicit terms such as "work," "worker," "labor," "job," or "employee," COVID collectors who explicitly focused on "life" or "experience," which constituted over 30 percent of respondents, inevitably contain more subtle investigations of social, reproductive, and waged labor and how the everyday is produced. Beyond this rich historical material that documents the pandemic through the lens of labor, COVID collections can also help incite organizing and solidarity among archivists and archival subjects. In what follows, I analyze the abundance of opportunities for collaboration among archivists, historians, community members, and the labor movement that emerged during the pandemic. By applying an archival lens to structural issues that the pandemic has aggravated, I aim to reveal how we might respond to our fullest potential.

Context

The meeting of New York–based historians and memory workers on April 2, 2020, is reminiscent of another gathering: the October 4, 2001, meeting of history professionals organized by the Museum of the City of New York and

the Smithsonian National Museum of American History, who sought to process and strategize their approach to documenting the events of September
11, 2001. In their retrospective article, James B. Gardner and Sarah M. Henry
describe the difficult process of dealing with the tragic aftermath of 9/11 while
also holding serious discussions around the ethics, safety, and imperative
behind contemporaneous collecting and historical work.[4] The crucial debate
over whether or not to collect, and then what ought to be collected, was—and
still is—steeped in the personal and professional discomfort of "working at
the intersection of grief and history," a position that remains unfamiliar for
most historians and archivists.[5] Gardner and Henry argued, in response to
the horror and confusion of 9/11, that historians needed to broaden their
methods to include emotional, empathetic labor. Rather than retreating into
"the safety of historical interpretation," they called upon their colleagues
to "respond to those challenges thoughtfully and positively, embracing the
opportunity to help our visitors understand these tragic events and contributing to the nation's healing."[6]

During the pandemic, memory workers were again in the complex position of having to deal with tragedy on a personal and professional level.
However, the fields of memory work have evolved since 9/11, particularly in
the emergence of community archives and user-centered archival practices
that represent a shift from practices emphasizing documents and records
to those that focus on people, collectives, and experiences.[7] The language
of community archivists, public historians, and oral historians has entered
the mainstream of historical discourse, advocacy, and outreach, and COVID
collections place emphasis on individual experience, the quotidian, and the
ephemeral.

At the core of these practices is the belief in shared authority and in the
decentering of the archival institution.[8] Shared authority considers the ways
records can have multiple provenances and stakeholders beyond the traditional concept of author and institution. Taking account of the community
and the subjects of records, not just their creators, expands the network of
archival relationships that inform the life cycle of records.[9] COVID collections
represent perhaps the largest, widest interpretation and implementation
of these community and user-centered practices thus far. This theoretical
groundwork was already laid by critical archival theorists and practitioners,
who now see their radical ideas put into place in universities, public libraries,
museums, historical societies, and heritage sites. This represents a monumen-
tal shift in possibility for the development of a critical archival practice that
draws attention to communities and their activities within larger structures
of power.

Scholars of critical disaster studies understand disasters as clarifying
moments, where underlying inequalities are brought to bear in new ways,

offering opportunity for radicalization and movement building.[10] The early efforts to bring about mass labor action during the summer of 2020 reflected this insight. Indeed, the intersection of COVID, labor and economic injustice, and racism and police brutality brought forth powerful mutual aid and grassroots efforts on a grand scale. Preserving stories of these efforts in support of their continuation requires collecting methods and historical approaches that are neither extractive nor violent in their surveillance.

The COVID Collections Project

The COVID Collections Project was born out of the Historical Approaches to COVID-19 Working Group, a National Science Foundation–funded endeavor to apply historical methods to understanding the pandemic's past, present, and future, and to develop archival materials and resources for future study of COVID-19. The project's mission is to create a clearinghouse for global COVID collections. Some versions of this project exist elsewhere, such as the American Historical Association's list or the International Federation for Public History's "Made by Us" interactive map of collections.[11]

What sets the COVID Collections Project apart is the extent of the collection and the future-oriented mission of the project. The COVID Collections Project not only draws together disparate resources to increase access, but it also seeks to make the information legible to audiences with various needs, questions, and positions. This type of resource was proposed at the Historians' Responses to COVID-19 conversation in April 2020; however, the group lacked the capacity to undertake such a project at that time.[12] Members of the history community thus sought collaboration with critical disaster scholars in order to create the NYU-UD collective.

A key feature of this interdisciplinary endeavor was the possibility of using the COVID Collections Project as a space for reworking the relationship between historians and archivists. The project's team was designed with the interests of traditional historians, public historians, and archivists in mind. After the initial discovery phase, where the team scoured the internet for project data, the bulk of the intellectual labor has been centered on thinking about information architecture. We reviewed literature from libraries, archives, and disaster history to try to design a survey that would anticipate the needs of future researchers of COVID collections. We also consulted with digital humanities specialists to brainstorm platforms and digital tools that would best suit our data set and our users' needs.

In the first months of the project, our whole team was focused on data gathering. During this crucial phase, we began to fill in a sketch of the COVID collections terrain. We oriented ourselves by beginning with smaller compilations and then snowballing from those leads. We also used structured search strategies to query multiple search engines on the open web. Ultimately, our discovery methods yielded a data set that highlights the commonality between projects and the COVID collecting practice broadly. In the database we began to build, we cataloged COVID collections' web presence and created descriptive metadata around the projects' stated goals, administrative and institutional affiliations, audience, collecting status, online collections status, and financial structure. We used this data to understand broad trends and categories across global COVID collections and steer the future of the project accordingly.

After spending months compiling and cataloging collections, we developed and launched a survey to 966 unique email addresses associated with the projects or institutions in our database and received 299 responses.[13] The purpose of the survey was to learn the definitions, objectives, scope, methods, and contents of COVID collections. We asked questions about the history of the collecting effort, the scope of the project in terms of material type or thematic focus, the extent of the materials, the project team's future aspirations for further collecting, the future accessibility of the collection for research, and the types of funding that make the project possible. This rich metadata bolsters our existing catalog by providing unique insight into the ways that collectors gathered their data and managed their projects.

The projects that we located and surveyed were largely interdisciplinary in nature and were structured around a number of key foci. Geography, occupation, population/group, and theme were the four major categories that survey respondents used to describe their collecting. Themes included daily life, art, masks, disability, and education. Other trends included encouraging participants to keep journals, record oral histories with their family members, and keep a photo diary of life under lockdown.

Many projects appeared to share a common language and spirit, reflecting a larger desire to express faith and explore futurity through archives. As archival theorist Scott Cline writes, "I believe that archives is a faith-based profession, not in the sense of religious faith, but rather as an organic, universal faith in the future of the species. At its deepest, most fundamental level, archives assume a genuine faith in humanity, a faith that there will be a future and generations to which archives will matter."[14] Cline argues that the absurdities and atrocities that have occurred in the twentieth century force us not to take for granted any future for humanity or any civilization where documentary records are privileged as a compelling source of truth. Still, despite this daunting reality, archivists toil away. In the midst of an unprecedented global pandemic, this deeply human impulse miraculously endured. COVID collections, in essence, expressed this archival faith in some uncertain future.

In an interview for the *New York Times Magazine* article "Three Years into Covid, We Still Don't Know How to Talk about It," sociologists Ryan Hagen and Denise Milstein described four new sociological concepts they developed from the more than two hundred oral history interviews their team conducted since 2020: ontological insecurity, agentic enactment, epistemic grounding, and repertoires of repair. These concepts revolve around individuals' experience of and strategies to cope with the grave disruption of normalcy during the pandemic. Ontological insecurity describes the breakdown of people's basic ability to feel safe in the world and make sense or narrativize their lives in a coherent way. Hagen and Milstein posit that their narrators developed strategic "repertoires of repair" to combat ontological insecurity via two distinct types of behavior: "'agentic enactment' (making a change to your environment) and 'epistemic grounding' (collecting or avoiding new knowledge)."[15]

Repertoires of repair are linked to Cline's concept of archival faith on three levels. First, there is the frantic groping around for some mechanism with which to narrativize and impose order on chaotic events. Second, there is the conflicting impulse to either destroy or preserve the memory, knowledge, and evidence of the bad with aspirations toward the imagined better future. Finally, there is the metacognition of the COVID collecting effort simultaneously aspiring to preserve material for future interpretation while yielding new insights in the present that confirm the absurd, traumatic, overwhelming ongoing impact of the pandemic on the world that individuals have little power to act on or resolve.

The hopeful urge to record COVID struck a chord with the general public, not just memory workers. Across the database of COVID collections, the word "story" appears in the title of a collection 114 times. The public's wide engagement with COVID collections as spaces for individuals to narrativize their experience speaks to the "epistemic grounding" impulse that Hagan and Milstein unearthed. In the collection titled "Telling Your Story: Documenting COVID-19," the local historical society frames the project in Cline's future-oriented language:

> A century from now when researchers, historians or even someone writing a Preserving the Past column want to know about the coronavirus, they should have far more resources than we have on past Wisconsin pandemics. There is a need to preserve the stories, photos and videos that chronicle the historic event of the COVID-19 pandemic in Manitowoc County.[16]

The work of COVID collecting was thus always in dialog with an imagined future. Whether in a Manhattan working group reflecting on 9/11 or in a Manitowoc County community center, memory workers are seeking new strategies for making sense of the past and present and ultimately making a historical claim on the future.

Embracing shared authority in archival collecting could have resounding consequences outside of COVID collecting. Theorists have linked the idea of *symbolic annihilation*—"the ways in which mainstream media ignore, misrepresent, or malign minoritized groups"—to archival representation, or lack thereof.[17] These same theorists propose a counter-concept of *representational belonging*: "the ways in which community archives empower people marginalized by mainstream media outlets and memory institutions with the autonomy and authority to establish, enact, and reflect on their presence in ways that are complex, meaningful, substantive, and positive to them in a variety of symbolic contexts."[18] If sharing historical authority through community-engaged archiving can develop representational belonging, I believe that local archives—long sites for the reproduction and performance of local hierarchies of power and privilege—can become a base of power for community organizing, healing, and movement building in areas such as racial, gender, and economic justice.

Because large research institutions make up a large proportion of the collectors, students and student workers are also often tapped to give accounts and facilitate interviews or outreach to other parts of the university or local community. University archives were the home of almost 35 percent of the collections in my sample pool. The role of student workers in archives has received increasing attention in the field recently, especially as the makeup of the libraries and archives workforce has become more flexible, causal, and temporary, and thus reliant on unpaid or low-paid students or interns to perform core archival duties.[19] COVID-19 accentuated these trends in archives, especially as departments experienced austerity measures such as hiring freezes and budget cuts, all while being expected to ensure continuity of services.

Working conditions in archives and libraries during COVID were an important part of my interviews with archivists and historians. Beyond the workplace, we also explored what kinds of labor went into COVID collecting as a practice. A common theme that emerged was the gap between archivists' capacity to perform their work and the demand for memory work to be performed contemporaneously in critical moments. This tension underscores the necessity of advocacy in archives and communities in order to support a more democratic, robust, and accessible form of contemporaneous collecting that will allow both collectors and subjects to understand themselves and their moment more completely. From my conversations with these practitioners and my familiarity with COVID collections projects, I am optimistic that this trend in collecting and archiving will resonate beyond the pandemic and change how archivists and historians understand themselves in relation to each other and to their subjects.

Archives during COVID: The Interviews

For this chapter, I reached out to respondents who indicated interest in working with us and who focused in some way on the relationship between labor and COVID-19 in their collecting or scholarship. Because the survey primarily covered collectors and not users, I also researched and networked to discover historians and scholars who would have a unique perspective on how COVID collections could be used toward labor research and issues. While there were over twenty collections in our sample that dealt with labor thematically, I chose to invite interview participants from projects that explicitly focused on workers and sites of labor during the pandemic. For some, their focus on COVID and labor was due to their subject expertise; for others, labor emerged as a central theme in their COVID archive because of personal experience, particularly with regard to labor and class as an intersectional issue that compounds with gender and race. Major themes that emerged from the interviews include the evolving role of archives in the history-making process, the ethical and practical issues that COVID collections pose, and the challenges and opportunities in archival labor during the pandemic.

Michael Koncewicz, Shannon O'Neill, and Weatherly Stephan are all connected to the NYU Special Collections COVID web-archiving initiative. Shannon and Mike, Tamiment Library curators, worked with Weatherly and the NYU web archivist to develop a web archive on COVID activism. Because Tamiment Library's focus is on the history of labor and the left, Shannon and Mike were particularly interested in the explosion of mutual aid work, labor organizing, and antiracist activism that occurred during 2020. Web archiving seemed to be the most appropriate way to document COVID-19 at the Tamiment due to issues of resource management, worker safety, and ethical concerns. The pandemic caused a university-wide hiring freeze and major cuts to departmental budgets, and the crunch for resources was compounded by the ongoing physical renovation of the library's Special Collections section. It was hard to justify bringing in new materials to the archive when the existing archives were in flux. The staff also worked remotely until late summer of 2020. Figuring out how to take stock of the COVID-19 pandemic as a historical moment was difficult when archivists' lives and regular duties were severely upended.[20]

Shannon emphasized that COVID collecting required deep consideration from an ethics standpoint. She described her thought process around contemporaneous collecting and crisis response, underscoring that while COVID collecting through journals, diaries, or community surveys wasn't necessarily extractive, it did give her pause:

> It was something that I was sitting with personally and how I think about archival collecting, which I think about, as always, first and foremost, being relational. And there's a tendency in archives to lean towards practices, whether this is intended or not, but to be extractive rather than to be in dialogue. And so, holding those kinds of thoughts and ethics in mind and also sensing the historicity of the moment and knowing that, you know, part of my job is to think about what records are being produced or have been produced and how those documents will be engaged in the present and in the future.[21]

The product of this thinking was a new policy that involved asking for permission to search websites, instead of simply collecting the data, and including a takedown policy. This shift from extractive to collaborative web archiving involved "reaching out to dozens and dozens of COVID-related organizations or any organization that we noticed was doing COVID-related activism in the Spring of 2020" before taking any digital preservation action.[22] It also made the creators of the websites aware that Tamiment would hold these records, which might become useful to them in the future.

By investing time and labor in clarifying and communicating their intent and process, Tamiment staff established new relationships with record creators and potential users of the collections. The curatorial work that Shannon described to me included forms of labor that are often devalued or invisible: deep listening, relationship building, and dialogic design. These practices can be seen as forms of care that reconfigure traditional archival dynamics of extraction and othering. Going above and beyond professional best practices and understandings of what a digital archiving endeavor might involve (that is, centering ethics and human connection over purely technological preservation considerations) requires significant time, effort, institutional support, and investment. To sustain these efforts, archivists and memory workers need to address how standards and best practices are being taught in professional programs as well as to conduct outreach to address record creators' perceptions and understandings of archival work and collaborative possibilities.

Rather than using COVID as justification for extractive collecting practices, the Tamiment COVID Activism Collection recognized the fact that COVID collections are as sensitive as they are informationally valuable. In thinking holistically, beyond the documentary or historical project that the archivist is attached to, they connect the real-world struggle of workers and marginalized people during the pandemic with the ongoing issues of power, representation, silence and belonging within the archive. The labor that goes into successful COVID collecting was another important part of our discussion. Both during the pandemic and in earlier historical moments, Tamiment staff who have worked on contemporaneous collections have prioritized relationship building as the basis for their collection development. Mike drew a connection to the contemporaneous archiving work performed by archivist Michael Nash in 2011. Nash's visits to Zuccotti Park helped him establish relationships with activists on the ground and ultimately led to the Tamiment's acquisition of a rich Occupy Wall Street collection. Not only does relationship building influence collection development, but it also expands the possibilities for rich description and research value.

Description is a core part of archival processing; recently, there has been major interest within archives in examining description practices in order to repair harmful language and challenge archival authority or neutrality by being transparent about context and positionality.[23] Sometimes this takes the form of allowing the creators or subjects of records to craft the description themselves about what records and collection material represent and who influenced them. When record creators, users, subjects, and archivists have closer relationships and understandings, the usefulness of documents and the impact of records is amplified.

When I asked Mike and Shannon about their predictions for the future use and significance of the collections, they pointed to the parallel question of whether COVID collections and COVID activism were exceptional or indicative of new trends. To Mike, both represented important developments but must be contextualized as part of a larger history of political movements in the United States. Because of his training as a historian of Cold War politics, Mike's curatorial perspective deemphasized current uses of the collection and prioritized the maturation of the materials to reveal change over time. As Mike wondered:

> How are people responding to periods of distress and what kind of community building has actually taken place? Will that last? Or is this just an exceptional period? I think that will be something that'll be interesting to track in our own collections. I think the predictable answer is that probably in most cases this will just be an exceptional burst of activity, but in some cases you'll see some forms of continuity. That's true of most waves of activism. And so I think that's another question that's worth studying on the relationship of COVID collections of labor in general.[24]

NYU's Weatherly Stephan echoed the need for time to pass before COVID collections could be employed to their fullest potential. Processing archivists work closely with newly acquired material in order to make it ready for research use and long-term care. Processing COVID collections during the pandemic demanded intense emotional labor from archivists:

I can't fathom asking people to work on things, to look retrospectively back at something while we're still living it. And while people are still dying in enormous numbers . . . like when we were stuck at home, . . . and [the archivists] were actively looking at the Transit Workers Union website, and seeing, like, more and more people die. And, like, the people in the Transit Workers Union kind of saying, 'Here's another one of our colleagues that we've lost'; it was really tough, and it continues to be tough. . . . I can't quite turn this around yet as, like, a historical moment, I feel like we're still living it.[25]

Weatherly's account demonstrates the value of the web archiving collection. An archived web page is not simply a stand-alone record of an organization's COVID response. Rather, the process of curating, preserving, and describing the record paints a larger picture of the pandemic and its impact on both the record creators and the archivists who interact with them. Further, this work opens up the possibility for solidarity and affinity between disparate groups that had vastly different pandemic experiences. So, despite physical and social distance, COVID collections offer up a new channel for both archivists and their communities to explore the collaborative work of history making.

The emotional labor integral to collecting during the pandemic that Weatherly described must be examined with gender in mind. The last industry-wide survey conducted by the Society of American Archivists in 2021 found that 71 percent of respondents were women. Archives are increasingly produced and maintained by women: there has been an 11 percent decrease in the proportion of men in the field and a 6 percent increase in the proportion of women in the field since the last survey in 2004.[26] Archivist Jessica Lapp proposed the idea of the archivist as "handmaiden of history" as a speculative tool to interrogate the feminization of archives amid major changes in the profession, which recognize archival work as "inherently political and interventionist."[27] For Lapp, handmaidens have "historically been the reproductive servants of the dominant class, but they have never been happy about it."[28] For archivists as handmaidens, our strength comes from subverting the very power structures and interests that we may be compelled to serve. No longer passive caretakers, archivists draw power from our strategic use of professional tools and resources to document and bear witness to histories that have been silenced, erased, or ignored.

The idea of *witnessing* is present in both the literature on emotional and trauma-informed archiving and in COVID collections language. Critical archival theorists like Marika Cifor have attempted to "reorient the archivist as a witness of historical events as well as historical and generational trauma. As a witness, the archivist engages in relationships of reciprocity and affective responsibility with archival stakeholders and responds and acts on emotional levels."[29] While bearing witness is a strategic and powerful tool for social and historical change, it generates complex affective situations that require empathy and attention. In the case of NYU processing archivists, witnessing the devastating death of transit workers during the pandemic through web archiving activated a traumatic relationship with a disparate population but also helped the archival workers make sense of the meaning and context of their labor. Could experiences like these lead to a shift in archivists' professional identities and activities? In this moment of disaster, could archival witnesses begin to identify commonality and foster solidarity across industries? Bonded by the experience of the pandemic, will the practice of doing history draw together a coalition of diverse workers who could support one another's organizing efforts and histories in new ways? In a so-called post-COVID world, these stakes should be the focus of archivists and memory workers within the labor movement who can be the go-between, activating the records, record creators, and themselves.

The pandemic's disparate, disproportionate impact on women's work (paid and unpaid), has been, of course, a central theme to critical studies of the pandemic. Librarian Abigail Goben sought to address and capture the gendered valences of the pandemic's impact by collecting material published online, from news articles to social media posts, in her COVID collection, "Women's Labor—COVID-19 Bibliography."[30] Collections like Goben's are valuable resources, especially in an age when information on digital media or the internet is vulnerable to total, permanent loss in ways that paper collections are not. As of January 2021, the collection had 1,199 entries. These entries were discovered through web crawls, nonautomated internet discovery, and crowdsourcing.

While the collection is named after Goben's three key search terms—"women's," "labor," and "COVID-19"—the collection actually reflects discovery via fuzzy language such as "mothers" and "childcare" or even "fathers."[31] This methodology reflects the strategies and challenges of discovery within a textual terrain characterized by the issue that Joan Scott raised more than thirty-five years ago: the conceptually immature interchangeable use of the concepts "women" and "gender."[32] Beyond the informational value of the collection itself, the bibliography and its methodologies offer researchers rich perspectives on the issues of women, gender, and labor during COVID. Not only are the experiences of the textual subjects and their authors preserved, but so too are the experiences of this researcher of women's labor. The dynamic of women's labor of social reproduction, memory, and care is thus captured and preserved in an artifact that attests to another ongoing aspect of structural inequality that the pandemic aggravated.

As a medical librarian, Goben's focus on issues of privacy informed both her perspective on COVID collecting activities broadly and her own research scope:

It was weird; it was weird to be in the middle of active trauma, which we all still are, and watching my university ask for performative trauma to then be shared with everyone. And, no, the students are in the middle of this; capturing it, documenting it for yourself, yes. But I was very concerned about the idea of these collections being shared without some sort of later review and re-consent in two years, in five years, by those same students. And I didn't see that kind of thoughtfulness going into this.[33]

Indeed, archivists have voiced concerns about privacy and ethics around COVID and other types of trauma response, contemporaneous collecting efforts. Goben worries about this even in her own work on public documents:

One of the things I do have in the data set that I have to figure out how to manage because I need to avoid this for my own work—I've captured a number of Twitter threads. They're powerful. They are absolutely powerful. They are equally or more impactful at reaching people than many of these news articles. Is it appropriate for me to retain those again? I did not ask permission. I do not have the consent of the original author.[34]

Eira Tansey's blog post "No One Owes Their Trauma to Archivists, or, the Commodification of Contemporaneous Collecting," was one of the first pieces to address COVID collecting ethics and has started many conversations within the field. Tansey's central critique was that some COVID collecting practices prioritized the completeness of the historical record over the impact of contemporaneous collecting on record creators: "Archivists have an ethical obligation to understand that respecting people's privacy and right to forget their own past means *accepting that we will lose parts of the historical record* that others may wish we had gone to great lengths to get." Furthermore, she questions the role of archivists within disaster response given the profession's lack of focus and training on issues of trauma: [Some archivists] "seem to have this cultural expectation that we are entitled to people's trauma in the service of constructing a comprehensive historical record, despite the fact that few of us have any meaningful training in trauma-informed practice."[35]

The example of the transit workers' web archive underscores the importance of trauma-informed practice, both for the well-being of the archival subjects and the archival workers themselves. Being trauma-informed requires practitioners to recognize how trauma impacts people's behavior. This recognition serves as the impetus for developing practices that address harm and seek to redress or reduce its effects. Armed with the knowledge and recognition of COVID's impact on the transit workers' community, archivists can practice solidarity by developing trauma-informed practices that help workers make sense of their history and feel historical authority.

My final interview was with Robert Snyder, who is working on a labor history of New York City during the pandemic as told through oral histories.[36]

His archives are digital oral history collections produced by institutions such as the New York Public Library, the Asian/Pacific/American Institute at NYU, and Brooklyn College. Snyder collaborates with collectors by transcribing audio interviews for his research that have not yet been made available.

When I asked him about what he would want archivists and collectors to be aware of in their work, he emphasized the need for collections to be available in multiple formats and through multiple entry points if they were to have the greatest possible impact.[37] This will be an important issue for archivists to think about as the life cycle of COVID collections records evolves. What are the additional commitments beyond collection and description that accompany contemporaneous collecting? How will professionals work together to facilitate access and use in a timely and appropriate manner? These concerns highlight the importance of archival labor and archival resources in movement building. In order to make the important historical materials that have been preserved throughout the pandemic accessible and usable in the labor movement, there needs to be broad support for public history and archival work.

Oral history has been an important part of labor and social history and literature because of the practice's subversion of existing hierarchies of historical authority and attention to overlooked historical subjects.[38] As a consequence of this, however, the field also grapples with questions of how to use and present collected voices in historical writing. The contemporaneous use of contemporaneous collections, according to Snyder, deters him from using traditional approaches to writing history like narrativization and periodization:

> As I proceeded with the interviews I've used, I have become ever more convinced that this documentary history that I'll compile will work best if the excerpts and interviews stand more or less on their own as primary sources. . . . I think that any narrative that I would add right now would inevitably be incomplete. And the pandemic's not over yet. I don't think there's an endpoint in sight; I don't think there will be a clear endpoint even by the time I finish the book. So I think any narrative, I think it would hurt the material very, very badly. And I think if I present interviews and excerpts and other documents on their own, you know with headnotes that set them in context and things like that, that they'll last a lot longer.[39]

Not only does Snyder recognize that narrativization would hurt his project, but he also simply acknowledges that certain aspects of historical perspective are inaccessible due to his current position as a subject of the pandemic. The impulse to narrativize the pandemic, searching for some certainty or hint of an ending, has recurred throughout COVID collections. Snyder's engagement with this impulse, and ultimately his resistance, crystalizes how contemporaneous memory work is in itself a valuable individual exercise and historical resource. Thus, his project can be looked at as another form of COVID collection—an academic journal of historically situated observations on the experiences of people around him, informed by his own pandemic context.

Snyder acknowledged, as did ninety-one of the collectors who responded to the COVID Collections Project survey, that he did not know when he would stop collecting, or in Snyder's case, when he would end the book. Sixty-six respondents said they would stop when the pandemic was over, but it is clear that the end is simply unknowable. In this sense, Snyder's book project is tied up with the collecting community's open-ended search for historical meaning during the pandemic, both in terms of methods and content. The lines between historian and archivist are increasingly blurred.

Conclusions

COVID collections have created significant chemistry between memory workers, historians, and archivists since the start of the pandemic. Furthermore, archivists themselves have emerged as more active members of their communities and of public history discourse. Understanding archivists as workers and the archives they build and shepherd as tools of the labor movement may generate fruitful projects and ultimately help build worker power in new communities beyond archives, even as the immediate crisis of COVID-19 wanes.

Archives are ripe for organization. Many underlying assumptions about archival labor were challenged by the need for remote work and social distancing during the pandemic. The pandemic troubled not only the foundations of in-person labor; it also pushed archivists to think about what access meant at a deeper level. Pandemic conditions also raised questions about archival authority and the role of the archivist or curator in relation to both donors and institutions. Fracturing traditional notions of archival authority also troubles the legalistic idea of a single entity holding archival custody or ownership of records as private property. As archival workers begin to reckon with both their waged relationship to their institutions and the existence of the plurality of relationships that records are enmeshed in across time and space to create a web of public good rather than private property, archives and archivists' position at a crux between the material and the historical or epistemic is honed into a compelling tool for revolutionary change.

For the labor movement, this means that archivists themselves are organizing and thinking collectively about workplace and profession-wide issues, many of which were change-resistant due to the history of the professionalization of archives.[40] While librarians and library assistants have longer histories of unionization in their professions, archivists have only recently begun to organize collectively as a distinct unit. Historical reasons for this include the physical and professional siloing and isolation of archivists within larger institutions and the casualization of archival work, with archivist's employment being contingent on a project-by-project basis.

However, in 2021 workers at the University of Michigan formed LEO-GLAM, the Lecturers' Employee Organization: Librarians, Archivists, and Curators bargaining unit. In an interview for the *Michigan Daily*, the sole archivist of U-M Flint, Colleen Marquis, said that poor working conditions exacerbated by the pandemic were the catalyst for organizing: "I think when COVID happened and the University started doing austerity measures, the librarians, archivists, and curators looked around in Ann Arbor and realized wow, nobody's got our back but us. . . . They started thinking about their colleagues at the other campuses and how they could help."[41] Indeed, parallel organizing efforts by archivists post-COVID are also ongoing at Wayne State University, University of Washington, and the Boston Public Library.

The labor movement can be bolstered further by workers' wider democratic engagement with historical material and deeper critical understanding of the politics and processes of knowledge creation. Critical information literacy and primary source literacy can be taught through initiatives like the COVID Collections Project; the study and popularization of this type of project might better equip future users with a tool kit to build upon and adapt during events of various scales.

As archivists engage in new dialogues about the future of archival labor, users of archives will encounter new types of relationships with these archivists, which may facilitate new forms of scholarship, organizing, and community building. Initiatives like the COVID Collections Project are starting points for collaborative efforts to bring together scholars, organizers, and users in novel configurations. The new records being added to archival repositories may tell more complete stories of life during COVID-19 and beyond. With rich description and context, the power of records can go beyond their extant boundaries and support labor activism and worker movements. Archives thus present a trifecta of opportunity that looks to the future from the COVID collections moment.

Notes

1. Robert Snyder, email to historians regarding "April 2 Zoom Conversation/ Historians' Responses to the Coronavirus," February 15, 2020.

2. Francis X. Blouin Jr. and William G. Rosenberg, *Processing the Past: Contesting Authority in History and the Archives* (Oxford: Oxford University Press, 2011), 7–8.

3. "COVID Collections Project—Initiative for Critical Disaster Studies," https://wp.nyu.edu/disasters/covid-collections-project/.

4. James B. Gardner and Sarah M. Henry, "September 11 and the Mourning After: Reflections on Collecting and Interpreting the History of Tragedy," *Public Historian* 24, no. 3 (2002): 37–52, https://doi.org/10.1525/tph.2002.24.3.37/.

5. Gardner and Henry, "September 11 and the Mourning After," 41.

6. Gardner and Henry, "September 11 and the Mourning After," 52.

7. Society of American Archivists, *Describing Archives: A Content Standard—DACS 2019.0.3* (Chicago: Society of American Archivists, 2020).

8. Michelle Caswell, Marika Cifor, and Mario H. Ramirez, "'To Suddenly Discover Yourself Existing': Uncovering the Impact of Community Archives," *American Archivist* 79, no. 1 (June 2016): 56–81, https://doi.org/10.17723/0360-9081.79.1.56/.

9. Michelle Caswell, "Dusting for Fingerprints: Introducing Feminist Standpoint Appraisal," edited by Elvia Arroyo-Ramirez, Jasmine Jones, Shannon O'Neill, and Holly Smith, *Radical Empathy in Archival Practice* 3, Special issue (2019): 2–36.

10. Jacob A. C. Remes and Andy Horowitz, *Critical Disaster Studies* (Philadelphia: University of Pennsylvania Press, 2021).

11. American Historical Association, "Collecting Initiatives: Past Pandemics and COVID-19," AHA Resource Library, March 21, 2021, https://www.historians.org/resource/collecting-initiatives-past-pandemics-and-covid-19/; Thomas Cauvin, "Mapping Public History Projects about COVID 19," *IFPH-FIHP* (blog), April 24, 2020, https://doi.org/10.58079/pvpe.

12. Robert Snyder in discussion with the author, February 4, 2022.

13. The survey is no longer accepting submissions, but the archived version is available to view: https://web.archive.org/web/20220413141632/https://delaware.ca1.qualtrics.com/jfe/form/SV_8bL6ZQrJeF6xNNY/.

14. Scott Cline, "'To the Limit of Our Integrity': Reflections on Archival Being," *American Archivist* 72, no. 2 (September 2009), 334, https://doi.org/10.17723/aarc.72.2.g0321510717r6j14.

15. Jon Mooallem and Photographs by Ashley Gilbertson, "Three Years into Covid, We Still Don't Know How to Talk about It," *New York Times*, February 22, 2023, sec. Magazine, https://www.nytimes.com/interactive/2023/02/22/magazine/covid-pandemic-oral-history.html.

16. Manitowoc County Historical Society, "Telling Your Story: Documenting COVID-19," https://www.manitowoccountyhistory.org/telling-covid19.

17. Caswell, Cifor, and Ramirez, "'To Suddenly Discover Yourself Existing'," 57.

18. Caswell, Cifor, and Ramirez, "'To Suddenly Discover Yourself Existing'."

19. Alexandra Bisio, Steve Duckworth, Helena Egbert, Emily Haskins, and Gayle O'Hara, "Archivist to Archivist: Employing an Ethics of Care Model with Interns and Student Workers," *Journal of Western Archives* 12, no. 1 (March 24, 2021), https://digitalcommons.usu.edu/westernarchives/vol12/iss1/2.

20. Weatherly Stephan in discussion with the author, January 14, 2022.

21. Shannon O'Neill in discussion with the author, February 28, 2022.

22. Michael Koncewicz in discussion with the author, January 14, 2022.

23. Alexis Antracoli and Katy Rawdon, "What's in a Name? Archives for Black Lives in Philadelphia and the Impact of Names and Name Authorities in Archival Description," in *Ethical Questions in Name Authority Control*, edited by Jane Sandberg, 307–336 (Sacramento, CA: Library Juice Press, 2019).

24. Koncewicz discussion with author, January 14, 2022.

25. Stephan discussion with author, January 14, 2022.

26. Makala Skinner and Ioana G. Hulbert, "A*CENSUS II All Archivists Survey Report" (Ithaka S+R and the Society of American Archivists, August 22, 2022), 64, https://sr.ithaka.org/wp-content/uploads/2022/08/SR-Report-ACENSUS -II-All-Archivists-Survey-08222022.pdf/.

27. Jessica M. Lapp, "'Handmaidens of History': Speculating on the Feminization of Archival Work," *Archival Science* 19 (2019), http://dx.doi.org/10.1007/ s10502-019-09319-7/, 216.

28. Lapp, "'Handmaidens of History,'" 230.

29. Taylor Wolford, "'Full of Emotions': Emotional Labor and Emotion Regulation Strategies in Archives Settings," 12, https://doi.org/10.17615/FXG6-8F06/.

30. Abigail Goben and Nell Haynes, "Women's Labor—COVID Bibliography," *Hedgehog Librarian* (blog), created May 4, 2020, updated January 18, 2021, https://hedgehoglibrarian.com/womenlaborcovidbib/.

31. Abigail Goben in discussion with the author, February 2, 2022.

32. Joan W. Scott, "Gender: A Useful Category of Historical Analysis," *American Historical Review* 91, no. 5 (December 1986): 1055–1056, https://doi.org/ 10.2307/1864376/.

33. Abigail Goben in discussion with the author, February 2, 2022.

34. Abigail Goben in discussion with the author, February 2, 2022.

35. Eira Tansey, "No One Owes Their Trauma to Archivists, or, the Commodification of Contemporaneous Collecting," June 5, 2020, https:// eiratansey.com/2020/06/05/no-one-owes-their-trauma-to-archivists-or-the -commodification-of-contemporaneous-collecting/; emphasis in original.

36. Robert Snyder, *Epicenter: The Pandemic in the Words of 42 New Yorkers* (Ithaca: Cornell University Press, forthcoming).

37. Snyder, in discussion with author.

38. Linda Shopes, "Oral History and Community Involvement," in *Presenting the Past: Essays on History and the Public*, edited by Susan Porter Benson, (Philadelphia: Temple University Press, 1986), 249–266.

39. Snyder, in discussion with author.

40. Terry Cook, "What Is Past Is Prologue: A History of Archival Ideas since 1898, and the Future Paradigm Shift," *Archivaria* 43 (February 12, 1997): 17–63.

41. Scarlett Bickerton, "UMich Librarians, Archivists and Curators Formally Join LEO," *Michigan Daily*, August 2, 2021, http://www.michigandaily.com/ news/administration/umich-librarians-archivists-and-curators-reach-formal -bargaining-recognition/. LEO is the Lecturers' Employee Organization (AFT Local 6244), and GLAM stands for Galleries, Libraries, Archives and Museums.

PART IV

The Healthcare Industry

9

COVID, Caregiving, and Coping

Nurses' Frontline Work through a Pandemic Year

MARIAN MOSER JONES

As Stephanie drove to her shift as an intensive care unit (ICU) nurse, she "could feel the adrenaline" pounding in her temples.[1] It was March 28, 2020, and the first COVID-19 cases had arrived at her Boston-area hospital. Even though this fifty-something veteran surgical ICU nurse felt she was "in great company" with colleagues who were all "facing this head-on," she admitted in her diary that she was "still scared." She spent the busy shift wearing PPE—personal protective equipment, including surgical masks—and, consequently, "not eating or drinking enough." Afterward, she realized she would "need to adapt my self-care" to these new working conditions. Three days later an email from hospital management informed ICU nurses that the hospital would be creating additional ICUs to handle the COVID-19 surge and that some general care nurses (who had no special training for ICU work) would be reassigned to augment the ICU staff. "WTF. Draining my reserves. 🤮🤮 🤮🤮🤮🤮🤮)," Stephanie wrote in her diary. The row of nine vomiting emojis expressed her anxiety. Even though she was a registered nurse (RN), with advanced training as an ICU nurse and experience as a nursing supervisor, she added, "I don't think I have the skill set to do what I am being asked."

The challenges and dangers of COVID-19 care soon became apparent. In early May, when a thoracic surgeon and a resident were "bronching" a critically ill COVID patient—looking down into the patient's airways with a slender lighted bronchoscope to see what mechanical obstructions might be impairing breathing—the patient went into cardiac arrest. While the bronchoscopy was "aerosolizing" the virus—causing particles to be released into the air—Stephanie's team of RNs and physicians rushed in to perform CPR as per standard hospital protocol for "coding" patients without a DNR (Do Not Resuscitate) order. The patient died anyway with no family nearby as no visitors were allowed.

Later, Stephanie reflected on what had happened. The CPR had not only involved strenuous exertion that became even more exhausting while wearing PPE; it had also proved ineffective and dangerous. She characterized this intervention as "prolonging the dying process and harming the patient" while noting that it had exposed at least ten healthcare workers (HCWs) directly to COVID-19. She would now have to "start my clock"—a phrase numerous RNs in this study used to describe a process of monitoring themselves for symptoms over the fourteen days following COVID exposure. Testing was not widely available at this point. Moreover, despite the careful personal disinfection rituals that Stephanie and other nurses followed before they entered their homes, their children, spouses, and other household members now faced a heightened risk of exposure to COVID-19—a virus that medical experts were barely beginning to learn how to treat. (As Stephanie wrote in her diary, treating COVID-19 in those early days was like "flying a plane while trying to build it.") After exposure, however, neither Stephanie nor the others were able to quarantine: they were urgently needed in the ICU.

Stories like Stephanie's have been featured in popular media since the pandemic's onset. Some accounts have lionized nurses as fearless "healthcare heroes," while others have painted a more nuanced picture.[2] Researchers have investigated the individual psychological impact of the pandemic on frontline nurses using surveys, diagnostic questionnaires, and other research tools.[3] But little analytic research or writing has centered on the voices of the nurses *as a group* without subordinating these voices to a larger, external agenda.

The study discussed in this chapter focused on listening to registered nurses' perspectives on their experiences working in the pandemic. The chapter involves analysis of diaries contributed by Stephanie and five other RNs who worked in US hospitals during the pandemic's first year. This chapter concentrates specifically on analyzing the nurses' writings to understand their pandemic-related occupational challenges and ways of coping.[4] It ends with conclusions and recommendations on how working conditions for RNs and other HCWs involved in nursing work can be improved to meet future crises.

Background: How the COVID-19 Pandemic Unfolded and Affected Nurses

To understand the experiences of specific US registered nurses during the COVID-19 pandemic, it is important to first briefly review how the pandemic unfolded and its overall reported impact on nurses and other HCWs. Although detailed pandemic timelines are available elsewhere, several early developments are worth noting here, as they set the stage for US hospital nurses' experiences.[5] First, in the fifty days between the US Centers for

Disease Control and Prevention's announcement of its first "laboratory confirmed" COVID-19 case in the United States on January 21, and the World Health Organization's (WHO) March 11 declaration of a pandemic, the US government, states, and localities did almost nothing to stem the spread of the virus within the United States or prepare to treat large numbers of very sick people.[6] In February, President Donald J. Trump assured Americans "we have it very well under control" and "it's going to disappear," while privately conveying to journalist Bob Woodward that this virus was five times more deadly than seasonal influenza and was airborne.[7] Meanwhile, a global shortage of PPE became apparent, due to "just-in-time" purchasing strategies that failed to account for unanticipated surges in demand and to COVID-related PPE factory shutdowns in China.[8] In response, WHO published guidance on efficient PPE use to prevent COVID-19 transmission. It directed all HCWs in direct contact with COVID-19 patients to use "gowns, gloves, medical masks and eye protection (goggles or face shield)" and specified that workers involved in aerosol-generating procedures wear N95 or equivalent respirators, along with gowns, gloves, and eye protection.[9] This combination of domestic unpreparedness and global PPE shortage created the conditions that RNs and other frontline pandemic HCWs faced beginning in March 2020.

A survey released in July 2020 by National Nurses United (NNU), the largest US union for RNs, found that 87 percent of hospital nurses reported reusing single-use respirators (N95 masks) or face shields, and that only 24 percent said their employer was providing a safe workplace. The survey of over twenty-one thousand union and nonunion RNs in fifty states, Washington, DC, and three US territories also found that only 23 percent reported being able to access COVID-19 testing for themselves. Additionally, only 31 percent reported that every patient in their hospital was screened for COVID-19, and 27 percent reported problems with inadequate staffing, while 30 percent said that since the pandemic's onset they had been reassigned to a new clinical care area that required them to possess "new skills or competencies." About a third of nurses surveyed reported increases in stress (42 percent), anxiety (38 percent), and sadness or depression (29 percent) during this period. In response to these results, NNU called upon healthcare systems to prioritize RNs and other HCWs for COVID-19 testing, requested the Occupational Safety and Health Administration to issue an emergency mandate requiring healthcare employers to provide adequate PPE for HCWs, and urged the president to immediately use the Defense Production Act to order US manufacturers to produce PPE to meet the shortage.[10]

In the fall a new COVID-19 surge strained the healthcare system. Hospitals continued to report PPE shortages while now also experiencing shortages of RNs. Some increased nurse-patient ratios to dangerous levels. North Dakota's governor began allowing asymptomatic COVID-positive nurses to remain at work, while other states competed to attract traveling nurses—RNs on short-term contracts from other states—with high pay and signing bonuses up to ten thousand dollars. (Many states relaxed RN and other HCW licensing requirements during the pandemic to recognize licenses from other states.[11]) The chief causes of the staffing shortage included nurses quarantining or recovering after COVID-19 exposure, nurses quitting after emotional burnout from the pandemic, and increased needs due to COVID-19 surges in rural areas where healthcare capacity was limited. This crisis augmented an estimated shortage of one hundred thousand RNs that had existed before the pandemic and had been concentrated in ICUs and other areas that demanded high skill levels and produced high levels of burnout.[12]

As the pandemic continued, the news about nurses worsened. A 2021 investigative report released by *The Guardian* and *Kaiser Health News* indicated that as of March 17, 2021, RNs and other nurses accounted for the greatest percentage of COVID-19 deaths among US HCWs.[13] In October 2021, WHO released a report estimating that 115,000 HCWs (including nurses) worldwide had died from COVID-19 between January 2020 and May 2021. The International Council of Nurses (ICN), a Geneva-based global nurses' advocacy organization, called this number a "damning indictment of governments for their failure to fulfill their duty of care to protect their most vital workforce during this period." The ICN also noted that this figure represented a conservative estimate of HCW deaths and warned that the pandemic had exacerbated a dire global shortage of skilled nurses.[14]

The Study: Six US Nurses Write the Pandemic

The study discussed in this chapter aimed expressly "to record the first-person testimonies of US registered nurses who [were] involved in the response to the COVID-19 pandemic as front-line witnesses to nursing history, and to understand these stories in the larger context of nursing and pandemic history," as stated in the participant consent form. After the principal investigator (the author) gained approval from the University of Maryland College Park Institutional Review Board, study recruitment began on April 24, 2020.[15] The study closed on April 23, 2021. Participants were recruited via email, referral, and social media. Prospective enrollees signed a written consent form and met with the principal investigator (PI) via video chat, during which they were invited to discuss their concerns and questions about the study or consent form and to show their nursing license and hospital ID badge to verify their eligibility.[16] They agreed to contribute writings, photographs, or expressive media (e.g., drawings, pictures, music lyrics) to a secure online folder for as long as they were able or willing to do so over the study period.

The PI enrolled in the study eight RNs from six states—Massachusetts, Maryland, Washington, Wisconsin, Pennsylvania, and California. All practiced in hospitals, some in designated COVID-19 units and others in specialty units to which COVID-19-positive patients were admitted. Six of the eight contributed substantial writings to the study. These six nurses all identified as female. All were US citizens. One identified as Black, one as Asian American, and the remaining four identified as white. Their ages ranged from mid-twenties to fifties, and some possessed advanced practice training beyond their nursing license. This small group, while far from a representative sample of the whole US nursing workforce, included a diverse array of participants.

In analyzing participants' contributions, the author employed a grounded theory approach, an inductive approach in which a close reading of the texts is conducted and then particular phenomena, such as ideas, events, phrases, and experiences, are labeled with a series of codes, or words with specific meanings. The codes are combined into loose thematic or topical categories, and different texts are related to one another to produce broader insights.[17] The following sections discuss key aspects of participants' reported pandemic-related work experiences that surfaced from this analysis. These include the nurses' experiences with the PPE shortage and how it influenced nurse–management relationships; these nurses' overall experiences with novel workplace hazards; the impact of the pandemic on these nurses' well-being; their pandemic-related challenges outside of the workplace; the nurses' experiences with the second and third waves, including ongoing struggles with management; and how they coped with and adapted to these challenges. To protect the privacy of the participants, along with patients and other HCWs, the nurses are identified by pseudonym only, and their hospitals are identified only by the state or major metropolitan area where they were located.

THE PPE DEBACLE

Participants' writings indicate that their fight for adequate PPE began almost immediately after COVID-19 came to their hospitals. In her March 23 diary entry, Jennifer wrote, "Tensions are already starting to get high as PPE supplies are limited and being rationed" at the Pennsylvania hospital where she worked. "We are to re-use our N95 masks, although our intensivist/Director of Critical Care is going through them like a box of tissues." The nurses were also being told that they did not need to wear "protective gowns or hair coverings," in contravention of WHO guidance. Meanwhile, at Stephanie's hospital, she reported that the CEO was asking the public to sew or make masks for HCWs to stem the shortage. At the Washington state hospital where

Helen worked, nurses were reusing single-use N95s and placing a surgical mask over a used N95, while "upper management" was "locking away" the cart of respirators and PPE because staff was allegedly "stealing or 'overusing'" its contents. At Liz's hospital, also in Washington state, the shortage of disposable masks with attached face shields led nurses to use "surgical masks with giant goggles that don't stay on your face," she wrote on March 21. Two weeks later, when the N95s were still being "locked up" by managers and were only to be used for aerosolizing procedures and CPR, Liz decided to wear N95s she had obtained from her husband's workplace. "I'm nervous to wear them and get in trouble, but when I asked another nurse to help me turn a [COVID-19] positive patient, I saw she had one under her paper mask," she wrote on April 4. "We wore the bouffant caps to hide the straps."

For these nurses, the handling of the PPE served as a painful indicator of their place in the hospital hierarchy and a sign of management's indifference. At Liz's hospital, hospitalists (physicians who are hospital staff) were given N95s, but nurses were provided them only for a "code situation"—a situation in which HCWs rush in to revive a patient in dire distress. "It is a weird feeling to be rationed supplies; like we are trusted with so much of patient care independently, but can't be trusted with a box of gloves," Liz wrote on April 2. When the hospital CEO sent the staff an email in late April blaming sinking revenues on "having to provide all this PPE" (in addition to having to cancel all elective surgeries), this also made Liz feel like the nurses were not being supported by "upper leadership," despite a supportive environment on her floor, the designated COVID unit. Helen similarly viewed the PPE rules as a sign that hospital management did not care whether the nurses got sick "as long as it doesn't affect their bottom line," she wrote in May. "The union negotiations [have] taught us all that," she added, suggesting that nurse–management relationships at her hospital had soured prior to the pandemic.

PPE recycling protocols also raised concerns about nurses' health and safety beyond COVID-19. At Jennifer's Pennsylvania hospital, and at Helen's and Liz's Washington hospitals, nurses were initially asked to place all used masks in a bin to be recycled and disinfected. Helen noted that nurses were then being asked to reuse these masks after the cleaning process, "when we don't understand if it is effective or safe for us to inhale the recycled mask." At Liz's hospital, the nurses' union fought in April "to have our recycled surgical masks NOT be sanitized with a chemical that causes breast cancer," she noted.

For Kat, working in a neurological unit of an urban Wisconsin hospital, the anger and frustration at the PPE situation extended to the hospital CEO, who "is just not listening," and to the federal government for failing to prepare for the pandemic. "The whole government thing with the PPE is just—it's just ludicrous," she explained in a May 9 audio diary entry. "We shouldn't have to fight for PPE. . . . It should just be 'Do you need supplies? Here you go.'" She noted that the United States had "plenty of time" to prepare and assemble supplies to meet the March surge, since the first US cases appeared in January. "And we are now paying the price for the selfishness," she added, "of certain leaders in our country who care more about their image than about America."

In the hospitals where the nurses in this study worked, the PPE shortages abated by June. But hospital management's handling of the initial situation, especially the rules restricting use of PPE by nurses and not physicians, seemed to set the stage for nurses' lingering bad feelings toward management. The continual and seemingly haphazard changes in PPE policy further undermined nurses' trust in upper management. At Liz's hospital these changes—from prohibiting COVID nurses from wearing N95s; to then requiring them to wear N95s and disposable face shields but to use a mask for at least four hours and reuse the shields; to then requiring N95s, a face shield, and a surgical mask, and not requiring their reuse—led her to view "higher ups" so skeptically that she hesitated to get vaccinated when the shots became available to her in December. "I just have a lot of mistrust about anything coming from my hospital," she wrote. This distrust and anger lingered into April 2021 as she contemplated quitting her job. "I'm angry at my employer for deciding how safe I get to be without asking me," Liz wrote. "I'm angry that they didn't take care of us and now everyone is quitting and they still aren't taking care of us because they know we will still show up. I don't want to show up anymore." While a paid leave of absence and employer-provided counseling sessions made Liz feel somewhat better about management, the hospitals' earlier handling of the PPE shortage left her and other nurses in this study with a lasting impression that they were not valued as workers.

PANDEMIC OCCUPATIONAL HEALTH HAZARDS, FROM "MASK-NE" TO PTSD

The restrictions on PPE, together with uncertainties of how COVID-19 was transmitted and delays in adapting safety protocols, meant nurses in the study realistically feared becoming infected and passing COVID-19 on to their households. As illustrated by Stephanie's story about doing CPR on a dying COVID-19 patient, nurses' everyday hospital responsibilities now entailed heightened risk of COVID-19 exposure. WHO recommendations that HCWs who were triaging possible COVID-19-positive patients remain at least a meter (3.28 feet) from them could not always be followed if nurses wanted to provide good patient care.[18] In Liz's hospital during the first COVID-19 wave, confusion and miscommunication about incoming patients, inconsistent testing, and lack of clinical knowledge about COVID-19 symptoms sometimes meant that HCWs were exposed to the disease from supposed "non-COVID" patients. "I helped complete the admission on a patient," Liz wrote in her diary on May 7. "Then two hours later, they decided to test her for the virus. I wore my surgical mask in the room, but that's it." The results had not come back yet when Liz clocked out and drove home to her husband and children. (After "starting her clock," she learned the patient was COVID-negative.)

Other nurses in the study also expressed persistent, exhausting worries about symptoms they feared were COVID-19. Jennifer, who wrote that she had no anxiety prior to the pandemic, now experienced persistent "underlying anxiety" at work and now suffered from acid reflux. Stephanie reported "anticipatory anxiety" about getting COVID-19 and dying. Eventually, this anxiety turned to exhaustion. "Just want to lay on the couch," Stephanie wrote in mid-May. "Don't want to cook, clean, or parent," she added. But she wondered if her exhaustion—ten days after the CPR exposure—signaled "the start" of COVID-19 or just fatigue from working in the COVID ICU for two months while caring for her teenagers at home.

For the nurses in this study, concerns about spreading COVID-19 to families and community sometimes produced more anxiety than the possibility of getting sick themselves. In early April, Liz canceled family plans to celebrate Easter and her younger child's birthday with her parents, because she was "just too nervous to pass anything on, especially in my own family." In September, when Liz's mother visited to provide long-needed help with childcare, Liz's older child developed a fever. Liz's mother went into "full panic" that the child had COVID-19 and had given it to her. (She tested negative.) Nurses' anxieties about being a vector of contagion for their families had to be balanced against the desire to see their extended families and to obtain relief from the heavy childcare burdens imposed by the pandemic. Kat's worries that she would pass on COVID-19 initially led her to keep her daughter out of daycare, even though she was exhausted from being pregnant with a second child and working in the hospital. "I feel I am considered a high risk [person] since I work at a hospital," Kat explained in a May 23 voice diary entry. "Out of the family, I'm the one that's exposed most and I don't want to catch something, be asymptomatic, bring it home and then accidentally give it to [my daughter] and then have her give it to the daycare people, so we're still trying to figure out the logistics of that." After Kat gave birth, her situation became "overwhelming" at home. COVID-19 case numbers were dropping, and Kat and her husband discovered that the COVID-19 safety protocols at daycare had become stricter, so she put her older child back in daycare. However, in early November, one of the teachers tested positive for COVID-19, and the daycare closed, leading Kat and her husband back to juggling full-time childcare and full-time work.

Hospitals' policies on visitors during the pandemic also produced stresses unique to nurses and nursing support staff. Helen noted in her diary that all the patients—not just those with COVID-19—were "dealing with emotional distress" and had a "higher need for emotional support from the nursing staff" given the fact that hospitals allowed no visitors in spring 2020. When patients wanted to communicate with their families via online platforms, they needed nurses (who were not trained in tech support) to set up the call and hold the tablet computer. In early April, Liz was assigned to set up a FaceTime call between a dying patient and his close family member. "I was given a phone number and told I only had one chance to make the call or the iPad would reset," she wrote. "I put on the yellow gown, surgical mask, reusable helmet and double gloves." Then she dialed the number, and, thankfully, the family member answered. As she held the iPad over the patient's bed and tried to keep it steady, the formerly unresponsive patient suddenly "tried to sit up and move [his] arms." Liz had to leave after the call and noted that the patient's family would not be allowed to visit and the patient "[would] die alone."

When the hospitals began allowing limited visitors in late May and June, this produced new difficulties for nurses. "Many of us are starting to feel like we're the mask police or the food police or the visitor police, where we have to make sure that it is actually one adult visitor per patient and the same visitor per 24-hour policy," Kat noted on May 25. Some nurses, to avoid upsetting patients' families, bent the rules and allowed more visitors in patients' rooms. But this increased the risk of two-way COVID-19 spread between patients and visitors and meant that when other nurses tried to enforce the one-visitor policy, they would "get met with backlash" by angry family members. On June 29, Kat reported that the nurses were still feeling "like hospital cops" for enforcing this policy. In Liz's hospital, the nursing supervisor eventually permitted more than one visitor for dying patients, but some families abused this policy. "Visitors are only supposed to visit for end-of-life situations like this once for a short time, but the family [of a dying patient] basically barricaded themselves in the room for 24 hours," she noted on January 1, 2021. They weren't "always wearing masks" and were "sneaking other family members in." The family members, moreover, seemed oblivious to the fact that they could be contracting COVID-19 and spreading it in their communities.

On top of these stresses, wearing PPE in negative-pressure isolation rooms for COVID-19 patients made nursing duties more physically taxing than before the pandemic. When the COVID-19 isolation rooms were first set up in Jennifer's hospital, with negative pressure machines that sucked the air out of the room, one of her colleagues was working in this environment for hours and "with only very minimal breaks from all his isolation garb."

He "started having chest pain, and we had to send him to the emergency dept," she wrote. "Nobody wants to call it a heart attack; instead, it was a mild cardiac event that kept him in the hospital overnight," she added. The loud noises made by negative pressure machines also made working in the rooms more difficult. "You have to yell" to be heard above the din, Liz noted on May 30. The installation of these machines in windows, with their large tubes that sucked air from the room to the outside, also meant that the windows could no longer be sealed shut. Years earlier, the windows on this upper floor had been sealed as a safety precaution after an employee had jumped out an open window and died. "It was interesting that having a negative air pressure machine in these private rooms, which could be easily pulled out of the window, suddenly became more important than that safety issue," Liz noted.

As the pandemic wore on, the nurses also experienced other mental and physical health problems. Liz developed a rash around her face and mouth from wearing the PPE and was prescribed medication from a dermatologist to treat the "mask-ne," as HCWs were calling it. Moreover, after three and a half months of working in a COVID unit, experiencing sleepless nights and frequent anxiety about going to work, Liz started to report that she was depressed. Most of her COVID-19 patients had died—some slowly, some quickly, and most alone. She also found it "depressing" that COVID-19 case numbers, which had dropped in the Northwest in May, had now begun to surge again due to the increase in public gatherings. "The COVID unit is full; the ICU in the city 2 hours away is full," she wrote on June 27. "They sent me an admit from this city who was at a family party 10 days ago and is now short of breath." She was upset that the paramedics had not informed the nursing staff that the patient's need for supplementary oxygen had increased rapidly during the transport to the hospital (an indication that his condition was worsening). They had kept him on the COVID floor rather than sending him immediately to the ICU, where his critical state could be better addressed. To add to the increased stress at work, the resurgence also meant that Liz had to cancel her children's play dates and once again have them stay home and watch movies while she tried to figure out which outside activities were safe.

Then one day in late July, just after she clocked in to work, Liz walked into an extremely upsetting situation. She heard another caregiver yell out from her patient's room, "He's not breathing!" She and another staff member grabbed their PPE and ran into the room. "We walked in and he was covered in blood from his mouth—he had either vomited blood or coughed it all up," she wrote in November, when she was finally "ready to write about" the episode. Just beforehand, his family "had called and asked to FaceTime using the hospital-provided iPad," Liz recounted. "The patient said he was too tired" and would call them later. Another staff member "and I had to prep his body for the morgue and spent a really long time trying to scrub all the blood out of his beard. Which is a lot harder than you think."

This episode not only illustrates how nurses and allied HCWs continued to provide care to patients even after death; it also shows how caring for COVID-19 patients could be traumatic for them. The unpredictable course of the disease; the painful and invasive nature of treatments like intubation; as well as the experience of seeing people unexpectedly "crash" and die, or linger for weeks and slowly die alone, proved wrenching for even experienced clinicians. "My coworkers are experiencing varying degrees of PTSD," Jennifer wrote on August 8. When it was time to extubate a patient who seemed to be improving, one of the nurses on her floor "practically had to be forced into the room to participate." It was "kind of like making a child get back on the bicycle they just fell off," she added. The fact that extubation released aerosol virus particles into the air, and could unexpectedly cause seemingly stable patients to crash, had likely made this nurse dread performing the procedure. Fortunately, the patient recovered. But many HCWs were suffering lasting mental health consequences from repeatedly facing situations like this one.

The nurses' reports of anxiety, sleeplessness, depression, and PTSD in this study appear consistent with larger reported trends. Researchers have thoroughly documented the impact of the global COVID-19 pandemic on nurses' and other HCWs' mental health. One "meta-review" published in January 2022 examined 40 systematic reviews of studies on the mental health of nurses and other healthcare professionals during the pandemic. This review, based on data from 1,828 studies published in English involving over 3.2 million participants in numerous countries, found that anxiety, depression, and stress/PTSD were the most prevalent COVID-19-related mental health conditions in HCWs, while sleep disorders, burnout, fear, obsessive-compulsive disorder, somatization (physical symptoms resulting from psychological stress), phobias, substance misuse, and suicidal thoughts also were reported among HCWs in relation to the pandemic.[19] Research specifically on nurses showed similar outcomes. A systematic review of 93 studies that examined the mental health of over 93,000 nurses in 28 countries from January through September 2020 found that about 43 percent reported stress over the time period, with stress prevalence peaking at 50 percent in April 2020. About 39 percent of frontline nurses and 32 percent of nurses overall reported anxiety, 35 percent reported depression, and 47 percent of frontline nurses and 37 percent of nurses overall reported sleep disturbances.[20] Even though these conditions also spiked in the general population during the pandemic, the levels found among nurses for all aspects of mental health conditions except depression were markedly higher than among the overall population.[21]

Pandemic Stressors Outside the Hospital Walls

For the nurses in this study, not all stressors came from work. Some lived in communities where groups actively protested pandemic-related restrictions or among friends and neighbors who began acting like the pandemic did not exist. For Liz, this situation led to a profound "disconnect" between her experiences in an urban hospital COVID unit, where patients were dying, and her off time, where neighbors in her bedroom community "tell me they think the virus is a conspiracy cooked up by Bill Gates and the government can't force them to wear masks and that sunshine and fresh air will kill it," she wrote on April 27, 2020. Her neighbors knew she worked in some sort of surgical unit, and she feared that if they learned she now worked with COVID-19 patients, "they will be scared to be near me or my family," she wrote. When she put on a mask and took her children to the dentist for a "time-sensitive" visit, she warily notified the front-desk staff about her job. "They said it was the least of their concerns, because I was probably the only one in our town wearing PPE and wearing it properly," she noted with relief. Amid the growing hostility to mask wearing, solidarity seemed to remain among HCWs across office and hospital contexts.

Other study nurses reacted with fury to those flouting or opposing restrictions. "I understand the frustration, fear for income, and dismay at normal life being disrupted," Helen wrote in May. "What I don't understand are the protests saying they have the right to get a haircut and how dare the government force this order. How dare those people? Is your haircut worth my life?" At Helen's hospital, the PPE shortage had resolved by May, but she worried (correctly) that the post-reopening surge caused by peoples' indifferent behavior would again strain supplies. Kat expressed anger similar to Helen's at the "complete selfishness" of people who "go to these protest rallies and then expose themselves [and their kids to COVID-19]." In a May 12 diary entry, she noted that large protests at her state capitol against the pandemic lockdown had been followed by a wave of COVID-19 among protesters. She found this development "infuriating," though "very much expected." Her anger, she indicated, was directed only at people who flaunted mask and stay-at-home orders and then expected to be able to show up at the hospital and have nurses and doctors take care of them. "I feel like we're being taken advantage of," she stated in May.

Liz expressed a slightly different view. While she said she felt angry at the people "protesting Walmart and Costco for requiring masks," as they clearly did not "get it" about the risks of COVID-19, she also expressed resignation at peoples' failure to do what was best for themselves and others. How many times in her nursing career, she reflected, "did I tell a patient not to eat a hamburger right after surgery and their family brought them McDonalds and then they threw up everywhere?" she wrote on July 17. "How many times have I said to take a stool softener with your opiates, so you don't get constipated and they refuse and then they are stuck at the hospital for an extra day waiting to poop?" She added, "I have spent my whole career making 'recommendations' that people never listen to. And why would they? We (the nurses) are always there to pick up the pieces." Four months into the pandemic, she continued, "Part of me wants to scream from the rooftop and educate, educate, educate like we were taught and the other part of me is so tired and says 'f*ck it. Let them learn the hard way.'"

Liz struggled with the fact that many in her community and her in-laws continued to insist that COVID-19 was a hoax and dismissed her own direct experience with COVID-19 patients. "I want to explain what I'm going through and what I've been seeing and why I'm so upset but no one really wants to know," she wrote on August 29. "They will read the news and pass on these crazy stories, but they don't really want to know what's happening when it's close to home. It also makes me feel like no one cares."

By summer's end, the resentments had begun to spill over into the hospital where Liz worked. In August, just as the staff was sorting out a "snafu" where a COVID-19 patient had been placed in a double room, other nurses informed Liz that a bomb had been placed in front of the entrance to the hospital's emergency room. Patients were diverted to other units while police (successfully) defused and removed it. Though it was not clear that this incident was directly related to community resentment against COVID-19 and restrictions, it certainly indicates a climate of hostility to HCWs. A more specific instance of hostility toward HCWs enforcing pandemic rules came weeks later in response to a requirement that patients wear masks when they leave their rooms. "My charge nurse asked a patient who was standing in the hallway outside his room to please wear a mask outside his room. He just looked at her and screamed," Liz wrote on September 10. When he kept screaming and refused to comply with her continued requests, security had to be called. With typical empathy, Liz added in her description of this incident that she could understand the patient's reaction because, with the pandemic and state of the world, she, too, felt like she wanted to scream sometimes.

"You're Either a Hero or Typhoid Mary"

While it may be tempting to view nurses as heroic for their continued willingness to treat patients in the face of probable COVID-19 infection and heightened hostility toward HCWs, none of the nurses in this study said they appreciated being called healthcare heroes. To the contrary, Kat vented in her audio diary on May 9, "Every time we get an email thanking us about being 'healthcare heroes,' I feel like it's more a slap in the face than an actual compliment because I feel like we are not heroes." Instead, she said, she viewed the nurses as an involuntary "last line of defense for COVID patients" and expressed anger at those who had contracted the illness through refusal to wear masks, social distance, or stay at home. "To put that kind of pressure on healthcare providers is completely unfair, especially when we have to worry about our own health and the potential to bring this disease into our own household," she said. Neither did Kat appreciate the thank-you notes for nurses. Instead, she preferred to be viewed as one among a group of workers who were just "doing our job." Liz expressed similar views in late April when she described reading an article about an ER doctor in New York who had died by suicide after working with COVID patients. In the article, another doctor had commented that "the clappers"—members of the public who stood on the sidewalks and clapped for healthcare workers as they entered or left the hospital—were "the hardest to hear." Liz indicated that she related to the second doctor's perspective. "I also don't feel like a hero; I didn't sign up for this," she wrote. Instead, she said she felt "expendable."

As COVID-19 cases in Liz's hospital climbed back up in July, the hospital decided that this time around, it would not cancel elective surgeries. This meant that staff from surgical units would not be redeployed to help in the COVID unit and the unit would struggle to find adequate nursing staff for the surge. "Why don't they cancel the elective surgeries again so we have the help again?" she asked her diary. Then she answered herself: "Because they are billion[s] of dollars in debt and don't care about us!!"

Liz came to dread going into work and even called in sick once in July when she was merely exhausted and depressed. This sick call left her wracked with guilt for letting down overburdened colleagues. As she prepared for her next shift and the anxiety mounted, she wrote that she felt like "a wimp" because she only worked flextime and others were doing this work full-time. She noted, however, that she had been "burnt out before COVID." She had already been struggling with a desire to quit nursing and stay home to be a full-time mother but had remained in her job due to the high pay, job security, and health insurance for her family, which balanced out her husband's career as a sole proprietor. Now she feared that the challenges of work with COVID-19 patients "might break me." Liz's inner conflict reveals the painful contrast between the public image of nurses as selfless superhuman caregivers—rescuing angels in the tradition of Florence Nightingale—and their lived realities as ordinary people who were struggling to do a hard job while themselves coping with elevated stress from pandemic parenting, caring for elderly parents, and their marriages. As Malia wrote in March 2021, "Hospitals and healthcare centers coined the cute term 'healthcare hero' with absolutely no benefit."

This chasm between public perceptions and private reality could even induce feelings of guilt and inadequacy as nurses watched patient after patient die without being able to save them. After Stephanie did her job according to hospital protocol and performed CPR on a patient in respiratory distress, she later lamented that she had only made the dying process worse. The deep emotional wounds created by these experiences, in which a worker must choose between two bad outcomes or go against their beliefs and values to do their job, have been termed "moral injuries." Research has only begun to examine the lasting negative effect of moral injuries on HCWs' mental health and well-being.[22]

The nurses additionally expressed concern about being stigmatized as vectors of contagion. While Liz feared that her family might be ostracized if neighbors discovered she worked with COVID-19 patients, others expressed concerns about being targeted for violence. Helen reported seeing a story on Instagram about a nurse who had been "beat up at a gas station" because the attacker believed she was spreading COVID-19. "Will my community fear me like this person did? Am I safe?" she wondered. Liz's coworkers experienced stigma in July when a massage place canceled their appointments after the owners found out they worked at Liz's hospital. "If you tell someone where you work, you are either a hero or Typhoid Mary," Liz quipped.

Coping and Resilience

Despite their limited PPE access, despite the deaths and suffering they witnessed, and despite the hostility they experienced inside and outside the hospitals, most nurses in this study persisted in their jobs during the first year of the pandemic. The nurses' diaries show that several factors helped them to continue. First, they reported being sustained by the mutual support and solidarity with other nurses and HCWs, including doctors. After a "rough shift" in which Liz's nursing supervisor decided to waive the one-visitor a day policy so a dying patient's young child could visit, Liz and the supervisor "walked to the parking garage together" and commiserated. In early September, Liz found support when she went hiking with another coworker and their children. "It was so nice to talk to someone who has EXACTLY the same experiences/emotions/situations," she wrote after the hike. Liz also drew strength from her coworker's ability to remain "so tough and so brave and so positive" in the face of multiple pandemic surges, she wrote in November. Similarly, Stephanie found support in the ability of her coworkers "to support one another" and to remain "in this together," while sometimes using gallows humor to maintain morale. She expressed pride at being "part of a mobilization" to meet the unprecedented emergency. "They lift me up,"

Stephanie wrote of general care nurses and "amazing" travel nurses brought in to bolster her ICU during the first surge. As previously noted, this solidarity could have a downside, as it exacerbated guilt that an exhausted nurse might feel in saying no to overtime or taking time off. But the nurses did not report being "shamed" by other HCWs for calling in sick or taking time off. Mainly, they reported support from and solidarity with others working on the floor.

The nurses in this study also may have been able to stay in their jobs because they prioritized self-care. Jennifer, who was finishing a nurse practitioner (NP) training program while her three children were all at home attending online school, quickly realized she would have to "do what I can to take care of my mental health during this time." She prioritized getting outside to get vitamin D and finding a low-stress clinical rotation for her NP program. Liz, meanwhile, sought counseling from a mental health provider paid for by the hospital, who helped her to release negative feelings and reframe some of her challenges. Being empathetic—where she felt patients' pain and suffering as her own—was "zapping all my energy," she realized. Instead, she tried to learn to be compassionate toward patients but not take their problems home. She also adapted the mantra "I can do hard things," from a popular book and decided to persist, for now, with nursing at some level, after requesting and obtaining a paid leave of absence. During this leave, she took runs in parks and hikes in the mountains. She found new appreciation in her ability to breathe, after seeing so many people with COVID-19 lose that ability. "I think all of this has shown me not to take for granted that big breath of fresh air. Not everyone gets to do that," Liz wrote in February 2021.

The Winter Surge and Vaccines

In November 2020, as COVID cases again surged, the exhausted nurses in this study prepared for another round of intense work. They had to prepare psychologically as well as logistically. "It has been like waiting for the other shoe to drop," Jennifer wrote on November 20. "The anxiety had almost become a distant memory, until it all came flooding back again." Even though her small unit now had six COVID-19 patients—all intubated—she found reason for optimism. "I desperately cling to the hope that we will be able to save people this time around," she wrote. No longer were the patients being given hydroxychloroquine and azithromycin, both of which had been demonstrated to be ineffective against COVID-19. Instead, the "go-to treatments" now included convalescent plasma from people who had recovered from COVID-19, along with remdesivir and dexamethasone—the two drugs that had famously seemed to produce a quick turnaround for President Trump in October 2020. Additionally, clinical teams had experience with "proning" patients—placing them on their bellies for sixteen hours, and then turning them on their backs for eight hours. Two patients undergoing proning, Jennifer reported, had high oxygen levels as well as other good signs. Both were "sedated and paralyzed so they don't fight against the ventilator and can let their bodies heal." Even with these clinical innovations, the winter surge proved very severe.

The announcement in December 2020 that HCWs were now eligible for vaccines could not have come at a more opportune time. However, the vaccines were new and had been tested in clinical trials that some perceived as rushed. After a year during which nurses felt that hospital management had been indifferent to their health and safety, some, like Liz, hesitated to get immunized against COVID-19, as they did not trust those in administration who were encouraging them to get vaccinated.

Since the study ended in April 2021, it provides no insights on how nurses' attitudes toward vaccination changed during the second pandemic year, or how subsequent pandemic waves, including the Delta and Omicron variants, affected nurses' mental health, well-being, and occupational satisfaction. However, the study does suggest that these waves crashed into a healthcare system and a nursing workforce that had already been struggling with heightened levels of anxiety, depression, PTSD, and pandemic-related burnout for more than a year. Subsequent studies will likely reveal more about the longer-term effects of the pandemic on nurses and other HCWs.

Conclusion: From Resilience to Resistance

This small study of writings from six nurses reveals some powerful insights about the state of US nursing in the pandemic. First, nurses have proven themselves flexible, resilient, and tough in their successful adaptation to a nightmarishly difficult and dangerous work environment. Their own sense of solidarity, mission, and purpose has made them stronger and able to withstand a great deal of occupational strain. However, these findings also suggest that working with COVID-19 patients has worsened nurses' mental health, has involved occupational traumas, and has produced moral injuries and PTSD. It is hard to know how much these conditions will resolve as the pandemic recedes. But it is likely that the pandemic has had deep and longlasting effects on nurses.

In a recent systematic review of research on nurses' mental health in the pandemic, the authors proposed that hospitals and other healthcare providers increase their psychological support and wellness services for nurses and do more to train nurse managers to address these issues proactively, as well as "improving manpower and resource allocations."[23] Certainly, it is difficult to see how the nursing profession will retain experienced hospital nurses without providing vehicles for healing and recovery, as well as enhanced work incentives such as student loan forgiveness and shorter shifts. However, the recent surge in strikes and threatened walkouts by nurses and other HCWs across the United States suggests that healthcare leaders and policymakers must move beyond individual-level solutions if they are going to meaning-fully address the problem of post-pandemic burnout among nurses and other HCWs.[24] This is a collective, population-wide problem that needs to be rem-edied at a systems level. As this study indicates, nurses did not just suffer from witnessing, and being powerless to prevent, many tragic but inevitable deaths from COVID-19. They also suffered due to hospital policies and practices that conveyed management's indifference to their health, safety, or well-being. And while the nurses in this study did not translate their frustrations into collective action during the study period, it has become apparent since then that many US nurses are doing so.

Since early 2021, US nurses and other HCWs have stepped up their orga-nized resistance to unsafe working conditions, inadequate pay, and unsafe staffing levels that compromise patient safety. Nurse strikes, once rare, had become common in the years leading up to the pandemic.[25] *Becker's Hospital Review* reported five "notable" nurse strikes in the United States in 2017, three in 2018, and five in 2019.[26] In 2021 the number shot up to at least ten.[27] While most involved walkouts of a day to a week, one group of nurses, from Saint Vincent Hospital in Worcester, Massachusetts, remained on strike for ten months between March 2021 and January 2022.[28] The striking Saint Vincent nurses told reporters that they had been driven to the picket line by the brutal coalescence of staffing cuts, furloughs, and unsafe working conditions that worsened during the pandemic. "They think that women will take it on the chin no matter what," striking nurse Marie Ritacco told the *Washington Post* in late 2021. "We are committed to our profession and to our patients, but the pandemic has proven to us that if we do not stand up for ourselves and our patients, no one is going to do that for us."[29] In their agreement with the hos-pital, the Saint Vincent nurses won guarantees of safer nurse:patient ratios, protective measures against all-too-common assaults by patients, including metal detectors in the hospital entrance, and improved pay and benefits.[30]

Since the Saint Vincent nurses' historic victory, nurse strikes have prolif-erated. *Becker's Hospital Review* reported fourteen notable nurse strikes in 2022, while the Bureau of Labor Statistics, which only tracks strikes involving at least 1,000 workers, reported that six nurses unions representing 32,800 nurses held strikes and that this number represented an increase over prior years.[31] In 2023 there were at least twelve nurse strikes. In January, 12,000 nurses at seven New York City hospitals threatened to walk off the job; then 7,000 went on strike for three days before reaching contract agreements with hospital management.[32] In June 2023, six months after a *New York Times* investigation revealed that the large, officially not-for-profit Ascension Health hospital chain had deliberately cut nursing staff down to unsafe levels ahead of the pandemic to raise profits, nurses at Ascension-owned hospitals in Kansas and in Austin, Texas, walked off the job for one-day strikes.[33] One nurse in the Austin picket line held a sign that read "Health Care Heroes Treated like Zeroes." Another's placard read "Essential, not Expendable."[34] In the nurses' clever hands, the blunt, hollow catchphrases used by management to keep them working in 2020 now became sharp-edged tools of resistance.

In this climate it would seem prudent for hospital management to work proactively to repair their relationships with nurses and rebuild trust. They can start with listening to nurses and their unions and professional organizations. Longer term, a possible avenue for addressing nurses' mistrust in management and need for improved working conditions is the well-honed model of labor–management partnerships, in which work teams of both frontline staff nurses and managers work together to solve problems and enact meaningful changes that improve work conditions. Such partnerships, when executed in good faith, empower frontline staff and have been shown to improve both staff working conditions and the well-being of patients.[35] Such improvements in staff–management relations may not only bring justice and respect to nurses but might also ensure that enough skilled and experienced nurses remain in the profession to handle the next pandemic.

Notes

1. All nurses in this chapter are identified only by pseudonyms. Some identifying details have been changed or omitted to protect their anonymity.

2. Karen Cunningham, "A City Nurse: Healing in the I.C.U. during COVID-19," *New Yorker*, May 4, 2020, https://www.newyorker.com/magazine/2020/05/04/a-city-nurse/; *Los Angeles Times* Staff, "Nurses Are the Coronavirus Heroes: These Photos Show Their Life Now," *Los Angeles Times*, April 17, 2020, https://www.latimes.com/world-nation/story/2020-04-17/nurses-are-the-coronavirus-heroes/.

3. Mohammed Al Maqbali, Mohammed Al Sinani, and Badriya Al-Lenjawi, "Prevalence of Stress, Depression, Anxiety and Sleep Disturbance among Nurses during the COVID-19 Pandemic: A Systematic Review and Meta-Analysis," *Journal of Psychosomatic Research* 141 (February 2021): 1–18, doi:10.1016/j.jpsychores.2020.110343/.

4. This publication focuses on licensed registered nurses (RNs), as all of the participants in the study were licensed RNs, and some also had advanced nursing training and credentials. However, when reporting upon the experiences of "nurses," the participants in the study did not always differentiate between RNs and other healthcare workers who perform nursing duties, including licensed practical nurses (LPNs) and licensed vocational nurses (LVNs) as well as certified nursing assistants (CNAs). Nor did they always differentiate between ordinary

RNs and advanced practice RNs, such as nurse practitioners (NPs), or those with a Doctor of Nursing Practice (DNP) degree. These all constitute important groups of healthcare workers.

5. For timelines, see "WHO's COVID-19 Response" (Geneva, World Health Organization, 2022), https://www.who.int/emergencies/diseases/novel-corona virus-2019/interactive-timeline#event-19/, and "CDC Museum COVID-19 Time-line" (Atlanta: US Centers for Disease Control and Prevention, 2022), https://www.cdc.gov/museum/timeline/covid19.html/.

6. WHO Timeline, CDC Museum Timeline.

7. "Timeline of Trump's COVID-19 Comments," FactCheck.org website (Phila-delphia, Annenberg Public Policy Center–University of Pennsylvania, 2020), https://www.factcheck.org/2020/10/timeline-of-trumps-covid-19-comments/. Robert Costa and Philip Rucker, "Woodward Book: Trump Says He Knew Coro-navirus Was 'Deadly' and Worse Than the Flu While Intentionally Misleading Americans," *Washington Post*, September 9, 2020, https://www.washingtonpost .com/politics/bob-woodward-rage-book-trump/2020/09/09/0368fe3c-efd2 -11ea-b4bc-3a2098fc73d4_story.html/.

8. Doug Bock Clark, "Inside the Chaotic, Cutthroat Gray Market for N95 Masks," *New York Times Magazine*, November 17, 2020, updated February 17, 2021, https://www.nytimes.com/2020/11/17/magazine/n95-masks-market-covid .html/.

9. World Health Organization, "Rational Use of Personal Protective Equip-ment for Coronavirus Disease (COVID-19): Interim Guidance, 27 February 2020," https://apps.who.int/iris/handle/10665/331215.

10. National Nurses United, "National Nurse Survey Reveals Devastating Impact of Reopening Too Soon," press release, July 28, 2020, https://www .nationalnursesunited.org/press/national-nurse-survey-reveals-devastating -impact-reopening-too-soon/.

11. National Conference of State Legislatures, COVID-19: Occupational Licens-ing during Public Emergencies, NCSL website, https://www.ncsl.org/labor-and -employment/covid-19-occupational-licensing-during-public-emergencies.

12. Tammy Webber, "Hospitals Competing for Nurses as US Coronavirus Cases Surge," *AP News*, November 2, 2020, https://apnews.com/article/hospitals -competing-nurses-virus-surge-0e1d92aa8002c1638d8bc9b692c01919/; Lianna Matt McLenon, "COVID-Related Nursing Shortages Hit Hospitals Nationwide," *CIDRAP News*, Center for Infectious Disease Research and Policy, University of Minnesota, November 30, 2020, https://www.cidrap .umn.edu/news-perspective/2020/11/covid-related-nursing-shortages-hit -hospitals-nationwide/.

13. Gabrielle Masson, "Nurses Account for Most Known US Healthcare Worker COVID-19 Deaths: Guardian, KHN," *Becker's Hospital Review*, March 17, 2021, https://www.beckershospitalreview.com/public-health/nurses-account-for -most-known-us-healthcare-worker-covid-19-deaths-guardian-khn.html/.

14. International Council of Nurses, "ICN Says 115,000 Healthcare Worker Deaths from COVID-19 Exposes Collective Failure of Leaders to Protect Global

Workforce," October 21, 2021, https://www.icn.ch/news/icn-says-115000 -healthcare-worker-deaths-covid-19-exposes-collective-failure-leaders-protect/.

15. University of Maryland College Park Institutional Review Board, "Approval Letter, New Project, [1593292-1] COVID, CAREGIVING, and COPING: U.S. Nurses Write from the Front Lines, Principal Investigator: Marian Moser Jones, Ph.D., M.P.H." Date Submitted: April 17, 2020. Publish Date: April 24, 2020.

16. The study investigators did not keep photos of these identifying documents in order to protect the participants' privacy.

17. Matthew B. Miles, A. Michael Huberman, and Johnny Saldana, *Qualitative Data Analysis: A Methods Sourcebook*, 3rd ed. (Washington, DC: Sage Publications, 2014), 69–92; Adele Clarke, *Situational Analysis: Grounded Theory after the Interpretive Turn* (Thousand Oaks, CA: Sage; 2018), xxiii–xxxii, 3–22.

18. WHO, Rational Use of Personal Protective Equipment for Coronavirus Disease (COVID-19): Interim Guidance, 27 February 2020 (Geneva, WHO, 2020), https://apps.who.int/iris/handle/10665/331215.

19. Muhammad Chutiyami, Allen MY Cheong, Dauda Salihu, Umar Muhammad Bello, Dorothy Ndwiga, Reshin Maharaj, Kogi Naidoo, et al., "COVID-19 Pandemic and Overall Mental Health of Healthcare Professionals Globally: A Meta-Review of Systematic Reviews," *Frontiers in Psychiatry* 12 (2021), doi:10.3389/fpsyt.2021.804525/.

20. Al Maqbali et al., "Prevalence of Stress, Depression, Anxiety, and Sleep Disturbance among Nurses."

21. Notably, this systematic review does not examine sleep disturbance levels among the general population. N. Salari, A. Hosseinian-Far, R. Jalali, A. Vaisi-Raygani, S. Rasoulpoor, M. Mohammadi, S. Rasoulpoor, B. Khaledi-Paveh, "Prevalence of Stress, Anxiety, Depression among the General Population during the COVID-19 Pandemic: A Systematic Review and Meta-Analysis," *Global Health* 16, no. 1: 57 (July 6, 2020), doi:10.1186/s12992-020-00589-w/. PMID: 32631403; PMCID: PMC7338126.

22. Anto Čartolovni, Minna Stolt, P. Anne Scott, and Riitta Suhonen. "Moral Injury in Healthcare Professionals: A Scoping Review and Discussion," *Nursing Ethics* 28, no. 5 (2021): 590–602, doi:10.1177/0969733020966776/.

23. Al Maqbali, et al. "Prevalence of Stress, Depression, Anxiety and Sleep Disturbance among Nurses," 14.

24. Kelly Gooch, "85 Strikes since 2021: Why Healthcare Workers Are 'More Emboldened to Act,'" *Becker's Hospital Review*, June 6, 2023, https://www.beckers hospitalreview.com/hr/85-strikes-since-2021-why-healthcare-workers-are -more-emboldened-to-act.html/.

25. Anita Catlin, "Nursing Strike, America, 2019: Concept Analysis to Guide Practice," *Nursing Outlook* 68, no. 4 (July–August 2020), 468–475, https://doi.org/ 10.1016/j.outlook.2020.03.002.

26. Kelly Gooch, "8 Notable Strikes So Far in 2017," *Becker's Hospital Review* (*BHR*), December 11, 2017, https://www.beckershospitalreview.com/hr/8 -notable-strikes-so-far-in-2017.html [5 nurses]; Gooch, "10 Notable Labor Strikes in 2018," *BHR*, December 20, 2018, https://www.beckershospitalreview.com/

hr/11-notable-labor-strikes-in-2018.html [3 nurses]; Gooch, "14 Labor Strikes in 2019," *BHR*, December 19, 2019, https://www.beckershospitalreview.com/hr/14-labor-strikes-in-2019.html [5 nurses]; Gooch, "7 Hospital Strikes in 2020," *BHR*, September 7, 2020, https://www.beckershospitalreview.com/hr/7-hospital-strikes-in-2020.html [4 nurses].

27. "Nurse Strikes 2021," Nurse Together website, https://www.nursetogether .com/nurse-strikes/. This website lists fourteen strikes in 2021, but with several it is not clear that nurses were among the hospital workers who went on strike. Becker's lists fourteen strikes in 2021 as well, but it is also not clear how many involved nurses. Kelly Gooch, "U.S. Healthcare Workers Walk Off the Job: 14 Strikes in 2021," *BHR*, December 7, 2021, https://www.beckershospitalreview .com/hr/us-healthcare-workers-walk-off-the-job-10-strikes-in-2021.html/.

28. Cyrus Moulton, "St. Vincent Hospital Nurses Overwhelmingly Approve Contract, Officially Ending Strike," *Worcester Telegram & Gazette*, January 3, 2022, https://www.telegram.com/story/news/2022/01/03/picket-line-ballot -box-nurses-st-vincent-hospital-worcester-weigh-contract/9078113002/.

29. Abigail Higgins, "These Nurses Have Been Striking for More Than 200 Days: The Pandemic Was a Breaking Point," *Washington Post* (The Lily), September 30, 2021, https://www.thelily.com/these-nurses-have-been-striking-for -more-than-200-days-the-pandemic-was-a-breaking-point/.

30. Aparna Gopalan, "Massachusetts Nurses Just Won an Epic 10-Month Strike, *New Republic*, January 6, 2022, https://newrepublic.com/article/164950/ st-vincent-hospital-nurses-strike.

31. Kelly Gooch, "U.S. Healthcare Workers Walk Off the Job: 18 Strikes in 2022," *BHR*, November 9, 2022, https://www.beckershospitalreview.com/hr/ us-healthcare-workers-walk-off-the-job-18-strikes-in-2022november9.html/; U.S. Bureau of Labor Statistics, "Major Work Stoppages Involving 1,000 or More Workers, 1993-Present," https://www.bls.gov/web/wkstp/monthly-listing.htm/; Associated Press, "How the NYC Nurses Strike Points to a Nationwide Problem with Staffing," *PBS News Hour*, January 13, 2023, https://www.pbs.org/newshour/nation/ how-the-nyc-nurses-strike-points-to-a-nationwide-problem-with-staffing.

32. Associated Press, "NYC Nurses Strike *PBS News Hour*," January 13, 2023.

33. Rebecca Robbins, Katie Thomas, and Jessica Silver-Greenberg, "How a Sprawling Hospital Chain Ignited Its Own Staffing Crisis," *New York Times*, December 15, 2022, https://www.nytimes.com/2022/12/15/business/hospital- staffing-ascension.html/; Olivia Aldridge, "Nurses Walk out of Austin's Ascension Seton in Historic Strike," *Texas Tribune*, June 27, 2023, https://www .texastribune.org/2023/06/27/texas-nurses-strike/; National Nurses United, "RNs Who Staged Historic TX and KS Strikes Now Locked Out by Ascension," press release, https://www.nationalnursesunited.org/press/rns-who -staged-historic-tx-and-ks-strikes-now-locked-out-by-ascension/.

34. Joe Timmerman, photo, in Aldridge, "Nurses Walk Out," *Texas Tribune*, June 27, 2023; Jaclyn Higgs, National Nurses United, photo, in Sasha von Oldershausen, "'The Worst It's Been': RNs in the Largest Nurse Strike in Texas History Describe

Their Workplace," *Texas Monthly*, June 28, 2023, https://www.texasmonthly
.com/news-politics/austin-nurse-strike-ascension-seton-medical-center/.

35. Peter Lazes and Marie G. Rudden, "Improving Working Conditions in
Turbulent Times: Expanding Unions' Toolkits," *AFT Health Care*, Spring 2022,
22–40.

10

Healthcare Social Workers on the Front Lines of the COVID-19 Pandemic

Cracks, Flaws, and a Vision for Social Healthcare

JENNIFER ZELNICK, LEIGH HOWARD, DORIS JOY, MAURA HAGAN, and SANDRINE ETIENNE

> I think social workers are important. I just want to bring that up. Our hospital is scrutinizing whether social workers are necessary or not. I think telling our story would help.—hospital social worker

> This pandemic has exposed the cracks in our systems, and it's exposed the cracks in our work system and exposed the flaws in management.—hospital social worker

While healthcare workers, especially doctors and nurses in the ED (emergency department) and ICU, have been widely profiled among the "essential" workforce identified during the COVID-19 pandemic, healthcare social workers have largely been absent from such discussions, their role obscured.[1] Like many workers who were called upon in New York City (NYC) during the COVID-19 pandemic, healthcare social workers saw a contradiction between their contributions and their treatment. The project described here grew out of the desire among healthcare social workers to tell their story. This process was facilitated by social workers' membership in their union, 1199SEIU, which provided an organizational structure to support this research, the narrative of the social work researchers, and their sense of their rights at work in general.[2]

In December 2020 a group of hospital-based, unionized social workers approached the New York City chapter of the National Association of Social

Workers (NASW-NYC), seeking support for their struggle to be recognized within the hospital as an essential workforce. This contact led to a town hall meeting of healthcare social workers, and a commitment of the NASW-NYC healthcare committee to collaborate with the 1199SEIU effort. Following the town hall meeting, a core planning group began to get together to discuss how to tell healthcare social workers' story. With assistance from a social work professor with a labor, policy, and occupational health and safety background, the group developed a participatory research approach.

Using principles from participatory action research, five healthcare social workers and a social worker/union representative were trained in focus group methods and thematic qualitative data analysis, considering their own positionality in addition to research skills. Our research team created a focus group protocol designed to elicit discussion about healthcare social workers' experiences during COVID-19, impact on social work roles, lessons learned from the pandemic experience, and advocating for healthcare social workers in the future. A snowball sampling approach using word of mouth was used to identify focus group participants; this process was facilitated by union activists who knew members from hospital and community settings. Three focus groups were scheduled in early 2021.

As a result of the 1199SEIU outreach, twenty-four healthcare social workers employed in hospitals, community-based agencies, or home health settings attended three focus groups conducted on Zoom. Focus group discussions were video-recorded and then transcribed. Focus group transcripts were analyzed by the research team using thematic codes generated from an initial review of the data; the codes were then applied to each transcript independently by each research team member; after this the team met to iron out differences and refine themes. The project was approved by the Institutional Review Board of the Touro College and University System in collaboration with 1199SEIU.

The social work profession studies itself poorly, preferring to research the problems of clients, families, and populations it serves. One dynamic of this "selflessness" is a tendency to be exploited, or to be a partner in our own exploitation. This point was driven home to us when, as part of our protocol planning process, a small group met with Canadian occupational and environmental health research and advocate Jim Brophy, who had written about Canadian healthcare workers during COVID-19.[3] He noted how our group's analysis easily reflected how healthcare social workers held things together, coped with chaos and deficits, and made "heroic" measures, but Brophy challenged our group to voice more explicitly the trauma of what was endured, the neglect and resource gaps, and to advocate for ourselves the way we would for clients. Informed by this mirror, we strived to make this project a window into healthcare social workers' experiences.

Social work in healthcare is part of a "policy driven" profession with deep connections to public attitudes toward the poor.[4] To contextualize our findings, we first introduce and discuss factors that structure healthcare social workers' working conditions and labor concerns. We also provide background on the initial COVID-19 outbreak in New York City in March 2020 and the protests following the George Floyd murder in May of the same year, events that social workers responded to in our focus groups. Finally, we introduce a critical social work perspective as a lens through which to understand our results.

Working Conditions for Healthcare Social Workers

Working conditions for social workers in healthcare are shaped by public policy and the political economy of public and nonprofit social service and healthcare sectors. The ideological attack on the US welfare state, privatization (as a mind-set as well as a set of specific practices), stigmatization of poverty, and the individualization of health and social problems shape the context of social work jobs.[5] The workforce is largely female and includes many workers of color; there is a legacy of lower wages, exploitation, and labor struggles characterized by these identities. Finally, labor union participation is weak, and social workers in labor unions often face being a smaller neglected segment in larger healthcare unions or being part of small, relatively ineffective unions in the contracted nonprofit sector, where their power is structurally constrained.[6]

Working conditions faced by healthcare social workers in hospital versus clinic-based mental/behavioral settings pose different challenges related to their histories, sectoral, and financial structures. Prior to the COVID-19 pandemic, hospital-based social work had experienced decades of decline characterized by the elimination of social work departments, a social work management and supervision structure, shifting of tasks onto nursing staff (especially discharge planning), and dwindling numbers of social workers employed in the hospital setting.[7] Overall, the decline of hospital social work has resulted in a smaller scope of discrete job tasks and a smaller workforce. This shift has been driven in part by (1) lack of billing codes specific to social work license in the hospital setting, (2) efficiency/cost-effectiveness studies that recommend social work staffing reductions, and (3) a general lack of recognition of the value of hospital social work. This has occurred despite growing recognition of the so-called social determinants of health, evidence of the readmission drivers of cost in healthcare that include mental health, opioid epidemic, trauma, community violence, and so forth (areas where social workers are trained), and hospitals need to improve their customer service and "patient-centered" care. The general backdrop of the shift in the hospital sector aimed at increasing market share and competition and decreasing costs also shape these trends.

In the clinic-based behavioral health setting, social workers' working conditions are constrained by the margins of the contracts under which they work.[8] These settings typically serve vulnerable, harder-to-reach populations that are reluctantly provided for in public policy.[9] Such clinics saw a boost under the Affordable Care Act, which concretized integrated behavioral and physical health, "health homes," and increased attention to behavioral and mental health parity. At the same time, community-based clinics and agencies that are organized to maximize scarce funding often sacrifice working conditions; contracting out clinical services (versus using full-time, permanent employees),[10] high caseloads, and high paperwork demands can introduce precarity, work stress, and may adversely impact service delivery as well as worker health and well-being.

Labor Concerns of Social Workers

UNDERSTAFFING, HIGH CASELOADS, LACK OF SOCIAL WORK LEADERSHIP

In acute care settings, social workers often lack enough staff to carry out their duties. Normally, these duties include psychosocial assessment of hospitalized patients; discharge planning; connection to community resources; bereavement counseling; psychiatric follow-up; ordering medical equipment; hospice, palliative, and end-of-life care and planning; family counseling; insurance company approval; interdisciplinary rounds; counsel on Medicaid eligibility and insurance limitations; and referral to child or adult protective services. Understaffing creates a negative feedback loop, contributing to overwork and adverse working conditions so that recruitment and especially retention become difficult. Lack of staff means an overload of less meaningful paperwork and discharge planning that involves calls and work on "the dashboard" but far less face-to-face time. After two years of the pandemic, this understaffing was hitting crisis proportions, with increasing numbers of social workers leaving to work in private practice.[11] Without hospital social work departments, clinical supervision—critically needed for social workers to advance their license—is no longer available in the healthcare workplace (most work under the nursing manager), compounding the challenges for retaining newly trained social workers.[12]

In the behavioral health setting, high caseloads are the hallmark of low staffing. In New York City some unionized behavioral health social workers carry as many as 130 cases at one time.[13] Despite many social workers in these settings wanting to fulfill a social justice mission through community-based work, and health benefits associated with agency work for unionized social workers, long-term pressures and two years of the pandemic (at the time of this writing) have led some to leave for private practice. In the words of one 1199SEIU representative, "Load 'em up, that's that. It feels intractable—there is no contract enforcement and it's hard to organize."[14]

More than this, when social work departments were eliminated and the remaining workforce folded into nursing, role definition eroded. The skills and value of social work failed to be recognized as distinct from nursing. Consultants used by hospital systems highlight the fact that there is no direct way to bill for social work services, and thus the value added of social work is unclear except insofar as social workers carry out a portion of nursing duties for lower pay. Unfortunately, at times this pits these two professions against one another, a "crabs in a barrel" scenario.

Two Pandemics:
COVID-19 and Structural Racism

The COVID-19 pandemic arrived in New York City in March 2020. Despite warnings from January 2020 onward, the city and its healthcare providers were unprepared for what unfolded over the next several months. New York City was an early epicenter in the United States. As of March 2022, New York City had 2,279,430 confirmed cases of SARS-CoV-2, and 39,924 deaths.[15] The bulk of deaths occurred between March and May 2020, peaking at 762 deaths per day on April 12, 2020; on that date there were more than 12,000 people hospitalized with COVID-19, just over 3,100 of them in intensive care units. The fatality rate among confirmed cases was 9.2 percent overall and 32.1 percent among hospitalized patients.[16] Incidence, hospitalization rates, and mortality were highest among Black/African American and Hispanic/Latino persons, as well as those who were living in neighborhoods with high poverty, 75 years or older, and with underlying medical conditions.

A second crisis unfolded after the murder of George Floyd in Minneapolis on May 26, 2020, by police officer Derek Chauvin while other officers watched and did nothing. The murder was followed by weeks of protests, confrontations with police, and curfews, including in New York City. Protests lasted until approximately the end of June. In response to these protests, schools, social service agencies, companies, and city departments—along with countless other groups and organizations—entered a period of what has been termed "racial reckoning," characterized by exploration, discussion, and focus on racism, antiracism, and white supremacy, as well as the role of police and other carceral systems in US society.

THE SOCIAL WORK DILEMMA

A core dilemma of social work, especially after decades of attacks on govern-ment social welfare programs and the people who use them, is that social work is often conducted within organizations that may, in part or by design, generate harm to many populations that use them. Schools, healthcare sys-tems, criminal justice, and child welfare systems are examples of structures that reflect, perpetuate, or generate inequality and harm. Social workers work on behalf of clients and families and often use their position to buffer or subvert systems and protect clients. A critical view of these processes is exemplified by the work of Paul Michael Garrett and his theory of dissent-ing social work,[17] and by the work of critical feminist Mimi E. Kim and her critique of social work's involvement with the carceral state in a movement toward abolition social work,[18] informed by the example of Angela Davis, among others.[19] While these approaches represent a critical flank of social work, many of the principles they uphold are not entirely remote from "main-stream" social work. Social work practice, both critical and mainstream, val-ues social justice, the dignity and worth of all people, and self-determination within systems and structures that do not always (in fact, often don't) share these values. Likewise, the importance of communication, positive mental health, and support are core to what social workers provide in healthcare settings, but the resources needed for these practices are not typically valued or available.

Results

Using the union activists to contact healthcare social workers, twenty-four participants were recruited: eight from community-based agency settings and sixteen from hospitals. Hospital-based participants worked at academic medical centers in Manhattan, the Bronx, or at a public hospital in Queens in inpatient, outpatient, and clinic settings. Community-based social work-ers worked in home care, agency, and private practice settings, focused on chronic health needs, people living with HIV, LGBTQ+, gender and sexuality, children, and families. Several mentioned services focused on the needs of BIPOC communities. Tenure at their jobs ranged from one to twenty-two years. Although we did not gather demographic data, participants men-tioned several diverse backgrounds, including Southeast Asian, Asian, His-panic, African American, Caucasian, and Haitian, as well as being part of the LGBTQ+ population.

In the sections that follow, we present our results categorized into four broad thematic areas: hospital and community experiences during COVID-19, lack of support, impacts on the workforce, and lessons learned. In each we explored hospital- and community-based perspectives and illustrated variety as well as agreement in perspectives. Through the process of analyzing this data, we noticed that despite heavy criticisms, social workers' perspectives also pointed toward a new, social vision of healthcare.

Hospital and Community Experiences during COVID-19

In the first week of March 2020, events outpaced understanding. Hospital services were quickly overwhelmed and chaotic, and the workplace became very tense. Hospital social workers expected something akin to the seasonal flu epidemics that occur each year but quickly realized this was something different, as services that normally managed fifty patients quickly doubled in size. Several conversations centered on the fact that working in a crisis was normal; however, the level of chaos was high, leading to feelings of "helplessness of not having answers for patients and families." The numbers of patients combined with high levels of uncertainty contributed to an extremely tense working environment; in the words of one hospital social worker: "My memory of the first wave was that the hospital was an extremely intense place. You [could] almost cut the tension with a knife the second you walked in there."

Social workers were also afraid for their own safety, especially as colleagues became sick or died. Palliative care social workers described being "speechless" and "terrified" when they learned they would have to work in a unit where COVID patients were going to die. They described difficult conversations with their families and the feeling that the situation was "beyond their pay grade." A social worker with one-year of experience was sent to work in an "open-air COVID ward" run by the military, a space of twelve to fifteen beds set up in the hospital lobby. This assignment came out of the blue, directly after she had learned of the death of a colleague.

The number of patients dying during the first wave of COVID-19 in NYC was a sustained mass casualty event, unlike anything the hospital staff normally encountered. In the words of one hospital social worker: "I never forgot, I was working weekends just after the second week, March 16 or March 20-something, I was by myself, the only social worker, and every 15 minutes we had rapid response. And I was told that literally no one, none of the patients survived."

COMMUNITY SETTING

In the community setting, the biggest change for many social workers was quickly converting to remote services and devising new ways to stay in touch with vulnerable clients. A social worker from a family service clinic in Queens remembered "being at work on a Monday, and by that Tuesday I was working at home, and have been ever since."[20] However, working from home was only one change; social workers described how "therapy stopped" as they stepped into the role of case managers, making sure that people had enough money and enough food and that they were taking safety precautions.

Social workers conducting home visits now needed to manage exposure risks. A fourteen-year veteran described how nothing in her past, including extreme squalor and hoarding situations, had scared her as much as walking into a home where she might be exposed to COVID. As social workers in the community learned of multiple clients and family members passing away, their fears for their own safety were compounded.

SHIFTING ROLES

Hospital-based social workers during COVID-19 became, in the words of one of them, "COVID care providers," doing whatever was needed and often unable to do what was normally done. Many were sent to work in newly set-up COVID wards. Social workers described acting as a communication bridge between hospitalized patients and their families and between these families and doctors. This bridging was, at times, an exaggerated form of what social workers often do in healthcare—translating medical terms into language that patients and families could understand: "creating that relationship between the family and the patient and the team in the context of a medical illness. . . . You really need people that can understand both sides. The medical side and then the family and patient dynamic side, and then bridge that together."

They also extended their practice of translating patients' psychosocial or culturally based needs to medical professionals to the COVID-19 situation. For example, one social worker described how medical providers misinterpreted a family member's emotional panic as a lack of language proficiency:

> I remember in one case, they were like, "I think she just doesn't understand English well." And I had been told that this was an English-speaking family member. So I start talking to her. She was perfectly fluent in English. The issue was that she never had to make decisions ever in her marriage. It was always the patient, who is now incapacitated. It really opened up her grief, being thrown into this.

In the context of COVID-19, when so many patients were not getting better, social workers also counseled medical professional colleagues on not raising false hopes. One social worker recalled hanging a sign in the unit with the word "better" crossed out, understanding that for families any indication of improvement might raise false hopes.

In the daily COVID-19 workplace, social workers often managed a white-board of patient family contacts to keep family members (who were forbidden to enter the hospital) informed. This activity at times transitioned to holding the phone for FaceTime/WhatsApp final moments with a loved one before they passed away. Social workers frequently encountered difficult end-of-life conversations that in the past had been relatively rare, such as discussing Do Not Intubate/Do Not Resuscitate (DNI/DNR) orders.

Palliative care stood out as a critical skill. Palliative care social workers in one academic medical center created materials to quickly train others on how to communicate with families about dying and death. With so many patients dying, end-of-life counseling extended to families, surviving patients in the hospital, and colleagues as they shouldered an almost unimaginable burden of death—more like a battlefield than a healthcare setting. The hopelessness and fear that many experienced was in part offset by the experience of working together, doing something, trying to help. Hospital social workers also described the therapeutic role they played with their colleagues, along with easing their burden of communication with distraught family members.

Community-based healthcare social workers were charged with shifting delivery of the counseling services they provided to a purely remote setting—trading their offices for computer Zoom sessions or phone calls. In some cases, online settings were challenging, especially working with teens and children. In other cases, this form of service provision was liberating—for example, with clients who had agoraphobia, for whom just traveling to the office was an ordeal. Community social workers working from home had to deal with new dimensions of work-life balance as their clients gained a window into their lives, families, children, and pets. In addition, the practice of creating "professional boundaries" was difficult to uphold, as one community social worker describes:

> Yeah, everybody meets my dog. And everybody at some point wants to see her or wants to meet her or, "Let's talk about your dog because we don't want to talk about anything else." We learned in school that you had to make sure there was a separation, you can't disclose so much information, you have got to be careful, but here I am doing video sessions. My mom sometimes is talking, the dog is walking in the background. I mean, you can't separate.

In one sense, the remote-from-home environment removed the professional boundary that often provides a safe buffer in such situations. At the same time, the shared experience of COVID-19 in New York City, the desire of people to help one another and connect on a human level, was facilitated by intimate interactions in a time of crisis. One social worker described a nine-year-old client reaching out to her at the end of a session, asking, "'So, miss. How was your week? Are you doing well this week?' It's crazy, here's this nine-year-old asking me this question. And I have to say, 'I had a great week, sweetheart. Thank you so much. It was good. Thank you for asking me.'"

Finally, as people sat at home with little else to do, no-shows virtually disappeared, leading to increases in workload but also increased billing for social work services. One agency social worker underscored a high point during the pandemic, where social work was elevated for bringing in extra revenue at a time when billing for medical services at their clinic all but disappeared.

Lack of Support: Poor Management, Scarce PPE, Working Sick, Feeling Invisible

LACK OF MANAGEMENT AND MANAGEMENT "DISCONNECT"

In the hospital, many participants observed that management—often working remotely without day-to-day experience of conditions—seemed out of touch and offered little serious guidance or leadership. Social workers in the hospital were frustrated as management seemed to pretend that everything was "business as usual." Social workers described a jarring disconnect between the crisis they witnessed, a serious, planned response to the crisis and management's actual response. Some reported that medical directors persisted in comparing the current outbreak to seasonal flu, stating, "You don't need to worry, we'll never get more than one unit of patients," or commenting on so-called patient zero, "Don't worry, that's in Westchester; you don't have to worry about anything here." One social worker with family who worked in healthcare in Italy tried to warn their managers about what they suspected was to come, but to no avail. Hospital social workers described how hard it was for management to pivot from their usual cost-driven concern with length of stay when patients were stuck, often on a ventilator, in the hospital. Out-of-touch managers would end remote meetings with a funny cartoon, or a recipe to try at home, reflecting a divide between what healthcare workers did during the pandemic and those who simply quarantined. Perhaps the hardest thing for our participants to bear was a sense that management might not truly care:

> They were trying to act as if things were just supposed to proceed as normal. They were saying that they know how crazy it was, but I felt like they were just kind of saying it just to say it. I feel like they didn't care that it was crazy. They were like "all right just do your job as normal, try and do it as normal as possible, please and thank you."

Social workers in the hospital felt like their job—its specific content and tasks and, by extension, the people they worked with—was not considered in the information provided by management. As they attended meetings about hospital protocol changes, they waited in vain for instruction about how their job and its tasks would be protocolized. Key information for social workers, such as the new processes set up for the Department of Homeless Services for COVID-positive patients,[21] or practices for discharge to nursing homes, were never included in such meetings. The invisibility of social work during normal times was compounded by the challenges of COVID-19.

Social workers felt at times like they were not treated as human beings by management and that there was little to no support for the crisis they had endured at work. There was no attention to feelings associated with trauma and grief and little attention to the need to debrief difficult situations, such as the death of a young patient or of a colleague. This lack of support was also perceived as a lack of compassion, which translated to failures around measures to keep employees safe: "It was a lack of compassion, imagination, when they think about their own employees. That's something unbelievable. I was in constant fight with management to try to get social workers safe," said one hospital social worker. Some social workers were incredulous over the lack of planning in a New York City hospital, given the prior SARS (severe acute respiratory syndrome) outbreak, recent experiences preparing for Ebola, and the 9/11 attacks. One social worker who had been through both 9/11 and the recent preparations for Ebola was shocked that masks were being rationed in spring 2020 and that there was seemingly no stockpile of PPE.

In a few cases, social workers made observations about the larger system that their patients and other healthcare workers encountered during COVID-19. In spring 2020, New York City experienced a devastating number of nursing home deaths, and it has subsequently been revealed that there were serious policy inconsistencies and coverups about the extent of the problem.[22] As many patients came from long-term care facilities, social workers also interacted with these facilities and their staff and noted aspects that management failed to grasp. Many patients could not be discharged without the help of their home health aides, but the home health aides were caught in the middle and often unable to protect their own health and jobs:

> People who are coming from long-term care with home attendants, and who had COVID, but they are well enough to go back home. And of course the agency said that the aide doesn't want to go, is afraid to be infected. There was anger, 'so what's the big deal she can wear a mask, what's the big deal'? And I'm like, oh my God, this is about people. That's a woman, maybe she has children, . . . this is reasonable that she's scared. She's not getting any PPE from her agency. Where is she going to get this PPE if we cannot get it in the hospital? It was like cold blooded with this. Really it would be illegal to convince this aide that this is absolutely safe to take care of this patient who had no idea if he's infectious or not.

PPE: "I FELT LIKE A CRIMINAL ASKING FOR THE PPE"

Despite prior experiences with SARS and infectious disease risk in healthcare settings, there was an acute lack of PPE and a lack of comprehensive policy. Social workers felt confused, unsupported, and hung out to dry by the lack of clear guidelines, concern, policy, and resources. There was some feeling that administration found wearing masks alarmist and were also concerned about scaring patients. A participant reported this event from March 13, 2020: Hospital staff including social workers were forbidden to wear masks and were told they would be written up if they did. One social worker reported how a charge nurse from China took charge: "Nobody in the hallways, keep everyone out. Masks. Shut every door, just make sure the patient is isolated," only to be reprimanded for overreacting.

As colleagues saw each other becoming ill, some even dying, the fights over PPE intensified. Social workers described fights over PPE as one of the most horrifying aspects of this phase of the pandemic, despite the fact that a majority of coworkers were infected with the virus. They worried about bringing the virus home to aging parents and young children and felt as if they were treated as criminals for trying to access PPE that was kept under lock and key. A social worker at a public hospital in Queens was told to wash and reuse her surgical mask and that she could use it for several days, a practice that persisted until somebody reported it to the health department.

WORKING SICK: "WE ARE HUMANS TOO, WE CAN GET SICK, WE CAN INFECT OTHER PEOPLE"

Like other hospital workers, some social workers were pressured to come to work with COVID. The absence of both rapid and PCR (polymerase chain reaction) testing in spring 2020 meant there was a gray area when it came to closing the information loop on quarantining.[23] As one social worker explained:

> I was infected with the virus. I would say, sixty percent of our staff members, social workers within that first week, we all had COVID. A few of us were out for several weeks, and I remember receiving a phone call from the occupational health director asking why I'm not at work. He's like, "Oh, you just need two weeks to recover and that's it. You need to come back. If you have a cough, that's fine. If you have chills, that's fine. If you're weak, that's fine. Come back and do the work."

Hospital social workers, like so many other essential workers, were forced to choose between protecting their health and their jobs.

SOURCES OF SUPPORT: "THAT BECAME OUR ROCK"

What was nearly universally mentioned by social workers in the inpatient and community settings was their intense sense of camaraderie during this period and the extent to which they relied on one another. Community-based social workers, who had less in-person contact with colleagues, described creating a WhatsApp group for work that quickly morphed into a support group. This became a place for dark humor, memes, and whatever was needed. As one Spanish-speaking social worker in the community noted, "That WhatsApp group? That became our rock." In one academic medical center, social workers started having weekly meetings, something that had not happened before. However, the experience of support and connectedness was not universal. Several social workers in the hospital reported feeling isolated during the pandemic, receiving appreciation from patients and families but not feeling connected to coworkers.

Impacts on the Workforce

WORKLOAD:
"I STARTED BURNING, LIKE, COMPLETE BURNOUT"

Whether in the hospital or community, the biggest immediate impact on working conditions was workload. In the hospital setting this was due to the swift and enormous influx of critically ill people without any change in staffing levels. As new ventilator units opened, one social worker wondered, "Who is going to take care of all these patients?" In addition, the extremely high death rate changed the nature of the work; for healthcare workers in general, the reward of a job well done is people getting better. This reward was in short supply during the initial wave of COVID-19. Hospital social workers were unaccustomed to dealing with so much death and described this situation using words like "horrible," "awful," and "nightmare."

Another factor that added to the intensified workload were new and sometimes strange demands that came from acting as a liaison between families and hospitalized loved ones. Because the normal processes of transfer to the morgue and funeral homes processing bodies were not functioning, social workers dealt with families demanding proof that their loved ones had died, sometimes asking, "Can someone go to the morgue and take a picture to prove it really happened?" Social workers in our focus groups reported sometimes talking to ten families a day as they tried to compensate for all the systems errors that were occurring. Social workers also took on additional volunteer tasks at home that added to the intensity of their work, including making phone calls to families in the evening when they were off work.

For social workers working from home, which included community-based social workers and some hospital social workers who were normally outpatient, the intensification of work took on a 24/7 dimension. One social worker said she didn't know when to stop working because everything seemed so important. Another became emotional as she reflected on everything she did:

> It felt like I was "on" 24/7 for a month. I was working 24/7. . . . If I wasn't working on the computer or on the phone, I was working at home with my mom and making sure she was okay, and my family was okay, and that our community was okay. I'm starting to get emotional.

For community-based social workers, workload also increased when COVID-19 exacerbated existing challenges and led to additional social issues that fall under the care of social workers. For example, this description of the challenges facing people living with HIV who also have mental health challenges captures the intersectional nature of social work client issues:

> My clients are worried because they're immunocompromised. So they were afraid that they were going to get infected. They were afraid to go outside. They were very angry with the world. First, before COVID, they were isolated because they're HIV-infected. And most of my clients were already afraid of the world. COVID only made it worse. Anxiety, depression . . . COVID exacerbated any underlying mental health issues that already existed. Everything became worse. Substance abuse, domestic violence got worse.

Finally, this overwork led to burnout for many. A social worker with a home visit caseload described how things fell apart for her: "I felt I needed to do more: more paperwork, more phone calls or I didn't reach a person that said I can speak to them at 3, okay it's 7 p.m. They have to pick up now. Let me call. I started burning, like, complete burnout."

TRAUMA: "I FELT THIS HUGE SENSE OF OVERWHELM THAT I'VE NEVER EXPERIENCED IN MY LIFE"

While social workers are trained to work with the effects of trauma, this is markedly different from working within the throes of traumatic events. In focus groups, many social workers relived these experiences and became triggered speaking about them. Social workers in our focus groups, especially those from Queens, where the death toll was highest during spring 2020, reflected on the fear, worry, anxiety, and grief they experienced. They relayed that as they saw so many Black and Latino community members suffering, they were both personally and professionally affected. Our focus groups occurred in 2021, and these experiences were raw. Social workers frequently cried or became unable to talk as they described events from 2020. In addition to the community trauma, some hospitalized patients experienced isolation from the death of their roommates. The dehumanizing experiences that came with this crisis also shaped patient experiences. As one hospital social worker told me:

> Then another layer of that was hearing the stories of my patients, while they were in the hospital, all the trauma that they had to deal with being isolated from their families. Having to deal with their roommate who passed away, who coded, it was just a lot. I remember feeling a lot of anxiety; I just feel like I'd never had these conversations, like people freaking out about worrying if their family member was left in a truck somewhere.[24]

For social workers acutely aware of the social justice issues facing their client population—for example, undocumented populations—the phenomenon of the Trump administration leadership during this crisis added another layer to their experiences. Spanish-speaking social workers reported that their undocumented clients were afraid to go to the hospitals and afraid to use services. For social workers of color, the disproportionate loss of life among people and communities of color was palpable in New York City and was intensified by the street protests and racial reckoning that began to occur in the aftermath of the murder of George Floyd. One community social worker used the word "jarring" to capture his experience of being a Black service provider during the loss of life among African Americans and the intense protests and racial reckonings. Another was alarmed by the prospect of being deployed to crisis situations; one suggestion that arose during early discussions was how to "defund the police." Social workers wondered how their profession could survive these demands:

> And what happens then? And not that any salary can ever protect you from being in danger, but something has to give, something has to be connected, where we are being recognized and accepted and seen. Have this profession be seen for what it is in the society that we're currently living in, with all the turmoil that it's going through. Pandemic, racial injustice, insane president.

Listening to and recording the stories of what social workers went through, many repressed their emotions and experiences to keep going through the motions. Reflecting in focus group discussion, many spoke about this repression, about what they were coming to recognize, and about their own challenge to face, process, and integrate these experiences. Some reported feeling numb during this time, an inability to process what was happening, feelings such as sadness and anger only arising long after the fact. For some it was just how wrong it was to have been the facilitator of the private moment for a loved one's death (witnessed through a FaceTime call, for example). Several social workers in our group were surprised that even after months, they found it difficult to describe what they had been feeling at that time: "I know that it was horrifying and horrific, but what was I actually feeling?" One community social worker described the ongoing trauma of reaching out to families:

> All these deaths. I was afraid of what I going to hear on the other end— "Oh, please don't tell my mom that my sister just died," or that "Oh, you know, by the way, my dad just died of COVID." Even calling families, just to gather information, you just don't know what kind of layers of trauma you will reveal.

"Lessons" Learned? Where Do We Go from Here?

MAKE SOCIAL WORK "VISIBLE": "MOST PEOPLE DON'T KNOW WHAT WE DO UNTIL THEY NEED US"

Social workers valued participating in this effort to portray social worker experiences in NYC during COVID-19. For some, the groups were therapeutic and an opportunity to review hard experiences in a supportive space. As participants discussed what was needed to elevate their jobs, the metaphor of visibility came up several times. One community social worker reflected that our conversation made him feel "seen," and it was moving for the group to experience this appreciation. ("I just want to say I so appreciate this conversation. I feel seen right now.") Regarding the nature of the work, our participants remarked on their use of self. Social workers expressed putting their whole selves into their jobs with phrases like "It isn't work, I'm using my soul," and "This job is so emotional and psychological."

Social workers also identified a need for advocacy and for a better understanding of what they do as a first step. Some described their role as "fixers" of problems ranging from lack of medical insurance, access to medication, substance abuse challenges, documentation, and mental and emotional health needs:

> We fix everything for everybody, no matter what it is. That's our job. We're the fixers. We're head soap and body wash and everything in between that.

> We fix lives and make it better and it needs to be promoted as such, we give everything every day to our clients.

RAISE PAY: "THE SALARY IS AT THE BOTTOM"

Low pay is a primary, objective reason for social workers feeling undervalued, particularly in the healthcare setting, where they receive lower pay than clinical healthcare staff. The experiences of intensified workload and overcommitment underscored these feelings. Social workers discussed working overtime without pay to make sure that client needs are met but agreed that their salaries were "at the bottom." Participants discussed how the history of social work as a "women's profession" set the stage for low pay but also bemoaned that they lacked the recognition of other professions that earn a decent salary, such as law or medicine. Social workers also admitted to being poor advocates for themselves, despite their ability to "move mountains" for their clients.

Several community-based social workers in our discussion struggled with the decision to leave agency work, with poor populations facing social justice challenges, for work in private practice, where they could earn more:

> I'm so burned out. I feel like I'm giving everything of myself. My essence. I can't move forward in my dreams or wherever my life needs to go, because here I am, giving everything to them. I don't have anything left for me. I love what I do, but what do I do now, where it's not going to take my whole soul? I can't do it being a psychotherapist unless I go into private practice. And do I really want to do that? I don't know. I feel like that's going to the dark side. How do I leave my undocumented Spanish-speaking families to go work with people that can pay me over $200 per session? I feel guilty. It feels like I'm not doing what I was supposed to do.

INCREASE STAFFING: "WE'RE HUMANS, AND WE CAN HANDLE ONLY A CERTAIN AMOUNT OF STRESS"

Social workers considered staffing not just in terms of workload but also in terms of having the time to do their jobs well. In the context of the hospital, this was described by multiple participants as "time to speak with families" and "the families wanted time." For example, one participant explained:

> When I have time to speak with families, the outcome is way better because I have time to answer questions, I have time to listen to them, I have time to explain, even from that certain medical point of view—like with stroke patients, what they can expect during recovery, what they have to prepare for. It's way easier to have successful discharge, or when you have complex patients with families, when we have time, than when we're in constant rush.

The COVID-19 experience in the hospital further made clear the value of time, as caseloads became impossible to manage, and intense discussions were often abruptly interrupted. Finally, social workers connected a lack of staff to a lack of time to attend to their own mental health needs.

RESTORE SOCIAL WORK LEADERSHIP IN HEALTHCARE: "WE DON'T HAVE ENOUGH SOCIAL WORKERS IN LEADERSHIP POSITIONS"

Social workers connected their lack of being respected to working under nursing directors who did not appreciate what social workers do. They described how "we have some social work managers, but our director is a nurse, and she reports to a VP who's a nurse, and in administration I don't know how well we're respected, how well they know what we do, and I think that's a really big problem." This is commonly found in the literature and was reflected in the discussion among this group that included several veteran hospital social workers who had witnessed this change firsthand. Social workers believed that without social work leadership in the hospital, their roles in these settings would be constrained, noting that social work in the hospital is "underutilized" but that without leadership in the organizational structure, it was hard to see how this situation could change.

THE POLITICAL ECONOMY OF CARE NEEDS TO CHANGE: "NONE OF IT (NONPROFIT, FOR-PROFIT, AGENCY WORK), I FEEL, IS ACTUALLY SUPPORTIVE TO US"

Some social workers identified that within a capitalist model, social workers would remain "used and abused." Another noted, ironically, that branding as a "life coach" would lead to higher pay.

During one discussion about possible solutions, participants considered a post-pandemic discussion of the "nonprofit industrial complex," where the field needs to go, and how the work should be better organized.

One community social worker who had recently moved from agency work into private practice viewed the structural problems of social work as a trade-off between different problems, regardless of setting:

> I feel I have a little bit more space now that I'm in a for-profit private practice. It's a very different animal and something else, to be a part of the capitalist system in a different way, being part of a for-profit business providing mental health services. And none of it (nonprofit, for-profit, agency work), I feel, is supportive to us. Regardless of our settings, what kind of work we're doing

RACIAL JUSTICE, SOCIAL JUSTICE, AND SOCIAL WORK: "WE'VE REALLY, REALLY FELT IT"

The disproportionate deaths of so many African American and Latinx New Yorkers followed by the racial justice uprisings created a visceral, immediate, embodied experience of racial injustice among many of our focus group participants. Social workers of color, especially the community-based social workers in our study, experienced the early days of the pandemic and the racial justice protests as "connected and intertwined on so many levels." This created intricate challenges. Even when well-meaning organizations wanted to respond, the burden on social workers of color was potentially magnified:

> I don't want to demonize [community-based agency]; I think it's a beautiful agency. I'm very proud to work there. But there was a moment, there was an invitation for diversity—not training, but let's talk about what's going on with racial injustice. And I just thought, No! You don't get to ask me. You need a warm-up.... To ask me to come to a meeting and I'm already burnt out. I can't do another Zoom call and I don't know if I trust you to be able to handle it. I don't even know if I can handle it. So, yeah, institutional ... we need a magnificent paradigm shift.

Social workers of color in the hospital setting reflected on the history of the profession and its goals, noting that the changes demanded by antiracist messages had meaning for the profession:[25]

> To add to what you were saying, in terms of patriarchy, I think also acknowledging the white supremacy at the foundation of Social Work. Like, who was it created to help? Who created it? Very good people were trying to do good things, but it continued to make anti-Blackness and anti-anyone-of-color more systemic in a lot of ways, and I think that that also needs to be acknowledged.

A SOCIAL VISION OF HEALTH AND WELL-BEING

Social workers in our study articulated a vision for social work in healthcare framed around educating and guiding patients and families through the healthcare system and times of illness. In part they saw their role as critical in compensating for the brokenness of the healthcare system and supporting patients to cope with this at the same time that they coped with possibly devastating and life-changing illness. It was described by one veteran social worker as follows:

> My favorite part of my job is providing education to patients and families about our healthcare system. I feel like you learn about how terrible our system is when you end up in the hospital or a loved one is in the hospital and you realize when your loved one needs twenty-four-hour care, "Oh, no, there's no one to help, except for you." My favorite part of my job is talking to patients and families about what's available, what's not available, and getting the information out there. And I feel like we don't have enough time to talk to patients and families. Because I'm spending an hour on the phone getting authorization for an ambulette or whatever I'm doing. There's so

much of the case management part of my job, and I feel like we could do more in terms of work with patients and families around counseling, self-care, health care proxies, and even end of life and all that stuff, and I feel like we're used more in just making referrals.

Healthcare social workers in our study also expressed more ambitious hopes: that the kind of attention paid to mental health, well-being, and human development that healthcare social workers specialize in should become essential to what we consider health to be; that social workers' role in this could be elevated; and that the stigma associated with social work and social services could be removed:

> I think social work needs to be from cradle to death. Like you said, it's something that needs to be like going to the doctor for an annual checkup. It's something that has to be like, I'm not going to a social worker because I just went through XYZ; I'm going through social work, because I'm doing fine, and I want to make sure I'm okay and I want to stay on this path, or I want to just talk about something that I need some help making decisions about or, I want to continue to improve my life. But not like, I went to a social worker because my parents got deported or I went to a social worker because I just got sexually assaulted or I'm poor and we're a family of five that lives in one bedroom in a shared apartment with two or three other families. It needs to be accepted from the beginning as part of your medical treatment. Like getting a vaccine, like you're going to the dentist, getting a medical annual check, it should just be that. And the more that we make it acceptable and normalize it, . . . it's not anything to feel stigma about.

At the same time, it was acknowledged that as they are currently characterized, mental health services remain stigmatized, which both hinders their uptake and adds to negative associations with the profession:

> But the way it is now? I get some families that ask me, "Oh, if they get therapy, is this going to be on their record?" I'm like, "What record do you think really exists out there that your adolescent is going to be. . . ." And then you have to explain to them. But yeah, God forbid, this adolescent decides to go into the Army or armed forces [and] there's a question. Did you have therapy? Did you have mental health services? Do you take medication? And that can make it or break it, and that's sad. I get why those questions are there, but that's not okay. There has to be a way for it to be different.

Discussion

Like other healthcare workers in New York City in the spring of 2020, social workers experienced a mass casualty event, were exposed to the SARS-CoV-2 virus, and worked under policies that failed to protect them. Like other healthcare workers of color, their experiences were compounded by the devastating losses in communities of color, the racial justice uprisings, and the urgency of attention to structural racism. What distinguishes social workers from other healthcare workers, however, is the nature of their jobs. Social workers' focus on psychosocial health and well-being, their role in guiding vulnerable people through institutions and social policies, and their attention to discrimination and oppression highlighted existing cracks and weaknesses in the healthcare system and the social work role within it.[26]

In this participatory, qualitative study, social workers developed a discourse about their experience during COVID-19 that explored their position and value as workers in the COVID-19 pandemic and the concurrent racial justice reckoning. Hospital social workers embodied experiences including witnessing firsthand the daily onslaught of illness and death in an environment of uncertainty, chaos, and tension. Despite having an intimate role in what happened in the hospital in the spring of 2020, they were frequently ignored in planning and protocols. Paradoxically, many felt they were part of the healthcare team and that what they did was more appreciated, but this also served to highlight the experience of feeling invisible. Their role in humanizing an extremely inhumane situation juxtaposed the nature of the institution with the priorities of social work.

Community-based social workers dealt with clients and their families in the home context and often felt a breakdown between the separation between "work" and "life." In this context, the twin pandemics of police violence against communities and people of color and COVID-19 made many acutely aware of the social justice issues that frame social problems. Many community-based social workers struggled to put their values into action while avoiding burnout and expending their whole selves in the process.

Participants in this study used the opportunity to make recommendations that expand a vison of social healthcare. Raising pay, increasing staffing, and making the role of social work visible and valued are not unique recommendations for this workforce; indeed, these demands mirror the demands of nurses, nurses' aides, home health aides, and others. However, the contradiction between trying to improve psychosocial functioning and well-being through understanding and attention suggest that time and attention to these aspects of patients' lives are non-negotiable conditions for effective practice. The need to humanize patient care was critical and fragile during the worst days of COVID-19 as social workers calmed desperate family members or facilitated last moments together on FaceTime. But these tasks also reminded social workers of what they typically do during the day-to-day and underscored its value.

After cataclysmic events there has been a societal tendency to revert to the idea of "strength" (i.e., "Boston Strong" after the 2013 marathon bombing) and "heroes" (first responders after 9/11, and the "healthcare heroes work here" following COVID-19) regarding the role of workers. During COVID-19, the idea of the "essential" worker has been added to the mix, both to denote importance and to decide policy (essential workers have received preference for protections from N95 masks to vaccines). In contrast to the overarching sense of abandonment felt by social workers in this study—from lack of PPE, lack of inclusion in management plans, lack of consideration from management, lack of social work leadership, low pay, and so forth—the notion of essentiality and heroics rings hollow, a poor substitute for institutions, social structures, public policy, and healthcare culture devoted to promoting safe and healthy working conditions for the healthcare workforce.

Among our participants, the lack of recognition for their profession within the larger healthcare system seemed connected to the social justice struggles of people who use the healthcare system. Healthcare social workers' experiences during COVID-19 suggest that organizing to improve working conditions among this workforce might lead to a holistic reconsideration of public healthcare policy and a new vision of a just healthcare system.[27] Our participants want readers to know that they have told this story to advocate for these goals.

Notes

1. For a deeper discussion of social work as essential, see Julie A. Cederbaum, Abigail M. Ross, Lisa de Saxe Zerden, Lilly Estenson, Jennifer Zelnick, and Betty J. Ruth, "'We Are on the Frontlines Too': A Qualitative Content Analysis of US Social Workers' Experiences during the COVID-19 Pandemic," *Health & Social Care in the Community* 30, no. 6 (2022): e5412-22, doi:10.1111/hsc.13963/.

2. SEIU stands for Service Employees International Union; 1199SEIU United Healthcare Workers East is a local union within the SEIU.

3. James T. Brophy, Margaret M. Keith, Michael Hurley, and Jane E. McArthur, "Sacrificed: Ontario Healthcare Workers in the Time of COVID-19," *New Solutions: A Journal of Environmental & Occupational Health Policy* 30, no. 4 (2021): 267–281, doi:10.1177/1048291120974358/.

4. Philip Popple and Leslie Leighninger. *The Policy-Based Profession: An Introduction to Social Welfare Policy Analysis for Social Workers* (New York: Pearson Education, 2019).

5. Mimi Abramovitz and Jennifer R. Zelnick, "The Rise of Managerialism in the U.S.: Whither Worker Control?" in *Working in the Context of Austerity: Challenges and Struggles,* ed. D. Baines and I. Cunningham, 193–216 (Bristol, UK: Bristol University Press, 2020).

6. For more discussion of the history of social work and labor unions, see Jennifer R. Zelnick, Sara Goodkind, and Mimi E. Kim, "'It would be foolish to pretend that our jobs aren't political': Social Workers Organizing for Power in the Nonprofit Sector," *Affilia: Feminist Inquiry in Social Work* 37, no. 1 (2022):

5–12; Jessica Rosenberg and Samuel Rosenberg, "Do Unions Matter? An Examination of the Historical and Contemporary Role of Labor Unions in the Social Work Profession," *Social Work* 51, no. 4 (2006): 295–302; Edward Scanlon and Scott Harding, "Social Work and Labor Unions: Historical and Contemporary Alliances," *Journal of Community Practice* 13, no. 1 (2005): 9–30.

7. For further discussion, see Michael Reisch, "The Challenges of Health Care Reform for Hospital Social Work in the United States," *Social Work in Health Care* 51, no. 10 (2012): 873–893.

8. For a discussion of privatization and human service contracting, see Jennifer R. Zelnick and Mimi Abramovitz, "The Perils of Privatization: Bringing the Business Model into the Human Services," *Social Work* 65, no. 3 (2020): 213–224.

9. For example, public policy for opioid treatment.

10. Contracted clinical employees are paid only for the time they are delivering services but are not compensated for planning, agency meetings, or supervision, which means either these activities are curtailed or clinicians end up donating their time.

11. Katie Johnson, "Human Service Agencies Face Staffing Crisis, Delaying Services for Those in Need," *Boston Globe*, October 2, 2021; Tim Williams, "New York's Mental Health Care System Faces 'Workforce Crisis,'" *State of Politics*, February 15, 2022.

12. Jennifer Van Pelt, "Making Caring Connections, Cutting Costs—Social Work in the Emergency Department," *Social Work Today*, November/December 2010.

13. Leigh Howard, 1199SEIU personal communication with author.

14. Leigh Howard, 1199SEIU personal communication with author.

15. New York City Department of Health and Mental Hygiene, https://www.nyc.gov/site/doh/covid/covid-19-data-archive.page.

16. C. N. Thompson, J. Baumgartner, C. Pichardo, et al., "COVID-19 Outbreak—New York City, February 29–June 1, 2020," *MMWR Morbity and Mortality Weekly Report* 69 (2020): 1725–1729.

17. Paul M. Garrett, *Dissenting Social Work: Critical Theory, Resistance, and Pandemic* (Abingdon, Oxon: Routledge, 2021).

18. Leah A. Jacobs, Mimi E. Kim, Darren L. Whitfield, Rachel E. Gartner, Meg Panichelli, Shanna K. Kattari, and Sarah E. Mountz, "Defund the Police: Moving towards an Anti-Carceral Social Work," *Journal of Progressive Human Services* 32, no. 1 (2021): 37–62; Mimi E. Kim, "From Carceral Feminism to Transformative Justice: Women-of-Color Feminism and Alternatives to Incarceration," *Journal of Ethnic & Cultural Diversity in Social Work* 27, no. 3 (2018): 219–233.

19. There is a strong tradition within social work exemplified by Mimi Abramovitz, "Social Work and Social Reform: An Arena of Struggle," *Social Work* 43, no. (1998) 512–526.

20. This focus group occurred in February 2021.

21. NYC has a right-to-shelter law and homeless patients would typically be discharged to the shelter system.

22. In order to meet demand for hospital beds early on in the pandemic, patients were discharged to nursing homes with dire consequences. This also led to a cover-up by the Cuomo administration and a state investigation. See https://www.nysenate.gov/newsroom/press-releases/sue-serino/bipartisan-coalition-continues-push-justice-nursing-home-victims/ for ongoing coverage of this issue.

23. It is interesting to note that during the Omicron outbreak in early 2022, hospital staffing became a serious issue due to testing protocols.

24. Referring to the refrigerated trucks that bodies were stored in. See Gina Cherelus, "'Dead Inside': The Morgue Trucks of New York City," *New York Times,* May 27, 2020.

25. Abigail M. Ross, Julie A. Cederbaum, Lisa de Saxe Zerden, Jennifer R. Zelnick, Betty J. Ruth, and Ting Guan, "Bearing a Disproportionate Burden: Racial/Ethnic Disparities in Experiences of U.S.-Based Social Workers during the COVID-19 Pandemic," *Social Work* 67, no. 1 (2022): 28–40, doi:10.1093/sw/swab050.

26. Lisa de Saxe Zerden, Abigail M. Ross, Julie Cederbaum, Ting Guan, Jennifer Zelnick, and Betty J. Ruth, "Race and COVID-19 among Social Workers in Health Settings: Physical, Mental Health, Personal Protective Equipment, and Financial Stressors," *Health & Social Work* 48, no. 2 (2023): 91–104, doi:10.1093/hsw/hlad002.

27. For a discussion about how healthcare work is linked to public health, see Emma K. Tsui, Emily Franzosa, Emilia F. Vignola, Isabel Cuervo, Paul Landsbergis, Jennifer Zelnick, and Sherry Baron, "Recognizing Careworkers' Contributions to Improving the Social Determinants of Health: A Call for Supporting Healthy Carework," *New Solutions: A Journal of Environmental and Occupational Health Policy* 32, no. 1 (2022): 9–18, doi:10.1177/10482911211066963/.

PART V

"New" Forms of Organizing

11

Beyond Austerity America

Labor Animates New Coalitions in the Age of COVID-19

PUYA GERAMI

On a sunny May Day morning in 2021, hundreds gathered outside the governor's mansion in Hartford, Connecticut. Diverse across race, age, gender, and occupation, the crowd had assembled to call for a state budget that would raise taxes on the wealthy and fund public investments to aid communities reeling from the pandemic. After marching on a loud and lively picket line that filled the street, protesters cheered on a series of speakers who shared painful stories about the ways the ongoing crisis had shattered their lives. Mostly Black and brown, women, and immigrants, the essential workers on the mic embodied the experience of communities that were paying the ultimate price during the pandemic, having borne the brunt of Connecticut's rising inequalities for decades. Many speakers contrasted their hardship with the ever-increasing prosperity of the state's elite residents—its dozen billionaires, for instance, who seized $13 billion in additional wealth during the pandemic's first year alone. At the climax of the rally, a minister initiated a moment of silence while protesters staged a die-in, lying down in the driveway and the road to symbolize the suffering and loss of life among working-class people.

As the colorful mix of flags and banners showed, this action was the work not of any single organization but rather an organization of organizations called Recovery For All (RFA). Bringing together more than fifty labor, community, faith, and nonprofit advocacy organizations, this new statewide coalition had launched several months earlier to demand that the state government take sweeping action to meet people's needs amid the most dire upheaval in nearly a century. In the short term, RFA sought to win immediate recovery measures that would guarantee ample and equitable relief for all residents, in particular the oppressed and most vulnerable. In the long term, the coalition sought to eliminate the extreme racial, economic, and gender inequalities that had long divided the wealthiest state in the world's wealthiest country, which the tragedy of the pandemic now exposed for all to see. Undertaking this ambitious mission, Recovery For All set out to unite as many organizations as possible around a strategy to shift the balance of political power at the state level away from the wealthy few and toward the multiracial, multigendered working-class majority.

Still in its first years, the coalition has started to bring its power to bear on the state budget process, advancing a politics against the dominant logic of racialized and gendered austerity and laying the foundation for a lasting alignment across the progressive movement ecosystem in Connecticut. The creation of RFA is an example of a much broader development, preceding and then accelerating during the pandemic: the growth of independent political organizations at the state and local levels, frequently coalitional formations joining together different unions and other base-building organizations. In many cases, these organizations taking off in the 2020s are anchored by local unions that practice the strategy of Bargaining for the Common Good, which itself took shape earlier in the 2010s.

This article recounts the development of RFA based on my experience as director during its inaugural three years. I will begin by examining the roots of the austerity approach that has defined policymaking for the last fifty years—not least due to the coordinated organizing of the political right and its wealthy donors—and that peaked during the Great Recession. In the years between that economic crisis and the pandemic, austerity wreaked havoc not only in strongholds of the Right but also in blue trifecta states like Connecticut—one of the country's wealthiest and most unequal places, a microcosm of the disparities that have widened in the era of neoliberal capitalism. The chapter will then turn to the case study of RFA, documenting previous coalition-building efforts in Connecticut and explaining how the pandemic pushed its founders to come together. I will provide an in-depth look at the coalition's vision of a more equitable state, its inside/outside strategy to build power, as well as the unique role that local unions have played. I will conclude this chapter by situating the case study of RFA within the larger context of independent political organizations emerging nationwide.

Starving the State

As the coronavirus devastated communities across the country and around the world, numerous commentators emphasized how earlier austerity policies had provided the ideal environment for the pandemic to spread. Soon it became a truism: the widespread suffering of working-class people, especially women and people of color, was the preventable result of neoliberalism's brutal calculus. The retrenchment and privatization of the American welfare state over half a century had depleted the resources required to weather the global pandemic.

Austerity policies enforced in the decade preceding COVID-19 played a crucial role in hastening the erosion of state capacity—specifically, the capacity of state and local governments. Indeed, the shock that the pandemic inflicted on the neoliberal social order is best understood in light of an earlier shock: the Great Recession. Lacking substantial federal aid, state and local governments chose to respond to that economic crisis with draconian spending cuts, sparking a "lost decade" for public investment. Funding dwindled for critical sectors of social reproduction, including healthcare, childcare, and education, as state and local government workforces shrank. All this amounted to a false recovery for working-class people, whose standards continued to stagnate, with Black and brown workers the hardest hit.

The prevailing austerity response to the Great Recession largely resulted from decades of concerted right-wing organizing. Starting in the 1970s, conservatives dedicated special attention to creating infrastructure and expanding political power at the state level. A spate of recent books have investigated how corporations and the ultra-wealthy financed a sophisticated organizational network within every state and across state lines to strengthen the Right and reshape public policy.[1] They used money power to construct state-level institutions such as think tanks, academic programs, and lobbying and advocacy organizations and to coordinate activities through national formations like the American Legislative Exchange Council, the State Policy Network, and Americans for Prosperity. Whereas the last quarter of the twentieth century was a time of marked fragmentation and retreat on the political Left, the nexus between these right-wing institutions and Republican elected officials helped lay the groundwork for the dangerous embrace of austerity.

This organizing paid off after the Great Recession, when the Republican Party rapidly captured state government trifectas—that is, one-party control over the governor's office, state senate, and state house—in more than half the country, an ascendancy unmatched in recent history. Republican elected officials passed deeply reactionary policies, many emerging as "model bills" from the state-based network built up in previous decades. Some elected officials, like Indiana governor and future vice president Mike Pence, had in fact cut their teeth working for this network. Their agenda aimed to slash public services, disenfranchise voters, restrict the rights of women and LGBTQ people, and strengthen the carceral state. Leaders of red trifecta states especially targeted public-sector unions, using the economic crisis as an opportunity to lower standards and gut collective bargaining.

But this alarming combination of trends—public disinvestment, growing inequality, and a rightward shift in the political terrain—was by no means confined to states languishing under the full control of the Republican Party. Connecticut has voted for the Democratic candidate in every presidential election since 1992 and for an entirely Democratic delegation in both chambers of Congress since 2009. Most important, a blue trifecta has existed at the state level since 2010, when voters elected their first Democratic governor in fifteen years. Here, in a state usually regarded as a blue stronghold, the years between the Great Recession and the pandemic proved a time when the Right vied for power, austerity budget-making deepened, and extreme inequalities skyrocketed.

As elsewhere in the country, one of the principal factors contributing to the politics of austerity in Connecticut was the persistent strength of right-wing forces. Although the Democratic Party maintained a trifecta throughout the 2010s, the Republican Party made rapid gains in the first half of the decade. By the time of Donald Trump's victory in 2016, the state legislature was effectively gridlocked between both parties. Moreover, the nonparty infrastructure advancing right-wing ideology wielded an outsized influence over the public debate surrounding the state's response to the Great Recession. The Yankee Institute for Freedom and Public Policy, established in the early 1980s as one of the State Policy Network's first affiliates, recycled policy prescriptions from red trifecta states in a consistent barrage targeting the public sector. Resident billionaires and multimillionaires, in addition to wealthy corporations affiliated with the Connecticut Business and Industry Association, wielded the threat of capital flight by threatening to migrate if the state government failed to limit public spending, cut taxes and regulations, and challenge public-sector unions.

As deficits mounted year after year, centrist Democrats leading state government warned of "permanent fiscal crisis," claiming that Connecticut had entered a "new economic reality" and prescribing a dose of spending cuts. Of course, progressive organizations interpreted this fiscal crisis as a manufactured crisis, since the state clearly possessed the resources to fund public services. Yet in the following decade, the state employee workforce shrank by more than 21 percent, fueling a staffing crisis across agencies and harming Connecticut's most vulnerable residents. And in 2017, centrist Democrats and Republicans united to enact the so-called "fiscal guardrails," a set of mechanisms centering on a mandatory spending cap that effectively enforced austerity.

To be sure, the progressive movement in Connecticut notched a number of notable victories throughout the 2010s. For instance, grassroots pressure yielded several policy wins, as Connecticut became the first state to raise the minimum wage to $10.10 and institute paid sick leave for all workers. Low-wage workers in the long-term care sector threatened strikes and won significant economic gains. In addition, membership organizations showed signs of growth. Unions scored major organizing victories in the healthcare, childcare, higher education, and gaming sectors, while new community organizations shot up after the 2016 elections too.

Some of the most promising work in the 2010s occurred in the electoral arena. The Working Families Party (WFP) launched in Connecticut four years after it was founded in New York in 1998. The party gained a track record of recruiting and electing progressive candidates, many emerging from the local labor movement and social movements. Since Connecticut is only one of a handful of states allowing fusion voting—where candidates may appear on the ballot in affiliation with multiple political parties—WFP usually uses its ballot line to cross-endorse Democratic candidates. This has proved a powerful political tool: in the key election of 2010, the total number of votes that the Democratic gubernatorial candidate received on the WFP ballot line was greater than the margin of victory over his Republican rival. While WFP typically chooses cross-endorsement, in two special elections the party went so far as to field candidates (both Black labor leaders) on its own ballot line alone and defeat corporate Democrats for state legislative seats. And in the capital, WFP succeeded in electing candidates on its own ballot line alone to replace the Republicans as the minority party on the city council. Meanwhile, another remarkable example of progressive victory at the ballot box occurred in New Haven. There, a coalition of labor and community activists anchored by UNITE HERE locals at Yale University created a new independent political organization called New Haven Rising, recruited a slate of candidates in city elections, and ran a powerful voter mobilization program that won a majority on the board of alders that continues to hold sway to this day.[2]

Yet these hopeful events proved exceptions to the general rule. For the most part, progressive organizations in Connecticut engaged in defensive struggles in the decade after the Great Recession. At the same time, Connecticut became a byword for extreme racial, economic, and gender inequalities. One report from the Federal Reserve rated Fairfield County—home to both affluent white towns like Greenwich and multiracial working-class cities like Bridgeport—as the most unequal place in America.[3] Under the reign of austerity, the Gold Coast had become the Gilded Coast.

Crisis Sparks Coalition Building

In the winter of 2019, at the end of Democratic governor Ned Lamont's first year in office, a group of labor, community, and faith leaders in Connecticut held a meeting in a local union hall. The latest legislative session featured a number of measures that the local Left had been aiming to win for some time, from the $15 minimum wage, to paid family and medical leave, to cannabis legalization. Yet these leaders harbored higher expectations from a Democratic trifecta, expressing shared disappointment with the lack of bold policymaking to address the state's extreme inequalities. The meeting also offered an opportunity for collective introspection. As long as the progressive movement remained fragmented at the state level, many leaders believed, then the Right would continue to peddle its noxious politics and centrist Democrats in top government posts would continue to stymie a transformational direction for the state. The meeting adjourned with a plan to further discuss the possibility of seeding a statewide progressive coalition.

The goal of building such a coalition in Connecticut was a recurring dream. In fact, some participants in the 2019 discussion had been key actors in previous attempts. One of the finest examples was the Legislative Electoral Action Program (LEAP) in the 1980s and 1990s. In an era when Democratic officials nationwide increasingly turned toward neoliberal ideology, several dozen organizations across Connecticut came together to create a vehicle for shared political action. LEAP included progressive unions, such as UAW Region 9A and 1199 New England, as well as up-and-coming community organizations, such as the Connecticut Citizen Action Group. The coalition managed to unseat powerful centrist Democrats in the state legislature by recruiting, training, and electing members from its own participating organizations. State legislators associated with LEAP soon formed a progressive caucus and led key victories on issues ranging from environmental protection to LGBTQ equality to workplace rights. They played a critical role in the passage of the state income tax in 1991, long considered a holy grail for the local Left. Over twenty years, LEAP distinguished itself as a formidable independent force in state politics, setting a precedent for future efforts.[4]

After LEAP dissolved in 2001, several similar statewide coalitions in Connecticut rose and fell. Whereas LEAP and the emerging Working Families Party worked primarily in the electoral arena, these new coalitions focused on campaigns oriented around the state budget. Each coalition took up the mantle of fighting for a moral budget to meet human needs, but each lasted for only a short period of time. Apart from these significant ventures, progressive organizations in Connecticut continued to operate in silos. As the state's extreme inequalities worsened, the local Left largely failed to coordinate around short-term actions or around a long-term strategy for social change. At a time of manufactured fiscal crisis, they were forced to fight for crumbs from a shrinking pie.

While the leaders in 2019 started with a commitment to found a new formation built to last, the fateful events of the next year intensified the urgency to forge unity. The arrival of the coronavirus pushed a long-standing crisis of need across Connecticut to spiral out of control. At the height of the pandemic, state officials reported that more than half of all deaths occurred in nursing homes, where workers were forced to wear garbage bags for lack of personal protective equipment. Mental health and addiction problems reached record highs. Public educators grappled with the challenge of supporting the rising needs of students during and after the lockdown. At the same time, wealthy corporations and individuals in Connecticut raked in astounding sums of additional wealth. On the national stage, the uprising after George Floyd's murder as well as increasing ecological disasters underscored how multiple crises converging with the pandemic were producing a moment of acute peril for working-class people. To make matters worse, the pandemic recession threatened state budgets, and many officials who had yet to receive an influx of federal aid responded with immediate cuts.

In 2020, with Connecticut's first budget session of the pandemic fast approaching, progressive organizations resolved to prevent a repeat of austerity. Whereas the so-called recovery in the 2010s deepened the concentration of wealth and power, these organizations sought a recovery in the 2020s that would truly improve the quality of life for all residents, not only those in the state's wealthy and predominantly white towns. The organizations eventually making up RFA featured unions, including locals of SEIU, AFT, AFSCME, UAW, CWA, UNITE HERE, and others, plus federations such as the Connecticut AFL-CIO and the State Employees Bargaining Agent Coalition; community organizations, especially those based in communities of color such as the New Britain Racial Justice Coalition, the HUSKY 4 Immigrants Coalition, Unidad Latina en Acción, Bridgeport Generation Now, and the Connecticut Tenants Union; nonprofit advocacy organizations such as She Leads Justice and the Universal Health Care Foundation of Connecticut; electoral vehicles such as WFP; and various faith leaders. They shared a basic vision of the common good—the dream of a future beyond austerity, where the state would fully fund the public resources that communities needed to survive and prosper. By 2021, what began as an informal group morphed into a public coalition eager for battle.

Envisioning an Equitable State

Over the first two state budget cycles of its existence (2021–2022 and 2023–2024), Recovery For All began molding a multifaceted set of demands to create a different kind of Connecticut. These demands represent the live issues that the coalition's affiliated organizations have been leading. The coalition's platform has centered on three kinds of expansion to eliminate inequalities and to provide material improvements in the quality of life for the majority of the state's 3.6 million residents. First, the coalition calls for the expansion of public investment in the woefully underfunded institutions so crucial to society before, during, and after the pandemic, such as mental health and addiction services; reentry services for the formerly incarcerated; and public schools, colleges, and universities. Other forms of investment intend to guarantee a living wage for essential service workers such as long-term care workers, childcare workers, and paraeducators—mostly women and people of color. Second, the coalition calls for the expansion of public benefits, such as the extension of the state's Medicaid program to cover all residents regardless of immigration status and the extension of paid sick leave to cover all workers. Finally, the coalition calls for the expansion of rights and protections for working-class people, such as rent caps, predictable scheduling, and stronger provisions for low-wage workers.

To finance these proposals, RFA has led the push to repair Connecticut's regressive tax system, a cornerstone of racialized and gendered austerity. Poor and working-class residents contribute a much greater share of their income than the ultra-wealthy to fund state and local public services. A recent tax incidence analysis from the state's Department of Revenue Services confirms this upside-down structure: more than 850,000 households earning annual incomes worth less than $45,000 contribute nearly 26 percent of their earnings in state and local taxes, while the tiny fraction of households earning tens of millions of dollars contribute less than 7 percent. Wealthy corporations make a similarly paltry contribution. The Economic Policy Institute reports that the majority of corporations in Connecticut, including, in some cases, those with federal taxable income exceeding a billion dollars a year, contribute nothing or next to nothing to the state.[5]

The regressive tax system not only reflects inequality but fuels it—by preventing greater funding for all sorts of investment to reduce racial, economic, and gender disparities. For many years, progressive organizations have viewed the broken tax structure as the main roadblock to progress on a variety of issues. Now, at a time when so many elected officials repeated the term *equity* to almost drain it of meaning, state senator Gary Winfield quipped, "Equity requires revenue." In other words, a more egalitarian future is impossible absent reforms that guarantee a sustainable revenue stream to support struggling communities. RFA has therefore linked its funding demands to tax proposals that would generate billions of public dollars by raising rates and introducing new taxes on the wealthy and corporations.

Beyond the regressive tax system, RFA has challenged the larger fiscal architecture propping up austerity. The pandemic showed how the state's fiscal guardrails enacted in 2017 functioned as a fiscal straitjacket. When federal aid and thriving stock market returns suddenly produced an enormous surplus in Connecticut, centrist Democrats and Republicans insisted on rigid adherence to the spending cap, forcing public money toward additional paydowns to state debt rather than toward desperately needed investments. This generated a perverse situation in which the state boasted a multibillion-dollar surplus and an overflowing rainy-day fund amid unprecedented levels of human need. Therefore, in addition to fighting for progressive tax reforms to generate new revenue, RFA has called for ways to work around and ultimately overhaul or outright eliminate the fiscal guardrails to ensure such revenue is allocated to tackle the state's inequalities in the future.

In its ongoing work, the coalition has combined these funding priorities and fiscal reforms into an overarching policy platform called the Equity Agenda—the first time in recent memory that dozens of organizations in Connecticut have united around such a comprehensive program. No mere laundry list of demands, the Equity Agenda constitutes a whole greater than the sum of its parts: a vision not only of a just recovery but of the kind of state that progressive organizations envision to make a reality.

The Inside/Outside Strategy in Action

To advance this vision, RFA has adopted an approach that an increasing number of organizers in the labor movement and the wider progressive movement call the inside/outside strategy: building and exercising power both inside and outside the electoral or legislative arenas. Proponents stand in contrast to others on the Left with markedly different perspectives. While some view electoral and legislative activities with skepticism or outright rejection, proponents of the inside/outside strategy view them as a crucial terrain to contest for political power at a time when the neoliberal consensus has unraveled. And while some on the Left focus on working inside these arenas exclusively, proponents of the inside/outside strategy emphasize a holistic orientation that connects organizing at the ballot box and the legislature with organizing in the workplace, the community, and other sites of struggle. In the case of Connecticut, coalition leaders define their version of the inside/outside strategy as a method to shape the state budget process by carrying out mass action inside and outside the legislative arena in particular.

Inside the legislative arena, RFA has advanced bills and budget items by mobilizing members of affiliated organizations to put pressure on lawmakers. Far from the mode of traditional lobbying, this set of tactics emphasizes mass action. For example, when the legislative committee responsible for tax policy scheduled a public hearing on proposals to increase taxes on the wealthy in 2021, more than three hundred people from many different organizations showed up to testify. This unusually high level of mobilization helped push the committee to ratify many of the coalition's favored policies and send them to the floor of the legislature. Moreover, leaders and members of RFA have linked their organization's specific demands to the larger Equity Agenda and consistently amplified each other's specific issues. Lawmakers accustomed to dividing and conquering competing demands must thereby face a united front of organizations presenting one vision of public investment.

The mobilizations that coalition leaders and members carry out inside the legislative arena have occurred in coordination with a bloc of several dozen allied elected officials in both chambers. The staunchest champions gained office in the last decade after emerging from affiliated unions, community organizations, and nonprofit advocacy organizations. Elected allies are not simply paper supporters—they strategize with coalition leaders on a regular basis, work to advance legislation, and show up in solidarity with coalition members engaging in direct action in the streets. Two relevant concepts entered the lexicon of the Left during the pandemic: co-governance and governing power.[6] The evolving relationship that RFA has built with its bloc of elected allies offers one example among many of how independent political organizations are enacting these concepts on the ground. It also points to another dimension of the inside/outside strategy: building power inside and outside the Democratic Party. RFA interacts with Democratic legislators and works closely with progressives in particular, yet remains completely independent of the party apparatus and frequently clashes with the centrist elected officials who lead it.

As RFA has made noise inside the halls of the Connecticut state capitol, it has concentrated most of its energy on organizing collective action outside the capitol. Leaders and members share an understanding that demonstrating strength in numbers, especially through the escalation of turnout and militancy, constitutes the fundamental source of the coalition's power. The purpose is to create a crisis for elected officials and the wealthy interests that control public policy through a diverse set of tactics, from rallies to car caravans, prayer vigils to marches, and even strikes and nonviolent civil disobedience. In another sense, creating a crisis that policymakers cannot ignore means drawing attention to the crisis of need and highlighting the concrete investments required to meet it. The coalition's actions have offered opportunities for organizations to mobilize members, deepen solidarity with one another, and collaborate on issues of shared interest for the first time. This commitment to showing people power outside the legislative arena is the chief route that the coalition has pursued to draw attention to its demands and cohere a disparate set of organizations.

While direct action in the streets has proved the coalition's most reliable means to broadcast its vision, RFA has engaged in other activities to change the common sense. The coalition has become a consistent voice articulating an anti-austerity message in the state's mainstream media. It has contributed to narrative change through the publication of its own reports directly taking on austerity's defenders and profiteers. A two-part report uncovered the destructive policy record and shadowy donors of the Yankee Institute, the state's leading right-wing think tank, while another laid bare the data on resident billionaires' soaring wealth during the pandemic. The coalition also gained attention for a poll showing that the vast majority of state residents favor higher taxes on the wealthy. In these ways, RFA has shifted the public debate over the state budget.

Of course, intertwining different kinds of mass action across multiple arenas requires a layer of rank-and-file leaders who are ready to lead their members into the fray. To recruit and develop this layer, the coalition has become a vehicle for political education through a new initiative called the Democracy School. The program brings together hundreds of rank-and-file leaders from across the coalition in a regular series of working people's assemblies.[7] Tenant union members and congregants from the Unitarian Church, domestic workers and professors—all joined together in a space that is truly multilingual, multigenerational, multiracial, and multigendered. The Democracy School offers a forum for rank-and-file leaders to discuss state politics through shared discussion and skill building. Even more important, the program enables these leaders to form deeper relationships and view themselves as a united movement across organizations. The Democracy School has proved one of the most exciting dimensions of the coalition's work—and a vital means to build the organizing capacity necessary to carry out the inside/outside strategy.

Unions as Anchors

As RFA has fought for material gains by applying the inside/outside strategy in the state budget process, some of its affiliated labor and community organizations have worked simultaneously to apply the Bargaining for the Common Good strategy in contract negotiations. The latter strategy, rooted in the experience of earlier struggles in labor history, first gained traction in the decade after the Great Recession. Several inspiring campaigns (most prominently in public education) applied key principles such as expanding the scope of bargaining beyond wages and benefits, coordinating short-term actions and forging long-term alignment with community allies, and embedding union demands within a larger vision of social justice. Trailblazing organizers from around the nation named the strategy, fleshed out its framework, and began the process of creating a formal network at a conference in Washington, DC, in 2014.[8] In Connecticut a core set of unions have practiced Bargaining for the Common Good in contract campaigns that coincide with the timeline of the state budget process and connect with the coalition's Equity Agenda. These unions represent workers in the public sector and workers in the private, nonprofit, and quasi-public sectors whose services rely on state funding. Several have embraced the strategy after electing labor leftists to positions of leadership. These unions illustrate the unique role that labor can play in tying workplace fights to electoral and legislative fights.

Perhaps the most advanced example of this practice during the pandemic was the work of SEIU 1199 New England (1199NE), a union of thirty thousand healthcare workers across the state and an indispensable affiliate of RFA.[9] Overwhelmingly women and disproportionately Black and brown, the members of 1199NE are essential workers who put their bodies on the line to keep society afloat despite the historic devaluation of their labor. Since its founding in the late 1960s as an offspring of the legendary union in New York, 1199NE has practiced a form of de facto sectoral bargaining by synchronizing negotiations with multiple employers to ensure that as many workers as possible can struggle—and even strike—at once. Remarkably, during the COVID-19 pandemic, 1199NE aligned contract expirations across the entire healthcare industry. Thus, at the same time that RFA agitated for the full Equity Agenda, members of 1199NE set a leading example in their fight to win investment in public health infrastructure.

The majority of 1199NE's membership are low-wage workers in long-term care—ground zero for the pandemic. Nursing home workers participated in countless job actions and threatened a statewide strike in 2021, winning huge steps toward a living wage, new racial equity measures on the shop floor, and higher staffing ratios to improve patient care. Nearly two thousand workers in group homes for intellectual and developmental disabilities ended up going out on a three-week-long strike in 2023 and winning desperately needed funding for this long-ignored sector of privatized work. RFA and its affiliated organizations consistently demonstrated solidarity with these workers' struggles, while the union consciously linked these fights with the coalition's demands to tax the wealthy and revitalize public investment.

At the same time, the approximately seven thousand members of 1199NE who provide healthcare in various state agencies joined together with allies to model an outstanding form of Bargaining for the Common Good and reverse the pattern of austerity measures that had stretched their services to the very limit. Rank-and-file leaders forged relationships with members of community and nonprofit advocacy organizations to formulate common good demands based on several criteria: whether the demand would address a gap in service, advance racial justice, and build the power of the union and community allies. For example, they called for reinvestment to guarantee comprehensive mobile crisis services in communities of color, ensuring that trained healthcare professionals, instead of police officers, respond to mental health emergencies. Under the banner "Expand Services to Save Lives," this campaign led to substantial economic gains, increased hiring to address the staffing crisis, and expanded public services to meet the rising needs of recipients.

In addition to the field of healthcare, the affiliated unions of RFA in the field of public education have used a Bargaining for the Common Good strategy and made the case for a moral budget. Connecticut's state universities and community colleges, which have suffered from years of disinvestment and tuition hikes, entered a time of crisis after the Lamont administration attempted to reduce funding despite the state's multibillion-dollar surplus. These institutions serve working-class students across Connecticut—disproportionately, or in some cases predominantly, students of color. Public higher education unions, including the 4Cs/SEIU Local 1973 in the community colleges and CSU-AAUP in the state universities, teamed up with one another and with student organizations to advance common good demands to fully fund services at these indispensable institutions of higher learning, winning over a $100 million to prevent dramatic cuts.[10]

The Rise of Independent Political Organizations

The Connecticut story constitutes one part of a larger pattern nationwide: the growth of independent political organizations at the state and local levels. These new formations aim to build the political power and ultimately the governing power of a mass base. Like RFA, many emerged through the collaboration of existing mass organizations, with unions playing a central role. While these formations vary in form and function, all share a commitment to the inside/outside strategy and advance a comprehensive vision of social justice taking aim at the interlocking structures of austerity, white supremacy, and gender oppression. Taken together, these efforts constitute a striking development in labor politics during the pandemic.

The labor movement and social movements for racial and gender liberation in the United States boast a long record of creating new organizational forms to lead fights inside and outside the two-party system. Today's independent political organizations arose amid the consolidation of the neoliberal social order, when the Right began its capture of the Republican Party and when the Democratic Party began to shed its nominal role in advancing the interests of the multiracial working class. Pioneering experiments such as WFP, California Calls, and New Virginia Majority got off the ground around the turn of the millennium. But the onset of the Great Recession and the Right's ascendancy precipitated a surge of new independent political organizations on the Left. For an outstanding example at the state level, consider Minnesotans for a Fair Economy, an alignment of seven different unions, faith organizations, community organizations, and worker centers started in 2011 that established a model for cross-organizational popular education and direct action. For an outstanding example at the municipal level, consider United Working Families—founded two years after the Chicago Teachers Union's seminal 2012 strike by that union, SEIU Health Care Illinois Indiana, Action Now, and Grassroots Illinois Action—which went on to elect former teacher Brandon Johnson on an anti-austerity platform in 2023.[11]

Some of the most hopeful results that independent political organizations in blue trifecta states have achieved during COVID-19 have been victories on tax reform. New Jersey set this trend in the first year of the pandemic when Democratic governor Phil Murphy signed a budget adding a "millionaire's tax" and expanding the Earned Income Tax Credit. The following year, the Invest in Our New York coalition won a state budget that raised more than $4 billion in annual revenue through various taxes on the wealthy and enabled pivotal investments, including a huge boost to underfunded public schools, emergency rental assistance for tenants, and a groundbreaking fund for immigrant workers who were excluded from federal relief. On the other side of the country, in the state of Washington, facing one of the country's most regressive state tax structures, the Balance Our Tax Code coalition won a capital gains tax that raised nearly a billion dollars in its first year alone. While most victories have been secured in the legislative arena, some formations have won through ballot initiatives. In 2022, the Raise Up Massachusetts coalition successfully led the passage of the Fair Share Amendment to the state constitution as millions of voters supported a tax increase on millionaires for the explicit purpose of funding public education and public transportation. Like RFA, many of these coalitions were anchored by strong labor, community, and other mass organizations.[12] Their victories show how the Left in various states has moved the needle on tax policy and challenged austerity during the pandemic.

From "Recovery For All" to "Connecticut For All"

On May 17, 2023, a little more than two years after hundreds had rallied outside the governor's mansion in one of the coalition's first actions, nearly two thousand supporters convened outside the state capitol to demand a moral budget. Inside the building, the coalition's elected allies in the state senate deliberated on how to translate this momentum into a strong push for the last phase of budget negotiations. Two weeks later, hundreds cheered on nearly sixty striking group home workers and their allies as they were arrested for blocking the intersection in front of the capitol. These bigger, riskier actions showed the coalition's growth. The coalition's embrace of a new name, Connecticut For All, signaled its maturation from a fledgling born in the chaos of the pandemic to an enduring force fighting to transform the state over the long haul.

By experimenting with the inside/outside strategy across multiple arenas, RFA and its affiliated organizations notched a number of policy wins during its first few years, including higher funding for long-term care and public schools, pandemic pay for essential workers, and expanded access to Medicaid for undocumented immigrant children. In one breakthrough, the coalition helped win a new provision requiring the governor to explain all future budget proposals based on how they mitigate inequality—a potentially important tool to shape fiscal policy. And although Governor Lamont has obstructed progressive tax reform, the coalition has brought this demand from the margins to the very center of the debate over the state budget.

Yet the value of the coalition's work over the last few years runs deeper than immediate policy changes. Most important, RFA has shown the potential of building strategic alignment across Connecticut's progressive movement ecosystem. To be sure, the coalition has encountered various limits. Externally, it has confronted the roadblock of fiscal conservatism upheld by corporate Democrats and the Right. Internally, it has grappled with the need to develop the organizing capacity of forces just beginning to deepen their relationships and move together from defense to offense. Despite these challenges, Recovery For All has started to cohere these progressive organizations into an overarching movement at the state level and exercise its fighting muscle. By raising a vision of a society where racial, economic, and gender inequalities are conquered, the coalition has made a sharp intervention in the public debate over the future of the state budget and of Connecticut itself.

More broadly, the growth of independent political organizations has proved a signature development in the politics of the pandemic. As COVID-19 rocked the neoliberal social order to its core, these organizations at the state and local levels are advancing a clear alternative to the ideology of racialized and gendered austerity and waging offensive struggles over public policy. Whereas right-wing formations have long dominated the contest over governance at the state level through organized money power, these progressive forces have begun to form a counterweight through organized people power. Often at the heart of these coalitions are unions that practice Bargaining for the Common Good, breaking down the artificial distinction between economic struggles at the workplace and political struggles at state capitols and beyond. By resourcing and leading new independent political organizations, these unions spur labor's revitalization, challenge the stranglehold of austerity, and propel the wider struggle to protect and expand multiracial democracy. While the seismic events of the 2020s prefigure an uncertain and foreboding future, new independent political organizations like RFA present a promise. Building these institutions will be one of the major tasks for organizers in the years to come.

Notes

1. Jane Mayer, *Dark Money: The Hidden History of the Billionaires behind the Rise of the Radical Right* (New York: Doubleday, 2016); Gordon Lafer, *The One Percent Solution: How Corporations Are Remaking America One State at a Time* (Ithaca: Cornell University Press, 2017); Nancy MacLean, *Democracy in Chains: The Deep History of the Radical Right's Stealth Plan for America* (New York: Penguin Books, 2018); Alex Hertel-Fernandez, *State Capture: How Conservative Activists, Big Businesses, and Wealthy Donors Reshaped the American States* (New York: Oxford University Press, 2019); Donald Cohen and Allen Mikaelian, *The Privatization of Everything: How the Plunder of Public Goods Transformed America and How We Can Fight Back* (New York: New Press, 2021); and Jacob Grumbach, *Laboratories against Democracy: How National Parties Transformed State Politics* (Princeton, NJ: Princeton University Press, 2022).

2. For more on New Haven Rising, see Jennifer Klein, "New Haven Rising," *Dissent* (Winter 2015): 45–54.

3. Jaison R. Abel and Richard Deitz, "Why Are Some Places So Much More Unequal Than Others?" Federal Reserve Bank of New York, *Economic Policy Review* 25, no. 1 (December 2019): 58–75.

4. For more on LEAP, see Louise Simmons, *Organizing in Hard Times: Labor and Neighborhoods in Hartford* (Philadelphia: Temple University Press, 1994); Bruce Shapiro, "Connecticut LEAP: A New Electoral Strategy," in *Building Bridges: The Emerging Grassroots Coalition of Labor and Community*, ed. Jeremy Brecher and Tim Costello, 135–143 (New York: Monthly Review Press, 1990); and Bill Fletcher Jr., "Debate: Inside or Outside the Democratic Party," *Labor Research Review* 1, no. 22 (1994): 86–97. See also Dan Clawson, *The Next Upsurge: Labor and the New Social Movements* (Ithaca: Cornell University Press, 2003).

5. Patrick R. O'Brien, "Connecticut's 2022 Tax Incidence Report: A High-Level Overview and Comparison to the 2014 Report," *Connecticut Voices for Children*, February 28, 2022; Josh Bivens, "Reclaiming Corporate Tax Revenues," *Economic Policy Institute*, April 14, 2022.

6. For more on co-governance, see Mark Engler and Paul Engler, "What Happens after Movement-Backed Politicians Take Office," *In These Times*, April 4, 2022. For more on governing power, see Bill Fletcher Jr., "How Socialists Can Govern," *Dissent* (Winter 2020), and Dan McGrath, Harmony Goldberg, and Grassroots Power Program, "Governing Power," published by the Grassroots Power Project and Grassroots Power Program in May 2023.

7. For more on the concept of working people's assemblies, see Bill Fletcher Jr. and Fernando Gapasin, *Solidarity Divided: The Crisis in Organized Labor and a New Path toward Social Justice* (Berkeley: University of California Press, 2009), and Sam Gindin, "Rethinking Unions, Registering Socialism," in *Socialist Register* 49 (2013): n.p.

8. See Joseph A. McCartin, "Bargaining for the Common Good," *Dissent* (Spring 2016); "Bargaining for the Common Good," special issue of *The Forge*,

especially Joseph McCartin and Merrie Najimy's "The Origins and Urgency of Bargaining for the Common Good," March 31, 2020.

9. Disclaimer: I served as an organizer and then as the education director at 1199NE for more than a decade, and my partner, Rebecca Simonsen, currently serves as vice president in charge of the union's State Division, and in that role led the Expand Services to Save Lives campaign described later in this section.

10. The 4Cs refers to the Congress of Connecticut Community Colleges, faculty and professional staff at the state's community colleges.

11. I wrote at length about this topic in "Independent Political Organizations: A Strategy in the Making," *Convergence Magazine*, November 27, 2023. See Daniel Cantor and Anthony Thigpenn, "Build an Independent Political Organization (But Not Quite a Party)," November 28, 2012, and Jon Liss, "Seize the Moment: Paving the Road for a Mass Left," June 9, 2019.

12. For the story on New York, see Sochie Nnaemeka and Nina Luo, "How We Won New Taxes on the Rich in New York," *The Forge*, October 21, 2021. For the story on Washington, see Galen Herz, "In Washington State, the Left Won a Major Victory for Taxing the Rich," *Jacobin*, May 15, 2021. For the story on Massachusetts, see Max Page, "Millionaire Tax Wins in Massachusetts," *Labor Notes*, December 16, 2022.

12

Rediscovering Class
EWOC and Pandemic Labor Activism

CONNOR HARNEY

The COVID-19 pandemic offered workers a common experience through which to articulate a discontent that had long been bubbling beneath the surface in the United States. While essential workers were told to make self-less sacrifices to maintain functioning supply chains, some of the wealthiest people on the planet reaped massive rewards while staying safe at one of their many homes. By exposing (in the most conspicuous of ways) a gross inequality that had been decades in the making while also revealing how workers were simultaneously so essential and precarious, the pandemic generated great anger and a growing sense of class among many working people. Where would this all lead?

This essay looks at the efforts of the Emergency Workplace Organizing Committee (EWOC) to seize upon this mood. EWOC is a partnership between the Democratic Socialists of America (DSA) and the United Electrical, Radio, and Machine Workers of America (UE) that emerged in the early days of the pandemic to provide resources for workers to fight for their own safety while building rank-and-file democracy. More than just an account of this relatively young institution, I try to place EWOC firmly within its own moment. In doing so, I hope to not only preserve the contributions the organization has made to working-class history but to also hold it up as a viable model for helping support workers' self-activity.

Much like the workers they have aided, EWOC has evolved over the three years from 2020 to 2023 from an organization whose very existence was prompted by the urgency of the pandemic to one that has collectively learned through class struggle. Out of that experience, they have become an organization that seeks to connect new organizers with labor movement veterans, combining formal training with strategic planning sessions. Reaching out through a campaign of mass texts and emails, the idea has been to help build up the experience of rank-and-file organizers rather than rely on professional organizers. While not opposed to working with already established unions, this independence has allowed EWOC to help those without a past relationship with the labor movement to learn how to operate with or without formal recognition.

EWOC's autonomy allows their organizers to think outside the traditional collective bargaining playbook while at the same time providing a place to share knowledge and skills that can possibly lead to formal recognition. The group's flexibility has been important to its success in forming a nationwide network of organizers across many different sectors and shops. These connections are helping to create a new generation of organizers who can operate in these increasingly lean and uncertain times, continuing the fight even in the face of the seemingly widespread acquiescence of Americans to powerlessness at work.

Through their efforts, EWOC tries to address the question of what is to be done to revitalize the labor movement. As commentators like Gabriel Winant have pointed out, while there may be valid criticism of organized labor, to ignore the full-frontal assault faced by unions from the end of the twentieth century forward is to miss just how asymmetrical the class warfare waged by bosses against workers has been.[1] This attack has been so successful partly because as union membership dwindles, they also have a diminished capacity to bring in new members and organize new shops. Organizing campaigns cost money that is paid out of union coffers, which often means having to choose prolonged battles over contracts for existing members at the expense of bringing in fresh recruits to the ranks of the labor movement.

By working primarily with a network of volunteers and funding itself through voluntary donations, EWOC is able to put young militants on a path that can converge with legacy unions. In providing training and education to workers to organize themselves, EWOC and its network are able to do things like free up those unions to fight what are often long, fierce battles for things like initial contract negotiations. Ideally, this effort that incubated during the pandemic will be part of bringing back "the mass spirit," one of the "two souls" of organized labor that needs to exist alongside its "reliable bureaucracy" in order to be successful.[2]

The Pandemic, the Working Class, and EWOC's Origins

By March 2020 it was clear that the COVID-19 pandemic was a world historic event, even if we were unaware of the extent to which it would transform our daily lives. In the first days of the pandemic, information was scarce and uncertainty defined the moment. As difficult as it is to remember at this point, in April 2020 Dr. Anthony Fauci predicted that it was possible we would be taking our summer vacations after flattening the curve over the course of the spring.³ However, even this optimistic forecasting did not resolve many of the pressing questions from those workers who were deemed an essential part of "critical infrastructure."⁴ How would they stay safe without the option to stay home, particularly in a country where workers' rights on the job are so limited? How would these workers ensure that their bosses were following proper health guidelines and providing protection at work? What would happen to these workers if they got sick?

Most workers were left to fend for themselves when addressing these questions. Some, like Chris Smalls and his coworkers at the Amazon warehouse on Staten Island, decided the best way to ensure their safety was to simply walk off the job.⁵ Self-activity like this functioned as a survival mechanism for working people who were used to highly regimented workplaces—disciplined by the clock or deadline, and overseen by the supervisor, manager, or, increasingly, the algorithm. Given the urgency of the moment, the state of labor relations, and the absence of labor unions in most workplaces, many workers were left to self-organize on relatively small scales in response to the challenges posed by the pandemic and employer callousness. Many would not have the wherewithal to do what Smalls and others did, not because of a lack of will or desire but because to do so in the United States in 2020 seemed impossible. Such was the state of class struggle.

EWOC came out of the collapse of Bernie Sanders's second run for the presidency—and the thousands who were inspired by his political message and the broader movement. Timing was key. Sanders suspended his campaign in early April after losing a string of primary contests to Joe Biden just as the seriousness of the COVID-19 pandemic began to sink in. With an army of supporters and engaged activists already mobilized, it is not surprising that many people focused their efforts on the class struggle posed by the pandemic. This includes the rather ad hoc formation of EWOC. It also came at the right time to become a bridge that different factions within the DSA could unite around for different reasons. While the dust had not yet settled around the Sanders campaign, and it would be its last gasps that provided some of the initial funding and experienced organizers for EWOC, there were clear fissures around the question of realignment that had been with the organization since the beginning. However, whether one believed in realigning the Democratic Party, creating a labor party surrogate within, or even that the DSA should be its own independent socialist party, their cause would need a revitalized labor movement with militant support no matter what. Helping workers organize themselves at their workplace was a way to do that.⁶

Whatever their leanings, organizing frontline workers during a world-wide pandemic was a clear unifying goal that could bring people of different persuasions together even if it was to achieve different stated ends. How to do it was the more difficult question to answer. Slowly but surely, organizers grasped at a strategy that had simple but serendipitous origins. Lead EWOC organizer, Megan Svoboda, recalls that while she was a member of the DSA's National Political Committee, she was working toward a COVID response for the organization. It was then that two leaders within the DSA, Eric Blanc and Jonah Furman, put out a Google Form to connect workers with an organizer. A simple form became the spark for what later became an organization. From there, Furman helped make the connection between UE and the DSA through the work he had done on the Sanders campaign (UE was one of the unions to endorse him nationally).[7] This partnership with UE has proved foundational in terms of both getting the project off the ground financially and providing a strong cadre of seasoned veteran organizers with decades of experience organizing workers. Their organizing chops have saved EWOC from having to cook up strategies from scratch, allowing UE organizers to pull from nearly a century of accumulated knowledge of rank-and-file unionism.[8]

Megan Svoboda captures the idea behind EWOC in the clearest terms as:

> a network that will support any worker regardless of industry, region, or workplace size, and connect them with a volunteer organizer who will support them to work with their coworkers to address inequalities at the workplace. Regardless of their ability to succeed at that, we support them to become lifelong organizers, people who will continue to either organize their workplace or help their family, friends, community members to fight for their own rights and their dignity at work.[9]

One of the lead organizers, Tristan Bock-Hughes, called it a "marriage" that brought people together to help workers save themselves from the "meat grinder" they were being thrown into to protect profits.[10] This relationship proved fruitful. UE's nonprofit arm was able to receive funds from the final Bernie push to help what would become EWOC's initial staff and get the project off the ground. It was not just the funds that helped kickstart their national organizing campaign. A mass text and email blast were sent out to Sanders's supporters across the country, providing an important Bernie bump at the beginning. From there they built up their intake form to aggregate data in a way that would help best connect workers to an organizer.

The staff also created a training program that would help educate prospective worker leaders after intake made initial contact. The training was a way to provide important insight into organizing as effectively as possible so that organizers were not continuously providing whoever they worked with a 101 crash course but could instead focus on the particular needs at that worker's shop. A lot of the first year was "trying to make systems work" and ensuring that EWOC was going to be something that would last beyond the crisis.[11] All of their systems building did not get in the way of EWOC scoring some early success helping workers win hazard pay and personal protective equipment (PPE). From Texas to Michigan, EWOC was able to help workers see, as worker Joshua Cano, of the grocery store Sprouts, put it, their "strength in numbers."[12]

As Tristan Bock-Hughes put it, workplace organizing has "a hundred steps from the first worker. Thinking about the need to make change in their workplace to, you know, winning a contract, a collective bargaining agreement that has a strong steward network to defend it." EWOC's "primary reason for being is to focus in with people in those first fifty steps because of the nature of resources."[13] What has that meant in practice? In the context of the pandemic, it meant helping workers to win real material victories so that they could see their own collective power—hazard pay, PPE, and sick leave were all things immediately obtainable with pressure from workers and their community together. It was a way that workers could protect themselves from paying the ultimate "price" for "$11 an hour."[14]

From its inception in early 2020 through 2023, 3,231 workers reached out to EWOC. Out of those who contacted the organization via its online form, about 943 were reached through a successful intake call. After that initial call, 405 potential worker organizers went through the six-session training series that EWOC put together in 2021 alone.

Each session of the training series covers the first steps workers need to go through on the path to organizing their workplace. The very first training focuses on identifying and developing potential worker leaders, while later trainings hone the organizers' ability to talk about joining their efforts and have conversations that prepare their coworkers to have a captive audience meeting with their boss(es). Each one builds off the previous, with the end goal of preparing the worker to put what they learned into practice.

On top of training attendance, EWOC kept track of workers who were assigned to a volunteer organizer's campaign. Of those who reached out, just about 97 percent made it to that step. This was made possible by the effort of EWOC's staff of volunteers, which number about 1,000 total, with about 165 considered regularly active. More difficult to quantify has been what rank-and-file organizers have accomplished on the ground. EWOC only recently began tracking this, so the data is incomplete and may paint an inaccurate picture. From the data they do have, it appears that of the 943, only 142 took any action—roughly a 15 percent conversion rate. However, EWOC's data accounts for only the 740 campaigns that they tracked using the data software Airtable, and much of the earlier information has yet to be backfilled. If we take 740 as our denominator, we are then looking at just under a 20 percent conversion rate—not where EWOC hopes to be eventually, but still, helping two out of every ten workers to act on their impulse to change their workplace is a good start.[15]

EWOC has shown continued growth, tapping into the wider excitement around the Amazon Labor Union's victory in April and the ongoing wave of Starbucks union drives that began in December 2021 with a Buffalo, New York, store. The total EWOC volunteer count reached 1,400 as of June 2022. Those volunteers helped 460 workers complete the initial form in the first six months of that year. From that initial contact, workers in 23 different workplaces made formal demands to their employees, with 13 holding union drives. These actions have affected the lives of 1,926 people. This success was only possible through the power of the workers themselves and the volunteer army of support staff behind them.

While those focusing on the training of organizers and organizing themselves played a major part in these victories, they were helped every step of the way by other volunteer organizers working in different capacities, including intake and tracking. Once cases have been logged, that information is analyzed by the EWOC data team, which helps ensure an effective use of the organization's limited resources. Other teams manage the organization's media presence, creating a newsletter and helping active campaigns deal with the press when necessary, while still others create targeted political education that serves those already involved with EWOC and, even more importantly, seeks to engage the wider public about how they can contribute to a renewed working-class struggle. Each piece is essential to making sure workers are as supported as they can be in this moment when the labor movement is still finding its feet in the face of a long decline.

Rank-and-File Movements

What do the first fifty steps of workplace organizing look like for those working with EWOC? This section covers three workplace campaigns at different stages, starting with (1) my own organizing efforts as an employee at Whole Foods, moving to (2) a more successful attempt to organize restaurant workers, and ending with (3) a successful attempt to unionize workers at a bookstore.

WHOLE FOODS

Like many other food service workers, I saw my hours increase significantly during the pandemic, though not enough to provide workers with health benefits. Indeed, Whole Foods cut healthcare for part-time employees just in time for the pandemic. In a "let them eat cake" moment, CEO John Mackey went as far as to say that people should not worry about healthcare, but instead, "The best solution is to change the way people eat, the way they live, the lifestyle, and diet."[16] This was a signal that not only did he not hear our concerns about safety but that also he was indifferent to them.

Those of us at the store at the start of the pandemic saw ourselves as working in the trenches. Retail is always a high turnover industry, but concerns for safety, long hours, and unpredictable schedules meant our management was always trying to find warm bodies for more cannon fodder. It was at this time that I got a text from former Bernie staffers saying they were connecting workers with organizers to help them organize their coworkers. Soon after expressing interest, I received a call from Terry Davis, a longtime organizer with UE who had volunteered to help mentor rank-and-file organizers. With her guidance and the organizing skills provided to me through EWOC's then-brand-new training program, I went to work trying to organize the employees at my store.

I knew going in that it would be difficult. It seemed that every time I got close to having an organizing committee in embryo, one key member left for better employment or just resigned over the unforgiving conditions at work. Eventually, I worked out a two-pronged strategy, which was to focus first on organizing my own department and concomitantly finding organic leaders in each of the other departments. The latter proved to be the more trying task, and the group that formed over the course of months remained unevenly representative.

However, the solidarity that our truck team formed over the course of my organizing effort is still something I take great pride in.[17] We held regular meetings and kept up communication in and out of work. For the majority of 2020 and the first half of 2021, our primary concerns centered on the pandemic and management's lack of transparency. By the end of the first year of the pandemic, mass automated texts telling us that someone in the store had contracted COVID were a regular occurrence. Each of these messages created a wave of anxiety and panic that would spread throughout the store because there was no clear-cut method of figuring out whether or not one of us had been exposed. Rather than rely on management to figure it out, we created our own contact-tracing network independent of management.[18]

Our team found out about the deceitful way in which management was handling who should be quarantined by chance. In January 2021 one of my truck team coworkers came down with COVID just as they put in their two-week notice to begin another job. We learned from this worker that management had made explicit that we would not be informed before more "contact tracing was done." Knowing our workflows, we concluded that we had been in close contact with this coworker. I tried to steer us toward either a walk-out or a callout, but the decision was made to wait and see what would be done the next day. When it became obvious that nothing was going to be done, a number of us came together and confronted management. Though we tried to prevent being broken up, we were forced to speak one-on-one with management and make our grievances known. After our appeal, they decided to further divide us by making us think we initially were not going to be quarantined until they had completed their "process." Almost immediately after each of our shifts, we were called and told not to come in for two weeks because we had indeed been exposed. We were also told not to tell any of our coworkers. Nobody honored that commitment, and by the end of the day, all of us who had been quarantined knew it.

Over the course of our time in isolation, we made plans to expand our organizing efforts and use our experience as an example for other teams in the store to show the power of solidarity. We were prepared for pushback from management. What we were not prepared for was the lengths they would go to keep us apart. Citing safety concerns, they completely changed my team's daily workflow so that there was little if no time with one another. That made communication nearly impossible anywhere except outside work, throwing a massive wrench into our plans. As a result of our exile, upon return our resistance to management appeared to be a pyrrhic victory, not the rallying action we had hoped it would be perceived as.

We were able to regroup over the following months, holding regular in-person meetings whenever we could—working closely with EWOC to develop new tactics for recruiting coworkers to our case along with actions we could take to show our strength. Even as we grew our numbers slowly and expanded outside of our initial core, the initial retaliation ended up being the death of our drive. A feeling of pessimism permeated throughout the store, and even our most committed found their best recourse was to flee to another job rather than stay and fight the boss. I eventually threw up my hands and called it quits when I was offered a full-time position at another job. My story may not offer a happy ending, but it does provide insight into the power (and limits) of worker-centered organizing and rank-and-file democracy. It also provides some of the context for my later analysis of the Great Resignation.

RESTAURANT WORKERS UNITE!

Not every organizing effort has ended with the tired resignation that mine did. In some shops, efforts are beginning to show real promise. At the start of 2022, I spoke with Ben DelSasso, a rank-and-file organizer outside of Chicago. Ben works at a locally owned restaurant with multiple locations. He and his coworkers have faced struggles that many workers will be able to recognize. Hit by heavy turnover, running short staffed has become the norm not the exception. Before the pandemic, the restaurant could afford to have a

constantly rotating cast of employees. However, in the COVID era, the pool
of applicants is not large enough to keep up with the rate at which workers
resign. According to Ben, the rate of people applying to open positions at his
restaurant is down about 60–70 percent, leading management to squeeze
the staff that it still has. These abuses acted as the catalyst for his coworkers
coming together. One particularly egregious practice consisted of having the
waitstaff arrive two hours early for their shift. Effectively, this meant that
those workers were being paid below minimum wage in order to prepare
food like rolls and other baked goods.[19]

It was this "buns and dumplings" incident that prompted Ben to sit down
with the CEO of the restaurant to find a remedy for the situation.[20] Unfortunately, his boss did not see eye to eye with him when it came to his complaint.
That his words fell on deaf ears pushed Ben to reach out to EWOC. Initially,
the most important thing that EWOC offered the staff was information. Ben
and his coworkers did not have previous union experience, so Tristan and
Terry together offered them counsel as to their rights on the job as well as
possible paths forward for organizing the restaurant.

Ben made an important observation about Tristan and Terry's work
together for EWOC that is refreshing, given the pervasiveness of generational conflict. He told me that in his opinion the vast wealth of experience
and wisdom that Terry brought to the table from her own organizing work
stretching back to the 1970s meshed well with Tristan's youthful energy and
his excitement for new ideas and strategy—in a way speaking to the strength
of the partnership between UE and the DSA. It was that combination that
brought them the confidence to craft a petition to bring to the boss. Of the
seventy-seven employees on schedule, fifty signed on to the list of demands.
Some of their demands were met right away while others were not.

The schedule at Ben's workplace was unpredictable, sometimes put out
only a few days ahead of when employees would have to work a shift and
typically for only a week at a time. Understandably, this threatened their
ability to have a life outside of work. More than this, employees' availability
was not being honored at all. Since the workers at Ben's restaurant presented
their petition, management has begun posting the schedule further ahead
of time and availability is being more faithfully honored. Yet, despite this
important concession, workers have yet to see an increase in pay. While the
restaurant prides itself on being "high-class," it pays its employees poverty
wages. The average back-of-the-house wage is around thirteen dollars an
hour, and bartenders make far less than the amount paid at similar restaurants
in the area.

Some progress has been made, however. Bussers, waitstaff, and hosts are
no longer sharing the same tip pool. Now hosts are separated and bussers

are given a flat wage rate. Another point of contention has been the services offered by the restaurant despite being short staffed. Weddings and other special events are still being held because they are an important source of revenue for the business. However, the restaurant does not have enough people to staff them. The justification is that by maintaining the revenue stream they will be able to bring on new staff—a promise that has yet to be delivered. For perspective, across the two main restaurant locations there are just under 80 employees. Before COVID there were 250 employees across all three locations. They are making do with less than half their pre-pandemic staff.

It was the workers who built their own organization, but it was the resources provided by EWOC that provided them a framework for understanding the organizing tools they had at hand. The importance of this information cannot be understated. What's more impressive about EWOC's ability to be a resource for rank-and-file workers in this case is their reach. Before reaching out to EWOC, Ben was not involved in any way with the DSA, nor was anyone else at his restaurant. It was googling "how to start a union" that made the fateful connection. Through its digital and media presence, the organization maintains social media accounts and a website that acts as a channel to connect with workers already in EWOC's orbit or those who may be unfamiliar with their mission.

UNIONIZING A BOOKSTORE

If Ben's restaurant represents a shop on its way to building long-term organization, the final example is of workers who won their union. Bookshop Santa Cruz is a case where concerns over safety led workers to take the step of unionizing their shop. On February 3, 2021, the bookstore's workers voted to unionize with CWA Local 9423. Their effort began toward the start of the COVID-19 as shelter-in-place orders were being lifted. Like many workers, they were offered the tough choice to either resign or come back to work. With only four days to make such an important decision, the store's employees opted to draft an email with their concerns over what safety measures the bookshop should take. Once they received a response, they recognized the strength they had when they came together.

As one worker-leader, Celeste Orlosky, recalled:

> I realized that organizing is not much more than just talking to your co-workers: finding out what's going on with each other, and we found that we had a lot of concerns in common. And for us in our workplace, it seemed like there was not any other way forward than forming a union. We wouldn't have legal protections any other way. And most of us don't have experience with unions. Maybe only a handful of us have had union jobs.[21]

EWOC provided Celeste and her coworkers with a spreadsheet that would help them map their workplace to gauge support for the union. Part of that process is determining organic leaders, whether a worker is for or against the union, and if they are for unionizing, to what degree they support doing so—whether they are active or passive.

In the case of Bookshop Santa Cruz, CWA required 70 percent support before voting, despite legally being required to have only 30 percent. The reason for this is simple. They expected the company to fight against unionization. Having more than 50 percent support to start means that when employers run anti-union campaigns, even if some supporters are scared off a majority still remains.

On December 11, 2020, Celeste and her coworkers signed union cards and presented a thirteen-point mission statement that called for, among other things:

- Just cause for termination
- No more at-will employment
- Dedicated, uninterrupted paid time for section work and professional development, especially with the holidays that we were going through
- Paid time off for part-time and full-time employees
- Improved scheduling procedures
- Big one: limiting the reliance on the Santa Cruz Police Department. That's something a lot of us feel really strongly about. George Floyd was murdered over the police being called for an allegedly counterfeit $20 bill. That was in a retail space.
- De-escalation training for all staff
- Tangible antiracist procedures and actions[22]

When their boss failed to meet these demands, they filed for a union election. Outside their store, they used a petition hosted on coworker.org to garner wider public support. Bookshop Santa Cruz employs about forty to fifty people, but they were able to obtain two thousand signatures total. The DSA provided another important pillar of support. Holding rallies helped show that the community was behind the bookstore workers.

After the initial filing, the election was held over three weeks in January 2021. During that time there was one captive audience meeting, and while some were reticent about the proposition of starting a union during a pandemic, and others just outright opposed it, the majority continued to favor the union. Upon winning their election, Celeste and her coworkers set to work putting together a bargaining unit to negotiate a contract. According to Celeste, it is clear that they want higher pay, more security, a stronger relationship with the community, and more *worker control* on the job.

The Great Resignation and the Future of Workers Organizations

Beginning in April 2021, millions of workers began telling their bosses to "take this job and shove it." Many of them came from the service sector—workers in restaurants, hotels, and grocery stores whose very jobs meant they sacrificed so that the world could keep turning during the pandemic. Less than ideal conditions prevail in these jobs in normal times. Underemployment, overwork, and safety concerns are all commonplace without the pandemic exacerbating them. Supply chain shocks and the spread of COVID meant that many people left stores and restaurants empty-handed or with empty stomachs—leaving what staff was there to deal with the frustration. These workers went from elevated essential workers to the target of irritated consumers' ire in a matter of months. It was no surprise that under such abusive conditions, many chose to take their chances looking for better work or taking time off to reassess their life's trajectory in 2021.

Whatever the scale and whatever the reason, the Great Resignation was something that any group of employees that seeks to organize their workplace had to contend with, as millions of workers continued to quit their jobs at elevated rates for the rest of 2021.[23] This is an issue that EWOC took very seriously, especially because many of the workers they had set their sights on organizing were those outside of traditionally unionized workplaces, and thus within the service sector. Seeing your coworkers leave out the revolving door alongside resignations en masse does not necessarily instill confidence to stay and fight for your rights on the job. For this reason, EWOC created explicit messaging geared at persuading these very people. Prominently, their home page asked the question "Thinking about Quitting Your Job? Here Are 5 Things You Can Do First."[24] What follows provides a basic framework for talking to coworkers, forming a committee on the job, and developing and presenting a petition to the boss. Links are embedded that would allow any interested worker to connect with an organizer who can help them to implement such a plan in their own workplace alongside other links to resources for would-be organizers.

The way lead organizer Megan Svoboda put it, if there is a high enough level of organization at a workplace that some people "are organizing everyone on their entire shift to leave together," and some are even "organizing all those people to get new jobs together," then we already have plenty of "organic leaders" on hand—they just may not have thought about it in those terms.[25] That is, if people are already prepared to leave together, it's clear that there is already a consensus that the way things are is untenable. The role of EWOC in that situation is to say, "We know you don't like your job, but what sucks about it?" "Can you change it?" "What would make it better?" "Do you want to?"[26] Posing these questions can help put the anti-work energy toward making life on the job better.

However, as Svoboda brought up in our conversations, many workers coming to EWOC are in a position where many of their coworkers already have one foot out the door. Changing their mind and getting them to stay is an uphill battle. At the same time, even when worker leaders are unsuccessful, it can still be seen as a step in the right direction. If these workers come out of their EWOC experience with a set of skills that they and their coworkers "can carry with them," that opens up future organizing opportunities as they find new jobs. Hopefully, it has also placed them in a wider network of workers who can communicate their collective experience across the country.[27]

While the Great Resignation offered opportunities for EWOC to expand its network of organizers, it also presented serious challenges. Much like the exhaustion with COVID itself, burnout bred feelings of hopelessness. Tristan Bock-Hughes described the process as "building a castle on shifting sands, and people are draining away because they're exhausted by what they're seeing with the total lack of engagement with the reality of COVID from their management," leading to the "recognition" for workers that they are "worth so little."[28] The problem with burnout like this is that it often leads people to give up before things have even gotten started. Organizing the kinds of workplaces that EWOC is trying to help organize has been a seemingly intractable problem for at least a century. Both the volunteer network and the rank-and-file organizers are trying to figure out a solution as they carry out the practical day-to-day work of organization building. It's difficult to get someone to commit to staying at a degrading job if it seems like there is no immediate win on the horizon—something that makes concrete the notion that "collective actions get the goods."[29]

Conclusion

For Tristan, the future for EWOC is building up the organization, forging stronger ties with other unions without compromising their commitment to internal democracy. Ideally, EWOC will be a "conduit for workers from across the country" that would prepare workers to tackle problems on their own so that union staffers can focus on getting workers formal recognition of their organizations. To achieve that end, he would like to eventually see a network of thousands of volunteers, thousands of organizers being able to help thousands of workers every single year. Megan gave a similarly optimistic prognostication when I asked her where she saw EWOC in five years. Her hope for the organization is to be "bigger and better," with "more union partners," "more staff," and "more on-the-ground nodes of organizing."[30]

Ultimately, the goal is to make EWOC into a massive virtual worker center on a national level. In this way they answer the question begged by Winant's article "Who Works for the Workers?" with "the workers themselves."[31] At the same time, they do this in a way that does fetishize spontaneous self-activity. While some people may be natural leaders, workers must learn to navigate the difficult terrain on which the struggle with their boss will be fought—each step littered with demoralizing obstacles meant to keep them caught in a quagmire. EWOC prepares workers the best they can so that they don't get bogged down.

There have been many efforts to revitalize the labor movement. The COVID-19 pandemic accelerated America's rediscovery of the working class, but what comes of that discovery remains to be seen. This is not the first time Americans have uncovered the importance of class. Some notion of class is common sense in American life, but what makes these moments unique is that they show signs of developing a universal language to articulate the role that class plays in structuring daily life. These moments offer an opportunity for forward-thinking organizers to seize on this common language to bring together people under the banner of class struggle. Part of optimizing the momentum these situations offer is thinking beyond the bounds of the past while taking its lessons.

When workers walked off the job in Detroit in January 1933, they could not have known what was in store from the Roosevelt administration or the Congress of Industrial Organizations in the years to follow. Those Briggs Manufacturing workers walked the picket line during a Michigan winter in protest of "dangerous conditions, the killing pace of operations, and repeated wage cuts."[32] Though it was ultimately "a lost cause," the twelve thousand workers on strike and the one hundred thousand more idled showed, according to Walter Reuther, "the most significant and encouraging developments in the history of the industry," the product of the Auto Workers Union's "years of constant and untiring propaganda work and agitation through the departmental committees, working secretly and under great pressure."[33] Despite Reuther's optimistic endorsement, as Steve Fraser reminds us, "No one alive in 1932 could have reasonably predicted what the country would be like a mere three years later."[34] What was accomplished in those years should serve to underscore the importance of building organization to prepare for those pivotal moments. When they come is not always up to us. How we meet them, however, is.

Notes

1. Gabriel Winant, "Who Works for the Workers?" *N+1* (blog), August 3, 2016, https://www.nplusonemag.com/issue-26/essays/who-works-for-the-workers/.

2. Winant, "Who Works for the Workers?"

3. Amanda Watts, "Americans May Be Able to Take Summer Vacations, Fauci Says," *CNN*, April 9, 2020, https://www.cnn.com/world/live-news/coronavirus -pandemic-04-09-20/index.html/; and Aylin Woodward, "It May Seem Like the US Isn't 'Flattening the Curve.' But It Takes 2 Weeks for Coronavirus Case Counts to Reflect Our Current Efforts, Anthony Fauci Said," *Business Insider*, April 8, 2020, https://www.businessinsider.in/science/news/it-may-seem-like-the-us -isnt-flattening-the-curve-but-it-takes-2-weeks-for-coronavirus-case-counts -to-reflect-our-current-efforts-anthony-fauci-said-/articleshow/75037843.cms/.

4. Christopher C. Krebs, "Memorandum on Identification of Essential Critical Infrastructure Workers during COVID-19 Response" (Washington, DC: U.S. Department of Homeland Security, March 19, 2020), https://www.cisa.gov/sites/ default/files/publications/CISA-Guidance-on-Essential-Critical-Infrastructure -Workers-1-20-508c.pdf/.

5. Irina Ivanova, "Amazon Fires Worker Who Organized Staten Island Warehouse Walkout," *CBS News*, March 31, 2020, https://www.cbsnews.com/news/ amazon-fires-chris-smalls-walkout-staten-island-new-york-warehouse/. Since this article was originally written, Smalls has gone on to help lead the first successful union drive at an Amazon warehouse. Not only that, but he and his coworkers achieved this through a newly formed independent organization called the Amazon Labor Union. Workers at a fulfillment center on Staten Island are in the process of casting their ballots for what would be second location organized by the ALU. Ultimately, they lost the second battle, and Amazon has made a concerted effort to ensure that other sites don't unionize. See Annie Palmer, "Amazon Labor Battle Continues as Union Vote Kicks Off at Second Staten Island Warehouse," *CNBC*, April 25, 2022, sec. Technology, https://www.cnbc.com/2022/04/25/ amazon-union-vote-begins-at-second-staten-island-warehouse.html/. Since the ALU's initial victory, EWOC held a joint online event with *Jacobin* magazine that teased out the lessons of this historic event in conversation with ALU organizers, including Smalls. After the event, EWOC began getting calls from Amazon workers seeking to organize their own workplace. Volunteers quickly got to work fielding their calls, putting together a phone banking effort to respond to influx of contacts. Here is a link to a recording of the event: Emergency Workplace Organizing Committee, *Amazon Workers Speak Out: Lessons for How to Win at Work*, 2022, https://www.youtube.com/watch?v=lC-w3rHJRWo/.

6. Here, "realignment" refers to the stance of the DSA toward the Democratic Party advocated by its founder, Michael Harrington, for most of his political career. The point of realignment was to unite the left wing of the party so that it could push conservatives like the Dixiecrats out of the party. A more recent model of realignment advocated by Seth Ackerman in a well-known *Jacobin* article published in 2016 called for the creation of a labor party surrogate within the Democratic Party that would someday break away once their ballot line outlived its usefulness. Other factions are more hostile to the Democratic Party and would like to see the DSA become an independent socialist party. Seth

Ackerman, "A Blueprint for a New Party," *Jacobin*, November 8, 2016, https://jacobin.com/2016/11/bernie-sanders-democratic-labor-party-ackerman/.

7. Interview with EWOC lead organizer Megan Svoboda by Connor Harney, January 5, 2022.

8. Founded in 1936 and one of the first chartered unions of the then-fledgling CIO, UE became known for its fiercely democratic unionism, which put a lot of purchase in rank-and-file participation in decision making from the shop floor to the negotiation table. At its height in the 1940s, the union represented 600,000 workers in the plants of major manufacturers like GE, RCA, and Westinghouse. However, differences over how to address the Taft-Hartley provision that required all unions to sign noncommunist affidavits brought about a schism within the CIO. Those like UE who opted not to sign it were ostracized from the labor movement and saw their numbers diminished during the red-baiting of the McCarthy era. Today, while the union represents only about 35,000 workers, it continues to hold to its principle of democratic participation through their immediate daily work and their partnership with the DSA, through which they seek to pass the torch of democratic unionism to a new generation of organizers. For further reading, see United Electrical, Radio, and Machine Workers of America (UE), *Them and Us Unionism* (Pittsburgh: United Electrical, Radio and Machine Workers of America, 2020), https://www.ueunion.org/ThemAndUs/; James Young, *Union Power: The United Electrical Workers in Erie, Pennsylvania* (New York: Monthly Review Press, 2017); and Ronald L. Filippelli and Mark McColloch, *Cold War in the Working Class: The Rise and Decline of the United Electrical Workers*, SUNY Series in American Labor History (Albany: SUNY Press, 1995).

9. Svoboda interview.

10. Interview with EWOC lead organizer Tristan Bock-Hughes by Connor Harney, December 15, 2021.

11. Svoboda interview.

12. Gus Bova, "Will Grocery Workers Still Be 'Heroes' When COVID-19 Subsides?" *Texas Observer*, May 1, 20202, https://www.texasobserver.org/grocery-workers-covid-19-texas/.

13. Bock-Hughes interview.

14. Bova, "Will Grocery Workers Still Be 'Heroes'?"

15. All of this data was obtained by me from EWOC's internal research team, January 11, 2022.

16. G. J. Harney, "Whole Foods' Hippie CEO and the Lie of Enlightened Capitalism," *Current Affairs*, March 12, 2021, https://www.currentaffairs.org/2021/03/whole-foods-hippie-ceo-and-the-lie-of-enlightened-capitalism/.

17. Our truck team was responsible for unloading the trucks of food coming into the store, breaking down the pallets, and then finally making sure the food made it to the shelves.

18. Fifteen minutes of continuous close proximity was their metric versus a cumulative contact across a shift.

19. Waitstaff are typically paid what is called cash wage plus tips per hour. However, when they are working without tips doing prep work like Ben described, they make only that cash wage, which is set at national minimum wage of $2.13 an hour.

20. Interview of restaurant rank-and-file organizer Ben DelSasso by Connor Harney, January 17, 2022.

21. Celeste Orlosky, "How to Organize a Bookstore: A Q&A with Worker Leader Celeste," interview by Eric Dirnbach and Tim Newman, March 10, 2021, https:// workerorganizing.org/bookstore-union-organizing-santa-cruz-1125/.

22. Orlosky interview.

23. Over four million workers have quit their jobs each month year after year from April 2021 to April 2022. For a breakdown of the number of workers quitting, which industries they are leaving, and what percentage of the total workforce has been leaving their jobs, see "Table 4. Quits Levels and Rates by Industry and Region, Seasonally Adjusted—2022 M04 Results," U.S. Bureau of Labor Statistics, June 1, 2022, https://www.bls.gov/news.release/jolts.t04.htm/.

24. "Emergency Workplace Organizing Committee," EWOC, https:// workerorganizing.org/; and "Thinking about Quitting Your Job? Here Are 5 Things You Can Do First," EWOC, https://workerorganizing.org/workers-quitting -jobs-great-resignation-2021/.

25. Svoboda interview.

26. Svoboda interview.

27. Svoboda interview.

28. Bock-Hughes interview.

29. Bock-Hughes interview.

30. Svoboda interview.

31. Winant, "Who Works for the Workers?"

32. Robert H. Zieger and Gilbert J. Gall, *American Workers, American Unions: The Twentieth Century*, 3rd ed. (Baltimore: Johns Hopkins University Press, 2002), 64.

33. Zieger and Gall, *American Workers*; and Walter Reuther, "Auto Workers Strike," *Student Outlook* 1, no. 4 (March 1933): 15.

34. Steve Fraser, *Mongrel Firebugs and Men of Property: Capitalism and Class Conflict in American History* (New York: Verso, 2019), 189.

13

The Pandemic Revolt of New York City's Immigrant "Small Business" Unions

ANDREW B. WOLF

In what would become an iconic image of the pandemic in New York City, Tipu Sultan climbed on top of a yellow taxicab on Broadway in front of city hall with a bullhorn. He raised his fist in the air and led hundreds of cabbies in a chant: "Debt forgiveness now! No more bankruptcies! No more suicides!" Tipu is a Yellow Cab driver and organizer with the New York Taxi Workers Alliance (NYTWA), a union of twenty-four thousand yellow and app-based drivers in the city. The NYTWA was protesting to demand that the mayor provide debt relief for medallion owner-drivers, whose medallions had been sold to them at artificially inflated prices. Medallions allow drivers to operate the city's iconic Yellow Cabs, which are the only vehicles that can pick up people who hail them on the street. Historically, about 30 percent of these medallions are owned by the driver themselves. The NYTWA argued that the city lied to the immigrant drivers about the value of the medallions, which then collapsed after the city allowed Uber to flood the market with thousands of new drivers. The pandemic was the final straw, as most drivers would lose their life's work and savings if the city did not act. The crowd of drivers were determined to win: "Driver power! Union power!"

This chant might strike some as peculiar since these drivers own their own cars and therefore are not employee/workers. The NYTWA insists that they are a union, but many drivers are—at least on paper—immigrant small business owners. Taxi drivers were not the only immigrant small business owners who organized "union style" movements that became militant during the pandemic, as app-based delivery workers, street vendors, and undocumented workers all formed powerful movements despite lacking formal employee protections. This chapter attempts to understand why immigrant small business owners organized "union style" movements and evaluates what factors account for the similarities and differences between the different pandemic movements.

Immigrant small business owners organize as workers because, for many, becoming self-employed was not a deliberate choice but a reality forced upon them. Immigrants choose to self-employ due to pull (positives) and push (negatives) factors deriving from their marginalization and the discrimination they face in the traditional labor market.[1] Pull factors are not the potential of massive windfall profits but, rather, the ability to carve out an existence with minimal majority white interference. This chapter adds an additional component to our understanding of immigrant self-employment push factors: deliberate firm strategy. This strategy takes two forms. The first is workplace fissuring, in which firms use contracting and misclassification to deny immigrants employee rights by labeling them proactively as independent contractors. Second, immigrant small businesses can find themselves dependent on the government due to restrictive licensing, which is often passed at the behest of larger, majority-dominated firms.

These two forms of forced immigrant entrepreneurship—misclassification and restrictive licensing—account for why immigrants working in "self-employed" jobs choose to form "union style" organizations. Based on years of ethnographic fieldwork and interviews, this chapter explores three such movements by organizations whose membership was pushed to the brink during the pandemic: the New York Taxi Workers Alliance, Los Deliveristas Unidos, and the Street Vendor Project. The form and strategies employed by these immigrant worker movements during the pandemic was driven by the logic of their industry, their memberships' immigration status, and their relationship to the question of whether their membership should be considered employees or not. While all three movements engaged in "union style" campaigns, the groups with more secure membership, in terms of industry structure and immigration status, more closely resembled traditional union structures.

The Creation of Dependent Immigrant Business Owners

The recent upsurge of immigrant activism during the COVID pandemic in New York City was decades in the making. When New York's political economy changed following the 1970s financial crisis, the city emerged reformed as a global city built around a bifurcated urban service economy with finance and real estate services at the top generating huge demand for low-end service jobs in industries like food service and domestic work. These service jobs were filled by a massive influx of new immigrants. Unlike previous European-dominated waves of immigration, these new immigrants were from all over the Global South. The impact was to racialize and gender these urban service occupations. This demographic change was due to passage of the 1965 Hart-Celler Act, which eliminated the country-of-origin quota system that had favored European immigration. This relaxation resulted in an explosion of immigrants from South and East Asia as well as Africa,[2] but the new immigrants primarily chose to settle in just a handful of America's largest cities. The urban concentration radically reformulated the demographics of cities like New York City and generated difficult questions about how to politically and economically incorporate these new arrivals.

Once they had settled in New York City, the post-1965 immigrants faced a wide variety of employment experiences. For immigrants, researchers find this process largely followed what is variously called ethnic networks, enclaves, or niches. Ethnic niche jobs are typically at the bottom of the employment opportunity ladder, and the social closure of immigrant networks allows groups to keep outsiders out.[3] These niches, while important sources of jobs, can also serve to limit immigrants' opportunities to enter other more-lucrative industries.

The post–Hart-Celler immigrants developed employment niches not only in traditional low-wage immigration service occupations but in different forms of self-employment at much higher rates than previous immigrants had. The choice of immigrants to pursue self-employment was driven by a combination of pull and push factors, which shape immigrants' opportunity structures. The dominant pull factor was the ability to operate in markets that were not in competition with the dominant majority-owned firms. This was accomplished by focusing on underserved or abandoned markets, markets characterized by low economies of scale, markets with unstable or uncertain demand, and markets for exotic goods.[4] Pull factors for immigrant self-employment, while they existed and still exist, provided smaller benefits than one might expect, given the risks. This history suggests the importance of considering the push factors driving self-employment for immigrants today.

At a broad level, the push factors driving immigrants to self-employment are all the social forces preventing immigrants from obtaining gainful incorporation into the traditional labor market. The lack of opportunities in the primary labor market makes the relatively weak pulls stronger. Push factors include lack of English proficiency, nontransferable home country education or skills, weak social networks, and racial discrimination. Understood in this framework, immigrant self-employment is not fulfilling an entrepreneurial American Dream but is a case of immigrants turning to their last resort.[5] Indicative of this reality, research finds that when presented with an alternative, most immigrants abandoned minority-neighborhood entrepreneurship.[6]

As noted previously, this chapter also focuses on the overlooked push factor of deliberate firm strategy. There are two dominant firm strategies driving precarity: misclassification and lobbying for restrictive licensing. These factors shape dependent self-employment and the individual strategies immigrants in each industry took in organizing. Following the financial crisis in the 1970s, firms devised new ways to exclude workers from labor protections through subcontracting and outsourcing.[7] Government's failure to modernize their laws in response to these changes have allowed them to persist. The logical extreme of this is the gig economy, where employment is outsourced to each individual worker.[8] In both the for-hire driver and food delivery worker cases, these apps misclassify their workers as independent contractors in order to avoid paying the minimum wage and unemployment insurance or giving them the right to form a union. Instead, these companies recast their workers as independent small business owners. These legal maneuvers serve to racialize workers' access to labor and employment protections. This denial of employment status contrasts with immigrant industries like domestic workers, where workers are clearly employees but are often denied rights given the informal nature of many domestic employment arrangements. This difference was reflected in Domestic Workers United's COVID efforts, which focused on worker and employer education offering models of negotiating COVID's impacts rather than campaigns directed at enacting legislative policy like the cases under study here.[9]

On the other hand, immigrant small businesses can find themselves dependent on the government due to restrictive licensing often passed at the behest of larger firms. Street vendors are not marginalized by misclassification but from the dominant white business associations lobbying the state to criminalize these businesses. In the case of street vendors, restrictive licensing requirements force workers to operate illegally. Here, immigrant entrepreneurs would like to be small business owners but are constrained by wider societal forces into a liminal position between worker and entrepreneur. Much as with the gig worker cases, the impacts of government dependence through restrictive licensing generates racialized impacts, given the concentration of undocumented immigrants in the vending industry in New York City. The process is also gendered. Where the gig worker misclassification primarily impacts male immigrant workers, the restrictive licensing primarily impacts female street vendors. Within street vending there is also further gendered division, as men are more likely to have access through holding or leasing a formal permit to operate in prime locations, while women primarily work unlicensed in the farther reaches of the city or in the city's subways. These gendered effects complicated responses to the pandemic by immigrants and people of color, as these families typically live in households with multiple frontline workers, with the women often working in nursing and domestic fields that remained opened during the pandemic, forcing male workers to take over primary care responsibilities.[10]

To combat these challenges during the COVID-19 pandemic, vendors worked to create de facto workers' organizations even though their dependence was not due to misclassification. Such "union style" small business movements in immigrant communities are not without historical precedent. In New York City's Chinatown during the Great Depression, the small family Chinese laundries, which represented the dominant industry in the community, organized the Chinese Hand Laundry Alliance (CHLA). CHLA formed in 1933 after the city imposed a twenty-five-dollar-a-year registration fee on businesses and a requirement that laundries post a one-thousand-dollar bond. This was done at the behest of large-scale white-owned laundries who were mad that the Chinese laundries undercut their prices. Chinese immigrants at the time faced extreme employment discrimination, leaving many with no other option than to engage in this marginal business.[11] The CHLA operated as a "union style" organization of dependent immigrant businessmen. In a more recent example, the independent lobstermen in Maine organized a union with the International Association of Machinists to combat the exploitation they faced from the buyers on the docks, who often work for multinational corporations.[12]

The Multiple Approaches to Immigrant Business Organizing

The pandemic represented a massive challenge to the livelihoods of all New Yorkers, but the effects were more concentrated on communities of color. Immigrants, both documented and undocumented alike, experienced uncertainties derived from their status as immigrants, which undermined their ability to manage their health, incomes, government interactions, and communities during the pandemic.[13] This forced them to attempt to keep working despite the public health threat, creating a reinforcing spiral of disease transmission in immigrant communities, turning their neighborhoods into what Queens council representative Daniel Dromm dubbed "the epicenter of the epicenter." As the *New York Times* reported, the seven square miles of central Queens, which is the center of immigrant New York, was the community hardest hit by COVID.[14] This small area had nearly as many COVID cases as did all of Manhattan.

The New York Taxi Workers Alliance, the Workers' Justice Project (WJP), and the Street Vendor Project (SVP) all achieved stunning victories during the pandemic. These "union style" movements were also unique in that they organized and fought primarily for workers who were, at least on paper, immigrant small business owners. Despite their similarities, these groups each took different approaches, given the unique challenges faced by the workers in each industry. A comparison of these movements can be found in table 13.1. In particular, the strategies and organizing objectives employed by each group were shaped by whether their members were misclassified or legally dependent, were documented or not, and the group's organizational form.

For all three groups the pandemic brought simmering conflicts for their membership to a boiling point. All movements were able to utilize their workers' newfound essential status to mobilize public support, and push long stalled organizational goals to victory. The experience of organizing during the pandemic, for all of these immigrant groups, showed their communities that victory is possible and has left them better connected and positioned to continue to advance their agenda.

THE NEW YORK TAXI WORKERS ALLIANCE

The New York Taxi Workers Alliance was born out of South Asian immigrant organizing in Queens in the early 1990s, which decided the only way to improve the community was to improve the industry that dominated it. The union first organized in 1998 against Mayor Rudy Giuliani's increased harassment of drivers through expensive "quality of life" tickets and his xenophobic demonization of drivers. The immigrant rights origins of the union shaped its focus of fighting for not just drivers but for their immigrant communities as well.

By the time the NYTWA had begun organizing, the New York City taxi industry had become a shell of its former self. Taxi driving had long been a steady middle-class job for the city's white-ethnic communities and was a popular job for working-class and middle-class kids looking for flexibility as they worked their way through college. In the late 1960s, taxi drivers unionized under the leadership of Harry Van Arsdale Jr., the powerful New York labor leader of the IBEW (International Brotherhood of Electric Workers) Local 3. Throughout the 1970s the industry went through a radical change mirroring the general fiscal crisis experienced by the city. Facing pressure from the rise of dispatch cabs, known as black cabs, the Uber of the day, and gradual financialization of the industry as garages transformed themselves into medallion brokers, the union lost power. By the end of the 1970s the union existed only in name, and taxi drivers had lost their employee status after the city legalized cab leasing.[15] As the industry declined, those who could got out. In their place, this newly diminished job was filled by the post–Hart-Celler immigrants from South Asia, the Caribbean, Africa, and China. By 2020, over 90 percent of drivers were foreign-born.[16] Taxi driving had become a classic example of an immigrant employment niche.[17] Drivers' reclassification as independent contractors due to the introduction of leasing also represented an example of forced independent immigrant businesses.

Table 13.1. Comparison of organizational form and pandemic responses along select characteristics

Industry	Taxi and App Drivers	Food Delivery, Domestic Work, and Day Labor	Street Vendors
Organization Form	Union	Workers' center	Advocacy group
Funding	Mostly membership dues and some foundation	Foundations, city contracts, and some membership dues	Formally connected to NGO and some membership dues
Workers Immigration Status	Overwhelmingly documented	Mostly undocumented	Mostly undocumented
Reason for Business Dependence	Yellow taxis (legal) & app (misclassified)	Misclassified	Legal
Employee Status Approach	Employee status	Unsure	Independent
Pandemic Organizing Goals	Debt forgiveness, employee status, and a union	Minimum wage, health & safety, enforcement, and representation	Legalize businesses through increased licensing and stop police harassment

The city's taxi regulatory body, the Taxi and Limousine Commission (TLC), had long been dominated by fleet interests. The NYTWA counteracted this through effective public protest and using the TLC's petition for a rule-making procedure to advance their demands and legitimate drivers' concerns. This petition process became a powerful tool for the taxi alliance, enabling them to secure economic and other material gains from the city and fleets without formal bargaining rights.[18] Over time, the alliance established de facto regular tripartite bargaining through the TLC.

The NYTWA has always maintained that it is a union. Scholars like Janice Fine have instead considered it a workers center, as they represent workers outside the protection of formal labor law.[19] A union/workers center hybrid is perhaps a more accurate description. When asked why it is important to consider themselves a union, union president Bhairavi Desai explained, "When you hear 'union' you think working class power, but 'workers' center' is more academic. . . . To us, a group of workers that bands together is a union, so that is what we are. Not to mention many unions are collective bargaining agents but not unions because they don't fight."[20] Owning the term "union" is empowering for drivers. Drivers did not choose to be small businesses; they were forced into this status by the introduction of leasing and Uber's misclassification. Calling themselves a union lets them own the term "workers" and make demands based on their class position.

The formation of a drivers union and their impressive gains through the establishment of informal tripartite bargaining all came under threat with the introduction of Uber. Uber entered New York City illegally in 2014, refusing to comply with local taxi regulations because they insisted they were a tech company, not a taxi service provider.[21] By 2019 Uber had exploded, with eighty-five thousand unique vehicles per month. Importantly, as the NYTWA argues, Uber reintroduced a more standard employment relationship to the industry. For NYTWA, Uber's algorithmic control of drivers is not indirect and constitutes an employer-and-employee relationship, meaning drivers are misclassified. As a result, the Yellow Cab membership more closely resembles dependent entrepreneurship through regulation while the app drivers represent dependence due to misclassification.

Immediately following the governor's emergency COVID shutdown order, in March 2020 the taxi industry was decimated. The alliance quickly focused on providing drivers and their communities with mutual aid and assistance in navigating public services, and engaged in a series of aggressive campaigns to defend drivers' rights. The two most prominent campaigns were fighting for app drivers to be considered employees under New York state's unemployment insurance system and fighting for debt forgiveness for medallion owner-drivers. These fights highlight examples of how "union style" campaigns are used to combat the two dominant forms of dependent immigrant businesses—those that are misclassified and those that are legally dependent.

Indicative of the complicated overlapping structures of US labor law, different statutes have different definitions of "employee." New York state's definition under its unemployment insurance law is particularly expansive. As a result, the NYTWA successfully sued the state for denying app drivers access to unemployment insurance benefits in 2018. Despite this ruling, Uber and other app companies refused to comply with the law and, when the pandemic hit, withheld wage data from the Department of Labor. The union again sued the New York State Department of Labor to force them to hold gig companies accountable and follow the department's 2018 determination. This lawsuit was successful and ensured that Uber drivers as employees were entitled to hundreds of additional dollars in benefits a week during the pandemic.[22]

The NYTWA approach to the employee status question is to unequivocally push for employee status for app drivers. This demand contrasts with the Deliveristas, discussed in detail below, who have not yet determined how to address this issue, given the largely undocumented workforce they represent. The alliance's position partly comes from the more secure immigration status of its members but also because, as Desai explains, "In New York, after our victories, it meant they are basically employees; New York is just excluding them from a few other rights [such as] paid sick leave, disability insurance and things like wage theft [protections]—these are benefits [and laws] that cost the least."[23] She went on to note that their victory during the pandemic, securing employee status for drivers under New York Unemployment Insurance law, had really highlighted for the membership the impact of fighting misclassification. It meant Uber drivers got hundreds of dollars more a week in benefits than they would have if they had only received Pandemic Unemployment Assistance under the CARES Act.

The pandemic also brought to a head the long-simmering medallion debt crisis. In the 2000s the city would sell these medallions through an auction system, for which the city was accused of artificially inflating their value. The influx of competition from Uber and the city's initial reluctance to regulate Uber resulted in the collapse of the medallions' value and drivers' earnings more generally. Those who own these medallions today have seen their life's work and investment fall by hundreds of thousands of dollars. This leaves the drivers underwater, as they still owe the banks the original amount. Faced with the burden of inflated medallion debts and declining fares due to the flood of Uber cars on the road, nine drivers took their own life.[24]

During this fight for medallion relief, the NYTWA developed new allies in the New York congressional delegation. Since many of the medallion mortgage lenders were federally regulated cooperatives, Senator Chuck Schumer and Representative Alexandria Ocasio-Cortez became intimately involved in attempting to find a solution to the debt crisis. The alliance got Schumer to include funding in Congress's COVID relief bill for the city to restructure the medallion owners' debt in accordance with the alliance's proposed program. Despite the federal money, Mayor Bill de Blasio instead attempted to institute his own plan, which was less generous to the drivers. The union called his plan a "bank bailout" and established a 24/7 protest camp in front of city hall, where they stayed for forty-five days despite dropping temperatures. But the city government would not budge, and on October 20 the union began a hunger strike that garnered international media attention. In total, six drivers fasted for fourteen days, with seventy-eight people, including city council members, joining the strike in solidarity at various points.[25] Throughout, the union engaged in civil disobedience, blocking traffic on the Brooklyn Bridge with their cabs and joining elected officials to block traffic on Broadway next to city hall. Pitching themselves as heroic essential workers who had helped doctors and nurses get to work in the early days of the pandemic, the alliance received broad public support and sympathetic editorials in the local press. On November 3 the alliance and the city reached an agreement that adopted nearly every detail of the drivers' plan. For some drivers, this victory meant relief of half a million dollars of debt. In the heart of the pandemic, when 90 percent of its members had to stop working, the union achieved two of its major goals: getting the New York State Department of Labor to enforce the ruling that app drivers were employees under unemployment insurance law and achieving debt relief for medallion drivers.

The pandemic had a profound impact on the NYTWA and served as a model galvanizing other immigrant movements during the pandemic. As Desai explained, "Our victories built worker and community trust." It was important for the union to have a pandemic campaign for both Yellow Cab and app drivers so that there was not tension between the membership. Desai explains winning for one group sends a message to the other that the union is how you advance your interests: "The number of app drivers watching that fight for medallion relief was impactful. It shows we are leaving no one behind. So many app drivers came to the victory party. It built pride and confidence. I feel the change myself in the members and the staff."[26]

THE WORKERS' JUSTICE PROJECT'S LOS DELIVERISTAS UNIDOS CAMPAIGN

The NYTWA was not the only group fighting for immigrant gig workers during the pandemic. The crisis saw the rise of a powerful movement of gig food delivery workers who called themselves Los Deliveristas Unidos. The Deliveristas began as informal networks of Latinx delivery workers who maintained WhatsApp groups to share information while working, to plan soccer games, and to provide emergency assistance when members faced bike robberies. During the pandemic, reliance on app-based food delivery exploded as restaurants closed and people stayed home and ordered food. For immigrant workers who worked traditional immigrant niche jobs like restaurants or construction, they found themselves without a job. Since many of these workers were undocumented, they could not apply for benefits. Working apps became a last-resort occupation for these workers during the pandemic. Given the demanding distances the apps require workers to travel, most are compelled to purchase e-bikes to complete this work. These e-bikes are very expensive, between one thousand and two thousand dollars. On the abandoned pandemic streets of New York City, these undocumented workers operating expensive e-bikes quickly became targets of a rash of armed robberies. Angry but afraid, these workers eventually turned to the Worker's Justice Project for assistance.

The Worker's Justice Project (WJP) was founded in 2010 as a Brooklyn-based Latinx worker center to organize domestic and day labor construction workers. WJP has since grown considerably and now has twelve thousand members and three offices. In an early victory to improve conditions for day laborers, WJP won a contract from the city to maintain a fair hiring hall for these workers. WJP provides numerous services for its members, including work training, health and safety classes, legal support, and mutual aid. It was Hurricane Sandy that cemented WJP's place in the community as their Herculean efforts to provide relief raised their stature with the community and in the eyes of the city.[27]

When the pandemic hit, WJP quickly attempted to mimic their Hurricane Sandy mobilization. WJP set up food pantries, raised cash relief, gave out PPE, and provided other basic essential services. As their membership is mostly undocumented, they had to find ways to fill the void left by the lack of access to social protections. As executive director Ligia Guallpa explained, "Overnight we had to turn from a workers center to an emergency relief center." They turned their Bensonhurst office into a food pantry, they got money to hire their members to make masks (turning their Sunset Park office into a factory), and the Williamsburg office became a centralized referral office. In March 2020 they raised over $2 million to provide cash relief. Given the amount of money raised, they asked their membership to recommend people in their communities who needed support, and someone offered, "There are these indigenous guys who all ride bikes."

This brought the Deliveristas into contact with WJP. Many Deliveristas are indigenous from Guatemala and Mexico. As such, some of them struggle with Spanish literacy and have limited or no English proficiency. They were marginalized within their own communities and had few connections outside of their immediate circles. Most of these workers were young men often living in crowded boardinghouses in Bensonhurst. As WJP members convinced these young men to come to the food bank and receive cash assistance from WJP, they began to build mutual trust. A full-scale organizing effort quickly took off. In April and May 2020, they began holding meetings in a park in Bensonhurst. Despite the picture that gig workers are isolated, they are, in fact, in constant contact. They were already organized, and they were upset. They just needed the WJP to help push them toward action. The biggest issues they faced were discrimination, lack of access to bathrooms, wage and tip theft, bike robberies, and lack of health care when they contracted COVID or experienced injuries. The robberies were particularly upsetting because of police inaction. As Guallpa explained, "They felt invisible and that agitated them. They feel they mean nothing to the government."[28] Unlike taxi and Uber driving, app delivery exploded during the pandemic, shaping difference in the two industries and organizing demands. The NYTWA drivers fought for access to social protections while the Deliveristas fought for basic workplace protections and a fair share of an exploding industry. These differences in demands were further magnified by the fact that NYTWA members are largely documented while the Deliveristas are largely undocumented.

WJP and the Deliveristas eventually decided to organize around a large protest bike ride. Much like taxi drivers, the Deliveristas felt no one was listening to immigrants during the pandemic. They had to protest to have their voices heard. The city was celebrating essential workers, but no one included delivery workers in this praise. The protest ride was held in August, beginning in the Upper West Side at Seventy-Second Street, where a large number of the robberies had occurred, and riding down Broadway to city hall to demand action. Nearly four hundred Deliveristas showed up. After the march, WJP committed much more organizing time and resources to supporting their efforts. In October they held another rally, this time to make public their specific demands. This rally drew thousands. As WJP political director Hildalyn Colón Hernández explained, "The role of protesting is significant. Showing your numbers shows you are mobilizing. The numbers matter and that is why these protests were so effective. It broke cultural barriers and helped us reach beyond the Latinos."[29] She went on to note that they learned from the failed gig worker organizing against Prop 22 in California that you had to win the customers' support. The marches were to educate the customers as well.

Coming out of these rallies, the WJP demanded that Deliveristas receive a minimum wage, have the right to use the bathroom at the restaurants they pick up orders from, have the apps provide safety equipment, limit the miles per order, and create greater pay and tip transparency. While the WJP had positive relationships with many council members, they had never attempted such a big lift. The NYTWA could appeal to the TLC with a formalized rule system to regulate for-hire vehicles in the city, but there was no such agency or institutional legacy the WJP could point to. The WJP worked to build their political capacity by building relationships with other unions like SEIU 32BJ, community groups like Transportation Alternatives, and local elected officials. In early 2021 the WJP partnered with the Cornell Worker Institute to conduct a survey of app delivery workers to put numbers to their campaign.[30] The report received wide media attention and garnered lots of public support. These efforts resulted in the successful passage of these bills in city hall. This established the first-in-the-nation minimum wage for app-based delivery workers. After a lengthy and delayed rule-making process, the Department of Consumer Protection set the app delivery minimum pay at $17.96 per hour.[31] The apps further delayed the law's implementation through a prolonged court battle against the law charging that the city's rule-making process was biased. Finally, the law was cleared by a judge in September 2023 and went into effect soon thereafter.[32] Other elements of the laws had already gone into effect long before.

While the WJP's Deliveristas campaign has been impressive, challenges remain. Unlike the NYTWA, most of the WJP's membership is undocumented. For the WJP, the campaign for the Deliveristas empowered the workers when they were most desperate to demand their dignity. It showed the workers that elected officials would respond if they organized. As Guallpa explained, "Before they wouldn't want to talk to [politicians] and now they go up to them at our events and make demands. Immigration status is important but focusing on it isolates ourselves. These workers are trying to say it is an aspect of my life but not my life. I'm a Deliverista first."[33]

The workers' immigration status has complicated WJP's approach to the employee status question. As Guallpa said, "Philosophically, I think they are employees and it's the right thing to do, but we need to understand the workers' reality. We don't want our members to lose their job. Independent contractor status has kept them working on the app."[34] Colón Hernández noted, "Many of these workers as immigrants have been considered workers at other jobs and still didn't get their rights. They don't care what you call them; they want rights."[35] WJP is trying to come up with a proposal that does not jeopardize their members' livelihoods but holds the apps responsible.

In terms of organizational form, WJP considers itself, and more closely resembles, a classic workers' center. Part of this stems from the fact that WJP is attempting to represent Latinx workers regardless of their industry. The Deliveristas is just one of the industries they organize. NYTWA, in contrast, represents many communities but organizes in only one industry. WJP hopes to build toward a union for the Deliveristas, but currently they must be a "laboratory to explore organizing innovation." As Guallpa explained, "Businesses are operating differently these days, so our organizing needs to evolve to match what we find. With some of our members this meant we had to become a co-op, with others a hiring hall, with others it meant health and safety committees. We will have to see what we need to become for the Deliveristas."[36] The WJP does not believe being undocumented prevents them from collective bargaining and is looking to successful models from farmworkers out west as they continue to evolve.

THE STREET VENDOR PROJECT

Street vending has always been throughout New York City's long history the industry of choice—or last resort—for those excluded from the formal economy. As the city industrialized and cars were introduced, vendors became viewed as a menace. The colorful pushcarts that once dotted Orchard Street were suddenly viewed as hostile to traffic and therefore modernity. Mayor Fiorello La Guardia, during the Depression, was the first mayor to crack down on the industry, attempting to remove vendors from the Lower East Side and regularize them through the establishment of markets, such as the famous Essex Street Market. This marked the turning point when immigrant small businesses were criminalized in the eyes of the city.

The contemporary fights over the status of street vending in New York City can be traced to the post-1970s crisis era when the city focused on rebuilding its economy around real estate. Mayor Ed Koch, the conservative Democratic mayor, stepped in and took aim at street vendors, passing Local Law 50 in 1979, which instituted the first cap on general merchants. In 1983 he expanded the cap to include mobile food permits as well. This cap was imposed at the urging of the white-dominated real estate and restaurant lobbies and mirrors the imposition of licensing fines on the Chinese laundries during the Depression. While driving and food delivery represent forced immigrant entrepreneurship through misclassification, street vending is forced out of desperation and then dependent due to legal constraints and criminalization.

These restrictive laws and the failure to increase the number of licenses over the years resulted in the vendors becoming highly dependent on exploitative brokers and city officials. The industry can be broken down into two parts: those who operate formally with a license and those who do not. For those who operate in the licensed sector, the restriction on the number of licenses has resulted in a thriving black market for permits, leading the industry to resemble the unfair taxi medallion system discussed above.[37] These vendors essentially—but not formally—have an employment relationship with brokers who lease vendors their carts and license to operate at exorbitant fees, often creating a system of debt patronage.[38] While exploitative, those who work in the licensed vending sector are more insulated from police harassment and have access to the prime vending locations in the city's tourist and business districts. The informal sector, on the other hand, is primarily comprised of immigrant women of color and men who have recently arrived in the country and are from less established immigrant communities without access to formal permits. Within the informal sector there is further gendering and racialization as women and the most marginalized operate in the least valuable locations in the outer boroughs of the city and in the subway system. The informal sector has also created unregulated marketplaces in places such as Fordham Road in the Bronx and Corona Plaza in Queens, which have become the sites of frequent battles with local businesses and police raids.[39] The exploitation in both the permitted and informal sectors of street vending is driven by the failure to increase the number of permits over time. Given the vendors' dependence on brokers and the city, both of which set the costs and conditions over the vendors' employment, it is unsurprising that vendors have taken to organize like workers. In contrast to the NYTWA or the WJP, though, street vendors have organized not to make workers' rights demands but to demand their right to be true independent business owners free of dependence.

Koch's cap did nothing to stem the growth of street vending in the city. The Street Vendor Project (SVP) was formed in 2001 to provide a voice for these increasingly criminalized and harassed immigrants. The SVP is a project of the Urban Justice Center, a mutual aid and legal service clinic that formed in East Harlem in 1984. While much of their funding comes from the Urban Justice Center and foundations, the SVP also has some dues-paying members. SVP, like the NYTWA, was formed in large part in response to Mayor Giuliani's "quality of life" campaign. As with taxi drivers, street vendors were viewed as a nuisance that needed to be cleaned up through police enforcement. Much like taxi drivers, street vendors viewed Giuliani's campaign as an attack on them as immigrants.

The SVP originally operated as a clinic providing legal assistance against unwarranted tickets and fines in the Giuliani era. Over time, they also engaged in political lobbying. An early successful campaign involved fighting Mayor Michael Bloomberg's 2006 quadrupling of penalties from a maximum of $250 to $1,000 per ticket for illegal vending. An SVP lawsuit got these fines temporarily suspended but needed the city council to make the rulings permanent. It took until 2012 when they finally got the bills passed. Over that time SVP made deeper relationships with the city council's "rising stars," building their political power. Today the SVP has grown to two thousand members out of the estimated twenty thousand vendors in the city. According to the SVP, vending added $300 million to the local economy and $71 million in tax revenue. Unlike taxi and food delivery, vending is a majority-female (57 percent) industry and has a much older worker force, with 67 percent of vendors being over fifty years old.[40] While vending is primarily a female occupation, it is immigrant men from the more established immigrant communities who have access to the formal permits that allow them to work in the best locations.

In contrast to the NYTWA, the SVP does not view itself as a union. Rather, it views itself as a vendor advocacy organization and couches its rhetoric in the language of protecting immigrant businesses' right to the free market. Additionally, SVP fights for the rights of its members to truly operate as independent businesses while the NYTWA and WJP are fighting for their members to have employment rights. They are a "union style" organization, as they organize more like a union than a business association and they make demands from a class position, much like the CHLA had, but unlike the misclassified workers discussed above, their goal is to fight the dependence of vendors' existence. As Kathleen Dunn notes, this treatment of vendors in New York City as small businesses is in contrast to much of the world, where vendors are seen as informal workers.[41] The International Labor Organization (ILO) refers to street vending as "own account workers," recognizing the relative dependence of this work.

As with the taxi and food delivery workers, the pandemic brought vendors' simmering issues to a crisis point. The pandemic decimated street vending in the city. By April 2020 nearly all street vendors had stopped work and only 26 percent had gone back by June. Vendors' earnings disappeared, as 98 percent reported zero earnings in April, and few vendors found government relief, with 63 percent denied food assistance and 26 percent reporting having not received a stimulus check.[42] Instead, 76 percent had to either borrow money, draw down their savings, or pawn their belongings during the pandemic. Much like the NYTWA and WJP, the SVP had to quickly reformulate themselves into a mutual aid organization. SVP quickly crowd-funded $147,000 in relief funds, which they distributed to 490 members. They later raised $300,000 from the Open Society Foundation for their undocumented members and a massive $2.25 million in relief funds from the Robin Hood Foundation and Morgan Stanley. SVP developed COVID education and safety training programs for their members. For those who were eligible, they helped them apply for public unemployment assistance and worked with a handful of New York–based foundations to provide small business loans that vendors otherwise would have been excluded from, given their lack of licensing. SVP also worked with elected officials in Queens to hire vendors to work as cooks in the large number of food banks the city worked to establish in immigrant neighborhoods. Additionally, as discussed below, SVP became a key member of the Excluded Worker Fund Coalition, which provided relief for its members.

Beyond the mutual aid efforts, SVP, much like the NYTWA, used the crisis and the workers' newfound "essential" status to move along stalled licensing reform. Their demands were formulated into Council Bill 1116. In addition to lifting the cap, the law would also move enforcement from the New York City Police Department to a civilian agency, the Department of Consumer and Worker Protection, which would also establish a Street Vendor Advisory Board. Since SVP is not organizing employees, their approach to their memberships' immigration status is to diminish interactions with authorities, which 1116 would help accomplish. The advisory board would regulate the industry and propose changes to laws similarly to what the TLC has for taxis. The advisory board holds the potential to generate a tripartite bargaining structure between the city, vendors, and the real estate/restaurant lobby, similar to what the NYTWA created at the TLC. Like the other immigrant pandemic movements, the SVP engaged in massive protests to garner attention and break through the invisibility that immigrants were feeling. The vendors led large and colorful marches over the Brooklyn Bridge carrying protest signs designed to look like iconic New York City street foods, such as pretzels, hot dogs, and coffee in the traditional blue Greco-Roman-style cups. The size of the protests and these visuals garnered media attention and public support. The real estate and restaurant lobbies were on the defensive and attempted to fight back by arguing that the timing was bad, given the pandemic. They also attempted to pit small mom-and-pop brick-and-mortar stores against vendors, arguing that an influx of new vendors would harm the devasted restaurant industry. SVP successfully countered that the bill would not increase the number of vendors but instead would legalize those already working in the shadows. Additionally, they commissioned an economic impact study, which showed that vendors do not compete with stores and that the city currently spends more on enforcement than it makes on vendors' fines. The SVP's lobbying efforts proved successful and the council passed Local Law 1116 on January 28, 2021.

The SVP as an advocacy organization, as opposed to a union or workers center, more closely resembles the CHLA. This difference from the other pandemic movements stems from their industry's status as dependent through law, not misclassification. While the SVP, like the NYTWA and WJP, found its membership recast as essential workers during the pandemic and used the crisis moment to push forward long-stalled reforms, it is the difference between misclassification and legal dependence that shaped its organizational form and strategy to organizing immigrant small business owners. Its "union style" reflects its membership's class position and dependence, not its direct exclusion from rights by an employer.

Conclusion

The three movements of immigrants—who are, at least on paper, small business owners—evaluated here challenge our conception of who forms a union and why. The movements show that unionism is a form that immigrant groups can employ to make demands around their work, given the communities' relative exploitation and marginalization. While these workers are not traditional workers, a union form is beneficial in advancing their struggles within the work-citizenship nexus. Immigrants face intersecting marginalizations, given both their labor market position and status as immigrants. These pandemic movements highlight that the archetypical immigrant small business might in fact be a myth. Cab drivers, Uber drivers, Deliveristas, street vendors, and excluded workers would all ideally like to work as employees and receive employment protections with the associated right to government social protections. These workers were funneled into these jobs by their immigrant networks because there were few other options available in the formal labor market. They became entrepreneurs out of necessity.

This chapter adds deliberate firm strategy to our understanding of the push factors that drive immigrant entrepreneurship. Two forms of this are considered: misclassification and restrictive licensing. Misclassification is when firms label workers as independent contractors when in truth they are economically dependent on the firm. Restrictive licensing is when majority-dominated firms lobby the government to criminalize and police immigrant businesses, turning their aims for independence into state dependence. The gig workers are an example of misclassified immigrant business owners, while the medallion drivers and street vendors are legally dependent immigrant businesses. This difference along with immigration status and the relative stability of the industry were the primary factors that account for the differences in movement form and strategy. The NYTWA, with a primarily documented, misclassified, and relatively economically lucrative profession, took a more union form with a more aggressive strategy and demands compared to the other groups. In contrast, the Street Vendor Project, with a female, undocumented, and informal industry of truly independent businesses, took a more legal advocacy form and strategy.

All of these movements were not just "union style" worker movements. They were immigrant community movements. These movements question who should be privileged in our understanding of community unionism. Is it the community or the union? While most studies of community unionism explore how unions fight for workers at both their job and in their community, these immigrant small business movements show that sometimes unionism is a movement form borrowed by communities whose advancement depends on improving conditions in an industry that dominates their community. These movements borrowed union forms because the logic of unionism reflected their perceived class position and exploitation in the work-citizenship nexus. Dependence is more important than legal label in determining who has the right to working-class organizational forms.

The immigrant pandemic revolt in New York City, which was led by these small business owner movements, was part of a larger trend toward greater social and political incorporation of the post–Hart-Celler immigrants. Beyond the groups discussed in this chapter, immigrants during the pandemic organized against racial discrimination and attacks, fought for free tuition at City University of New York, engaged in a massive mobilization against Donald Trump's efforts to undercount their communities during the census, and secured the right of noncitizens to vote in local elections. The crisis of the pandemic catalyzed a broad immigrant movement into action. The three movements studied here were prominent parts of a broader political awakening in these post–Hart-Celler immigrant communities who are demanding greater political and social incorporation.

Notes

Disclosure: The author was hired as a consultant by the New York City Department of Consumer and Worker Protection, discussed herein, to advise on their survey of app-food delivery work in the city.

1. H. E. Aldrich and R. Waldinger, "Ethnicity and Entrepreneurship," *Annual Review of Sociology* 16, no. 1 (1990): 111–135.

2. M. Zhou and C. L. Bankston III, *The Rise of the New Second Generation* (Cambridge: Polity Press, 2016).

3. R. Waldinger, *Still the Promised City? African Americans and New Immigrants in Postindustrial New York* (Cambridge, MA: Harvard University Press, 1996).

4. Aldrich and Waldinger, "Ethnicity and Entrepreneurship"; I. Light, *Ethnic Enterprise in America: Business and Welfare among Chinese, Japanese, and Blacks* (Berkeley: University of California Press, 1972).

5. R. Ward, "Small Retailers in Inner Urban Areas," in *Business Strategy and Retailing*, ed. Gerry Johnson, 275–287 (Chichester, UK: Wiley, 1987).

6. T. Bates and A. Robb, "Small-Business Viability in America's Urban Minority Communities," *Urban Studies* 51, no. 13 (2014): 2844–2862.

7. D. Weil, *The Fissured Workplace: Why Work Became So Bad for So Many and What Can Be Done to Improve It* (Cambridge, MA: Harvard University Press, 2014).

8. A. Wolf, "Who's the Boss? Digitally Mediated Employment's Impacts on Labor Markets and the Nature of Work," in *The Platform Economy and the City: Urban Peril and Promise in the New Digital Economy*, ed. Z. Spicer and A. Zwick, 50–79 (Montreal: McGill-Queen's University Press, 2021).

9. National Domestic Workers Alliance, "Coronavirus Resource Center," https://membership.domesticworkers.org/coronavirus/.

10. A. Wolf, "COVID and the Risky Immigrant Workplace: How Declining Employment Standards Socialized Risk and Made the COVID-19 Pandemic Worse," *Labor Studies Journal* 47, no. 3 (2022): 286–319.

11. P. Kwong, *Chinatown, New York: Labor and Politics, 1930–1950* (New York: New Press, 1979).

12. B. Fitzsimons and R. Lurie, "How Lobstermen Formed a Union Co-op to Claw Back Fair Prices," *Labor Notes*, February 7, 2022, https://labornotes.org/2022/02/how-lobstermen-formed-union-co-op-claw-back-fair-prices/.

13. Wolf, "COVID and the Risky Immigrant Workplace."

14. A. Correal and A. Jacobs, "A Tragedy Is Unfolding: Inside New York's Virus Epicenter," *New York Times*, April 9, 2020; D. Khullar, "The Essential Workers Filling New York's Coronavirus Wards," *New Yorker*, May 1, 2020.

15. G. R. G. Hodges. *Taxi! A Social History of the New York City Cabdriver* (Boston: Johns Hopkins University Press, 2020).

16. TLC—Taxi & Limousine Commission NYC, *TLC Factbook 2020*, https://www1.nyc.gov/assets/tlc/downloads/pdf/2020-tlc-factbook.pdf/.

17. Douglas Massey, Rafael Alarcon, Jorge Durand, and Humberto Gonzalez, *Return to Aztlan: The Social Process of International Migration from Western Mexico* (Berkeley: University of California Press, 1987).

18. M. Gaus, "Not Waiting for Permission: The New York Taxi Workers Alliance and 21st Century Bargaining," in *New Labor in New York: Precarious Workers and the Future of the Labor Movement*, ed. R. Milkman and E. Ott, 246–265 (Ithaca: ILR Press, 2014); H. Johnston, "Workplace Gains beyond the Wagner Act: The

New York Taxi Workers Alliance and Participation in Adminstrative Rulemaking." *Labor Studies Journal* 43, no. 2 (2019): 141–165.

19. Janice Fine, *Worker Centers: Organizing Communities at the Edge of the Dream* (Ithaca: Cornell University Press, 2006).

20. Personal interview with Bhairavi Desai, February 23, 2022, in New York City by Andrew Wolf.

21. A. Wolf, "City Power in the Age of Silicon Valley: Evaluating Municipal Regulatory Response to the Entry of Uber to the American City," *City & Community* 21, no. 4 (2022): 290–313.

22. Noam Scheiber, "Uber and Lyft Drivers Win Ruling on Unemployment Benefits," *New York Times*, July 28, 2020.

23. Desai interview, February 23, 2022.

24. G. Roberts and A. Woods, "Lyft Driver Found Dead in Back of Car as Cabbie Suicide Epidemic Continues," *New York Post*, March 23, 2019.

25. M. Crabapple, "How the Taxi Workers Won," *The Nation*, December 13, 2021, https://www.thenation.com/article/society/taxi-driver-strike/.

26. Desai interview, February 23, 2022.

27. Personal interview with Ligia Guallpa, February 7, 2022, in New York City by Andrew Wolf.

28. Guallpa interview, February 7, 2022.

29. Personal interview with Hildalyn Colón Hernández, February 25, 2022, in New York City by Andrew Wolf.

30. M. Figueroa, L. Guallpa, A. Wolf, G. Tsitouras, and H. Hernández, "Essential but Unprotected: App-Based Food Couriers in New York City" (Cornell ILR Worker Institute, 2021), https://ecommons.cornell.edu/items/7236a5cb-ebf7-4629-bf02-505efd1ce1d5/.

31. S. Chen, "New York City Sets New Minimum Wage for Food Delivery Workers," *New York Times*, June 12, 2023, https://www.nytimes.com/2023/06/12/nyregion/nyc-delivery-workers-minimum-wage.html?smid=url-share/.

32. K. Browning and A. Ley, "Judge Affirms Pay Raise for Food Delivery Workers in New York," *New York Times*, September 28, 2023, https://www.nytimes.com/2023/09/28/nyregion/food-delivery-workers-pay-raise-nyc.html; C. Irizarry Aponte, "Judge Delays Rollout of Delivery Worker Minimum Wage Law," *The City*, July 7, 2023, https://www.thecity.nyc/2023/7/6/23786444/doordash-grubhub-uber-sue-delivery-minimum-wage/.

33. Guallpa interview, February 7, 2022.

34. Guallpa interview, February 7, 2022.

35. Colón Hernández interview, February 25, 2022.

36. Guallpa interview, February 7, 2022.

37. D. Gonzalez, "$20,000 for a Permit? New York May Finally Offer Vendors Some Relief," *New York Times*, January 29, 2021, https://www.nytimes.com/2021/01/29/nyregion/street-vendors-permits-nyc.html/.

38. For an excellent depiction of the world of exploitative street vending license leasing, see the movie *Man Push Cart* (2005), directed by Ramin Bahrani.

39. J. Stratman, "Street Vendors Ousted from Fordham Road as NYC Cracks

Down across the Five Boroughs," *NY Daily News*, May 20, 2023, https://www
.nydailynews.com/2023/05/20/street-vendors-ousted-from-fordham-road-as
-nyc-cracks-down-across-the-five-boroughs/.

40. Women in Informal Employment: Globalizing and Organizing (WIEGO),
Urban Justice Center Street Vendor Project, *COVID-10 Crisis and the Informal
Economy: Street Vendors in New York City, USA*, January 2021, https://www.wiego
.org/sites/default/files/publications/file/WIEGO_FactSheet_NYC_SVP_web
.pdf.

41. Kathleen Dunn, "Decriminalize Street Vending: Reform and Social Justice,"
in *Food Trucks, Cultural Identity, and Social Justice*, ed. J. Agyeman, C. Matthews,
and H. Sobel, 47–66 (Cambridge: MIT Press, 2017).

42. WIEGO, COVID-10 Crisis and the Informal Economy.

14

Cannabis, COVID-19, and Racial Capitalism

Unionization in an Era of Inequality

ERIC D. LARSON

Jobs disappeared. And so did people. Many workers, particularly Black and brown workers, were forced to report to work, despite the spread of a lethal disease.[1] The COVID-19 pandemic illuminated, and exacerbated, the inequalities at the heart of US racial capitalism, but it also meant shifts in the economic order, many of those discussed in this volume. The rise of legal cannabis is one of those significant changes.

Cannabis is critical to understanding the working class in the COVID-19 pandemic. It intersects with a wide variety of social issues and ancillary industries—from drug policy to healthcare, and from agriculture to Amazon. The legal industry is one of the few that grew during the lockdowns and restrictions of the early years of the pandemic. Even now, with legal cannabis still prohibited in many US states, cannabis workers outnumber firefighters or machinists, historically powerful unionized industries, and many analysts project the growth of the sector to skyrocket.[2] While unionization in the industry is still in its initial stages, a string of union victories in 2020 and 2021 helped drive the broader surge of retail unionization in recent years.[3] Yet despite the promises of diversity and social equity from many elected officials and cannabis executives, the outline of the industry's workforce replicates a fundamental inequality at the heart of the US economy in general: Black and brown workers are on the bottom, and white managers and owners—almost exclusively men—are on the top.[4]

This chapter seeks to build on the emerging scholarship on legal cannabis and economic and racial justice by focusing on one component: union organizing in the legal cannabis industry during the COVID-19 pandemic.[5] Using interviews with cannabis dispensary workers and managers, as well as with cannabis organizers and advocates, this chapter traces the COVID-era growth of the industry; the efforts of the United Food and Commercial Workers to organize cannabis workers; and persistent barriers to create pathways for Black and brown workers in the industry, despite frequent proclamations of social equity by elected officials and cannabis executives.[6]

Legal Cannabis and the COVID-19 Era

The legal cannabis industry is unique in many ways. It operates in a legal gray area, still as a Schedule 1 substance federally but now fully legal in twenty-five US states. Cannabis is sold in highly regulated dispensaries, yet those stores operate alongside a "legacy market" of vendors, many who have been selling cannabis for years in ways unregulated—and criminalized—by the state. Because of its federal illegality, cannabis businesses can't partake in federal tax deductions for their business expenses. They are unable to engage in basic banking activities and credit card transactions, so exchanges are done in cash or debit card. They can't access federal grants for research and development. They were locked out of most federal COVID-19 stimulus funding.[7]

Yet for all its exceptional qualities, cannabis rapidly became a major US industry during the COVID-19 years. While the pandemic tends to be associated with economic contraction and loss, legal cannabis enjoyed spectacular job growth during the period.[8] The legal cannabis industry has been predicted to grow "faster than smart phones."[9] It will soon account for $70 billion of international commerce each year.[10] Eight states legalized adult-use cannabis in 2020 and 2021 alone, nearly doubling the total number at the time. Tax revenue from cannabis surged during the pandemic years, reaching more than $11 billion in 2022.[11]

A variety of factors explain why the COVID-19 crisis galvanized the legal cannabis industry. As state governments navigated the budget crises of the era, elected officials saw new value in taxing cannabis for revenue.[12] Medical cannabis markets continued to grow. More people began to use cannabis during the pandemic years.[13] In the era of the George Floyd uprising and the Movement for Black Lives, more and more economic and racial justice organizers saw legalizing cannabis as a crucial step in repairing the harms of the racist war on drugs, which disproportionately imprisoned Black and brown community members, particularly in working-class areas.

In addition to its sheer size, the legal cannabis industry is crucial for understanding workers and the COVID-19 crisis because it operates at the center of a variety of crucial forces of US racial capitalism. It exists within and beside a fundamentally unfair and exclusionary healthcare system. It exists intermeshed with the criminal legal system, which historians Elizabeth Hinton and DeAnza Cook have identified as a central "engine of American inequality."[14] The policing of cannabis has been fundamentally racist. The war on drugs policies of the last fifty years have disproportionately resulted in the incarceration of Black and brown people, particularly those in working-class communities, despite statistics that consistently indicate that whites use and distribute cannabis at the same rate as other groups.[15] The prohibition and policing of the production of cannabis also sits amid the illicit international trade of mind-altering substances. Indeed, the war on drugs has always been directed at the Global South.[16]

Cannabis Sector Organizing and COVID-19

Would COVID-19 lead to more union organizing? Early in the pandemic, some observers addressed the scenario with a gloomy outlook. Isolation, social distancing, fear, work mandates for "essential" workers—all those factors led some to think unionization would take a hit. Yet the way employers responded to the pandemic, as well as the militancy of everyday workers, proved many of the skeptics wrong.[17] Waves of workers opted for safety and community over work. Others stood up to even the largest employers. The public is more positive about unions than it has been in decades.[18]

Cannabis was no exception, even if the early days of the pandemic were destabilizing and uncertain. "I mean, there was no time or energy for strategic thinking," said Megan Carvalho, the cannabis organizing director for the United Food and Commercial Workers (UFCW) union. "I was frankly just happy to have a campaign that I could work remotely," she said, as she juggled having two kids (one of them a baby) at home, while her spouse also worked remotely at the residence. "I felt grateful for that and that this was a group of workers that was receptive to organizing," she said, speaking of the cannabis dispensary and warehouse workers she was helping to organize in Massachusetts.[19]

The UFCW has been organizing cannabis workers since 2010, starting with the medical marijuana facilities in states during the wave of medical marijuana legalization in the early twenty-first century.[20] By the end of 2022 it represented workers in nineteen states in both retail dispensaries and cultivation and processing sites, many of them added in the preceding three pandemic years, particularly in the adult-use industry. In 2022 the UFCW and cannabis workers at Greenleaf Compassion Center in Rhode Island won raises of up to 22 percent for some employees, time-and-a-half pay for Sunday shifts, a thousand-dollar ratification bonus, and other benefits. The employees had voted 21–1 to join the union in 2021 and launched a one-day strike that year to protest the termination of an employee.[21]

The UFCW's work also helped get legal cannabis off the ground. Unlike many industries, union–management cooperation was crucial in getting cannabis legalized. Many of the major cannabis employers, instead of immediately resisting unions, made overtures to them. In a suspect and illicit industry, they thought they needed unions to gain legitimacy and legal standing from the public and from elected officials.[22] They were new businesses in a newly legalizing industry. That means they didn't have their own lobbying forces. They didn't have relationships with politicians or regulators.[23]

The union's political will and early organizing successes also helped provide some early momentum for broader cannabis legalization. In 2012 the UFCW endorsed the initiative to legalize adult-use cannabis in Colorado amid significant resistance from business leaders and influential state-level politicians.[24] The union's former director of cannabis organizing, T. J. Lauritsen, suggested that the union endorsement proved to be a critical piece for securing its passage, since it only narrowly passed. As early as 2013 the UFCW supported an end to federal prohibition of cannabis. By then it enjoyed scattered representation in the medical marijuana industry.[25]

But it was the pandemic years that led to an upsurge in cannabis union organizing. UFCW leaders and organizers suggest that the COVID-19 pandemic actually helped them organize unions in the cannabis workplaces. Carvalho said, "I think 2020 was busier than the previous 13 years that I had been an organizer." She got a call from medicinal dispensary workers in early March 2020. "They were terrified. Right? You know, Governor [Charlie] Baker had shut down the adult use cannabis stores and left open the medicinal ones." "In the beginning," she said, "everybody was kind of panicking."[26]

The president of UFCW Local 328, Tim Melia, said the pandemic completely changed the union's approach.[27] Donald Trump closed the National Labor Relations Board (NLRB) during the early months of the pandemic, even as abuses of essential workers multiplied. When Trump reopened the NLRB in April, the UFCW was the first to file a case—now in a new, virtual format. That case was part of its successful effort to organize the Hanover, Massachusetts, Curaleaf dispensary.[28] The union had relied on face-to-face contact to organize, primarily in the grocery and food services industry. As with other unions, its approach was guided by house visits and servicing everyday members. Yet the move to virtual communication with workers may have given them an advantage. They used WhatsApp. They used text message chains. They used Zoom meetings. Employers often block union organizers from accessing their workforces, but electronic communication made it easier.[29] For one Massachusetts dispensary worker, it was the pandemic and the employer's lack of effort to protect workers from sickness that created the "last straw" for many to support the unionization effort.[30]

The UFCW's national cannabis campaign, called Cannabis Workers Rising, was also particularly busy—and successful—during the early pandemic years. Lauritsen, who retired in November 2020, termed the cannabis worker organizing in 2020 a "tidal wave." They were getting calls from workers all over the place, he said. Cannabis stories on the UFCW website exhibit a strong uptick in articles then, particularly in 2020 through mid-2021. The national UFCW media relations officer told me that taking calls about cannabis was one of his main tasks in 2022. The tide turned partly because of the union's success in lobbying for labor peace agreements as part of legalization legislation.[31] Although varied, these agreements tended to require owners to agree not to interfere with employee unionization efforts as a condition for acquiring a license to operate a business. Those were state-level laws, but, nationally, major companies agreed to labor peace agreements.[32] Before the pandemic there were only a couple of states that had adopted labor peace agreements, but several states adopted them in 2020 and 2021. Organizers in Colorado and Washington faced stiff resistance to the proposal in earlier efforts.[33]

Cannabis Sector Organizing:
A "Wolf in Sheep's Clothing"

The application for a job at Wendy's fast-food restaurant said it all. The application, pinned to the wall at a Massachusetts cannabis dispensary by the manager, sent a constant message to the employees. It said, "Hey, wow, you can work [at Wendy's] if you don't like the work conditions here."[34]

The rhetoric of the war on drugs reduced the highly variegated cannabis plant—with its multitude of uses in many different cultures—to a mere "drug." Yet cannabis sector workers have been deeply invested in both the product and their customers. Cannabis workers, as Carvalho said, "tend to love the product and love the industry." Others during COVID may have traded higher-status occupations for work in cannabis due to seeking more meaningful experiences in work.[35] One Arizona "budtender" told me that he left his position in medical records to begin working at cannabis dispensaries. Understanding medical coding, he said, helped orient him to the medical uses of cannabis. Many cannabis workers have come from experiences in low-wage retail and service work or have worked in other aspects of cannabis.[36]

As UFCW organizer Marvin stressed, there tends to be a "honeymoon" period for cannabis employees. "There's been a huge demand to get into this industry," he said. Workplaces can be "flooded with applications, as workers see this as the industry to join, that these were going to be careers." Though many adult-use (or "recreational") facilities have been allowed to open only recently, workers in medical marijuana have already been working in the industry for years. And, Carvalho said, the excitement was waning in the early pandemic years. "[The employees] were like, 'Okay, this is great,'" when they got into the industry. But they began to "notice they should be treated better," she said. To be clear, the cannabis industry has also been characterized by high levels of turnover, much like the rest of the COVID-era US economy.

Especially in the early months of adult-use legalization, lines outside dispensaries were long. One manager told me they tend to hire two or three employees at a time to save on training costs. "We've spent a full day training a new hire," he said. "And then we never saw them again." One budtender told me she was a regular customer at a dispensary, and one day a staff member offered her a part-time job. They desperately needed employees, she said.[37]

Despite interviewing them in their workplaces, several budtenders indicated to me the difficult work conditions. Dispensaries tend to be very busy, and one Arizona budtender who previously worked in California was disappointed to find that budtenders in Arizona receive only a thirty-minute lunch break if their shifts are of a certain length. Shorter shifts grant only ten-minute breaks, unlike in California. "Labor laws protect you less [here]," she said.[38] Budtenders stand for long periods of time, are assigned to customers, and earn a wage as well as accept tips. Many dispensaries serve both medical and recreational patients, and budtenders are expected to be both "healers and dealers." Dispensaries sell hundreds of products, and budtenders are expected to be familiar with all of them and face pressure to purchase products on their own to familiarize themselves with their qualities.[39] Given surging demand and highly regulated supply chains, select products and brands are frequently out of stock, making customers irritable and demanding.[40]

The COVID pandemic exacerbated already tense conditions in many cannabis dispensaries. "What we've heard from workers during the pandemic," Marvin said, "is that there was a lot of poor communication, [and] changing policies." In some cases, "we heard from workers, [that employers] just weren't doing [contact tracing], or weren't doing it extensively enough." It was the same with PPE and social distancing. "There were just a lot of issues, where [workers] . . . didn't feel safe or felt that the employer didn't do enough to keep them safe."[41] For cannabis workers in many states, they enjoyed little or no paid leave. In addition, dealing with masking and COVID-19 rules with customers wore the workers down. "Just because people are consuming cannabis doesn't make them chill as customers," Carvalho said.[42] One Massachusetts worker died due to inhaling cannabis dust and mold; her employer had refused to move her to another position even after she complained.[43]

Resistance to unionization has often been stiff but sometimes in ways unique to the industry. The associations many people have with cannabis has proven to be one obstacle. Melia recounted how early discussions of cannabis organizing received smirks and quizzical looks at national UFCW meetings.[44] More recently, employers have manipulated stereotypes about "mellow stoners" to affirm the idea that cannabis workers are not serious employees with serious concerns.[45]

Yet Marvin attests that workers are often tired of hitting a "ceiling." There is little upward mobility in an industry with substantial levels of turnover—despite the popularity of the career. Now that some have a few years of experience working in this new industry, they expect more. "We've seen too that employers don't often view their employees as who they are, which is professional, highly skilled, highly knowledgeable, both on the back . . . where they are guiding patients and customers to meet their needs."[46] As the Wendy's sign attests, employers have dared employees to complain, knowing that many other community members would be happy to try a job in the cannabis industry.

Other union-busting tactics have resembled those in other industries.[47] "They do the same things as they do elsewhere," Melia said. Employers held one-on-one meetings with workers before union meetings or offered them one-time benefits to keep them from voting to unionize. Carvalho said the same union-busting lawyers that other executives use are the ones used in cannabis. While both small employers and large have proven resistant to unionization, large employers have been particularly tough. Unions and workers have filed several NLRB grievances in the last few years against Curaleaf and Vesco.[48] Companies have forced the UFCW to spend lots of money on lobbying and have often reneged on pledges.[49]

Still others have resorted to firing pro-union employees.[50] In an ongoing case in Maryland, one worker is arguing that two Black managers were laid off without cause because, she argues, they supported a unionization campaign earlier that year. The (Black) worker herself was later fired after she asked why she was paid less than her white counterparts. In a preliminary ruling, a judge found evidence of a pattern of racist employment practices at the dispensary. Among other reasons, the employer is using the COVID-19 pandemic, and the economic uncertainty it created, to justify its layoffs.[51]

Ultimately, as essential workers, cannabis sector workers put their health on the line to go to work but got little for it. As Marvin said, "It's kind of like how it was, like, 'Thank our grocery workers and all that stuff. And then, you know, later all that goodwill and grace was gone, and it was back to capitalism."

Unfair Access to Jobs

Despite legalization and decriminalization, the cannabis industry continues to be highly interwoven with the criminal legal system.[52] As has been widely documented, the war on drugs and the policing of cannabis have been carried out in fundamentally racist ways, resulting in the disproportionate incarceration of communities of color.[53] The ways cannabis remains criminalized significantly affects who can get jobs in the industry. While state-elected officials and their supporters have gained political capital by claiming they support legalizing cannabis to repair the harms of the war on drugs (and not solely to acquire the additional tax revenue), much of that social equity work has had very uneven results.[54] Many workers from impacted communities continue to face highly exclusionary hurdles to work in the industry, making access to jobs an important racial justice matter for legal cannabis.

The first, and most widely noted, of these has been the continued racist policing of cannabis use. Where cannabis is now "legal," it is in fact still criminalized in certain ways. You can consume it without restriction in or on a private property you own, but renters often face restrictions, as do people on probation or parole.[55] Public spaces often have bans or limitations on consumption (especially smoking), and cannabis use is highly restricted in public housing. Police patrol working-class communities of color at increased rates regardless of whether cannabis is legal or not, and in some states with legal cannabis they can still justify intrusive searches solely based on the perceived odor of cannabis.[56] Perhaps it should be no surprise, then, that racial disparities in cannabis arrests remain the same, or have even been exacerbated, in states that have legalized or decriminalized cannabis.[57] In short, even in states that have publicly accepted arguments that the risk of cannabis is minimal, or that the plant has important medicinal affects, people continue to get arrested for it—and endure the stigma of a criminal record when they seek jobs.

Much less noted has been how past criminal convictions, including of cannabis possession or use, restrict access to participating in the legal cannabis industry. For workers who have already served their time, they continue to face the punishment of a burden of a criminal record. Rules about who may work in the industry (as opposed to who may own businesses) are likely to be made by state regulatory bodies, with limited participation of the public. Aside from the exception of Washington and California, all states require background checks for any aspiring cannabis employees. Far from being mere formalities, most states have decided to use background checks to automatically disqualify people with certain kinds of criminal records, without allowing them the chance to explain their histories or discuss their rehabilitation.[58] This includes states that paired legalizing cannabis with the creation of cannabis social equity programs, which are programs with stated objectives of creating diversity or reparatory actions in the legal cannabis industry. In some more recent legislation, as in Colorado and Rhode Island, state cannabis officials have more discretion about which convictions can be used to disqualify potential workers, partly by determining if the conviction is "substantially related" to work at a cannabis establishment.[59] Because of these rules, people with past felony convictions who have already served their sentences face an uphill battle if they seek to work in the industry.[60] In limited cases, cannabis businesses that acquire state subsidies by qualifying as official "social equity" businesses are required to meet social equity hiring goals. Those rules mandate they hire from communities harmed by the war on drugs. But financial and regulatory burdens have made it difficult for social equity businesses to actually open.[61]

In theory, cannabis convictions themselves shouldn't be a major obstacle in many legalizing states, because those states implemented expungement policies when they ended cannabis prohibition policies. Acknowledging how criminal records make it difficult for workers to get jobs, acquire loans, and find housing, recent legislation has extended opportunities to delete or "expunge" cannabis convictions from state files. Yet expungement in many states has been limited and contradictory.[62] Many efforts require applicants to formally petition the state and pay required fees, compelling some applicants to hire lawyers. The eligible convictions are limited to select, nonviolent offenses. One recent study indicates that only 6.5 percent of people eligible for expungement succeed in the process.[63] In Rhode Island in 2021, activists in the Formerly Incarcerated Union (supported by the UFCW and other organizations) carried out extensive lobbying to ensure that expungement would be "automatic" and "state-initiated." Those and other recent efforts may lead to more effective expungement results in future years.

Even if applicants' records are deemed acceptable by state agencies, that doesn't mean employers won't discriminate against them in hiring decisions. In an era of social media and online records, the stigma of a criminal conviction circulates far beyond official state records and amplifies labor market discrimination based on race and other factors.[64] In addition, cannabis job markets are increasingly competitive, partly because of emerging questions of professionalization and credentialing. Today working-class job applicants are often competing for jobs with people who have attained expensive certificates or cannabis degrees from local colleges or independent certifiers. Or they are competing against workers with years of experience in the medical marijuana sector. That sector has been characterized by especially stringent background check policies, few social equity efforts, and locations in census tracts of predominantly highly educated white communities.[65]

One of the unique opportunities to confront these exclusions is the idea of cannabis apprenticeships. Instead of expecting potential applicants to pay for their training, apprenticeships allow workers to "earn while they learn." For cannabis specifically, the UFCW and several major union employers are in the midst of creating a Joint Apprenticeship Training Program. The program, organizers argue, will create pathways to jobs, promotions, and continuing education college credits.[66] Organizers held an opening summit in April 2021 and initiated monthly meetings in subsequent months. Structural racism, noted the UFCW's Lynne Dodson, is built into the current hiring practices of cannabis owners. Some look for employees through friends and from their social networks. Some use computer programs, whose algorithms rank and sort job applications. These approaches tend to direct opportunities to white workers, whose access to social capital or traditional forms of training and education will lock out workers of color and many precarious workers.[67] These "apprenticeships will help level the playing field for the folks who have been penalized the most by the failed war on drugs," a UFCW leader said. "This will be an opportunity for people of color to really thrive, because it's the skills that will get you there, not your gender or color,'" the UFCW's Jeff Ferro has argued.[68]

The joint apprenticeship program is being led by a national joint union-employer committee. The committee consists of ten multistate operators and twelve UFCW locals, as well as UFCW Canada. The companies have agreed to put money into a trust to fund the apprenticeships. The apprenticeships will be run by local union-management committees. Unlike in a typical dispensary job search, these committees will select apprentices, and the UFCW hopes to make the prerequisites be minimal—for instance, a driver's license and a high school degree. They may join with local community organizations to place people in the internships. The apprenticeships will consist of on-the-job training, paired with (paid) outside class sessions. They will help "raise the floor," creating a pipeline to higher-paying work and wage progressions. Already, in some union contracts, too, local unions have bargained for employer funds for training, which could be steered into apprenticeships. The progress and results of this apprenticeship program will be an important topic for future research. At the time of this writing, one state-level apprenticeship program through the UFCW is in operation, in the state of New Jersey.[69]

• • •

Legal cannabis took shape as a significant economic and political force in the COVID-19 era. A variety of political interests converged in several states to end state-level cannabis prohibition, with the UFCW seeking to gain a union foothold in what promises to be a growing industry. It was also a moment of renewed calls for racial justice, with the Movement for Black Lives pressuring for change in all levels of society, including in questions of labor and employment and including in the cannabis sector. The context helped inspire bold and new calls for unions to take more active roles in fighting for racial justice, calls that included recognizing that union members are also community members with needs outside of the workplace. Such a recognition will be critical for unions to intervene in some of the challenges mentioned above and to help ensure that legal cannabis offers pathways to repair the harms of cannabis prohibition and the war on drugs.[70]

If—or when—cannabis is decriminalized at the federal level, the industry will likely radically change. That means that the COVID-19-era developments discussed in this chapter could constitute an exceptional moment in an industry that will likely transform itself in coming decades. Or it could mean—as the UFCW would prefer—that labor organizers created a crucial union foundation before larger, more mainstream interests gained a foothold. Given how the cannabis industry is highly interwoven with crucial issues for the working classes—issues such as policing, drug policy, and healthcare—the fate of cannabis workers will likely have repercussions far beyond cannabis itself.

Notes

1. Tiana N. Rogers et al., "Racial Disparities in COVID-19 Mortality among Essential Workers in the United States," *World Medical & Health Policy* 12, no. 3 (2020): 311–327, https://doi.org/10.1002/wmh3.358/.

2. There are nearly 450,000 workers in the legal cannabis industry in the United States. See Jenna Pletcher, "Labor Protections under Federal Cannabis Prohibition and the Future of Cannabis Unions," SSRN Scholarly Paper, November 3, 2022, https://doi.org/10.2139/ssrn.4267483/.

3. Robert Combs, "Cannabis Workers Make Retail Sector a New Union Haven," *Bloomberg Law*, March 17, 2022, https://news.bloomberglaw.com/bloomberg-law-analysis/analysis-cannabis-workers-make-retail-sector-a-new-union-haven/. Cannabis unions launched twenty-six NLRB union elections in 2021, winning eighteen of them.

4. The federal government does not collect data about race in the cannabis industry, but some state governments do. Numerous surveys have indicated how white men dominate the industry ownership. See Amiah Taylor, "Black Cannabis Entrepreneurs Account for Less than 2% of the Nation's Marijuana Businesses," *Fortune*, April 25, 2022, https://fortune.com/2022/04/26/black-cannabis-entrepreneurs-marijuana-businesses-marijuana-laws/. The racial inequality in both ownership and in the workforce is perhaps most evident in Illinois. "Black" and "Hispanic" employees are most prominent in part-time positions (11 percent and 10 percent of the total, respectively), even as they are 15 percent and 18 percent of the state total population. Only 10 percent of full-time "frontline employees" are Black, and 7 percent of "middle managers" are Black. Only 1 percent of "majority owners" are Black. See Kyle Jaeger, "Illinois Regulators Detail Lack of Marijuana Industry Diversity and Preview Equity Plans in 2022 Report," *Marijuana Moment* (blog), September 27, 2022, https://www.marijuanamoment.net/illinois-regulators-detail-lack-of-marijuana-industry-diversity-and-preview-equity-plans-in-2022-report/. In Massachusetts, women who identified as "African American" or "Latina" constitute only 2 percent of the legal cannabis industry's "senior positions," a category that includes both executives and low-level managers. See Samantha M. Doonan et al., "Racial Equity in Cannabis Policy: Diversity in the Massachusetts Adult-Use Industry at 18-Months," *Cannabis* 5, no. 1 (2022): 30–41, https://doi.org/10.26828/cannabis/2022.01.004/.

5. While research on cannabis equity is growing, few works address workplace rights or unionization. Some important exceptions are Marty Otañez and Jassy Grewal, "Health and Safety in the Legal Cannabis Industry before and during COVID-19," *New Solutions* 30, no. 4 (2021): 311–323; Pletcher, "Labor Protections under Federal Cannabis Prohibition and the Future of Cannabis Unions"; Margaret Gray and Olivia Heffernan, "Cannabis: A New Frontier for Union Jobs," *New Labor Forum* 32, no. 2 (2023): 38–45, https://doi.org/10.1177/10957960231170227/. Other works that have influenced my understanding of cannabis equity and justice include Robert Chlala, "Misfit Medicine and Queer Geographies: The Diverse Economy and Politics of Cannabis in Carceral Los Angeles," *Environment and Planning C* 38, no. 7–8 (2020): 1180–1197; M. Polson and H. Bodwitch, "Prohibited Commoning," *Elementa: Science of the Anthropocene* 9, no. 1 (2021): 00054; Kaitlin P. Reed, *Settler Cannabis: From Gold Rush to Green Rush in Indigenous Northern California* (Seattle: University of Washington Press, 2023); and Shaleen Title, "Fair and Square: How to Effectively Incorporate Social Equity into Cannabis Laws and Regulations," SSRN Scholarly Paper, December 6, 2021, https://doi.org/10.2139/ssrn.3978766/. See also Dominic Corva and Joshua S. Meisel, *The Routledge Handbook of Post-Prohibition Cannabis Research* (New York: Routledge, 2021).

6. For this chapter I conducted ten interviews with cannabis employees and managers in Arizona and Massachusetts, six interviews with UFCW leaders and staff, and three interviews with industry observers. I also conducted site visits to three Massachusetts dispensaries and ten dispensaries in Arizona.

7. Jeff Smith, "Marijuana Companies Mostly Shut Out of $2T Coronavirus Stimulus Package," *MJBizDaily* (blog), April 9, 2020, https://mjbizdaily.com/marijuana-companies-mostly-shut-out-of-2-trillion-coronavirus-stimulus-package/.

8. T. J. Lauritsen, former UFCW director of cannabis organizing, telephone interview with the author, January 7, 2022. See also "How Section 280E Is Hindering the Cannabis Industry," https://www.bakertilly.com/insights/how-section-280e-is-hindering-the-cannabis-industry/.

9. "Marijuana Market Poised to Grow Faster Than Smartphones," *The United Food & Commercial Workers International Union* (blog), November 5, 2013, https://www.ufcw.org/marijuana-market-poised-to-grow-faster-than-smartphones/.

10. Courtney Connley, "Cannabis Is Projected to Be a $70 Billion Market by 2028—Yet Those Hurt Most by the War on Drugs Lack Access," CNBC, July 1, 2021, https://www.cnbc.com/2021/07/01/in-billion-dollar-cannabis-market-racial-inequity-persists-despite-legalization.html.

11. Marijuana Policy Project (MPP), "Cannabis Tax Revenue in States That Regulate Cannabis for Adult Use," MPP, accessed January 13, 2023, https://www.mpp.org/issues/legalization/cannabis-tax-revenue-states-regulate-cannabis-adult-use/.

12. International Tax Review (ITR), "Cannabis Could Boost Government Tax Revenue Post-Crisis," June 3, 2020, https://www.internationaltaxreview.com/article/2a6a5vgquljqsway9w7pc/cannabis-could-boost-government-tax-revenue-post-crisis/.

13. Luke Winkie, "How the Pandemic Created a New Generation of Stoners,"

The Guardian, March 30, 2022, sec. US News, https://www.theguardian.com/us-news/2022/mar/30/pandemic-marijuana-use-increase-covid/.

14. Elizabeth Hinton and DeAnza Cook, "The Mass Criminalization of Black Americans: A Historical Overview," *Annual Review of Criminology* 4, no. 1 (2021): 261–286, https://doi.org/10.1146/annurev-criminol-060520-033306/.

15. Michelle Alexander, *The New Jim Crow: Mass Incarceration in the Age of Colorblindness*, rev. ed. (New York: New Press, 2012); Elizabeth Danquah-Brobby, "Comment: Prison for You. Profit for Me. Systemic Racism Effectively Bars Blacks from Participation in Newly Legal Marijuana Industry," *University of Baltimore Law Review* 46, no. 3 (May 1, 2017), https://scholarworks.law.ubalt.edu/ublr/vol46/iss3/5/.

16. I thank a former NORML staff member for some of these insights. Former NORML staff member, confidential interview with the author, June 14, 2022. See also Isaac Campos, *Home Grown: Marijuana and the Origins of Mexico's War on Drugs* (Chapel Hill: University of North Carolina Press, 2012).

17. Steven Greenhouse, "Will COVID-19 Spur a Wave of Unionization?" *Dissent*, Summer 2020, https://www.dissentmagazine.org/article/will-covid-19-spur-a-wave-of-unionization/.

18. Gallup Inc., "U.S. Approval of Labor Unions at Highest Point since 1965," Gallup.com, August 30, 2022, https://news.gallup.com/poll/398303/approval-labor-unions-highest-point-1965.aspx/.

19. Megan Carvalho, director of cannabis organizing, UFCW, telephone interview with the author, July 1, 2022.

20. It was active in the legislative arena for legalization of medical and adult use as well. Lynne Dodson, director of workforce development, UFCW, Zoom interview with the author, December 13, 2022.

21. Josh Fenton, "Union Says RI Compassion Center Retaliated and Fired Worker, Sparking Strike," *Providence Journal*, June 28, 2021, https://www.golocalprov.com/news/union-says-ri-compassion-center-retaliated-and-fired-worker-sparking-strike/.

22. Samuel P. Jacobs and Alex Dobuzinskis, "Shrinking U.S. Labor Unions See Relief in Marijuana Industry," *Reuters*, February 6, 2013, sec. Retail—Drugs, https://www.reuters.com/article/usa-marijuana-unions-idUSL1N0ATFBD20130206/.

23. Tim Melia, UFCW Local 328 president, interview with the author, June 27, 2022, Providence, RI; Lauritsen, interview with the author.

24. "Unlikely Allies behind Marijuana Votes in Washington, Colorado," *Los Angeles Times*, November 11, 2012, https://www.latimes.com/archives/la-xpm-2012-nov-11-la-na-marijuana-20121111-story.html.

25. Don McIntosh, "Labor Backs Effort to Stop Discrimination against Ex-Offenders," *Northwest Labor Press* 115, no. 13 (July 4, 2014): 4. See also Gregory DeFreitas, "New Labor Organizing in a New Industry: Cannabis," *Regional Labor Review*, Fall 2022, https://www.hofstra.edu/sites/default/files/2022-12/new-labor-organizing-new-industry-cannabis-fall22.pdf/.

26. Carvalho, interview with the author.

27. Melia, interview with the author.

28. Sam Marvin, UFCW Local 328 organizer, telephone interview with the author, June 29, 2022.

29. Carvalho, interview with the author; Marvin, interview with the author.

30. Massachusetts cannabis employee 1, confidential telephone interview with the author.

31. UFCW, "NEW REPORT: Cannabis Workers Unionizing Leads to Higher Quality Jobs and Increases Standards in Fast-Growing Industry," press release, September 20, 2021, https://www.ufcw.org/press-releases/new-report-cannabis-workers-unionizing-leads-to-higher-quality-jobs-and-increases-standards-in-fast-growing-industry/.

32. Jeff Smith, "Unionization of Labor in the Cannabis Industry Is Encouraged," *MJBizDaily* (blog), December 16, 2019, https://mjbizdaily.com/unionization-of-labor-in-the-cannabis-industry-is-encouraged/.

33. Robert Iafolla and Joyce E. Cutler, "Cannabis Economy Peace Laws Spread, Fertilizing Union Growth," *Bloomberg Law*, May 13, 2021, https://news.bloomberglaw.com/daily-labor-report/cannabis-industry-peace-laws-spread-fertilizing-union-growth/; Jeff Smith, "What Are the Business Implications of Labor Peace Agreements for the Cannabis Industry?" *Marijuana Business Daily*, May 24, 2022, https://mjbizdaily.com/business-implications-of-labor-peace-agreements-for-the-cannabis-industry/. In 2019 northeastern US governors agreed to a framework for a regional adult-use cannabis market, suggesting need for social equity but without mentioning labor or labor peace agreements. See Jeff Smith, "Northeast Governors Take Big Step toward Regional Cannabis Coordination," *Marijuana Business Daily*, December 17, 2021, https://mjbizdaily.com/northeast-governors-take-big-step-toward-regional-cannabis-coordination/.

34. Marvin, interview with the author; Massachusetts dispensary worker 3, confidential telephone interview with the author, July 1, 2022. The "wolf in sheep's clothing" reference comes from Naomi Diaz/For CU-CitizenAccess, "'Wolf in Sheep's Clothing': Cannabis Workers Describe Pushback against Unionization Efforts," *CU-CitizenAccess.Org* (blog), February 10, 2022, https://cu-citizenaccess.org/2022/02/wolf-in-sheeps-clothing-cannabis-workers-describe-pushback-against-unionization-efforts/.

35. Polson and Bodwitch, "Prohibited Commoning." Others in cannabis cultivation have found meaning and escaping the "fucking desk life."

36. Interview with Arizona budtender, Tempe, Arizona, January 3, 2023; Marvin interview. One young Arizona budtender told me he had worked in every facet of cannabis, from cultivation to processing. A Massachusetts budtender and several in Arizona told me they worked in the retail and service sector before entering the cannabis industry.

37. Interview with store manager, Phoenix, Arizona, January 6, 2023; Interview with Arizona budtender, Glendale, Arizona, January 8, 2023.

38. Interview with Arizona budtender, Glendale, Arizona, January 7, 2023.

39. Lauritsen interview.

40. Interview with Arizona assistant store manager, Phoenix, Arizona, January 8, 2023.

41. Marvin, interview with the author.

42. Otañez and Grewal, "Health and Safety in the Legal Cannabis Industry before and during COVID-19." The authors detail health risks in cultivation and processing.

43. Chris Roberts, "Report: Legal Cannabis Industry Worker Died after Breathing Marijuana Dust," *Forbes*, October 3, 2022, https://www.forbes.com/sites/chrisroberts/2022/10/03/report-legal-cannabis-industry-worker-died-after-breathing-marijuana-dust/.

44. Melia, interview with the author.

45. Marvin, interview with the author. See also David Schlussel, "'The Mellow Pot-Smoker': White Individualism in Marijuana Legalization Campaigns," *California Law Review* 105, no. 3 (2017): 885–927, https://doi.org/10.15779/z38pz51k8d/. See also Gray and Heffernan, "Cannabis."

46. This sentiment was also explored in the author's confidential telephone interview with Massachusetts dispensary worker 2.

47. Mark Miller, "Toward a More Perfect Pot Union," *High Times*, November 16, 2022, https://hightimes.com/news/toward-a-more-perfect-pot-union/.

48. Jeff Smith, "Cannabis Labor Peace Requirements Expand, Sometimes Sparking Conflict in Legal Marijuana Markets," *Marijuana Business Daily*, 2021, https://mjbizdaily.com/unionization-of-labor-in-the-cannabis-industry-is-encouraged/.

49. Smith, "What Are the Business Implications of Labor Peace Agreements for the Cannabis Industry?"

50. Lauritsen interview.

51. Debra Borchardt, "Maryland's Blair Wellness Claps Back at Allegations," *Green Market Report*, June 6, 2022, https://www.greenmarketreport.com/marylands-blair-wellness-claps-back-at-allegations/.

52. Hinton and Cook, "Mass Criminalization of Black Americans," 1.

53. Danquah-Brobby, "Comment"; Alexander, *New Jim Crow*.

54. Title, "Fair and Square"; Minority Cannabis Business Association, "MCBA National Cannabis Equity Report," 2022.

55. Eli Hager, "People on Probation and Parole Are Being Denied Perfectly Legal Medical Weed," The Marshall Project, January 17, 2020, https://www.themarshallproject.org/2020/01/17/people-on-probation-and-parole-are-being-denied-perfectly-legal-medical-weed/.

56. "A Whiff of Pot Alone No Longer Airtight Probable Cause for Police to Search Cars in Several States," *Washington Post*, June 27, 2021, https://www.washingtonpost.com/national-security/marijuana-police-probable-cause/2021/06/26/9d984f8e-d36c-11eb-a53a-3b5450fdca7a_story.html/. While some states have ruled that cannabis odor alone should no longer constitute probable cause for a search, courts in other states have disagreed. In Rhode Island, legalization legislation fails to mention the matter, making the issue a legal and regulatory gray area.

57. Caislin L. Firth et al., "Did Marijuana Legalization in Washington State Reduce Racial Disparities in Adult Marijuana Arrests?" *Substance Use & Misuse* 54, no. 9 (2019): 1582–1587, https://doi.org/10.1080/10826084.2019.159

3007/; Brynn E. Sheehan, Richard A. Grucza, and Andrew D. Plunk, "Association of Racial Disparity of Cannabis Possession Arrests among Adults and Youths with Statewide Cannabis Decriminalization and Legalization," *JAMA Health Forum* 2, no. 10 (October 29, 2021): e213435, https://doi.org/10.1001/jamahealthforum.2021.3435/.

58. Minority Cannabis Business Association, "MCBA National Cannabis Equity Report."

59. In Colorado state officials must weigh several factors, including the time elapsed and the relationship of the conviction to their proposed work in the cannabis industry, to determine if the applicant's "criminal history indicates that he or she is not of good moral character," and thus unqualified for an employee license. See "Section 44-10-307—Persons Prohibited as Licensees—Definition," 44-10-307 Colo. Rev. Stat § (2018), https://casetext.com/statute/colorado-revised-statutes/title-44-revenue-regulation-of-activities/marijuana-regulation/article-10-regulated-marijuana/part-3-licensing-procedures/section-44-10-307-persons-prohibited-as-licensees-definition/.

60. The kinds of felonies vary by state. Six states exclude cannabis offenses now legalized under state law (Minority Cannabis Business Association 2022, p. 27.)

61. In most states these social equity licenses are only available to cannabis dispensaries, not cultivation or processing sites. The 2018 Cannabis Equity Act in California creates incentives for localities to produce social equity plans that can include, among other things, hiring goals. The same is true in Massachusetts.

62. Beau Kilmer et al., "Cannabis Legalization and Social Equity: Some Opportunities, Puzzles, and Trade-Offs," *Boston University Law Review* 101, no. 3 (May 2021): 1003–1041; Corey Kilgannon and Wesley Parnell, "Clean Slates Promised under New York Marijuana Law Prove Complicated," *New York Times*, February 11, 2023, sec. New York, https://www.nytimes.com/2023/02/11/nyregion/marijuana-legalization-law.html/.

63. J. J. Prescott and Sonja B. Starr, "Expungement of Criminal Convictions: An Empirical Study," SSRN Scholarly Paper, March 16, 2019, https://doi.org/10.2139/ssrn.3353620/. People with criminal records tend to avoid governmental agencies and "fly below the radar" for fear of encountering additional repercussions for their record. See Sarah Esther Lageson, "Found Out and Opting Out: The Consequences of Online Criminal Records for Families," *ANNALS of the American Academy of Political and Social Science* 665, no. 1 (May 1, 2016): 127–141, https://doi.org/10.1177/0002716215625053/. The problems with the implementation of expungement led activists in the District of Columbia to petition to amend the legislation and specify databases and organizations to help effectively implement it. Doni Crawford, "First in Line: A Reparative Approach to Recreational Cannabis Policy," *DC Fiscal Policy Institute* (blog), February 16, 2021, https://www.dcfpi.org/all/first-in-line/.

64. Sarah E. Lageson and Shadd Maruna, "Digital Degradation: Stigma Management in the Internet Age," *Punishment & Society* 20, no. 1 (January 1, 2018): 113–133, https://doi.org/10.1177/1462474517737050/; Devah Pager, "The Mark

of a Criminal Record," *American Journal of Sociology* 108, no. 5 (March 2003): 937–975, https://doi.org/10.1086/374403/.

65. Chinazo O. Cunningham et al., "Availability of Medical Cannabis Services by Racial, Social, and Geographic Characteristics of Neighborhoods in New York: A Cross-Sectional Study," *BMC Public Health* 22, no. 1 (April 6, 2022): 671, https://doi.org/10.1186/s12889-022-13076-1/; Martha S. Rosenthal and R. Nathan Pipitone, "Demographics, Perceptions, and Use of Medical Marijuana among Patients in Florida," *Medical Cannabis and Cannabinoids* 4, no. 1 (December 22, 2020): 13–20, https://doi.org/10.1159/000512342/.

66. No author, "UFCW's JATC Will Raise Standards in the Cannabis Industry," *UFCW: For Local Unions*, May 10, 2021, http://forlocals.ufcw.org/2021/05/10/ufcw-establishes-jatc-to-raise-standards-in-cannabis-industry/.

67. Dodson interview.

68. Robin Abcarian, "Cannabis Workers, Once Facing Legal Peril, Get the California Seal of Approval," *Los Angeles Times*, April 23, 2017, https://www.latimes.com/local/abcarian/la-me-abcarian-marijuana-technician-20170423-story.html/.

69. Kimberly Redmond, "NJ's Retail Cannabis Worker Apprenticeship Program Now Accepting Apps," *NJBIZ* (blog), June 29, 2023, https://njbiz.com/njs-retail-cannabis-worker-apprenticeship-program-now-accepting-apps/.

70. "Home—Bargaining for the Common Good," accessed October 4, 2023, https://www.bargainingforthecommongood.org/; "Critical Race Feminism and Common Good Unionism," Non Profit News | Nonprofit Quarterly, September 28, 2022, https://nonprofitquarterly.org/critical-race-feminism-and-common-good-unionism/. For other new visions of union organizing, see Erica Smiley and Sarita Gupta, *The Future We Need: Organizing for a Better Democracy in the Twenty-First Century* (Ithaca: Cornell University Press, 2022); Jane McAlevey, *A Collective Bargain: Unions, Organizing, and the Fight for Democracy* (New York: HarperCollins, 2020).

Epilogue
The Return of the Strike,
the Return of the Working Class?

NICK JURAVICH and
STEVE STRIFFLER

On September 26, 2023, Joe Biden became the first sitting president to join a picket line when he visited striking United Auto Workers (UAW) workers in Michigan. In his brief remarks, the president noted that workers had saved the industry, sacrificed considerably when the auto companies had been struggling, and deserved payback now that they were doing well. It was time for a contract that reflected their sacrifices and kept pace with corporate profits. His remarks tapped in to the frustration that workers across the country had been experiencing for years—indeed, they echoed Biden's remarks on the campaign trail for the vice presidency in 2008 and 2012—but that intensified during the pandemic. It was, in part, the renewed popularity of the labor movement, coupled with the inability and unwillingness of corporations and government to adequately protect and provide for working people in the first year of the pandemic, that helped sweep Biden into the White House, where he promised to be "the most pro-union president in history."[1]

As the chapters in this volume demonstrate, the pandemic exposed inequality and government ineffectiveness and, in doing so, led workers to quit, question career paths, rethink their work-life balance, walk off the job, organize in new ways, demand better from employers, and rethink the very function of government. To be sure, the labor movement has been building toward this upsurge for decades in some sectors. The campaigns launched since 2020 reflect those efforts, from long-running movements for union democracy in the Teamsters and UAW to the more recent revival of social movement unionism and "bargaining for the common good" among educators. The inspiration provided by political movements, including Occupy Wall Street, Bernie Sanders's presidential campaigns, and the massive growth of the Democratic Socialists of America (DSA), played a role as well. All of these movements generated pressure that helps explain why Biden was politically comfortable, and even obligated, to join the UAW picket line, as well as to promise a pro-worker presidency. Working people insisted on it and gave him the necessary political base to seek such political gains for the working class.

But the pandemic remains key for understanding labor's current moment, as we argued in chapter 1, for two reasons. First, since the shocks of March 2020, it has been clear that neither the bosses nor the politicians whose pockets they line will protect working people. The same billionaires who saw their fortunes grow at record rates in 2020 and 2021 spent 2022 engaged in sustained and unrepentant public union busting at Starbucks and Amazon. Despite having the "most pro-union president in history" in the White House and control of both houses of Congress, the Democratic Party could neither pass the Protecting the Right to Organize (PRO) Act, labor's primary legislative goal, nor preserve the expanded Child Tax Credit, which halved child poverty in just over a year.[2] The Supreme Court demonstrated its continued willingness to reduce the power of workers and their unions in the *Glacier Northwest* case, and to keep millions of Americans mired in debt—and thus yoked to their jobs—when it struck down student loan forgiveness.[3] The Federal Reserve, as Samir Sonti discusses in chapter 3, has worked to discipline workers' power and reduce their wages through its monetary policies since 2021. And as discussed in chapter 1, even Biden and his labor secretary, Marty Walsh, a former union leader, opted for a "return to normal" when they preemptively celebrated a settlement and shut down the possibility of a railroad workers' strike in the fall of 2022.

Despite the limits of our political system, the power of capital, and the numerical weakness of organized labor (relative to the preceding century), the three pandemic years studied in this book reveal a second overarching experience. The chaos, crises, and disjunctures of the pandemic's first year, coupled with the many ways workers responded then and since, have made clear that another world is possible. Tens of thousands of workers struck or walked out during the first weeks of the pandemic, showing themselves and the wider public that infection and death on the job were political decisions that could be resisted and refused. While the response of elected officials was nowhere near sufficient, the eventual influx of welfare-state spending in the summer and fall of 2020 demonstrated that it is entirely possible for our government to provide for people, both those who are out of work and those who need protections on the job.

As workers' new awareness of the power of organizing grew, individual actions like quitting or switching jobs gave way to new organizing in many jobs often thought to be "unorganizable" until recently. This wave of new organizing targeted some of the world's biggest brands, including Amazon, Target, Whole Foods, and Starbucks, but it impacted workplaces across the country. As we have seen in this book, the food and hospitality, education, and healthcare industries were at the center of this, but few sectors of the economy were left untouched. Significantly, much of this organizing was driven by a genuine grassroots upsurge coupled with the work of a "militant minority" drawn from the ranks of radical and socialist formations like the Emergency Workers Organizing Committee, discussed in chapter 12. Some of it took place within established unions, but some took the form of independent unionism, including at Amazon, Trader Joe's, and many small restaurants, cafés, and bakeries. Within established unions, these organizing efforts often represented major departures from past practices, from SEIU Workers United's model of support for Starbucks Workers United to the doubling of the UE's membership through landslide academic worker elections at universities.[4] At the same time, those unions that were already committed to social movement unionism, like the Graduate Employees' Organization at the University of Michigan or the Boston Teachers Union (discussed in chapters 6 and 7), showed how these models could effectively respond to the overlapping suffering experienced by educators and those they served.

While the Biden administration and Democratic Party failed to deliver on many of their 2020 campaign promises, the president earned his "most pro-union president in history" title (admittedly a low bar) in one crucial respect: through the appointment of an aggressively pro-labor National Labor Relations Board, including the firing of Peter Robb on his first day in office and the subsequent appointment, in July 2021, of Jennifer Abruzzo as NLRB general counsel.[5] Despite a deadlocked Congress and hostile Supreme Court, Abruzzo and the NLRB not only supported the explosion of new organizing efforts through their choices of cases, their rulings and key rule changes; they were also vocally pro-worker and pro-union. This rhetoric from a key site of government interaction with labor reinforced and emboldened the statements and positions of union leaders and organizers, encouraging them to articulate big demands and working-class consciousness in ways that are, as of this writing, connecting specific union campaigns to a wider mobilization of working people *as* working people.

The impact of these two pandemic experiences—the bosses' push for "normalcy" and the power of organizing—became clear in 2023, the year of the (large) strike. Around four hundred thousand workers had gone on strike by November, with large, established unions taking the lead. Nearly two hundred thousand actors and writers went on strike at the start of the summer, the first time they went out together since 1960 (when Ronald Reagan was president of the Screen Actors Guild).[6] Two of the largest private sector labor unions in the country—the Teamsters and the UAW—then put the strike more firmly on the table, making bold demands with a level of militancy that harkened back to an earlier era. It was a militancy that had been building for years as workers witnessed record corporate profits, saw few of the benefits, and became increasingly frustrated not only with their bosses but with a complacent union leadership as well.[7] They were poised to break from business unionism and, in fact, had been organizing to do so from within unions for years, even decades. And they were now ready to once again utilize the strike as weapon to make demands.

It is no wonder, then, that both the Teamsters and the UAW framed their demands by juxtaposing the meteoric growth of corporate profits and CEO pay on the one hand with stagnating worker pay on the other—and have routinely referenced the pandemic as a moment when such inequality reached a breaking point. Such a framing resonates not only with truck drivers and autoworkers but also with a public—including many Republican voters—that has overwhelmingly supported the strikes. This support comes in part from the fact that most Americans still believe that anyone who works hard should be able to live a comfortable middle-class life—and that this "American Dream" has become increasingly unattainable. It is incumbent upon labor to explain why this has happened, and what we can do about it, in ways that make sense to (and mobilize) working people, and to thereby seize this once-in-a-generation opportunity to unite diverse groups of working people around fundamental shared interests.

Importantly, both unions have prioritized the question of long-term working-class survival by addressing inequality within their own ranks. They have done so by attempting to roll back contract language that protects the benefits and pay of existing workers while allowing new workers to be hired under far less generous terms, creating "tiers" of workers.[8] These tiers had been agreed to by the unions themselves in earlier contracts—indeed, they had become commonplace in contracts across several industries—but were no longer palatable to the restive rank and file who elected these new leaders.[9] Equally important, these unions and their leaders now felt sufficiently empowered to say "No to Tiers" that would degrade the entire labor force over time, leaving more and more workers poorly positioned to survive the next crisis.

This fight against tiers, and for the rights and dignity of all workers in hitherto stratified workplaces, resonates across many sectors. In academia, fourteen thousand graduate workers joined the UE alone in the first four months of 2023.[10] They joined tens of thousands organized, or organizing, with unions including SEIU, AFT, and the newly militant UAW, in which fifty thousand academic workers struck for six weeks in the University of California system in 2022.[11] For these academic workers, just as for United Parcel Service delivery drivers and Big Three autoworkers, a "return to normal" would mean returning to hierarchical workplaces with steep, narrow ladders to middle-class stability that most workers would never climb. Although wage tiers in manufacturing and logistics contracts and the precarity of graduate and postdoctoral workers have vastly different origins, the broader fight, these workers realize, is much the same. Instead of distant promises, working people need solidarity to win contracts that lift everyone to strong and stable futures.

While it is still far too early to declare that the tide has turned in labor's favor, encouraging developments have emerged from this strike wave. Teamsters president Sean O'Brien and UAW president Shawn Fain—both elected with the support of Democratic and left reformers in their unions—have not only built militant, strike-based strategies that delivered massive contract gains, they have also consciously articulated a broader working-class consciousness in many ways: explaining their contract demands (particularly around ending tiers), attacking corporate greed, going toe-to-toe with legislators in congressional hearings, and appearing regularly in the media, sporting such messages as Fain's now-iconic "Eat the Rich" T-shirt.[12] In doing so, they have joined labor leaders including Sara Nelson of AFA-CWA and SAG-AFTRA's Fran Drescher and political allies including Bernie Sanders, Rashida Tlaib, and Alexandria Ocasio-Cortez. Beyond building the public profile of labor and working-class consciousness, these unions have indicated strong public support for one another's actions, exemplified by Teamsters Local 399 in Hollywood's vocal support for SAG-AFTRA and Writers Guild of America strikes.[13] There are also encouraging examples of labor's growing political power at the state and local level, as discussed by Puya Gerami in chapter 11, and witnessed most spectacularly in 2023 by the election of Brandon Johnson, a former Chicago Teachers Union member, as mayor of Chicago.[14]

These developments suggest the possibility not just of a continued labor upsurge but also of the building of something resembling a wider working-class consciousness, one rooted in the lessons of the pandemic but that overcomes the early divisions we discussed in chapter 1. This is not an uncontested task, as right-wing and centrist politicians have tried to exploit the divides between frontline workers and those who either worked from home or became unemployed. Spurious attacks on unionized educators for "closing schools" are attempts to divide working people and pit them against one another, as are attacks on student loan forgiveness and expansions of welfare state services more broadly. A return to normal, for the bosses, means a return to a working class divided by race, gender, and geography, as well as by sector, job, and prescriptive notions of who is "deserving" of living wages, job security, and government assistance.

We believe the chapters in this book light a different path. When workers talk to one another, record and share their stories, and use these grassroots experiences as the foundations for new organizing, they construct the capacity to overcome these divides. The further we get from the initial shock of 2020, the clearer it is that workers across many sectors and experiences not only demand rights and respect at work but also believe in the power of organizing to deliver them. Absent bosses escaping COVID-19 on yachts and squabbling politicians did not protect working people or their communities in the years between 2020 and 2023: they protected one another. Turning that insight into a lasting solidarity with the power to win at the bargaining table and the ballot box is a steep challenge, but there is real hope that working people and their unions in this country understand this to be the task and that they are increasingly up to it.

Notes

1. "ICYMI: President Biden: I'm 'the Most Pro-Union President in American History. And I Make No Apologies for It,'" AFL-CIO statement, June 29, 2023, https://aflcio.org/statements/icymi-president-biden-im-most-pro-union-president-american-history-and-i-make-no/.

2. Hamilton Nolan, "The Good Years May Be Over, and Labor Didn't Get Much," *In These Times*, November 14, 2022, https://inthesetimes.com/article/midterms-labor-union-biden-democrats-house-gerrymandering/; "One Year On: What We Know about the Expanded Child Tax Credit," Policy Update, Center on Poverty and Social Policy at Columbia University, November 15, 2022, https://www.povertycenter.columbia.edu/news-internal/2022/child-tax-credit-research-roundup-one-year-on/.

3. Jane McAlevy, "How Should Workers Respond to the Supreme Court's Ruling in Glacier Northwest?" *The Nation*, June 1, 2023, https://www.thenation.com/article/politics/supreme-court-glacier-northwest-workers/; Adam Liptak, "Supreme Court Rejects Biden's Student Loan Forgiveness Plan," *New York Times*, June 30, 2023, https://www.nytimes.com/2023/06/30/us/student-loan-forgiveness-supreme-court-biden.html/.

4. "14,000 Graduate Workers Join UE in First Four Months of 2023," *UE News*, June 3, 2023, https://www.ueunion.org/ue-news-feature/2023/14000-graduate-workers-join-ue-in-first-four-months-of-2023/.

5. Bryce Covert, "Meet the Activist Championing the Rights of Workers from the Inside," *The Nation*, February 13, 2023, https://www.thenation.com/article/society/jennifer-abruzzo-national-labor-relations-board/

6. Jesse Steinmetz, "Hollywood's Writers and Actors Strike Together for the First Time in over 60 Years," *WGBH*, August 7, 2023, https://www.wgbh.org/news/local/2023-07-21/hollywoods-writers-and-actors-strike-together-for-the-first-time-in-over-60-years/.

7. Luis Feliz Leon, "Inside the Teamsters' Historic Contract at UPS," *American Prospect*, July 25, 2023, https://prospect.org/labor/2023-07-25-teamsters-historic-contract-ups/; Nelson Lichtenstein, "UAW Strikers Have Scored a

Historic, Transformative Victory," *Jacobin*, November 1, 2023, https://jacobin.com/2023/11/uaw-strike-contract-fain-victory/.

8. Alexandra Bradbury, "UPS Teamsters to Vote on Contract That Ends Driver Tiers, Lifts Part-Timer Pay," *Labor Notes*, July 27, 2023, https://labornotes.org/2023/07/ups-teamsters-vote-contract-ends-driver-tiers-lifts-part-timer-pay/; Dustin Dwyer, "Behind the Push to 'End Tiers,' a Precarious History of Solidarity in the UAW," *Michigan Radio*, October 3, 2023, https://www.michiganradio.org/economy/2023-10-03/behind-the-push-to-end-tiers-a-precarious-history-of-solidarity-in-the-uaw/.

9. Alex Press, "How Two-Tier Unions Turn Workers against One Another," *Washington Post*, August 29, 2018, https://www.washingtonpost.com/outlook/2018/08/30/how-two-tier-unions-turn-workers-against-each-other/.

10. "14,000 Graduate Workers Join UE in First Four Months of 2023," *UE News*, June 3, 2023.

11. Rafael Jaime and Yunyi Li, "How University of California Workers Won the Biggest Higher-Ed Strike in US History," *Jacobin*, September 2, 2023, https://jacobin.com/2023/09/uc-uaw-2865-strike-california-contract-student-researchers/.

12. David Streitfeld, "New U.A.W. Chief Has a Nonnegotiable Demand: Eat the Rich," *New York Times*, October 5, 2023, https://www.nytimes.com/2023/10/05/business/economy/shawn-fain-uaw-profile.html/. On efforts to articulate a broader working-class struggle, see Daniel Denvir, "Seizing Labor's Moment w/Alex Press & Eric Blanc," *The Dig*, September 9, 2023, https://thedigradio.com/podcast/seizing-labors-moment-w-alex-press-eric-blanc/.

13. Jeff Schuhrke, "Cross-Union Solidarity Is Fueling the Historic Summer Strike Wave," *In These Times*, July 25, 2023, https://inthesetimes.com/article/wga-sag-aftra-ups-teamsters-hollywood-union-strike-wave/.

14. Barbara Ransby, "Chicago's Rich Organizing Tradition Paid Off, Delivering Victory for Brandon Johnson," *The Nation*, April 13, 2023, https://www.thenation.com/article/politics/brandon-johnson-movement-organizing-chicago/.

Contributors

CARLOS ARAMAYO is the president of UNITE HERE Local 26, the union for hospitality workers in the greater Boston area and Rhode Island. In addition to his work in the union, he is a member of the Massachusetts Convention Center's Board of Directors and a member of Massachusetts governor Maura Healy's Advisory Council on Latino Empowerment. He first became involved with the labor movement as a rank-and-file organizer with the Graduate Employees and Students Organization (now Local 33) at Yale University, where he earned a PhD in Latin American history.

KATHLEEN BROWN is a PhD candidate in American culture at the University of Michigan and a member of the Graduate Employees' Organization, AFT Local 3550. She is interested in the dialectical relationship between labor and social movements throughout history. Her dissertation examines the 1930s US-American solidarity movement with Republican Spain during the Spanish Civil War.

SANDRINE ETIENNE is a licensed social worker based in the New York City area with sixteen years of experience in the healthcare field. She works directly with patients and their families who are dealing with chronic and debilitating illness with a focus on providing resources that can help them adapt to life-changing events.

ISMAEL GARCÍA-COLÓN is a professor of anthropology at the College of Staten Island and the CUNY Graduate Center. He is a historical and political anthropologist with a focus on immigration and colonial migration, guest-workers, farm labor, US empire, Puerto Rico, and US ethnic and racial histories. García-Colón is the author of *Colonial Migrants at the Heart of Empire: Puerto Rican Workers on U.S. Farms* (University of California Press, 2020), and winner of the 2020 Frank Bonilla Book Award from the Puerto Rican Studies Association.

PUYA GERAMI is an organizer and writer who lives in Connecticut. He served as director of Recovery For All from 2020 to 2023. He previously served as an organizer and then the education director at SEIU 1199 New England. He is currently completing his doctoral dissertation at Yale on the history of public sector unionism and privatization.

MAURA HAGAN is the licensed clinical social worker and mental health coordinator at the Gunnar Esiason Adult Cystic Fibrosis and Lung Program at NYPH/Columbia University Medical Center. Maura is responsible for assessing the mental health needs, advocating for, making referrals, and providing resources to patients to help them cope with chronic illness. She has worked at the Adult CF Center for three years and has been employed as a medical social worker at NYPH for twenty-one years. She has experience working with chronic illness in multiple areas, including end-stage renal disease and liver transplantation.

CONNOR HARNEY is a history PhD student at the University of North Carolina Greensboro. His work focuses on race, class, and suburbanization in the South after the Second World War as part of the history of capitalism, with a particular interest in the transitionary moment of the long 1970s.

DEVAN HAWKINS is an assistant professor of public health at the Massachusetts College of Pharmacy and Health Sciences. An epidemiologist by training, his research focuses on how work-related factors contribute to different health challenges including COVID-19, drug overdoses, and suicides. He previously worked for the Massachusetts Department of Public Health.

LEIGH HOWARD, LCSW-R, began her career as a clinical social worker and psychotherapist primarily with the LGBTQ community. She transitioned into the labor movement in order to fight for workers' rights and is currently a vice president at 1199SEIU, United Healthcare Workers East. She lives in Brooklyn, New York.

DORIS JOY, LCSW-R, RN, ACM, is a medical social worker with over twenty years of experience working in an acute care hospital setting. She is former 1199SEIU union delegate and a newly licensed nurse. Her interest lies in how the presence and work of social workers supports quality care in US healthcare.

NICK JURAVICH is an assistant professor of history and labor studies and the associate director of the Labor Resource Center at UMass Boston. His first book, *Para Power: How Paraprofessional Labor Changed Education*, was published by the University of Illinois Press in 2024.

ERIC D. LARSON is author of *Grounding Global Justice: Race, Class, and Grassroots Globalism in the U.S. and Mexico* (University of California Press, 2023). He edited *Jobs with Justice: 25 Years, 25 Voices* (PM Press, 2013). He is associate professor of crime and justice studies at the University of Massachusetts Dartmouth.

KATHRYN M. MEYER is a lecturer in the Department of Teaching, Learning, and Educational Leadership at Binghamton University. Her teaching and research focus on enacting critical pedagogy to honor the strengths, lived experiences, and access needs of disabled and multiply marginalized teachers and students across K–12 and higher education. Kathryn also works with other disabled educators to build anti-ableist curricula and pedagogy that celebrates disability histories and positive conceptions of disability.

MARIAN MOSER JONES is an associate professor at Ohio State University in the College of Public Health, Division of Health Services Management and Policy, and the History Department. She also currently serves as an associate editor of the *American Journal of Public Health*. She is the author of *The American Red Cross from Clara Barton to the New Deal* (Johns Hopkins University Press, 2012), as well as numerous articles on the history and sociopolitical context of nursing, maternal and child health, homelessness, and other topics.

SAMIR SONTI is an assistant professor at the CUNY School of Labor and Urban Studies. He is an editor of *New Labor Forum* and is writing a book on the politics of inflation in the United States.

STEVE STRIFFLER is the director of the Labor Resource Center and professor of anthropology at UMass Boston. He writes on labor and the left in Latin America and the United States, including *Solidarity: Latin America and the U.S. Left in the Era of Human Rights* (Pluto, 2019) and (with Aviva Chomsky) *Organizing for Power: Building a Twenty-First-Century Labor Movement in Boston* (Haymarket Books, 2021).

LIA WARNER is a reference and instruction associate at New York University's Bobst Library. She is interested in archival labor practices, especially the ways that archivists can work with community members to create meaning and foster historical memory. Currently she works closely with undergraduate students and is passionate about critical information literacy, teaching with primary sources, and community engagement.

ANDREW B. WOLF is an assistant professor in the Department of Global Labor and Work at Cornell University's School of Industrial and Labor Relations. His research focuses on immigrant and gig worker organizing.

JENNIFER ZELNICK, MSW, ScD, is a professor and social welfare policy chair at the Touro College Graduate School of Social Work in New York City. Her research and scholarship investigate topics of importance to the health and social service workplace, beginning with the premise that quality health/ social services depend on sustainable work environments. Dr. Zelnick has a background in labor/community organizing, occupational health and safety policy, and public health social work in the United States and South Africa.

Index

Abruzzo, Jennifer, 311
Ackerman, Seth, 268–69n6
Action Network, 110
Action Now, 250
Adverse Effect Wage Rate, 85, 86, 92n25
Affordable Care Act (2010), 213
African American workers. *See* Black/
    African American workers
AFSCME Local 1583, 135
agriculture/farmworkers, 79–90;
    Adverse Effect Wage Rate and, 85,
    86, 92n25; Bracero Program with
    Mexico, 81–82; climate change as
    risk for, 89–90; COVID-19 infection
    and mortality rates, 36–37, 83, 87;
    deaths of despair and, 41; H-2A visas
    and, 83–87, 89; lack of health insur-
    ance and sick leave, 87; local workers
    as, 82, 84, 89; nativist responses to,
    81–83; personal protective equip-
    ment and, 86–87; social distancing
    and, 86–87; symbolic anthropol-
    ogy and, 80–81; temporary migrant
    workers and, 80, 81–82; unemploy-
    ment rate in 2020, 88; working and
    living conditions of, 84–85, 87–88
alcohol, deaths of despair and, 39, 40
Amazon, union organizing at, 3, 10–11,
    16, 21–23, 45, 114, 124, 256, 259,
    268n5, 310–11
American Farm Bureau, 86

American Federation of Labor–Con-
    gress of Industrial Organizations
    (AFL-CIO), 21–22, 43, 108, 155, 243.
    See also Congress of Industrial Orga-
    nizations (CIO)
American Federation of Teachers
    (AFT), 4, 123–25, 127–40, 155, 312
American Historical Association
    (AHA), 169
American Hotel and Lodging Associa-
    tion, 97
American Legislative Exchange
    Council, 239
American Rescue Plan Act (2021), 53,
    118n33
Americans for Prosperity, 239
Americans with Disabilities Act (ADA)
    (1990), 150, 156–57, 159
Ann Arbor (Mich.) Public Schools, 129
Aramayo, Carlos, 95–119
archival workers, 165–81; authority
    within archives, 166–67, 180; critical
    archival theory, 176–77; feminization
    of archival work, 176; methodolo-
    gies in, 166; organizing by, 180–81;
    representational belonging and, 172;
    symbolic annihilation and, 172; wit-
    nessing and, 176–77. *See also* COVID
    collections
Archives and Public History Program,
    New York University (NYU), 167

The University of Illinois Press
is a founding member of the
Association of University Presses.

———————————————————

Composed in 10.5/13 Mercury Text
with Avenir display
by Jim Proefrock
at the University of Illinois Press

University of Illinois Press
1325 South Oak Street
Champaign, IL 61820-6903
www.press.uillinois.edu